Strengthening Global Innovation Policies Through Innovative Virtual Open Incubators Cluster

Ilan Bijaoui
Bar Ilan University, Israel

IGI Global
Scientific Publishing
Publishing Tomorrow's Research Today

Vice President of Editorial	Melissa Wagner
Director of Acquisitions	Mikaela Felty
Director of Book Development	Jocelynn Hessler
Production Manager	Mike Brehm
Cover Design	Jose Rosado

Published in the United States of America by
IGI Global Scientific Publishing
701 East Chocolate Avenue
Hershey, PA, 17033, USA
Tel: 717-533-8845 | Fax: 717-533-7115
Website: https://www.igi-global.com E-mail: cust@igi-global.com

Library of Congress Cataloging-in-Publication Data

Names: Bijaoui, Ilan author
Title: Strengthening global innovation policies through innovative virtual open incubators cluster / Ilan Bijaoui.
Description: Hershey, PA : IGI Global Scientific Publishing, [2026] | Includes bibliographical references and index. | Summary: "This book examines how virtual open incubator clusters can accelerate disruptive innovation across key sectors-from agriculture and healthcare to microelectronics, energy, and defense-while strengthening global innovation policy frameworks and advancing sustainable economic development"-- Provided by publisher.
Identifiers: LCCN 2026002379 (print) | LCCN 2026002380 (ebook) | ISBN 9798337373508 hardcover | ISBN 9798337373515 paperback | ISBN 9798337373522 ebook
Subjects: LCSH: Technological innovations--Economic aspects | Disruptive technologies | Business incubators
Classification: LCC HC79.T4 B536 2026 (print) | LCC HC79.T4 (ebook) | DDC 338/.064--dc23/eng/20260313
LC record available at https://lccn.loc.gov/2026002379
LC ebook record available at https://lccn.loc.gov/2026002380
British Cataloguing in Publication Data
A Cataloguing in Publication record for this book is available from the British Library.

Table of Contents

Preface

High-technology exports have become a defining structural component of Israel's economic architecture, representing more than 50 percent of total national exports in 2023. This proportion not only underscores the scale of the country's technology sector but also reflects the centrality of innovation to Israel's growth model, external trade balance, and international competitiveness. Over the past decade, the internal composition of these exports has undergone a significant transformation, marked by a decisive shift from goods-based production toward knowledge-intensive services.

In 2013, software and digital services accounted for approximately 40 percent of Israel's high-technology exports. By 2023, their share had expanded to roughly 71 percent, indicating a structural reorientation of the export base. This transition highlights the declining relative weight of traditional high-technology manufacturing segments—such as electronics and hardware—alongside the rapid expansion of software development, cybersecurity solutions, fintech platforms, artificial intelligence applications, and cloud-based services. The growing prominence of these digital sectors reflects broader global trends toward dematerialization, platformization, and the increasing value of intangible assets in international trade.

The rise of knowledge-intensive services is closely linked to Israel's comparative advantages in human capital formation, research intensity, and entrepreneurial dynamism. Israel consistently demonstrates high levels of investment in research and development relative to GDP, coupled with strong university-industry linkages and a dense venture capital ecosystem. These institutional characteristics facilitate rapid commercialization of scientific research and enable firms to scale efficiently into global markets. Unlike capital-intensive manufacturing, digital services rely predominantly on intellectual capital, enabling firms to achieve high productivity with comparatively limited physical infrastructure.

Moreover, the scalability of software and digital exports enhances Israel's resilience within the global economy. Knowledge-based services can be delivered across borders with minimal logistical constraints, reducing exposure to trade disruptions and supply chain vulnerabilities. This structural advantage has strengthened Israel's integration into global value chains while reinforcing its reputation as a leading innovation hub.

PRINCIPAL HIGH-TECHNOLOGY AND INNOVATION DOMAINS IN ISRAEL

Cybertechnology and Homeland Security

Israel's leadership in cybersecurity and homeland security technologies is deeply embedded in its national security architecture and long-standing investment in military research and intelligence capabilities (Israel Innovation Authority, 2024). Elite units within the Israel Defense Forces—most notably Unit 8200—have functioned as critical incubators of advanced cyber talent. These institutional pathways facilitate the transfer of technological expertise from defense frameworks into civilian innovation ecosystems, creating a distinctive civil-military synergy that underpins Israel's comparative advantage in cybertechnology.

Cybersecurity is treated as a strategic national asset and supported through targeted public policies, including R&D grants, government-backed incubators, and venture capital incentives administered by bodies such as the Israel Innovation Authority. As of 2024, Israel hosts more than 300 companies active in cybertech and homeland security. These firms develop advanced solutions spanning automated border control systems, biometric identification technologies, UAV and IED jamming systems, intelligent video surveillance, and sophisticated intelligence-gathering platforms.

Financial indicators further confirm sectoral strength. In 2024, Israeli cybersecurity firms raised approximately $3.8 billion, representing 36 percent of total national technology funding, with median investment rounds significantly exceeding the broader high-tech average.

Major acquisitions, including CyberArk's acquisition of Venafi (Cyberark, 2024) and Wiz's, Dazz and Gem acquisitions (Orbach, 2024) illustrate both consolidation and global integration within the ecosystem.

Agriculture and Food Technology

Israel's agricultural technology sector reflects decades of innovation driven by resource scarcity, arid climatic conditions, and the strategic imperative of food security. The sector encompasses advanced crop management systems, automated packaging technologies, silage and feed machinery, poultry production systems, precision spraying tools, transplanting equipment, and automated horticultural sorting and packing platforms.

By 2025, sectoral innovation increasingly centered on precision agriculture, artificial intelligence–driven decision support systems, sustainability, and alternative protein development. Precision agriculture integrates AI, sensor networks, and big data analytics to optimize irrigation, fertilization, and pesticide application. Sustainability initiatives emphasize regenerative farming practices and climate adaptation, while alternative protein research spans insect-based and cellular agriculture solutions.

A foundational actor in this ecosystem is Netafim, pioneer of modern drip irrigation technology since the 1960s, which continues to operate as a global leader in water-efficient agricultural systems. The sector's evolution demonstrates Israel's capacity to transform environmental constraints into exportable technological solutions addressing global climate and food security challenges.

Cleantech and Environmental Technologies

Israel's cleantech ecosystem comprises approximately 400 companies operating across renewable energy and water technologies. Core domains include energy storage and advanced battery systems, carbon capture and sequestration (both technological and nature-based), hydrogen technologies and renewable gases, solar photovoltaic systems (panels, inverters, tracking systems), and wind energy solutions.

Multinational corporations—including Google, Microsoft, and Volkswagen Group—participate through local R&D centers, strategic investments, and collaborative partnerships with Israeli startups. With over 430 multinational firms operating domestically, Israel functions as an experimental platform for scalable sustainability solutions, reinforcing its integration into global environmental innovation networks.

Software and Digital Technologies

Software and digital technologies remain the backbone of Israel's high-tech economy. The sector attracts substantial multinational R&D activity, leveraging Israel's expertise in artificial intelligence, data analytics, cybersecurity, fintech, SaaS platforms, and digital advertising technologies.

Major multinational corporations maintaining significant Israeli operations include Google, Microsoft, Nvidia, Amazon, and Intel, particularly in semiconductor and AI-related research.

Prominent Israeli-founded firms—such as monday.com, Mobileye, Wix, CyberArk, eToro, Riskified, and HiBob illustrate the ecosystem's capacity to generate globally competitive digital platforms. Collectively, these actors reinforce Israel's identity as a digitally driven innovation hub embedded within global capital and technology flows.

Automotive and Mobility Technologies

Israel's automotive innovation ecosystem concentrates on vehicle performance optimization, electrification, road safety systems, and environmental sustainability. Israeli firms maintain strategic collaborations with leading global automakers, including Volkswagen Group, Toyota, Ford Motor Company, Volvo, and Renault.

Technological partnerships—such as StoreDot with Volvo (Globes, 2022), ElectReon with Toyota and Denso (Foster, 2023), and Innoviz Technologies with Volkswagen Group (Innoviz Technologies, 2024) demonstrate Israel's role as a preferred R&D destination for next-generation mobility systems. The sector benefits from the cross-fertilization of software, semiconductor, and AI expertise originally cultivated in defense and digital industries.

Life Sciences and Health Technologies

Israel's life sciences sector encompasses approximately 1,800 health-technology companies employing around 80,000 professionals as of 2024. Recent growth has been driven primarily by digital health and medical device startups, while investment in capital-intensive biotechnology segments has remained comparatively moderate.

The ecosystem integrates competencies in electronics, communications, and electro-optics to deliver innovations in medical imaging, laser-based therapies, telemedicine platforms, diagnostics, surgical technologies, and medical education systems. Multinational pharmaceutical and medical technology firms—including Philips, Roche, Johnson & Johnson, and Pfizer—maintain active participation, alongside technology firms such as IBM, Oracle, and Cisco. This convergence of medical and digital expertise positions Israel at the forefront of integrated health innovation.

Financial Technology (Fintech)

Israel's fintech ecosystem comprises approximately 250 companies operating across payments, lending, wealth management, cross-border transfers, digital currencies, and financial planning technologies. By 2025, the sector demonstrated sustained global competitiveness, driven by AI adoption, embedded finance models, and advanced fraud detection systems.

Leading firms such as BioCatch, Forter, Payoneer, Rapyd and Melio (Orbach, 2025) exemplify scalable payment infrastructures and risk-management solutions.

Increasing consolidation, IPO readiness, and strategic partnerships—particularly with Gulf markets—signal the sector's maturation into a globally integrated financial innovation hub.

These domains illustrate the structural diversification and technological sophistication of Israel's innovation economy. While each sector exhibits distinct technological trajectories, they share common foundations: strong human capital formation, dense public-private collaboration, significant R&D intensity, and deep integration into global markets. Together, these characteristics sustain Israel's position as one of the world's most dynamic and export-oriented high-technology ecosystems.

DYNAMIC CLUSTERING AS A MECHANISM FOR INNOVATION DEVELOPMENT

Israel has institutionalized a dynamic clustering strategy as a central mechanism for fostering innovation-driven growth. This model is anchored in the establishment of open innovation incubators and technology hubs, many of which emerge from demonstrated scientific or commercial capabilities and receive structured support from IIA. Rather than operating as isolated accelerators, these incubators function as systemic coordination nodes that catalyse the gradual formation of sectoral and cross-sectoral innovation clusters.

At the core of this framework lies an open innovation logic. Incubators facilitate structured interaction among startups, established corporations, universities and research institutes, venture capital funds, and public-sector institutions. Through these sustained interactions, the system promotes knowledge diffusion, collaborative experimentation, and the recombination of technological and organizational capabilities. Such recombination is particularly significant in Israel's innovation environment, where defense technologies, digital systems, life sciences, and mobility platforms often intersect, generating spillover effects across domains.

In contrast to traditional cluster models—typically grounded in fixed geographic concentration—Israel's dynamic clustering model emphasizes functional connectivity over spatial proximity.

Although geographic hubs such as Tel Aviv and Haifa remain important, the primary organizing principle is network density rather than territorial boundaries.

Clusters are therefore adaptive and reconfigurable, capable of evolving in response to technological disruption, capital market shifts, and global demand fluctuations. This flexibility enhances systemic resilience and reduces path dependency.

The principal strategic objectives of Israel's dynamic clustering approach include:

- Promoting cross-domain innovation and knowledge exchange – By encouraging collaboration across technological fields, the model facilitates the integration of complementary competencies (e.g., AI with healthcare, cybersecurity with fintech, or mobility with semiconductor technologies).
- Building scalable and globally integrated ecosystems – Clusters are designed to accelerate startup growth and enable rapid insertion into global value chains through partnerships with multinational corporations and international investors.
- Supporting balanced regional development – While reinforcing Israel's global competitiveness, clustering initiatives also seek to distribute innovation activity beyond core metropolitan areas, leveraging universities and regional development programs to stimulate localized economic growth.

From a theoretical perspective, this approach reflects elements of evolutionary economic geography and innovation systems theory, where adaptability, institutional coordination, and network embeddedness are central determinants of long-term competitiveness.

By institutionalizing dynamic clustering, Israel has constructed a flexible innovation architecture that combines public policy coordination with private-sector dynamism, thereby sustaining high levels of technological output, export performance, and global integration.

ORGANIZATION OF THIS BOOK

Chapter 1: Models of Economic Development

In this opening chapter, I situate incubators and open incubator systems within the broader intellectual lineage of economic development theory. I trace their conceptual roots to the classical insights of industrial organization, where localized production systems and knowledge spillovers first emerged as engines of growth. Building on the Industrial Districts framework and the cluster-based logic of competitive advantage, I argue that contemporary incubators are not merely institutional supports for startups but sophisticated coordination mechanisms. They embed entrepreneurial ventures within dense innovation networks, enabling the circulation of knowledge, capital, and market access. In doing so, they represent a structural evolution from geographically bounded production systems toward more dynamic, networked innovation ecosystems.

Chapter 2: Agriculture-Based Products and Water Treatment

Here, I explore how structural constraints—particularly water scarcity and arid environmental conditions—can catalyze innovation rather than impede it. I demonstrate how an integrated ecosystem linking scientific research, entrepreneurial ventures, and state policy has transformed these constraints into competitive advantages. Advances in crop science, biotechnology, and digital agriculture illustrate a systemic shift toward efficiency, resilience, and sustainability. At the same time, water innovation, especially desalination and precision irrigation, emerges not as a supporting sector but as a foundational pillar. This chapter shows how necessity, when institutionalized through innovation systems, becomes a powerful driver of technological leadership.

Chapter 3: Food Technology (FoodTech)

In this chapter, I examine the transformation of food systems through technological innovation, with a particular emphasis on alternative proteins, microbiome science, and sustainable materials. I argue that FoodTech represents a convergence of agriculture, biotechnology, and digital systems, where nutritional functionality, environmental sustainability, and production efficiency intersect. From plant-based proteins to microalgae fermentation and personalized nutrition platforms, these innovations reflect a reconfiguration of how food is produced, consumed, and conceptualized. The integration of smart technologies and biodegradable packaging further illustrates the systemic nature of this transformation, positioning food not only as sustenance but as a domain of high technological sophistication.

Chapter 4: Healthcare Innovations in Israel

This chapter presents healthcare as a deeply integrated innovation system, where digital technologies, molecular biology, and engineering converge to redefine diagnosis and treatment. I explore how artificial intelligence enhances imaging, how non-invasive diagnostics shift the paradigm toward early detection, and how decentralized monitoring technologies bring healthcare into the home. Pharmaceutical innovation, too, is reimagined through targeted therapies and advanced delivery systems. Collectively, these developments signal a transition from reactive to predictive and personalized medicine, where precision and accessibility become central organizing principles of modern healthcare systems.

Chapter 5: Telecommunication and Security

In examining telecommunications and cybersecurity, I highlight the emergence of a highly interconnected technological ecosystem that spans communication infrastructure, cloud computing, and digital security. I show how innovations in satellite systems, voice-over-IP technologies, semiconductor design, and real-time navigation collectively underpin the architecture of the modern digital economy. At the same time, cybersecurity emerges as an indispensable counterpart to connectivity, safeguarding increasingly complex and distributed systems. This chapter underscores how integration across technological domains—not isolated breakthroughs—drives systemic innovation and global competitiveness.

Chapter 6: Management Platforms and Tools

This chapter shifts attention to the operational backbone of technological ecosystems: management platforms and digital tools. I argue that innovation is not only about breakthrough technologies but also about the systems that enable their development, deployment, and governance. From retail management systems to DevOps platforms and no-code security automation, these tools facilitate coordination across complex organizational environments. They reduce friction, enhance scalability, and democratize access to advanced capabilities. In this sense, management technologies become critical enablers of innovation, shaping how firms operate and compete in increasingly digitalized industries.

Chapter 7: Microelectronics

In this chapter, I explore the foundational role of microelectronics in enabling modern technological systems. I trace key innovations in memory storage, data transfer, and signal processing, demonstrating how these developments underpin a wide range of applications—from computing to telecommunications and automotive systems. By examining technologies such as non-volatile memory and high-speed data exchange protocols, I show how advances at the micro level generate transformative effects across entire industries. This chapter emphasizes that seemingly small-scale innovations in semiconductor design often serve as the invisible infrastructure of the digital age.

Chapter 8: Digital Imaging and AI Applications

Here, I examine the evolution of digital imaging into a broader ecosystem of artificial intelligence applications. Beginning with early breakthroughs in digital printing and image processing, I trace how these capabilities expanded into advanced computer vision systems. I argue that this progression reflects a deeper trajectory: from visual representation to intelligent interpretation. Across sectors such as healthcare, agriculture, and autonomous mobility, AI-driven image analysis enables new forms of decision-making and automation. This chapter highlights how foundational expertise in imaging has positioned the ecosystem at the forefront of the global AI revolution.

Chapter 9: Energy

In this chapter, I analyze innovation across the entire energy value chain, emphasizing the transition toward more sustainable, efficient, and flexible systems. I explore technologies ranging from waste heat recovery and desalination-linked energy systems to advanced storage solutions and wireless power transmission. These innovations reflect a shift from centralized, fossil-based systems to distributed, multi-source energy architectures. I argue that the future of energy lies not in a single breakthrough but in the integration of diverse technologies that collectively enhance resilience and sustainability.

Chapter 10: Defense

This chapter examines how persistent security challenges have driven the development of a highly advanced and integrated defense innovation ecosystem. I explore the convergence of unmanned systems, missile defense, artificial intelligence, and communication technologies, demonstrating how these capabilities are designed to operate in complex and dynamic environments. The emphasis on precision, adaptability, and real-time intelligence reflects a broader trend toward technologically intensive defense strategies. In this context, innovation is not optional but existential, shaping both national security and technological advancement.

Chapter 11: The Open Incubators Cluster Model for Discontinuous and Disruptive Innovations

In this chapter, I extend the discussion of innovation systems by introducing the Open Incubators Cluster Model as a framework for fostering disruptive technological change. I analyze how policy instruments, particularly state-supported R&D incentives, have enabled a bottom-up innovation ecosystem characterized by entrepreneurial diversity and rapid commercialization. At the same time, I critically assess the limitations of this approach, particularly in terms of strategic coordination.

I propose that future development requires a more data-driven and integrated policy framework capable of aligning innovation efforts with long-term societal challenges.

Chapter 12: Domains of Potential Regional Cooperation of MNCs in the Middle East

This chapter shifts the focus to regional dynamics, exploring how multinational corporations and governments collaborate to address shared challenges in water, energy, food, and ecosystem security. I examine how large-scale infrastructure projects and digital connectivity initiatives serve as mechanisms for both economic development and geopolitical stability. The integration of AI and cloud technologies further enhances these efforts, illustrating how technological cooperation can transcend traditional political boundaries. I argue that such collaborations represent a new model of regional development grounded in shared resource management.

Chapter 13: Multinational Corporations and Innovation Ecosystems in the Middle East

In this chapter, I provide a comparative analysis of innovation ecosystems across key Middle Eastern economies. I explore how multinational corporations interact with local institutions to drive digital transformation, industrial modernization, and energy transition. Each country presents a distinct model shaped by its economic structure, policy framework, and strategic priorities. Together, they illustrate the diversity of pathways through which innovation ecosystems can emerge and evolve within a rapidly changing global economy.

Chapter 14: Innovative Activities of Multinational Corporations in the Middle East

Here, I examine the role of multinational corporations as catalysts of technological change and economic diversification. I argue that their contributions extend beyond capital investment to include knowledge transfer, workforce development, and integration into global value chains. By analyzing their activities across different national contexts, I show how MNCs facilitate the diffusion of advanced technologies and managerial practices, accelerating the transition toward knowledge-based economies.

Chapter 15: MNCs and Innovative Virtual Open Incubators Cluster (IVOIC) Promoting Peace in the Middle East

In this chapter, I explore the intersection of innovation, economic development, and geopolitical stability. I introduce the concept of the Innovative Virtual Open Incubators Cluster as a mechanism for fostering cross-border collaboration and reducing conflict through shared economic interests. By examining urban innovation hubs and institutional reforms, I demonstrate how technological ecosystems can contribute to peace-building efforts. Innovation, in this context, becomes not only an economic imperative but also a strategic tool for regional cooperation.

Chapter 16: The Resource Curse Debate and Rent Capture

This chapter turns to the paradox of resource-rich economies that struggle to achieve broad-based development. I examine the structural and institutional factors underlying the resource curse, focusing on issues of governance, rent distribution, and economic diversification. Through the lens of African economies, I argue that natural resource wealth, in the absence of effective institutions, can hinder rather than promote development. This analysis sets the stage for a deeper exploration of extractive industries in subsequent chapters.

Chapter 17: Leading Mining MNCs in Africa

In this chapter, I analyze the dominant role of multinational mining corporations in shaping Africa's extractive sectors. I explore how their control over capital, technology, and global value chains influences production structures and knowledge flows. While these firms bring significant capabilities, their dominance also reinforces asymmetries in value distribution. This chapter highlights the complex interplay between global corporate power and local economic development.

Chapter 18: Chinese Companies in Africa's Extractive Industries

Here, I examine the transformative impact of Chinese investment in Africa's resource sectors. I analyze how infrastructure financing, trade agreements, and long-term resource access strategies are integrated within a broader geopolitical framework. Through case studies, I explore the implications for governance, development, and knowledge transfer. This chapter provides a nuanced assessment of both the opportunities and challenges associated with China's growing presence in Africa.

Chapter 19: Indian and Japanese Companies in Africa's Extractive Industries

In this chapter, I compare the distinct strategies of Indian and Japanese firms operating in Africa. I show how differences in investment models—ranging from direct ownership to partnership-based approaches—shape outcomes in terms of control, risk, and knowledge transfer. This comparative perspective reveals the diversity of global engagement strategies and their implications for local development.

Chapter 20: European Companies in Africa's Extractive Industries

This chapter examines the historical and contemporary role of European firms in Africa's resource sectors. I analyze how their emphasis on governance and sustainability frameworks contrasts with other global actors, while also acknowledging the of structural inequalities in global value chains. The chapter highlights both progress and persistent challenges in aligning corporate practices with developmental objectives.

Chapter 21: North American Companies in Africa's Extractive Industries

Here, I explore the contributions of North American firms, emphasizing their technological capabilities and structured investment approaches. I argue that while these firms play a significant role in resource development and revenue generation, they also exemplify the broader limitations of externally driven industrialization. The chapter underscores the need for greater local integration and capacity building.

Chapter 22: Brazilian Companies in Africa's Extractive and Energy Sectors

In this chapter, I present Brazil's engagement as a distinctive model of South–South cooperation. I analyze how Brazilian firms integrate extraction with infrastructure development and technical collaboration, creating more holistic value chains. This approach offers an alternative to traditional Western and Chinese models, highlighting the potential for more balanced and cooperative forms of global economic engagement.

Chapter 23: African Companies in Mining and Energy Sectors

This chapter shifts the focus to African-owned enterprises, examining their growing role in managing and developing the continent's natural resources. I explore how these firms combine local knowledge with strategic capabilities, contributing to a gradual rebalancing of control within the extractive sector. While challenges remain, their emergence signals an important step toward greater economic sovereignty.

Chapter 24: Australian Companies in Africa

In this chapter, I analyze the role of Australian firms, emphasizing their integration within a broader ecosystem of mining services and technical expertise. I show how their engagement extends beyond extraction to include knowledge transfer and operational support, shaping local industry practices. This highlights the importance of ancillary services in the development of extractive economies.

Chapter 25: Main African Mines

Here, I examine key mining operations and the role of state-owned enterprises in resource governance. Through specific examples, I explore how state participation can enhance value capture while also confronting challenges related to efficiency and governance. This chapter illustrates the evolving landscape of resource control and the increasing diversification of actors within the sector.

Chapter 26: The Innovative Virtual Open Incubators Cluster (IVOIC) Adaptation to African Mining

In the concluding chapter, I extend the IVOIC framework to the context of African mining, proposing a model for transforming extractive economies into innovation-driven systems. By leveraging virtual collaboration platforms, the model overcomes the limitations of geographic clustering, enabling knowledge exchange across borders. I argue that this approach can facilitate technological upgrading, support diversification, and create more sustainable development pathways. In doing so, the chapter brings the book's central themes full circle, linking innovation systems, global collaboration, and economic transformation.

REFERENCES

CyberArk. (2024). *CyberArk to Acquire Venafi Seamlessly securing all identities.* https://s203.q4cdn.com/693570796/files/doc_presentation/Investor-Presentation-Final.pdf

Foster, J. (2023). Electreon to develop wireless charging technology with Toyota and Denso. *Electric Charging and Infrastructure.*

Globes. (2022). Volvo invests in fast-charge EV battery co StoreDot. *Globes.* https://en.globes.co.il/en/article-volvo-invests-in-fast-charge-ev-battery-co-storedot-1001409715

Innoviz Technologies (2024). Innoviz Technologies Accelerates Delivery of Newly Designed LiDAR Platform to Volkswagen Autonomous Mobility to Equip a Fleet of ID. Buzz AD Shuttles in 2025. Innoviz Technologies.

Israel Innovation Authority. (2024). 2024 Annual Report The State of High-Tech. Israel Innovation Authority. https://innovationisrael.org.il/wp-content/uploads/2024/06/2024-Annual-Report-The-State-of-High-Tech.pdf

Orbach, M. (2024). Wiz acquires Dazz for $450 million to strengthen AI-driven cloud security. *Calcalisttech.*

Orbach, M. (2025). Zealand's Xero acquires Melio for up to $3 billion, marking one of Israel's largest tech exits. Calcalist.

Chapter 1
Models of Economic Development

ABSTRACT

Incubators and open incubator systems have emerged as central instruments in contemporary economic development strategies, particularly within knowledge-driven economies seeking to enhance entrepreneurial dynamism, employment generation, and technological upgrading. These institutional mechanisms are designed not merely to support firm creation, but to embed startups within structured innovation networks that facilitate knowledge transfer, capital access, and market integration. Their conceptual foundations can be traced to earlier theories of regional industrial development, most notably the Industrial Districts (ID) framework. The ID model, associated with the work of Alfred Marshall and later expanded by scholars such as Giacomo Becattini, emphasized the economic advantages derived from geographic concentration, specialization, and localized learning. The Cluster Model advanced by Michael Porter highlighted the competitive advantages generated by geographically proximate and interconnected firms operating within related industries.

INTRODUCTION

Incubators and open incubator systems have emerged as central instruments in contemporary economic development strategies, particularly within knowledge-driven economies seeking to enhance entrepreneurial dynamism, employment generation, and technological upgrading. These institutional mechanisms are designed not merely to support firm creation, but to embed startups within structured innovation networks that facilitate knowledge transfer, capital access, and market integration.

DOI: 10.4018/979-8-3373-7350-8.ch001

Their conceptual foundations can be traced to earlier theories of regional industrial development, most notably the Industrial Districts (ID) framework.

The Industrial Districts model, associated with the work of Alfred Marshall and later expanded by scholars such as Giacomo Becattini, emphasized the economic advantages derived from geographic concentration, specialization, and localized learning. Within this paradigm, spatial proximity enabled informal knowledge spillovers, labor market pooling, and cumulative innovation dynamics. Industrial growth was therefore understood as a socially embedded process in which tacit knowledge circulated through dense local networks, reinforcing collective efficiency and regional competitiveness.

Subsequent theoretical developments broadened and formalized these insights. The Cluster Model advanced by Michael Porter highlighted the competitive advantages generated by geographically proximate and interconnected firms operating within related industries.

Porter's framework underscored the role of supplier-buyer linkages, specialized institutions, and competitive rivalry in stimulating innovation and productivity growth. In this view, clusters function as strategic ecosystems that enhance firm performance through both collaboration and competition.

SCOPE AND STRUCTURE OF THE CHAPTER

Further refinement emerged in the Clust-ER Associations framework, which institutionalized structured inter-firm collaboration based on the principle of "co-opetition"—the simultaneous coexistence of cooperation and competition among firms operating in overlapping technological or market domains. Unlike earlier models that relied primarily on spontaneous agglomeration, Clust-ER systems emphasize formal coordination mechanisms, shared governance structures, and public-private partnerships designed to accelerate innovation diffusion and joint capability development.

Building upon these theoretical foundations, the Open Incubator Cluster Model represents an evolutionary extension of cluster-based development strategies. Rather than confining incubation to narrowly defined technological cores, open incubator systems intentionally integrate adjacent and complementary sectors. This cross-sectoral orientation encourages knowledge recombination, interdisciplinary experimentation, and the emergence of hybrid innovation domains. By connecting startups with established firms, universities, research institutions, investors, and policy agencies, open incubators serve as adaptive coordination platforms within broader innovation ecosystems.

From a systemic perspective, this model enhances resilience and long-term competitiveness by promoting flexibility, reducing technological lock-in, and enabling rapid reconfiguration in response to shifting market conditions. The integration of cross-domain capabilities strengthens both regional and national innovation systems, ensuring that economic development strategies remain responsive to technological disruption and global competition. In this sense, open incubator clusters embody a dynamic and network-based approach to economic development, rooted in classical agglomeration theory yet adapted to the complexities of the contemporary knowledge economy.

The remainder of this chapter explores the central dimensions of modern incubation and clustering frameworks, with particular focus on the following themes:

- Physical and virtual incubation models;
- Open incubators and the core operational functions of virtual open incubators;
- Industrial Districts (IDs) and Clust-ER Associations;
- Cluster-based development models, including the role of supporting industries, related sectors, and infrastructure and service providers;
- Virtual clusters and Virtual Open Incubator Clusters (VOICs);

Innovative Virtual Open Incubator Clusters (IVOICs) implemented under Israel Innovation Authority (IIA) policy, including their governance structures, operational mechanisms, strategic advantages, and targeted technological domains.

PHYSICAL AND VIRTUAL INCUBATORS: A COMPARATIVE PERSPECTIVE

Modern incubation frameworks encompass both physical and virtual modalities, each designed to facilitate entrepreneurial development while responding to different operational and strategic imperatives. Physical incubators traditionally provide a shared, co-located environment in which early-stage startups or small and medium-sized enterprises (SMEs) operate under structured organizational and managerial conditions. Typically hosting twenty to thirty ventures, these incubators enable participants to access common infrastructure, including office space, laboratories, and prototyping facilities, alongside essential services such as mentoring, administrative support, legal and accounting guidance, and specialized technical assistance from both in-house staff and external experts. Co-location fosters informal knowledge exchange, social learning, and collaborative problem-solving, reinforcing the interactive processes highlighted in Industrial Districts and cluster theories (see Exhibit 1).

In contrast, virtual incubators deliver comparable advisory, financial, and networking support without necessitating physical co-location. Startups participating in virtual incubation programs operate from geographically dispersed locations while interacting with incubator staff, mentors, and peer firms through digital platforms, virtual workshops, and structured remote engagements. This modality leverages contemporary information and communication technologies to maintain high-intensity interaction, knowledge transfer, and resource accessibility across spatial boundaries.

Virtual incubators are often sponsored by diverse actors, including venture capital funds, public authorities, or private corporations, each with distinctive objectives. Private-sector sponsors typically prioritize commercial outcomes, portfolio performance, and accelerated scaling, whereas public-sector sponsors emphasize regional economic development, entrepreneurial skill formation, and broader socioeconomic impact.

The comparative advantages of each model reflect underlying strategic trade-offs. Physical incubators excel in fostering dense interpersonal networks, tacit knowledge exchange, and hands-on support for technology-intensive ventures. Virtual incubators, by contrast, maximize geographic reach, scalability, and flexibility, enabling participants to access specialized expertise and international markets without the constraints of co-location. Hybrid models increasingly integrate physical and virtual components, combining on-site facilities with remote mentorship, virtual learning, and online networking to exploit the benefits of both approaches.

Together, these incubation modalities form the operational foundation for more complex clustering frameworks, including open incubators, Virtual Open Incubator Clusters (VOICs), and Innovative Virtual Open Incubator Clusters (IVOICs). These frameworks extend the traditional incubator model by emphasizing cross-sectoral collaboration, networked innovation, and adaptive governance structures, thereby reinforcing the resilience and global competitiveness of national and regional innovation ecosystems. Figure 1 provides a synthesized overview of the core characteristics, functional components, and comparative dimensions of physical and virtual incubator models.

Figure 1. Incubator

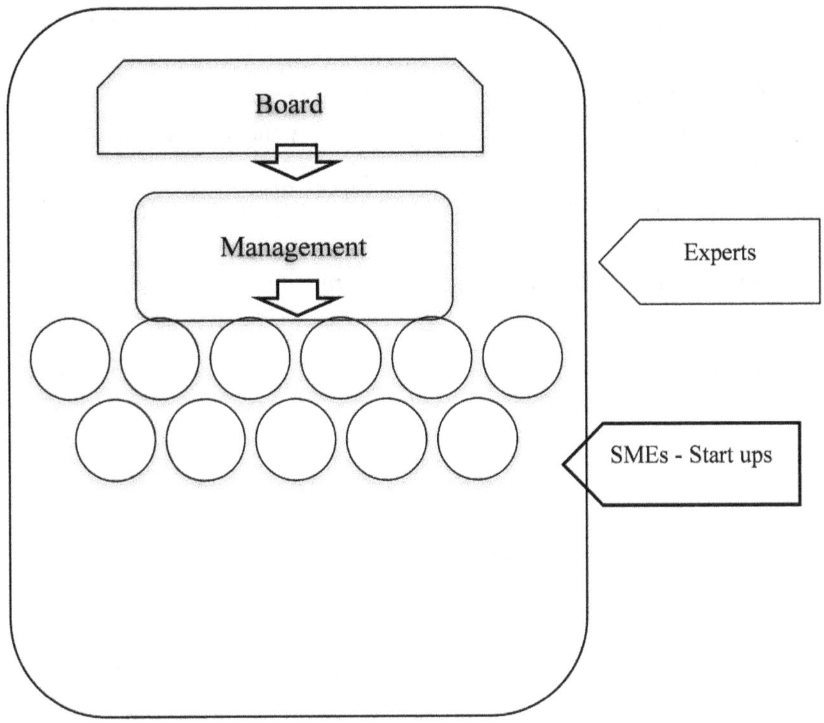

The Open Incubator Model

The Open Incubator Model constitutes an advancement of the conventional incubation framework, distinguished by its expansion of both participant diversity and the breadth of support mechanisms. Traditional incubators typically focus on firms physically hosted within their facilities, providing co-location, mentorship, and shared infrastructure. In contrast, open incubators extend their activities beyond resident startups to include a broader ecosystem of stakeholders. These encompass graduated ventures, external companies operating in complementary or supporting sectors, and organizations offering specialized infrastructure, professional services, or technological capabilities aligned with the incubator's industrial or technological domain (see Figure 2).

By integrating diverse actors into a unified innovation platform, open incubators facilitate structured cross-sector interaction, promote accelerated knowledge diffusion, and strengthen the coherence and resilience of regional innovation systems. The deliberate linkage of early-stage ventures with established firms, service providers, research institutions, and enabling organizations fosters collaborative experimentation, capability recombination, and co-development of novel technologies and solutions.

This systemic approach enhances the scalability and impact of innovation outcomes. Startups benefit not only from direct support but also from the extended network of actors capable of providing complementary expertise, market access, and strategic resources. Consequently, open incubators expand the reach of entrepreneurial activity, reinforce ecosystem connectivity, and contribute to the long-term Figure 2 illustrates the structural configuration of the Open Incubator Model, highlighting the relationships among resident ventures, ecosystem participants, and enabling institutions within a coordinated innovation framework.

Figure 2. The open incubator

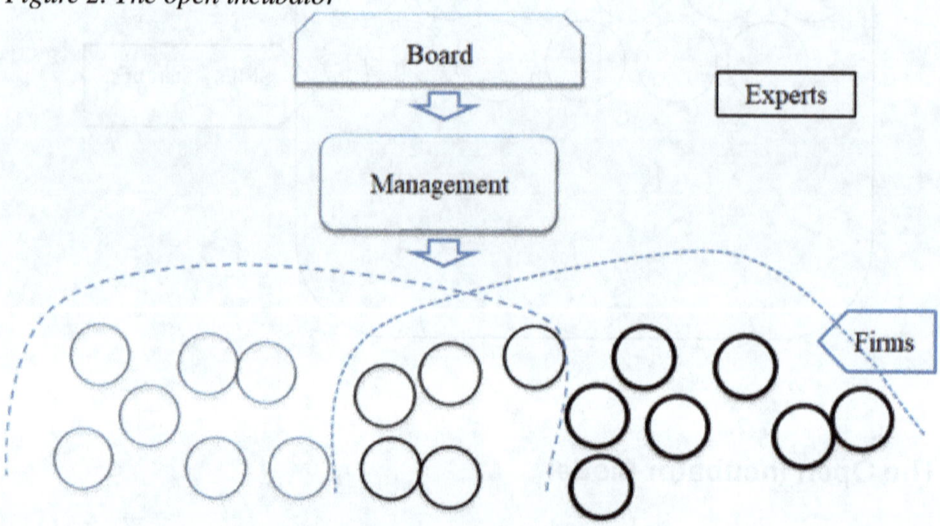

Governance and Management of Open Incubators

The effective operation of Open Incubators depends on a dual structure of strategic governance and operational management, designed to align incubation activities with broader economic development objectives while ensuring the efficient delivery of services to entrepreneurial participants.

Board Structure

The governance of an Open Incubator is overseen by a board comprising representatives from local and national authorities, industry stakeholders, and other relevant ecosystem actors (see Figure 3). The board functions as the principal strategic decision-making body, guiding the incubator's mission and ensuring alignment with regional and national economic priorities. Typical board composition includes:

- Local and national authorities: Government delegates provide policy oversight, propose financial and professional support measures, and ensure that incubator programs advance public-sector objectives.
- Infrastructure service providers: Organizations operating in sectors such as energy, water, transportation, finance, insurance, and education contribute to strategic planning, assist in program implementation, and monitor outcomes.
- Professional associations: Sectoral associations—for example in agriculture, healthcare, food processing, and microelectronics—offer technical guidance, validate operational standards, and ensure adherence to industry best practices.
- Customer organizations: Representatives from relevant customer associations, NGOs, and private or public enterprises provide market insights, user feedback, and guidance on adoption pathways for innovations developed within the incubator.

The board's oversight ensures that strategic priorities, resource allocation, and stakeholder interests are systematically integrated into incubator operations.

Management Responsibilities

The management team operationalizes the board's directives and oversees the daily functioning of the incubator. Core responsibilities include:

Entrepreneur Selection and Monitoring:

- Identify and select startups with potential to reinforce existing industries or develop capabilities in strategic sectors.
- Monitor progress throughout the incubation period, providing support tailored to each venture's developmental stage.
- Facilitate post-incubation integration into wider economic networks, ensuring continuity of support after graduation.

Stakeholder Engagement:

- Coordinate with external actors—including industry mavens, connectors, and sales professionals from supporting and related sectors—as well as infrastructure providers.
- Ensure that startups have access to technological expertise, market insights, and business development resources.

Expert Support:

- Engage technical, financial, and business specialists to advise management and strengthen the outcomes of incubation.
- Address gaps in startup development, providing targeted interventions to enhance commercial and technological readiness.

Development and Expansion of the Open Incubator

A central objective of the Open Incubator is to catalyse the growth of related and supporting industries, as well as essential infrastructure services within its technological or industrial domain. This is accomplished through sustained collaboration with board members, local authorities, and key economic actors, ensuring that incubator initiatives reinforce broader ecosystem development while generating tangible economic and technological spillovers.

The Open Incubator model also serves as a scalable blueprint for replication across regions and sectors. New incubators are established in alignment with the technological or industrial focus of the original incubator, preserving strategic coherence while adapting to local conditions and stakeholder networks (see Figure 3). Each successive incubator implements its own dedicated programs to support successive generations of entrepreneurs, providing structured mentorship, access to technical and business expertise, and integration into wider innovation networks.

Through this replication and expansion process, the Open Incubator model achieves several critical outcomes:

Ecosystem Scaling: By replicating incubators within complementary sectors, the model facilitates systemic growth, creating a network of interconnected innovation nodes that mutually reinforce each other.

Continuity of Support: Successive incubators ensure sustained developmental pathways for entrepreneurs, maintaining knowledge flows and support structures over multiple startup generations.

Resilience and Adaptability: The distributed and networked nature of the incubator system enhances the resilience of the innovation ecosystem, enabling rapid adaptation to technological changes, market dynamics, and policy shifts.

In effect, the Open Incubator model transforms incubation from a single-site support mechanism into a replicable, ecosystem-level strategy that fosters long-term, scalable, and sustainable innovation-led economic development.

Figure 3. Structural overview of the open incubator model

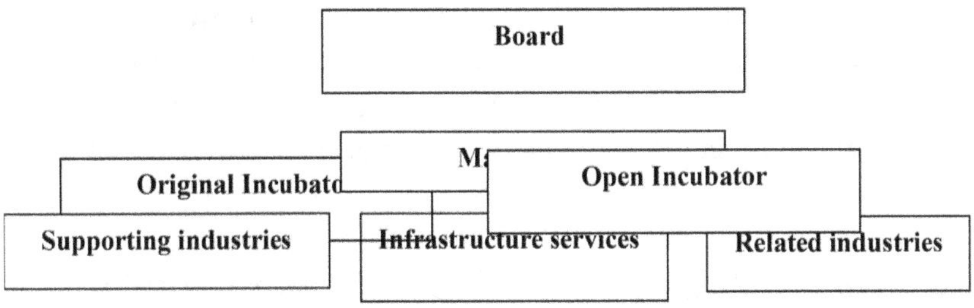

Virtual Open Incubators

Virtual incubators are specialized support structures designed to deliver funding, mentorship, and professional guidance to entrepreneurial ventures distributed across geographically dispersed locations. Typically established by venture capital firms, private corporations, or public institutions, virtual incubators provide flexible, digitally mediated platforms for startup development. The objectives of sponsoring entities differ: private sponsors primarily seek accelerated business growth and financial returns, whereas public organizations, such as the Israel Innovation Authority (IIA), emphasize regional and national economic development outcomes.

Under Israel's Law for the Encouragement of Industrial Research and Development (1984), the IIA predominantly supports individual firms. However, exceptions exist for group-based initiatives in strategic domains such as space technology, applied research consortia, and pilot programs co-funded with government partners. Building on this framework, domain-specific virtual incubators are proposed, in which participating firms collaborate with local enterprises, service providers, and public-sector institutions. These virtual clusters enable joint proposal submissions for funding, targeting tangible economic impacts in their regions. Within this model, incubator management establishes strategic priorities for technological and business initiatives, while participating firms guide the engagement of local economic actors and supporting service providers.

Industrial Districts (IDs)

Industrial Districts (IDs) trace their origins to Alfred Marshall's early-20th-century analysis of the economic advantages of geographic concentration (Markusen, 1996). These districts typically aggregate specialized skills, advanced machinery, and leading firms, fostering localized competitive advantages. The ID model emphasizes a division of labor among small and medium enterprises, combining competitive and complementary activities, and represents a form of regional specialization in which inter-firm interactions stimulate innovation and industrial dynamics (Becattini, 1990).

In Italy, IDs became prominent in the 1970s, characterized by flexible specialization, differentiated processes or products, and a deepened division of labor (Rabellotti, 1995; Schmitz, 1995; Rabellotti & Schmitz, 1999). Cooperation within these districts is reinforced by institutional support (Bellandi, 1996), geographic proximity facilitating knowledge spillovers (Garnsey, 1998), and social embeddedness encouraging collective learning and resource sharing (Dei Ottati, 1994; Harrison, 1992). Becattini (1990) identified four critical dimensions underpinning IDs: institutional frameworks, local culture and values, social capital, and human resources. These dimensions are operationalized through business support services, collective marketing, entrepreneurial promotion, and advocacy with government authorities (Alberti, 2001; Provasi, 2002; Marini, 2000; Scarlato, 2001; D'Antonio & Scarlato, 2000).

Over time, traditional Italian IDs evolved into hub-and-spoke cluster structures, where dominant firms coordinate networks of smaller enterprises, consolidating regional innovation capacity and sustaining competitive advantage (Carbonara, 2002; Belussi & Bertini, 1998).

Clust-ER Associations

Clust-ER Associations are collaborative networks composed of public and private actors—including research centers, firms, and training institutions—designed to enhance the competitiveness of strategic production systems, particularly in the Emilia-Romagna region. These networks leverage regional innovation capacities by linking research laboratories and invention centers within the High Technology Network to companies and higher education institutions, facilitating joint problem-solving, strategic project development, and identification of new business opportunities (InvestinEmiliaRomagna, n.d.).

The Clust-ER ecosystem currently includes seven core clusters: Agrifood, Build, Create, Greentech, Health, Innovate, and Mech. Two additional networks focus on Motorvehicle and Big Data. In 2022, Clust-ER Tourism and Clust-ER Urban were added to accommodate emerging sectors. Collectively, the Clust-ER system comprises 757 members, including 411 enterprises, encompassing 32 value chains, and is coordinated by ART-ER, the regional consortium for innovation and technology transfer.

These associations exemplify structured, networked approaches to innovation, combining research, industry, and institutional resources to strengthen regional and sectoral competitiveness, and providing a model for integration into broader virtual incubator and cluster-based frameworks.

Cluster Model

A cluster is defined as a geographic concentration of interconnected companies, institutions, and organizations operating within a specific sector, often encompassing related and supporting industries that collectively sustain competitive advantage (Porter, 1998). Clusters enhance access to specialized labor, suppliers, knowledge, and market intelligence, strengthening firms' competitiveness both locally and globally (Enright, 1996, 2000; Rosenfeld, 1996; Saxenian, 1994). By fostering proximity, shared expertise, and dense inter-firm linkages, clusters create environments conducive to innovation, efficiency, and dynamic growth.

Supporting Industries

Supporting industries provide essential inputs that enable production, service delivery, and market competitiveness. These include:

- Suppliers of raw materials, components, and machinery: Deliver critical inputs necessary for manufacturing and production processes.
- Subcontracting services: Offer specialized capabilities that complement in-house operations, such as precision fabrication or assembly.
- Infrastructure services: Logistics, utilities, and communications networks facilitate efficient operations and market access.

By supplying expertise, resources, and operational support, supporting industries improve efficiency, reduce costs, and underpin the growth and sustainability of clusters.

Related Industries

Related industries share common technologies, materials, or customer bases with core cluster activities, enabling cross-sectoral knowledge transfer, resource sharing, and collaborative innovation. Examples include:

- Similar raw materials: Pineapple and apple juice production within the beverage sector; wood used in furniture, construction, and paper manufacturing.
- Similar technologies: Laser applications spanning metal fabrication, medical devices, and telecommunications; AI solutions applied in education, healthcare, and defense.
- Similar customer segments: Books targeted at children, medical professionals, or engineers; furniture designed for homes, offices, or warehouses.

Integration with related industries strengthens a cluster's technological versatility, market reach, and innovation potential.

Infrastructure Services

Infrastructure services are foundational to cluster functionality, supporting both operational efficiency and inter-firm connectivity:

- Water management and treatment: Ensures quality, reduces waste, and supports industries such as food, pharmaceuticals, and metals.
- Energy supply: Shared power networks facilitate chemical, plastics, cold storage, medical, and semiconductor production.
- Transportation: Integrated shipping, rail, road, and air logistics—including warehousing—enhance supply chain efficiency.
- Telecommunications: Fiber optics, satellite links, cloud computing platforms, servers, and digital networks enable virtual collaboration, knowledge exchange, and cluster integration.

  By combining core firms with related industries, supporting industries, and robust infrastructure services, clusters create synergistic ecosystems that reinforce competitive advantage, innovation, and sustainable economic growth.

Virtual Clusters

The emergence of digital technologies and online professional networks has transformed the traditional geographic basis of clusters into virtual clusters. These networks enable organizations to collaborate across dispersed locations, leveraging information and communication technologies (ICT) for knowledge sharing, joint problem-solving, and innovation activities (Passiante et al., 2002). While virtual clusters may reduce some local economic spillovers, they expand access to a broader array of supporting and related industries, allowing firms to tap expertise, resources, and markets beyond their immediate region.

The Virtual Innovation System (VIS) concept conceptualizes innovation as a non-linear, multi-directional process, emphasizing person-based interactions over strict place-based linkages (Romano & Passiante, 1997; De la Mothe & Paquet, 1998). VIS underscores the importance of connectivity, knowledge flows, and distributed collaboration in generating and applying innovative solutions.

Virtual Open Incubator Cluster (VOIC) Model

The Virtual Open Incubator Cluster (VOIC) model integrates principles of traditional cluster theory with virtual collaboration, extending the advantages of co-location to distributed networks. Unlike conventional clusters that rely on geographic proximity, VOICs connect startups, research institutions, supporting industries, and infrastructure providers through ICT platforms. This configuration enables the translation of radical scientific and technological innovations into practical applications by linking innovators with firms capable of bringing breakthrough ideas to market—both domestically and internationally.

Governance: VOIC Board

Each VOIC is governed by a board comprising representatives from local and national authorities, industry stakeholders, and the broader entrepreneurial and academic ecosystem. Board composition and responsibilities typically include:

- Local and national public authorities: Ensure policy alignment, implement strategic initiatives, and allocate resources.
- Economic stakeholders: Represent industries within the VOIC's domain, providing market insights and sectoral guidance.
- Academic and entrepreneurial representatives: Facilitate knowledge transfer, research collaboration, and innovation strategy integration.
- Board responsibilities focus on:
- Coordinating the execution of innovation strategies at local and national levels.
- Deploying financial instruments and professional support programs to strengthen startup development.

Ensuring that cluster activities align with regional and national priorities, maximizing systemic impact and scalability.

Management Responsibilities

The VOIC management team operationalizes the cluster's strategic objectives and coordinates day-to-day activities. Key responsibilities include:

- Identifying initiatives for IIA support: Selecting projects and programs requiring funding or guidance from the Israel Innovation Authority.
- Defining collaboration domains: Establishing cross-sector cooperation with related clusters and industry networks to enhance knowledge exchange.
- Coordinating joint initiatives: Managing collective projects that leverage shared resources to generate measurable economic and technological outcomes.

By integrating multiple open incubators into a cohesive network, the VOIC framework accelerates innovation-driven growth. Each incubator focuses on its strategic domain while benefiting from expertise and support provided by complementary industries and service providers.

Impact and Acceleration

Embedding open incubators within a networked VOIC framework extends their influence beyond immediate participants. Key benefits include:

- Cross-pollination among sectors: Facilitates knowledge exchange and collaboration across related and supporting industries.
- Strengthening national innovation systems: Enhances coherence, efficiency, and alignment of the broader innovation ecosystem.
- Promoting regional economic development: Establishes interconnected hubs that stimulate entrepreneurship, job creation, and technology diffusion.

Adaptability and Continuous Evolution

To remain effective in rapidly evolving technological and market environments, VOICs emphasize:

- Continuous strategic alignment: Regular updates to cluster priorities to match changing market demands, emerging technologies, and policy objectives.
- Feedback loops: Structured mechanisms linking startups, experts, authorities, and market actors to monitor performance and identify new opportunities.

- Adaptive capacity: The ability to pivot, reconfigure activities, and integrate emerging technologies or innovation opportunities, ensuring sustained competitiveness and systemic resilience.

Through these mechanisms, the VOIC model operationalizes a dynamic, networked, and technology-enabled approach to innovation, bridging the advantages of traditional clusters with the flexibility and reach of virtual collaboration.

Innovative VOICs (IVOICs) under IIA Policy

Building on Israel's Law for the Encouragement of Industrial Research and Development (1984), current innovation policy administered by the Israel Innovation Authority (IIA) primarily targets individual high-tech projects. To achieve greater system-level impact and stimulate sector-wide innovation, this study proposes the development of Innovative Virtual Open Incubator Clusters (IVOICs), which extend support from single firms to networked clusters of interrelated actors.

IVOIC Initiative

Objective:

- To expand IIA support beyond individual firms, creating integrated VOICs that cluster strategic domains and connect complementary actors across the innovation ecosystem.

Mechanism:

- Firms applying for IIA support are invited to join a relevant VOIC aligned with their technological or industrial domain.
- Each VOIC is governed by a dedicated IIA board responsible for project selection, defining incentive structures, and coordinating cross-firm initiatives.
- The board ensures alignment with national innovation priorities, monitors cluster performance, and facilitates collaborative activities among participants.

Benefits:

- Enhanced system intelligence: By connecting related innovations and fostering knowledge sharing, IVOICs strengthen the collective understanding of technological trends and market opportunities.

- Efficiency and accelerated diffusion: The cluster structure reduces duplication of effort, streamlines R&D activities, and promotes rapid dissemination of technologies across firms and sectors.
- Scalability and market integration: By linking complementary projects and actors, IVOICs facilitate the scaling of innovations and their integration into domestic and international markets.

Targeted VOIC Domains

Initial implementation of IVOICs focuses on strategically significant sectors where Israel maintains competitive advantage or seeks to foster systemic innovation:

- Agriculture and Water Treatment: Precision agriculture, irrigation technologies, and sustainable water management solutions.
- Food Technology: Novel ingredients, processing systems, and alternative protein innovations.
- Healthcare: Digital health, medical devices, and telemedicine platforms.
- Telecommunications and Security: Cybersecurity, data networks, and communication infrastructure.
- Energy: Renewable energy technologies, storage systems, and cleantech solutions.
- Microelectronics: Semiconductor design, embedded systems, and advanced electronics.
- Management Platforms and Tools: Enterprise software, workflow solutions, and decision-support systems.
- Artificial Intelligence (AI) Applications: Machine learning, data analytics, and domain-specific AI solutions.
- Defense Technologies: Innovative solutions for homeland security, autonomous systems, and advanced defense platforms.

By systematically integrating these sectors within a VOIC framework, IVOICs are positioned to amplify the strategic impact of IIA programs, enhance collaboration across the national innovation ecosystem, and accelerate Israel's global technological competitiveness.

REFERENCES

Alberti, F. (2001). The governance of industrial districts: a theoretical footing proposal. *Liuc Papers, 82*(5).

Becattini, G. (1990). The Marshallian industrial districtindustrial district as a socio-economic notion. In *Industrial Districts and Inter-Firm Co-operation in Italy*. International Institute for Labor Studies.

Bellandi, M. (1996). On entrepreneurship, region and the constitution of scale and scope economies. *European Planning Studies*, *4*(4), 421–438. DOI: 10.1080/09654319608720356

Belussi, F., & Bertini, S. (1998). Evoluzione, apprendimento e modelli di acquisizione delle conoscenze: due sistemi locali a confronto nel settore del mobile imbottito. *Economia e Società Regionale*, (1998/2).

Carbonara, N. (2002). New models of inter-firm networks within industrial districts. *Entrepreneurship and Regional Development*, *14*(3), 229–246. DOI: 10.1080/08985620210136027

D'Antonio, M., & Scarlato, M. (2000), Capitale umano e sviluppo economico un modello di equilibrio economico generale per il Centro-Nord e il Mezzogiorno d'Italia. Dipartimento di Economia, Università degli Studi di Roma Tre, Collana di Economia, Working Paper, n.16.

De la Mothe, J., & Paquet, G. (1998). Local and Regional Systems of Innovation as learning socio-economies. In *Local and Regional Systems of Innovation*. Kluwer Academic Publisher. DOI: 10.1007/978-1-4615-5551-3_1

Dei Ottati, G. (1994). Trust, interlinking transactions and credit in the industrial district. *Cambridge Journal of Economics*, *18*, 529–546.

DiGiacinto, V., & Nuzzo, G. (2006). Explaining labour productivity differentials across Italian regions: The role of socio-economic structure and factor endowments. *Papers in Regional Science*, *85*(2), 299–320. DOI: 10.1111/j.1435-5957.2006.00072.x

Enright, M. (1996). Regional clustersclusters and economic development: A research agenda. In U. Staber, N. V. Schaefer, & B. Sharma (Eds.), Business Network Prospects for Regional Development. *de Gruyer*.

Enright, M. J. (2000). Survey of the characterization of regional clusters. Initial results. Institute of Economic Policy & Business Strategy. Competitiveness Program Working Paper, University of Hong Kong.

Gamsey, E. (1998). The genesis of the high technology milieu: A study of complexity. *International Journal of Urban and Regional Research, 22*(3), 361–377. DOI: 10.1111/1468-2427.00146

Harrison, B. (1992). Industrial districts: Old wine in new bottles? *Regional Studies, 26*(5), 469–483. DOI: 10.1080/00343409212331347121

Marini, M. (2000). *Le risorse Immateriali. I fattori culturali dello Sviluppo economico*. Carocci Editore.

Markusen, A. (1996). Sticky Places in Slippery Space: A Typology of Industrial Districts. *Economic Geography, 72*(3), 293–313. DOI: 10.2307/144402

Passiante, G., Elia, V., & Massari, T. (2002). Digital innovation. Imperial College Press.

Porter, M. E. (1998). Clusters. *Innovation, and Competitiveness: New Findings and Implications for Policy*.

Provasi, G. (2002). *Le istituzioni dello sviluppo economico*. Donzelli.

Rabellotti, R. (1995). Is there an industrial district. *World Development, 23*(1), 29–41. DOI: 10.1016/0305-750X(94)00103-6

Rabellotti, R., & Schmitz, H. (1999). The internal heterogeneity of industrial districts in Italy. *Regional Studies, 33*(2), 99–128. DOI: 10.1080/00343409950122909

Romano, A., & Passiante, G. (1997). Innovation Territorial System as Learning Organization of Local System Innovation Virtual System. Paper presented at the Regional Science Association 37th European Congress, Rome.

Rosenfeld, S. (1996). Bringing Business Clusters into the Mainstream of Economic Development. *European Planning Studies, 5*(1), 3–23. DOI: 10.1080/09654319708720381

Saxenian, A. (1994). *Regional Advantage: Culture and Competition in the Silicon Valley and Route 128*. Harvard University Press.

Scarlato, M. (2001). Capitale sociale e sviluppo economico: Un'analisi empirica per le province italiane. *Economia Pubblica, 2001*(1).

Schmitz, H. (1995). Collective efficiency: Growth path for the small-scale industry. *The Journal of Development Studies, 31*(4), 529–566. DOI: 10.1080/00220389508422377

Chapter 2
Agriculture-Based Products and Water Treatment

ABSTRACT

Emerging from structural constraints, particularly arid climate conditions and limited freshwater resources, the ecosystem has evolved into a globally competitive innovation hub linking research institutions, startups, multinational firms, and government policy frameworks. In crop production, technological advances focus on enhancing quality, resilience, and efficiency across the value chain. Biotechnology also drives innovation in medical and ecological plants, including genetic optimization of cannabis and industrial crops for pharmaceutical, cosmetic, and sustainable material uses. Digital agriculture technologies further enhance precision and resource efficiency. AI-driven irrigation systems developed by companies such as Netafim optimize water use, while precision pollination platforms. Animal genetics research complements plant innovation through molecular diagnostics and developmental regulation technologies that enhance livestock productivity and health.

INTRODUCTION

Emerging from structural constraints, particularly arid climate conditions and limited freshwater resources, the ecosystem has evolved into a globally competitive innovation hub linking research institutions, startups, multinational firms, and government policy frameworks.

In crop production, technological advances focus on enhancing quality, resilience, and efficiency across the value chain. Innovations in fruit and vegetable processing—including sugar-reduction technologies, advanced freezing, robotic

DOI: 10.4018/979-8-3373-7350-8.ch002

handling, and controlled dehydration—improve shelf life, nutritional value, and export competitiveness.

Biotechnology also drives innovation in medical and ecological plants, including genetic optimization of cannabis and industrial crops for pharmaceutical, cosmetic, and sustainable material uses. In parallel, microbial fertilization, biologically integrated pest management, and sensor-based nutrient monitoring systems reduce chemical inputs while maintaining productivity, reinforcing ecological sustainability.

Digital agriculture technologies further enhance precision and resource efficiency. AI-driven irrigation systems developed by companies such as Netafim optimize water use, while precision pollination platforms like BeeHero improve crop yields and pollinator health through real-time data analytics. Controlled-environment agriculture, hydroponics, and sustainable fertilizer technologies contribute to high-density production with minimal environmental footprint.

Animal genetics research complements plant innovation through molecular diagnostics and developmental regulation technologies that enhance livestock productivity and health.

Water innovation remains foundational to the ecosystem. Large-scale reverse osmosis desalination—exemplified by the Sorek Desalination Plant—alongside atmospheric water generation and emerging energy-water nexus solutions, secures national water supply while supporting agricultural expansion.

The evolution of Israel's agricultural sector reflects a long-standing culture of innovation, shaped initially by European immigrants who introduced diverse cultivation techniques, market knowledge, and consumer preferences. Contemporary agricultural advancement is largely driven by the integration of scientific research with commercial practice, as research centers collaborate closely with growers, agribusiness firms, and technology providers to translate discoveries into scalable, market-ready solutions.

Within fruit and vegetable production, innovation in Israel manifests along two primary dimensions. The first focuses on product characteristics, including smaller size, enhanced sweetness, extended shelf life, seedless varieties, higher nutritional content, and improved processing efficiency (e.g., ease of peeling or sorting).

The second dimension emphasizes technological and process innovations, encompassing advanced seed genetics, optimized water and nutrient management through precision irrigation and fertilization, and biologically informed plant protection strategies. Together, these approaches illustrate Israel's systemic and technology-driven strategy for increasing agricultural productivity, quality, and sustainability.

FRUIT AND VEGETABLE-BASED INNOVATIONS

Israel's fruit and vegetable processing sector exemplifies the integration of advanced technologies to enhance product quality, extend shelf life, reduce post-harvest losses, and access global markets. Innovations span chemical, mechanical, and digital interventions:

- Sugar Molecule Removal (BlueTree Technologies): BlueTree has developed a patented method to selectively reduce sugars such as fructose in natural fruit juices without affecting taste or nutritional content. This technology addresses public health concerns, supports low-sugar beverage markets, and has been licensed internationally (BlueTree, 2026).
- Advanced Freezing Technology (Juran's Fresh Defrost™): This system preserves the texture, flavor, and nutritional quality of frozen produce, reducing post-harvest waste and enabling extended cold-chain export (FreshdeFrost, 2018).
- Automated Pomegranate Processing (Juran's ArilSystem™): Robotics-based extraction of pomegranate arils maximizes yield without damaging fruit, supporting applications in cosmetics, pharmaceuticals, and high-value nutrition.
- Semi-Dried Cherry Tomatoes (Supree, NRGene): Self-drying techniques produce semi-dried tomatoes with concentrated flavor and prolonged shelf life. Strategic partnerships with technology providers accelerate commercialization for premium export markets (Solomon, 2024).

MEDICAL AND ECOLOGICAL PLANTS

Israeli agriculture also emphasizes high-value medicinal and ecological crops:

- Cannabis: Israel has led medical cannabis research since the 1960s, developing controlled indoor and greenhouse cultivation systems to optimize cannabinoid profiles for therapeutic use across neurological, oncological, and pain management applications (Chandra et al., 2017).
- Jojoba Oil: Advanced cultivation and extraction techniques enhance oil yield and purity, supporting cosmetic, pharmaceutical, and dermatological applications while promoting sustainable agriculture in arid regions (Zahid et al., 2023).
- Kenaf: A fast-growing fiber crop, kenaf serves ecological and industrial purposes, including bio-composites, biodegradable packaging, insulation, and

soil remediation, illustrating cross-sector innovation in cleantech and circular economy initiatives (Kiron, 2021).

PLANT GENETICS AND DISEASE MANAGEMENT

Genome Regulation (miRNAs): MicroRNAs regulate gene expression post-transcriptionally, influencing plant development, stress tolerance, and disease resistance. For instance, the miR482 family modulates NBS-LRR immune receptor genes, balancing growth and defense mechanisms (Yu et al., 2026).

Tomato Brown Rugose Fruit Virus (ToBRFV): First detected in Israel in 2014, ToBRFV overcomes traditional $Tm\text{-}2^2$ resistance, causing mosaic leaf patterns, fruit deformation, and yield losses. Israeli research produced resistant rootstock and scion varieties, exemplifying rapid applied plant disease management (Salem et al, 2023).

Ripening Inhibitor (RIN)

The RIN transcription factor regulates tomato fruit ripening by coordinating processes affecting texture, color, and flavor. Mutations or silencing of RIN disrupt normal ripening patterns, while post-transcriptional modulation by miRNAs and viral interference further influences fruit development and susceptibility to disease (Slugina, 2021). Israeli studies first characterized RIN mutants in 1976, providing early molecular evidence of genetic control over fruit ripening (Yang et al., 2023).

Digital and AI-Driven Crop Monitoring Israeli agriculture has adopted advanced digital and AI-driven platforms to monitor crop health, optimize inputs, and enable precision breeding. Leading technologies include: CropX: Combines soil sensors with AI-driven agronomy to optimize irrigation, nutrient supply, and salinity control, providing daily recommendations via dashboards or mobile apps (CropX, 2022). Taranis: Utilizes high-resolution aerial imagery and AI to detect pests, diseases, weeds, and nutrient deficiencies, producing real-time alerts and actionable treatment maps for row crops (Taranis, n.d.). Prospera Technologies: Offers smart greenhouse and open-field monitoring, integrating AI with irrigation systems to optimize plant growth and resource efficiency (Prospera Technologies, 2026).

SeeTree: Employs drone, plane, and satellite imagery to assess orchard health, creating "Tree IDs" for citrus, avocado, and olive crops, linking productivity, health, and yield potential (SeeTree, 2019). MyCrops: Provides camera-based greenhouse monitoring using computer vision to detect growth anomalies, pests, and irrigation needs, enabling rapid decision-making for farm managers (MyCrops, 2020).

Plant Nutrition, Breeding, and Pest Control Innovations

Israeli agriculture demonstrates a systemic approach to enhancing crop productivity, sustainability, and resilience through microbial, digital, and precision technologies, integrated with advanced breeding and ecological pest management.

Plant Nutrition and Microbial Fertilization

Microbial solutions optimize nutrient availability while reducing chemical fertilizer dependence:

- Nitrogen-Fixing Microbes (Rhizobium, Azotobacter) convert atmospheric nitrogen to bioavailable forms, improving soil fertility and reducing emissions (Sumbul et al, 2020).
- Microbial Bio-Products (Groundwork BioAg, Evogene) enhance phosphorus uptake, drought tolerance, nitrogen fixation, phosphate solubilization, and disease resistance (GroundWork BioAg, 2024).
- Controlled-Release Fertilizers (Multicote™ CRF, ICL Polysulphate) synchronize nutrient release with plant demand, reducing leaching and improving efficiency (Haifa Group, 2019).

Digital Decision Support and Sensor-Based Management

Precision platforms leverage AI, IoT, and real-time data to optimize fertilization and irrigation:

- NutriNet (Haifa Group): Cloud-based fertigation planning integrating climate, soil, and crop data.
- Croptune™, DOTS, Sensoil, Sol-Chip, LeafSens: Sensors and AI tools for real-time nutrient, moisture, and stress monitoring, enabling precision nutrient management and minimizing resource waste (Croptune, 2026; Han et al, 2024; Sol-Chip, 2025; Sensoil, 2024).

Personalized Plant Breeding

Israel leads in climate-adapted, non-GMO, and CRISPR-assisted breeding:

- Equinom (2024), NetaGenomiX (2026), PlantArcBio (2026), Morflora (Shiny Aura, 2025), Pheno IL: Platforms and high-throughput phenotyping enable rapid trait selection for drought, salinity, pest resistance, protein content, and flavor optimization.

Biocontrol and Integrated Pest Management (IPM)

Ecological pest suppression reduces chemical reliance:

- Microalgae and Cyanobacteria (Haematococcus, Leptolyngbya, Oscillatoria, Anabaena, Chlorella) enhance plant growth, deter pests, and suppress soil-borne fungi and nematodes (Mutale et al, 2023):
- BioBee IPM integrates predatory species, pollinators, and minimal chemical inputs for sustainable pest control.
- Crop Monitoring Platforms (Prospera Technologies) combine AI, climate, and sensor data for real-time plant health management.

Pollination and Bee Health Innovations

Advanced technologies counter pollinator decline while enhancing productivity:

- BeeHero – PIP: AI and sensor-based real-time pollination monitoring (BeeHero, n.d.).
- Beewise Robotic Beehives: Autonomous hive management reducing colony collapse, increasing yield, and minimizing labor (Beewise, n.d.).
- Bee-io Honey: Lab-grown honey reduces pressure on natural bee populations (bee-io, 2023).
- Edete Precision Technologies & Bumblebee AI: Robotic and artificial pollination devices improve yield, pollen viability, and fruit quality.
- ToBe – Hivemaster: Smart miticide delivery integrated with hive monitoring targets Varroa mites effectively.

SMART AGRICULTURE EQUIPMENT, SYSTEMS, AND ANIMAL GENETICS INNOVATIONS

Israeli agricultural innovation integrates precision irrigation, AI-driven aquaculture, hydroponics, automated quality assessment, and molecular animal genetics, emphasizing sustainability, efficiency, and productivity.

Precision Irrigation and Water Management

N-Drip Connect: Gravity-powered drip irrigation enabling precision nutrient and water delivery without electricity, optimizing yield and reducing costs (CTech, 2023).

AI-Driven Aquaculture Management

GoSmart: Edge-AI sensors monitor biomass, oxygen, temperature, and behavior in ponds and RAS systems, providing SaaS-based recommendations for feed optimization.

Yamim: Microbial live feed production reduces artificial feed reliance and nitrate accumulation; AI-driven optimization improves feed conversion by up to 15%.

Nobify: Multi-sensor, AI-guided bird deterrence systems reduce predation losses by up to 30% (Nobify, 2017).

Hydroponics, Controlled Environment Agriculture, and Organic Fertilizers

GrowPonics: Automated, pesticide-free hydroponic greenhouses recycling ~80% of water; year-round cultivation with extended shelf life.

AlgaeNite: Carbon-negative organic bio-ammonia fertilizer for agriculture, feed, cosmetics, and bioplastics.

TAPKIT Hydroponic Systems: Modular, climate-controlled NFT greenhouses with AI monitoring, producing high-yield leafy crops.

AgwaFarm / AgwaGarden: Compact autonomous hydroponic units for home or vessel-based cultivation, minimizing water and energy use.

Neolithics Light Automation: AI and optical sensing for rapid, non-destructive quality analysis, grading, and sorting of produce.

Animal Genetics and Molecular Innovation

- miRNA-Based Diagnostics and Therapeutics:
- Rosetta Genomics / Genoptix: miRNA diagnostics for cancers of unknown primary origin.
- BioGenCell: Blood-based miRNA assays for cardiovascular and immune disorders.
- NeuroGenesis: miRNA-driven regenerative therapies for post-stroke and cognitive disorders.

Sex Detection and Manipulation in Poultry:

- NextHen & Soos Technology: Early-stage sex determination and incubation manipulation achieving 60–65% female hatch rates (NextHen, 2024).

- Soos Technology: AI-guided incubation system using temperature, humidity, CO_2, and sonic vibrations to induce female development in male embryos; early trials achieved 60–65% female hatch rates.
- Golda Hen (Volcani / Huminn): CRISPR-mediated female-only embryos using light-activated gene switches; commercial deployment anticipated in 2–3 years (Leichman, 2022).
- eggXYt: Fluorescent tagging for day-zero male egg detection, enabling ethical culling (eggxyt, n.d.).
- Electro-Optical Broiler Chick Sexing (Eshet Eilon): Camera-based system achieving ~95% accuracy at industrial scale (~50,000 chicks/hour) (Doughman, 2022).

INNOVATIONS IN WATER TREATMENT AND DESALINATION

Israel has emerged as a global leader in water treatment and desalination technologies, leveraging advanced engineering, renewable energy integration, and chemical-free treatment systems. These innovations are critical for arid-region agriculture, precision irrigation, industrial water reuse, and municipal water security, making them ideal candidates for inclusion in Innovative Virtual Open Incubator Clusters (IVOICs) in agro-business and water treatment domains.

Reverse Osmosis (RO)

Reverse osmosis is a membrane-based filtration method widely applied to seawater and brackish water desalination, as well as industrial water purification (Cohen & Glater, 2010). Israeli firms have developed energy-efficient, deep-sea RO systems:

Flocean and OceanWell: Pilot RO systems deployed on the ocean floor at depths exceeding 400 m utilize ambient water pressure to reduce energy consumption by approximately 40% (Flocean, 2025).

Closed-Circuit Desalination (CCD / CCRO)

Closed-Circuit Desalination recycles brine concentrate in a closed loop, preventing membrane fouling while achieving exceptionally high-water recovery rates of 90–98% with lower energy inputs.

Desalitech: Founded in 2008, Desalitech commercialized CCD/NCRO technology achieving up to 98% water recovery with 20–60% lower costs than conventional RO systems. Pilot projects include brackish water desalination at Dead Sea Works

(600 m^3/day at 0.65 kWh/m^3). Acquired by DuPont in 2019, Desalitech is scaling CCD systems globally.

Vacuum Freezing Vapor Compression (VFVC)

Developed in 1964 by Alexander Zarchin, VFVC enables desalination through freeze and vapor compression cycles, reducing energy requirements to roughly one-seventh of conventional evaporation (Jewish Federation Los Angeles, 2021). While large-scale deployment is limited by space and vacuum control requirements, VFVC is suitable for coastal or cold-region communities and for producing ultrapure water for pharmaceutical and microelectronics applications.

Atmospheric Water Generation (AWG)

AWG systems extract water from ambient air via condensation, offering solutions for remote, arid, or emergency contexts:

- Watergen (founded 2009, Arye Kohavi): Uses the GENius™ heat-exchange system to produce 20–6,000 L/day, deployed in over 90 countries, including schools, hospitals, and military facilities.
- H2OLL (Technion): Employs an absorption-desorption cycle for low-energy water extraction from air. Full-scale deployment in the Negev Desert earned the Water Europe Innovation Award (H2OLL, 2026).

On-Site Water Treatment and Disinfection

HPNow – Peroxide UltraPure™: Generates hydrogen peroxide on-site using waste heat and renewable energy. Applications include:

- Blueberry Plantation (12 ha): Eliminated biofilm in drippers, restored uniform irrigation, and improved yields.
- Pig Farm: Provided pathogen-free drinking water, improving livestock health and feed conversion.
- Melon Packing House: Sanitized surfaces and equipment, enhancing shelf life and reducing reliance on chemical disinfectants.

Integration into IVOICs in Agro-Business and Water Treatment

These water treatment innovations exemplify cross-sectoral synergies suitable for inclusion in Virtual Open Incubator Clusters (IVOICs) targeting:

- Water-efficient agriculture: Precision irrigation, desalination, and AWG integration.
- Sustainable aquaculture and livestock management: Pathogen-free water and resource optimization.
- Industrial and municipal water reuse: CCD systems and on-site H_2O_2 generation.

By linking these technologies with Israeli innovations in agritech, plant nutrition, hydroponics, and precision irrigation, IVOICs can:

- Accelerate knowledge diffusion and innovation scalability.
- Promote eco-friendly, sustainable solutions for arid and semi-arid regions worldwide.

Herewith, the Agro-Business and Water Treatment IVOICs framework (Figure 1).

Figure 1. Agro business and water treatment IVOICs

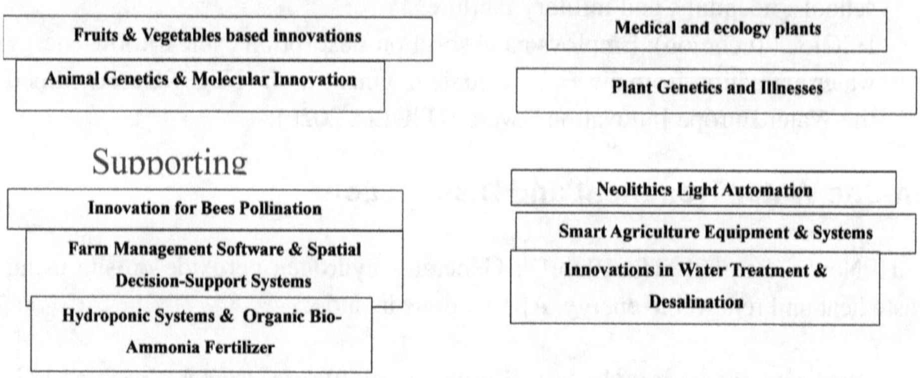

REFERENCES

bee-io. (2023). *Home.* Bee-Io.com. https://bee-io.com/

BeeHero. (n.d.). BeeHero. https://www.beehero.io/

Beewise. (n.d.). *Home.* Beewise.ag. https://beewise.ag/home

BlueTree. (2026). *Leaving Nature In, Taking Sugar Out.* Bluetree-Tech.com. https://bluetree-tech.com/

Chandra S., Lata H., ElSohly M.A., Walker L.A., & Potter D. (2017). Cannabis cultivation: Methodological issues for obtaining medical-grade product. *Epilepsy & Behavior, 70*(B), 302-312.

Cohen, Y., & Glater, J. (2010). A tribute to Sidney Loeb—The pioneer of reverse osmosis desalination research. *Desalination and Water Treatment, 15*(1–3), 222–227. DOI: 10.5004/dwt.2010.1762

Crop, X. (2022, March 23). *CropX Technologies.* CropX Technologies - Data-Driven Farming. https://cropx.com/

Croptune. (2026, March 9). *Your personal nitrogen meter - Croptune.* Croptune. https://www.croptune.io/

CTech (2023). Cleantech startup Tipa acquires Bio4Pack in $8 million deal. *CTech.*

Doughman, E. (2022). Automating the broiler sex sorting process in the hatchery could help improve bird growth, welfare and uniformity. *Watt Poultry.*

eggXYt. (n.d.). *Count Your Chickens Before They Hatch.* Eggxyt. https://www.eggxyt.com/

Equinom. (2024). *Consistent Quality, Smarter Milling!* Equi-Nom.com. https://www.equi-nom.com/

Flocean. (2025). Flocean. https://www.flocean.green

FreshDefrost. (2018). FreshDefrost. https://freshdefrost.wixsite.com/website

Groundwork BioAg. (2024, July 9). *Mycorrhizal Fungi, Carbon Sequestration & Removal Inoculants.* Groundwork BioAg. https://groundworkbioag.com/

H2OLL. (2026). *H2OLL Cyclic Absorption Atmospheric Water Generation.* H2oll.com. https://www.h2oll.com/

Haifa Group. (2019). Haifa Group. https://www.haifa-group.com/

Han, X., Wan, S., He, L., Zou, J., Mavric, A., Wang, Y., Piotrowski, M., Bandela, A. K., Samorì, P., Wang, Z., Leydecker, T., & Thumu, U. (2024). Tunable Emissive $CsPbBr_3/Cs_4PbBr_6$ Quantum Dots Engineered by Discrete Phase Transformation for Enhanced Photogating in Field-Effect Phototransistors. *Advancement of Science, 11*(32), 2401973. Advance online publication. DOI: 10.1002/advs.202401973 PMID: 39189467

Jewish Federation Los Angeles. (2021, June 28). Home. Jewish Federation Los Angeles. https://www.jewishla.org/

Kiron, M. I. (2021, May 10). *Kenaf Fiber: Properties, Cultivation, Production, Uses and Advantages*. Textile Learner. https://textilelearner.net/kenaf-fiber-properties/

Leichman, A. K. (2022, December 28). *Golda, the Israeli hen that lays only female eggs - ISRAEL21c*. ISRAEL21c. https://archive.israel21c.org/golda-the-israeli-hen-that-lays-only-female-eggs/

Mutale-J., C., Sbabou, L., & Hicham, E. A. (2023). Microalgae and Cyanobacteria: How Exploiting These Microbial Resources Can Address the Underlying Challenges Related to Food Sources and Sustainable Agriculture: A Review. *Journal of Plant Growth Regulation, 42*(1), 1–20. DOI: 10.1007/s00344-021-10534-9

MyCrops. (2020). *Farm Management software simplified*. Mycrops.ag. https://www.mycrops.ag/

NetaGenomix. (2026, February 10). *Revolutionizing Plant Genetics*. NetaGenomiX. https://netagenomix.com/

NextHen. (2024, December 9). *Pioneering Poultry's Future*. NextHen. https://www.nexthen.net/

Nobify. (2017). Nobify. https://www.nobify.ai/

Orbach M. (2021). Israeli agtech startup Prospera acquired by Valmont for $300 million. Calcalist, Tech, 05.05.21

PlantArcBio. (2026, January 19). *Home*. Plantarc. https://plantarcbio.com/

Prospera Technologies. (2026). *Founder Led Custom Software Development | Prototype Before Contract or Payment*. Prospera Technologies. https://prospera-technologies.com/

Salem, N. M., Jewehan, A., Aranda, M. A., & Fox, A. (2023, September 5). Tomato Brown Rugose Fruit Virus Pandemic. *Annual Review of Phytopathology, 61*(1), 137–164. DOI: 10.1146/annurev-phyto-021622-120703 PMID: 37268006

SeeTree. (2019). *SeeTree: Intelligence network for Trees*. Seetree.ai. https://www.seetree.ai/

Shiny Aura. (2025). 100 Types of Flowers: The Ultimate Guide to Names, Meanings, and Gardening Tips [Review of 100 Types of Flowers: The Ultimate Guide to Names, Meanings, and Gardening Tips]. MorFlora. https://morflora.com/

Slugina, M. A. (2021). Transcription Factor RIPENING INHIBITOR and Its Homologs in Regulation of Fleshy Fruit Ripening of Various Plant Species. *Russian Journal of Plant Physiology: a Comprehensive Russian Journal on Modern Phytophysiology*, *68*(5), 783–799. DOI: 10.1134/S1021443721050186

Snesoil. (2024, June 4). Sensoil Protecting Groundwater by Monitoring the Vadose Zone. Sensoil. https://sensoil.com/

Sol-Chip. (2025, June 27). Sol-Chip. https://sol-chip.com/

Solomon, S. (2024, February). Defying war's wreckage, self-drying cherry tomatoes ripen near Gaza. *Times of Israel*, 25.

Sumbul, A., Ansari, R. A., Rizvi, R., & Mahmood, I. (2020, December). Azotobacter: A potential bio-fertilizer for soil and plant health management. *Saudi Journal of Biological Sciences*, *27*(12), 3634–3640. DOI: 10.1016/j.sjbs.2020.08.004 PMID: 33304174

Taranis. (n.d.). Crop & Farm Management Software | Precision Agriculture Technology. Taranis. https://www.taranis.com/

Yang, K., Fu, R., Feng, H., Jiang, G., Finkel, O., Sun, T., Liu, M., Huang, B., Li, S., Wang, X., Yang, T., Wang, Y., Wang, S., Xu, Y., Shen, Q., Friman, V. P., Jousset, A., & Wei, Z. (2023). RIN enhances plant disease resistance via root exudate-mediated assembly of disease-suppressive rhizosphere microbiota. *Molecular Plant*, *16*(9), 1379–1395. DOI: 10.1016/j.molp.2023.08.004 PMID: 37563832

Yu, Y., Wang, H., You, C., & Chen, X. (2026). Plant microRNA maturation and function. *Nature Reviews. Molecular Cell Biology*, *27*(1), 55–70. DOI: 10.1038/s41580-025-00871-y PMID: 40681920

Zahid, A., Asif, H. M., Zahid, R., Firdous, M., Idrees, H. M., Hasnain, M., & Bashir, U. (2023). Jojoba oil: A best-in-class assessment as cosmetics and forthcoming opportunities. *Journal of Pharma and Biomedics*, *1*(1), 27–34.

Chapter 3
Food Technology (FoodTech)

ABSTRACT

Israeli FoodTech focuses on plant-based and functional protein innovations. Companies such as InnovoPro and ChickP specialize in chickpea-derived protein concentrates and isolates characterized by improved digestibility and functional versatility. Brevel advances microalgae-based protein production through light-driven fermentation processes, contributing to climate-resilient and resource-efficient protein systems. Emerging companies such as MyBiotics Pharma develop microbiome-targeted probiotic formulations designed to improve metabolic, digestive, and immune functions. Food automation systems and smart kitchen technologies further contribute to personalized nutrition and reduced food waste, reinforcing the intersection between digital innovation and food systems. Israeli FoodTech extends into innovations in sustainable packaging, addressing the environmental footprint of food distribution. Developments in fungi-based biomaterials offer biodegradable alternatives to petroleum-derived plastics.

INTRODUCTION

Israeli FoodTech has emerged as a strategic pillar of the country's innovation economy, integrating biotechnology, food engineering, and sustainability science to address global challenges related to nutrition, health, and environmental resilience. Supported by a dense ecosystem of research institutions, venture capital, and innovation platforms such as The Kitchen FoodTech Hub, the sector advances three interconnected objectives: enhancing nutritional value, supporting human health, and promoting environmental and ethical responsibility.

The development of animal-free products, encompassing both cultivated and plant-based alternatives. Israeli companies have positioned themselves at the forefront

DOI: 10.4018/979-8-3373-7350-8.ch003

of cellular agriculture. Aleph Farms and Future Meat Technologies have pioneered scalable methods for producing cultured beef through cell proliferation and tissue engineering. Precision fermentation technologies developed by Remilk enable the production of dairy-identical proteins without reliance on livestock. Complementing these advances, plant-based innovators such as Redefine Meat employ advanced formulation and 3D-printing technologies to replicate the sensory and structural attributes of conventional meat. Collectively, these approaches aim to mitigate greenhouse gas emissions, reduce land and water consumption, and address ethical concerns associated with industrial animal agriculture.

Israeli FoodTech focuses on plant-based and functional protein innovations. Companies such as InnovoPro and ChickP specialize in chickpea-derived protein concentrates and isolates characterized by improved digestibility and functional versatility. Brevel advances microalgae-based protein production through light-driven fermentation processes, contributing to climate-resilient and resource-efficient protein systems. Emerging companies such as MyBiotics Pharma develop microbiome-targeted probiotic formulations designed to improve metabolic, digestive, and immune functions. Food automation systems and smart kitchen technologies further contribute to personalized nutrition and reduced food waste, reinforcing the intersection between digital innovation and food systems.

Israeli FoodTech extends into innovations in sustainable packaging, addressing the environmental footprint of food distribution. Developments in fungi-based biomaterials offer biodegradable alternatives to petroleum-derived plastics.

ANIMAL-FREE PRODUCTS

Israeli FoodTech has positioned itself at the forefront of animal-free protein innovation through both cellular agriculture and plant-based engineering. Companies such as Aleph Farms and SuperMeat advance cultivated beef and poultry technologies designed to replicate conventional meat while significantly reducing land use, greenhouse gas emissions, and animal slaughter. In parallel, Redefine Meat and Plantish develop plant-based whole-cut meat and seafood analogs that address sustainability challenges, including overfishing and intensive livestock production.

Animal-free dairy innovation follows similar trajectories. Remilk utilizes precision fermentation to produce milk-identical proteins without cows, enabling environmentally efficient dairy alternatives. Complementary plant-based approaches are represented by Tamiz, which develops almond-based cheeses and desserts, and Yofix Probiotics, which formulates soy-free probiotic yogurts targeting gut health. Together, these ventures demonstrate the integration of sustainability, nutritional design, and microbiome science in reshaping dairy consumption.

PLANT-BASED AND FUNCTIONAL PROTEINS

Israel has diversified protein sources through legume- and microalgae-based innovations. InnovoPro (Vegconomist, 2023) and ChickP produce high-purity chickpea proteins suitable for beverages and functional foods, enhancing digestibility and formulation performance. Microalgae-based initiatives such as AlgaeCore Technologies (Spampinato, 2025) and Wanda Fish further expand sustainable protein systems through spirulina-derived products and hybrid seafood technologies. These approaches reinforce nutritional density while reducing ecological pressures on terrestrial and marine ecosystems.

Functional Food Applications

Functional FoodTech in Israel integrates protein innovation with health-oriented applications. MyBiotics Pharma develops clinically validated probiotic formulations targeting gastrointestinal and immune health, while fermentation platforms such as MyCrobe support tailored microbiome solutions. In parallel, companies including Mediterranean Food Lab enhance plant-based flavor complexity through fermentation-derived systems, enabling clean-label meat alternatives.

Sugar-reduction technologies constitute another major segment. Better Juice, DouxMatok, and Amai Proteins apply enzymatic, delivery-based, and computational protein design methods to significantly lower sugar content without compromising taste, addressing metabolic health concerns.

SMART FOOD SYSTEMS AND AUTOMATION

Beyond ingredient innovation, Israeli FoodTech advances food processing and distribution efficiency. ANINA repurposes surplus produce into ready-to-cook vegetable-based meal capsules, reducing food waste (Levit, 2023). Hyper Food Robotics and Kitchen Robotics develop autonomous kitchen systems that optimize labor, energy use, and production consistency (Kitchen Robotics, 2023).

INNOVATIONS IN FOOD PACKAGING

Food packaging innovation in Israel emphasizes sustainability, product safety, and quality assurance through biodegradable materials, bio-based composites, and real-time analytical monitoring systems. These technologies contribute to extended shelf life, reduced food waste, and strengthened consumer protection, aligning with circular-economy and regulatory compliance frameworks.

Fungi-Based Biomaterials

A notable development in sustainable materials is advanced by MadeRight, founded in 2022 by Rotem Cahanovitc and Yotam David. The company cultivates fungi on industrial biowaste streams such as wood chips, extracting mycelium-derived compounds that are blended with bioplastics to produce functional pellets for packaging applications.

Key technological attributes include:

- Replacement of fossil-based additives while maintaining oxygen and light barrier performance
- Full biodegradability and compostability from renewable sources
- Inherent antimicrobial and protective properties derived from fungal metabolites

Applications span protective food packaging, cushioning materials, and flexible food-contact wraps. By utilizing low-energy biological growth processes and valorizing industrial byproducts, this approach reflects a circular and resource-efficient packaging model.

Packaging Analytical Monitoring (PAM) for Heat-Sealed Products

Beyond material innovation, Israeli companies are advancing non-destructive, real-time inspection technologies to ensure seal integrity and product safety in heat-sealed packaging systems.

Yoran Imaging has developed Thermal-PAM, an inline thermal imaging solution designed to evaluate induction- and heat-sealed containers without disrupting production speed. The system detects overheating, insufficient sealing, foil misalignment, and cap integrity failures, supported by dashboards, statistical process control tools, and predictive alerts.

Similarly, DIR Technologies employs high-resolution infrared thermography for continuous 100% inline inspection of form-fill-seal packaging. Its Induction Integrity Verification System (I2VS) identifies defects such as wrinkles, gaps, and foreign contaminants, enabling comprehensive process control. DIR Technologies operates as a spin-off of SemiConductor Devices (SCD), jointly owned by Rafael Advanced Defense Systems, Elbit Systems, and SCP Vitalife.

Impact of PAM Systems

Packaging Analytical Monitoring technologies generate measurable operational and safety benefits by:

- Extending product shelf life and reducing spoilage rates
- Minimizing recalls and consumer health risks
- Enhancing production efficiency through real-time process control
- Supporting compliance with stringent food safety and quality standards

Figure 1. FoodTech IVOICs

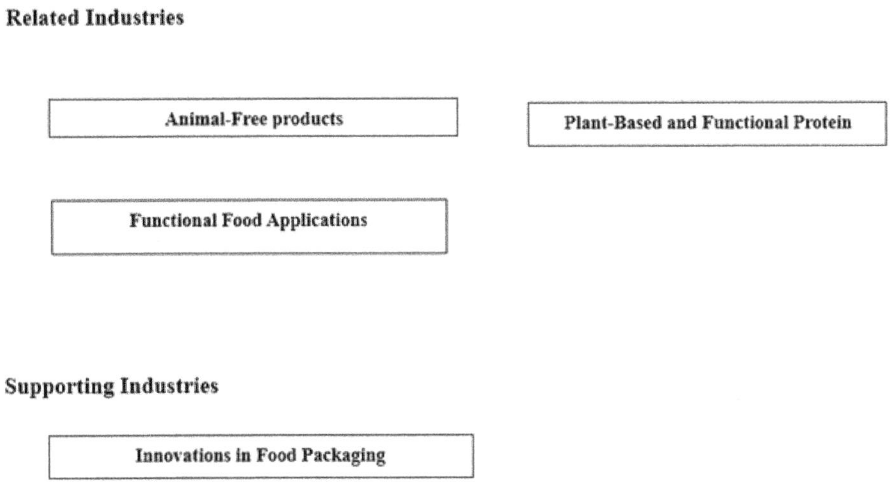

REFERENCES

Kitchen Robotics. (2023). Kitchen Robotics Launches an AI-Driven Culinary Revolution for its robotic kitchen Beastro™. *Cision PR Web,* Dec 05, 2023

Levit, M. (2023). ANINA Will Make You Forget Everything You Know About Ready-Made Meals. *Asif.*

Spampinato, E. (2025). Israeli plant-based firm SimpliiGood will commercialize its smoked salmon spirulina analog. *Plant-Based & Cell-Based. Sea food source.*

Vegconomist. (2023). InnovoPro Presents Nutritious Chickpea Solutions for Bakery and Coffee Shop Industries at Fi Europe 2023. *Vegconomist.*

Chapter 4
Healthcare Innovations in Israel

ABSTRACT

This chapter examines the multidimensional transformation of the healthcare sector through advances in diagnostic technologies, artificial intelligence, pharmaceutical development, regenerative medicine, and decentralized care systems. Innovation is increasingly characterized by the integration of digital tools, molecular science, and biomedical engineering to enhance precision, accessibility, and efficiency. Imaging technologies such as AI-enhanced CT and MRI systems have shifted diagnostics from visual interpretation to data-driven analysis, enabling earlier detection and improved clinical decision-making. Non-invasive disease detection methods, including liquid biopsy platforms such as Guardant360 and breath-based molecular analysis systems, illustrate the move toward precision oncology and personalized medicine. The expansion of at-home monitoring technologies—developed by companies such as Biobeat and EarlySense—demonstrates the decentralization of healthcare delivery.

INTRODUCTION

This chapter examines the multidimensional transformation of the healthcare sector through advances in diagnostic technologies, artificial intelligence, pharmaceutical development, regenerative medicine, and decentralized care systems. Innovation is increasingly characterized by the integration of digital tools, molecular science, and biomedical engineering to enhance precision, accessibility, and efficiency.

Imaging technologies such as AI-enhanced CT and MRI systems have shifted diagnostics from visual interpretation to data-driven analysis, enabling earlier detection and improved clinical decision-making. Artificial intelligence platforms further support automated scan interpretation, biomarker quantification, and predictive modeling, significantly strengthening diagnostic accuracy and workflow efficiency.

DOI: 10.4018/979-8-3373-7350-8.ch004

Non-invasive disease detection methods, including liquid biopsy platforms such as Guardant360 and breath-based molecular analysis systems, illustrate the move toward precision oncology and personalized medicine. These tools reduce reliance on invasive procedures while enabling real-time monitoring of disease progression.

The expansion of at-home monitoring technologies—developed by companies such as Biobeat and EarlySense—demonstrates the decentralization of healthcare delivery. Continuous remote monitoring supports chronic disease management, reduces hospital admissions, and promotes aging-in-place models.

Pharmaceutical innovation, including landmark therapies such as Copaxone, continues to evolve through nano-based drug delivery systems and targeted biological treatments. Parallel advances in regenerative medicine, stem cell platforms, and robotics-assisted therapeutic equipment further expand treatment capabilities.

Collectively, these developments signal a transition from reactive, hospital-centered care toward predictive, personalized, and patient-centric healthcare systems. The convergence of AI, molecular diagnostics, digital monitoring, and advanced therapeutics defines the contemporary healthcare innovation landscape and shapes the future trajectory of global medical practice.

Israel has established itself as a global hub for healthcare technology innovation, driven by the integration of artificial intelligence, advanced imaging hardware, and non-invasive diagnostic platforms. The ecosystem is strongly aligned with precision medicine and digital healthcare models, making it highly suitable for deployment within Innovative Virtual Open Incubator Clusters (IVOICs).

IMAGING-BASED DIAGNOSTIC TECHNOLOGIES

Advanced Imaging Hardware

Israeli contributions to medical imaging have significantly improved diagnostic precision and patient safety. Early innovations include Elscint Ltd, which developed the world's first multi-slice CT scanner and Linear Velocity Imaging Tomography (LVIT) for enhanced breast imaging with reduced radiation exposure (Yu and Wang, 2008).

Modern systems such as GE Healthcare CT scanners, partially developed through Israeli R&D centers (e.g., at Sheba Medical Center), have reduced radiation exposure by up to 82% while maintaining image resolution.

AI-Enhanced Diagnostic Platforms

Artificial intelligence is widely deployed in radiology workflows:

- Aidoc – Real-time CT triage for stroke, brain hemorrhage, and pulmonary embolism.
- Zebra Medical Vision – FDA-cleared AI imaging analytics with ~92% breast cancer detection accuracy (Ravet, 2021).
- Quibim – Quantitative MRI/CT/PET biomarker analytics for personalized diagnostics.
- Deepc and Dia Imaging – Multi-organ AI diagnostic applications.

Specialized AI systems include DENISE AI (MICA AI) for contrast mammography optimization and iCAD Systems for dense breast tissue cancer screening.

Non-Invasive Biomarker and Molecular Diagnostics

Israel leads in breath, blood, and cellular biomarker diagnostics (Zachari et al, 2024):

- Technion – Israel Institute of Technology – VOC-based organoid cancer detection and nano-sensor "artificial nose" technologies.
- Ben-Gurion University of the Negev – Breath nanosensor arrays for breast cancer detection.
- Savicell Diagnostics – ImmunoBiopsy immune profiling with ~91% cancer detection sensitivity.

Liquid biopsy technologies include:

- ResultMed – Circulating tumor cell (CTC) analysis.
- Guardant Health – cfDNA genomic panels covering 70+ cancer-related genes.
- Sheba Medical Center – High-resolution ctDNA tumor monitoring.

Early Detection of Neurological and Developmental Disorders

Early behavioral and neurological diagnostics are advancing (Zoppe, 2025):

- Mifne Center and Bar-Ilan University – Eye-tracking and behavioral AI models for autism detection in infants aged 4–6 months.

AI-based electronic health record predictive analytics further enhance developmental risk screening.

Capsule Endoscopy and Robotic Diagnostics

Minimally invasive diagnostic robotics represent another Israeli strength:

- Given Imaging (now part of Medtronic) – PillCam swallowable imaging capsule, with millions of units deployed globally.
- Check-Cap Ltd – Prep-free colon imaging capsules.
- Microbot Medical – Endovascular robotic surgical systems. Ben-Gurion University-developed microbots (ViRob, TipCAT) enable targeted drug delivery and minimally invasive visualization.

Israeli healthcare innovation demonstrates strong convergence between artificial intelligence, biomedical engineering, and precision diagnostics. The ecosystem is characterized by early detection technologies, minimally invasive diagnostics, and digital healthcare platforms that collectively enhance clinical efficiency and patient outcomes. These innovations provide strong foundations for future global healthcare transformation and open innovation cluster models.

AT-HOME MONITORING TECHNOLOGIES

A major paradigm shift in modern healthcare is the movement from hospital-centered medicine toward continuous home-based monitoring. Israeli companies have pioneered wearable, contactless, and AI-enabled monitoring technologies that allow clinicians to observe patient health trajectories over time.

Wearable biosensing technologies developed by Biobeat enable continuous measurement of blood pressure, oxygen saturation, and pulse dynamics. Similarly, EarlySense has developed under-mattress monitoring systems that analyze physiological and movement signals without physical attachment to the patient. These systems are particularly valuable in intensive care and elderly care environments.

Contactless sensing technologies have further expanded with radar-based health monitoring systems developed by Neteera Technologies, which can measure respiration and cardiac rhythms through clothing or bedding materials. Behavioral and safety monitoring platforms developed by Sensi.AI and Essence SmartCare use artificial intelligence to detect anomalies in elderly patients living independently.

Voice biomarker analysis represents an additional innovation domain. Vocalis Health applies computational linguistics and acoustic signal processing to detect respiratory and neurological disease markers from speech patterns.

ADVANCED DRUG DELIVERY AND PHARMACEUTICAL INNOVATION

Pharmaceutical innovation in Israel combines biotechnology, nanomedicine, and immunotherapy platforms. One of the most successful examples of immunomodulatory therapy is Copaxone, widely used in treating multiple sclerosis by reducing immune-mediated neural damage and relapse frequency.

Nanotechnology has enabled sustained-release ophthalmic therapies that improve treatment outcomes for chronic ocular diseases. These nano-layered drug delivery platforms enhance medication absorption while reducing dosing frequency and systemic side effects.

Biotechnology startups have also advanced antimicrobial therapy development. BiomX develops bacteriophage cocktails targeting antibiotic-resistant bacteria. Complementary research by Omnix Medical focuses on synthetic immune-mimicking peptides.

To address global antimicrobial resistance, AI-driven drug discovery platforms such as Pepticom and CytoReason analyze molecular interactions and immune responses using machine learning models.

Diagnostic support for antibiotic stewardship is provided by MeMed, which differentiates bacterial from viral infections to guide appropriate treatment decisions.

HEMOSTASIS, INFECTION CONTROL, AND CRITICAL CARE THERAPEUTICS

Severe infection and trauma management remain major global health challenges. Enlivex Therapeutics has developed immune modulation therapies for sepsis and hemorrhagic shock conditions.

Blood and coagulation management technologies developed by Omrix Biopharmaceuticals (acquired by Johnson & Johnson on Nov 2008) provide surgical fibrin sealants that improve intraoperative bleeding control. Similarly, plasma-derived therapeutic products produced by Kamada Ltd address coagulation disorders and immune deficiencies.

These innovations reduce surgical mortality risks and improve emergency trauma care outcomes.

REGENERATIVE MEDICINE AND ADVANCED BIOLOGICAL THERAPIES

Regenerative medicine represents one of the fastest-growing sectors of Israeli biomedical research. Stem cell-based therapies and tissue engineering platforms are being developed for neurological, reproductive, and orthopedic disorders.

Neurosurgical therapeutic innovations include deep brain stimulation technologies pioneered globally through platforms similar to Medtronic, which are used to treat Parkinson's disease, epilepsy, and psychiatric disorders.

Stem cell engineering approaches combine biomaterial scaffolds, neurotrophic growth factors, and electrical stimulation to promote spinal cord regeneration. Cellular membrane coating technologies improve targeted drug delivery to tumor sites and damaged tissues.

In reproductive medicine, microfluidics-based sperm selection technologies provide new treatment pathways for male infertility. Public health applications extend to vector disease control through biological mosquito sterilization techniques that reduce disease transmission rates.

SURGICAL ROBOTICS AND ASSISTIVE MEDICAL DEVICES

Robotics and automation are transforming surgical precision and rehabilitation medicine. Mazor Robotics provides robotic guidance for spinal surgery procedures, improving surgical accuracy and reducing recovery time.

Interventional robotics developed by XACT Robotics enable minimally invasive catheter-based treatments with real-time navigation capabilities.

Surgical ergonomics and laparoscopic innovation are supported by HandX Medical, which enhances surgeon precision during minimally invasive procedures.

Telemedicine robotics platforms such as Temi Global support remote clinical consultations and elderly patient monitoring.

LIFE SUPPORT TECHNOLOGIES AND PORTABLE MEDICAL SYSTEMS

Portable medical systems are expanding access to advanced therapies outside traditional hospitals. Artificial respiratory technology inspired by biological systems enables environmental monitoring and underwater respiratory support.

Portable hyperbaric oxygen therapy systems developed by companies such as Macy Pan Medical provide therapeutic oxygen treatment for neurological, wound healing, and cognitive performance applications.

Smart infusion technologies such as Avoset Health enable cloud-based medication delivery monitoring, improving patient safety in home care environments.

Figure 1. Healthcare IVOICs

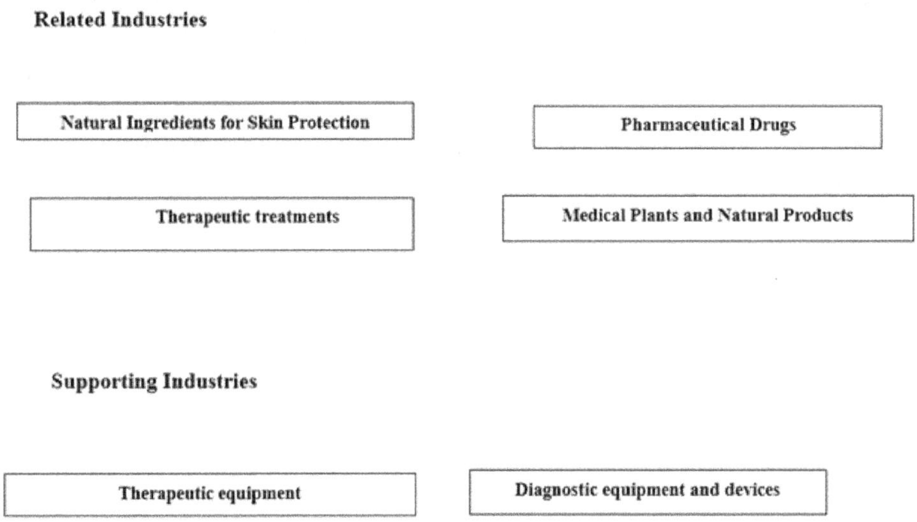

REFERENCES

Ravet, H. (2021). Israel's Zebra Medical acquired by Nanox for just $200 million. *Calcalist Tech,* 10.08.21 https://www.calcalistech.com/ctech/articles/0,7340,L-3914640,00.html

Yu, H., & Wang, G. (2008). A general scheme for velocity tomography. *Signal Processing, 88*(5), 1165–1175. DOI: 10.1016/j.sigpro.2007.11.007 PMID: 19412317

Zakari, S., Niels, N. K., Olagunju, G. V., Nnaji, P. C., Ogunniyi, O., Tebamifor, M., Israel, E. N., Atawodi, S. E., & Ogunlana, O. O. (2024). Emerging biomarkers for non-invasive diagnosis and treatment of cancer: A systematic review. *Frontiers in Oncology, 14*, 1405267. DOI: 10.3389/fonc.2024.1405267 PMID: 39132504

Zoppé, H., Trocmet, L., Rambault, A., Abtroun, Y., Defresne, D., Ansoborlo, M., Hazard, M., & Bonnet-Brilhault, F. (2025). Early detection of neurodevelopmental disorders in children with delayed milestones: Navigating between overlapping trajectories and the limits of a single-diagnosis categorical approach (A Preliminary Study for the CONDOR Cohort). *Asian Journal of Psychiatry, 109*(July), 104561. DOI: 10.1016/j.ajp.2025.104561 PMID: 40466582

Chapter 5
Telecommunication and Security

ABSTRACT

Israel's telecommunications and digital infrastructure sector has produced foundational innovations across satellite connectivity, VoIP, semiconductor networking, GPS navigation, cloud computing, cybersecurity, and automotive safety systems. Companies such as Gilat Satellite Networks advanced satellite broadband through VSAT technology, while AudioCodes, Viber, and Fring helped accelerate the global adoption of IP-based voice and messaging platforms. Networking hardware and semiconductor innovation were strengthened by RAD Group, Galileo Technology, Broadcom (with major Israeli R&D), and Anapurna Labs in cloud-optimized processors. In navigation and data analytics, Waze transformed real-time GPS applications, while cybersecurity leaders such as Orca Security, Wiz, and Sanctum strengthened cloud and web protection. Together, these innovations reflect an integrated ecosystem spanning end-to-end communication systems, cloud infrastructure, and secure digital and automotive networks, positioning Israel as a strategic contributor.

INTRODUCTION

Israel's telecommunications and digital infrastructure sector has produced foundational innovations across satellite connectivity, VoIP, semiconductor networking, GPS navigation, cloud computing, cybersecurity, and automotive safety systems. Companies such as Gilat Satellite Networks advanced satellite broadband through VSAT technology, while AudioCodes, Viber, and Fring helped accelerate the global adoption of IP-based voice and messaging platforms. Networking hardware and semiconductor innovation were strengthened by RAD Group, Galileo Technolo-

DOI: 10.4018/979-8-3373-7350-8.ch005

gy, Broadcom (with major Israeli R&D), and Anapurna Labs in cloud-optimized processors.

In navigation and data analytics, Waze transformed real-time GPS applications, while cybersecurity leaders such as Orca Security, Wiz, and Sanctum strengthened cloud and web protection. Together, these innovations reflect an integrated ecosystem spanning end-to-end communication systems, cloud infrastructure, and secure digital and automotive networks, positioning Israel as a strategic contributor to global telecommunications and cybersecurity architecture.

Israel has played a transformative role in the advancement of global telecommunications, contributing foundational innovations across satellite communications, Voice over Internet Protocol (VoIP), mobile devices, network protocols, global positioning systems (GPS), data centers, cloud computing, and automotive safety systems. These technologies constitute critical infrastructure for modern digital communications and represent key areas for integration into Innovative Virtual Open Incubators Clusters (IVOICs) focused on telecommunications and network solutions. Israel's contributions demonstrate the capacity of a small, innovation-driven economy to influence global technological standards and operational practices.

END-TO-END COMMUNICATION SYSTEMS AND SOLUTIONS

Battle Resource Optimization (BRO) – Omnisys

The BRO Mission Management Suite, developed by Omnisys, provides a modular platform for mission planning, real-time execution, and post-mission evaluation. The system comprises three primary components—Planner, Commander, and Debriefer—which collectively streamline resource allocation, reduce cognitive workload, and optimize operational outcomes.

Established in 2000 by former Israeli Air Force personnel and Ministry of Defense experts, Omnisys has emerged as a leader in artificial intelligence-enhanced mission lifecycle management. The BRO suite supports:

- Tactical planning and allocation of resources
- Operational guidance with real-time decision support
- Post-mission performance evaluation and feedback

The BRO system has achieved global relevance through strategic partnerships with European governments, NATO, and leading defense technology providers. Its adoption illustrates the practical application of Israeli expertise in the integration of AI and communications technology within defense operations.

Satellite Bandwidth and Connectivity – Gilat

Gilat Telecom, established in 1991, specializes in satellite-based, fiber, and radio communication services for mobile operators, internet service providers, corporations, and government agencies. The company has pioneered several innovations in satellite communications, including:

- The development of the first Very Small Aperture Terminal (VSAT) technology, enabling reliable satellite connectivity in remote regions
- The deployment of the Faraway satellite telephony system and the DialAway service
- Strategic acquisition of Spacenet in 1998, with General Electric acquiring a 30% stake

Gilat's technological contributions have facilitated high-bandwidth communications in underserved regions, disaster zones, and for multinational enterprises. The company exemplifies Israel's capacity to deliver scalable satellite communication solutions with significant commercial and humanitarian applications.

Mobile Handset Design – Emblaze

In partnership with Partner Communications, Emblaze Mobile developed the Alpha 8 and Alpha P8 mobile devices in 2004. These handsets integrated video, multimedia, 3D gaming, and advanced user interface functionalities, reflecting a convergence of telecommunications and digital entertainment technologies. Key features included:

- Video recording capabilities exceeding 30 minutes and high-resolution still photography
- Large, color displays (2.2 inches, 65,000 colors)
- Java-based gaming and customizable user interface skins
- Support for multimedia messaging (MMS), email, and seven-way conference calls

These devices provided mobile carriers with enhanced control over handset software and value-added services, establishing a precedent for the integrated, multifunctional mobile experience that defines contemporary smartphones.

NETWORK TECHNOLOGIES

Cross-Platform Instant Messaging (IM) and VoIP – ICQ

The Israeli company Mirabilis, founded in 1996 by Yair Goldfinger, Sefi Vigiser, Amnon Amir, Arik Vardi, and Yossi Vardi, developed ICQ, one of the earliest text-based instant messaging platforms to achieve global adoption. The platform, whose name is derived from the English phrase *"I Seek You"*, enabled real-time communication across platforms, integrating instant messaging with VoIP capabilities (Kan, 2024).

ICQ's technology was initially distributed free of charge, representing an early model of rapid technology diffusion. The platform achieved commercial success, culminating in its acquisition by AOL in 1998 for USD 287 million, with additional performance-based payments of USD 120 million over three years. In 2010, ownership transferred to Mail.Ru Group. The original ICQ service was officially discontinued on June 26, 2024.

The contemporary iteration, ICQ New, continues as a modern cross-platform IM and VoIP client, available on Windows, macOS, iOS, Android, and web platforms, offering chat, voice/video calls, and group collaboration features. ICQ represents a seminal contribution of Israeli innovation to real-time networked communication technologies and global digital infrastructure.

Early Mobile VoIP Platforms: Fring and Viber

Israel has been instrumental in the development of mobile Voice over Internet Protocol (VoIP) applications. Fring, later acquired by Genband, was among the first mobile VoIP and messaging applications. Developed in Israel, Fring enabled free voice calls over data networks well before the emergence of platforms such as WhatsApp or FaceTime.

Similarly, Viber, founded by Israeli entrepreneurs Talmon Marco and Igor Magazinnik in Tel Aviv in 2010, emerged as a major VoIP and messaging platform. Although headquartered in Cyprus, its original research and development activities were Israeli-based. Viber supported instant messaging, voice and video calls, group chats, stickers, and cross-platform synchronization across mobile and desktop devices. The platform's early adoption and acquisition by Rakuten Japan underscore the global impact of Israeli innovation in mobile communications.

VoIP Infrastructure: AudioCodes

AudioCodes is a leading Israeli provider of VoIP hardware and software, offering carrier-grade solutions including session border controllers, media gateways, IP phones, and VoIP network management tools. Its systems integrate with enterprise collaboration platforms such as Microsoft Teams, Zoom, and Genesys.

While VocalTec pioneered consumer-side VoIP applications, AudioCodes established the backbone for enterprise and carrier VoIP networks. Its solutions enable real-time voice over IP in large-scale telecommunications environments, highlighting Israel's dual role in both consumer-facing and infrastructure-level innovations.

Network Voice Protocol (NVP) and Foundations of VoIP

Israeli-American computer scientist Danny Cohen played a foundational role in the development of the Network Voice Protocol (NVP) at the University of Southern California's Information Sciences Institute (USC/ISI). In August 1974, Cohen and his team conducted the first voice transmission over a computer network, connecting USC/ISI and MIT Lincoln Laboratory using packetized voice. This early experiment demonstrated the feasibility of real-time digital voice communication and laid the conceptual groundwork for later packet-based protocols, including UDP, RTP, and contemporary VoIP systems (Cohen, 1974).

From the 1970s to the 1980s, NVP and associated experimental protocols influenced the development of modern VoIP technologies. In 1995, Israel's VocalTec, founded by Alon Cohen and Lior Haramaty, released InternetPhone, the first commercial VoIP software for personal computers. InternetPhone allowed users to make voice calls over IP networks, reducing the cost of long-distance communication and establishing a commercial model for subsequent platforms such as Skype, Zoom, and Google Meet.

RAD Group: Modems, Multiplexers, and Enterprise Networking

RAD Group revolutionized telecommunications hardware with compact modems capable of operating solely from telephone line power. Subsequent innovations included fiber-optic products, multiplexers, network adapters for servers and security appliances, and video conferencing infrastructure. RAD emphasizes carrier-edge networking and AI-powered solutions, providing enterprises with advanced diagnostics, real-time performance monitoring, and secure network-embedded communications. Its contributions enabled voice services across hybrid IP/TDM networks and early enterprise networks, positioning Israel as a leader in integrated telecommunications hardware.

Comverse: Voice Mail and Value-Added Services

Founded in 1984, Comverse Technology (originally Efrat, 1983) emerged as a global pioneer in voice mail technology. Led by Kobi Alexander, the company specialized in delivering value-added communication services to telecommunication providers, particularly mobile network operators. Most of Comverse's research and development occurred in Israel.

By the late 1990s and 2000s, Comverse developed voice mail, call completion, and IP messaging systems, which ultimately integrated into IP Multimedia Subsystem (IMS) VoIP architectures. These innovations facilitated the transition of global mobile operators from Public Switched Telephone Networks (PSTN) to VoIP/SIP systems, underscoring Israel's pivotal role in the evolution of networked voice communications.

Waze: Crowdsourced GPS Navigation

Waze is a GPS-based navigation platform that integrates real-time, crowdsourced traffic data to enhance routing accuracy and situational awareness. The application combines advanced map-routing algorithms with user-reported alerts, such as traffic congestion, road hazards, and law enforcement presence.

Founded in 2008 in Israel by Uri Levine, Ehud Shabtai, and Amir Shinar, the company was initially called LinQmap. Shabtai identified a critical limitation in existing GPS systems: while they were effective for routing, they lacked real-time traffic intelligence. By mapping Israel and mobilizing a community of drivers to report incidents, the Waze team created a dynamic, crowd-powered navigation system.

In June 2013, Google acquired Waze for USD 1.15 billion, marking one of the highest valuations ever for a consumer application at that time and highlighting Israel's influence on global high-tech ecosystems (Levine, 2023).

Semiconductor and Infrastructure Software Solutions

Broadcom Inc. is a global leader in advanced semiconductor and infrastructure software solutions, with Israeli engineering talent contributing significantly to its R&D operations. Key personnel, such as Asad Khamisy (VP of R&D, Core Switch Products) and Nafea Bshara (Distinguished Engineer at AWS, co-founder of Annapurna Labs), exemplify Israel's influence in semiconductor design and high-performance computing.

Broadcom's product portfolio spans semiconductors, networking, storage, and enterprise security solutions. Its technologies connect a wide array of industries, enabling customers to build scalable infrastructure while maintaining operational efficiency. The company's engineering depth and global scale have positioned it as a central player in networked communications and data center technologies.

DATA CENTER OPERATORS AND ACCELERATOR TECHNOLOGIES

UnifabriX has developed the RPU™ (Resource Processing Unit™), enabling data center operators to maximize computational speed, density, and scalability. Its CXL™-based products optimize bare-metal and virtualized environments for high-performance computing (HPC), artificial intelligence (AI), and database workloads.

Avigdor Willenz is a key figure in Israeli semiconductor and data communications innovation. Beginning his career at Elbit in the early 1980s, Willenz contributed to the computer infrastructures of the Lavi and F-16 combat aircraft. In 1997, he took Galileo Technologies public and later sold it to Marvell Technology for USD 2.7 billion, establishing Galileo as a leading provider of data communications systems on silicon (Gilad, 2023). Willenz has since invested in multiple Israeli startups, including proteanTecs, Lightbits Labs, and Quantum Machines.

Annapurna Labs, co-founded by Technion alumni Billy Hrvoye and Nafea Bshara, accelerates cloud server performance through custom silicon solutions. Acquired by Amazon in 2015 for over USD 300 million, Annapurna Labs developed the Nitro processor, integral to AWS EC2 P5 instances used in AI workloads. The company's innovations have enabled Amazon to save an estimated USD 5 billion in server costs, reflecting Israel's strategic impact on global cloud infrastructure (Bishop, 2023).

PHYSICAL AND CLOUD SECURITY TECHNOLOGIES

Orca Security: Agentless Cloud Protection

Orca Security, led by CEO Gil Geron, provides agentless cloud security solutions. The platform offers comprehensive visibility into misconfigurations, malware, and exposed data across cloud environments without requiring software installation on individual workloads. Orca exemplifies Israeli innovation in cloud-native cybersecurity architectures.

Wiz: Cloud Infrastructure Security

Founded in 2020 by Assaf Rappaport, Yinon Costica, Roy Reznik, and Ami Luttwak, Wiz, Inc. is an Israeli–American cloud security company headquartered in New

York City. The founders previously created Adallom, a cloud access security broker acquired by Microsoft in 2015. Wiz has emerged as a leader in cloud infrastructure security, reflecting the continued influence of Israeli cybersecurity entrepreneurs in shaping global enterprise security standards (Shulman, 2025).

Sanctum: Web Application Firewalls and Vulnerability Assessment

In 1997, Gili Raanan and Eran Reshef founded Sanctum, developing AppShield, one of the earliest Web Application Firewalls (WAFs), and AppScan, the first web security vulnerability assessment tool. AppShield filtered, monitored, and blocked HTTP traffic to prevent attacks such as SQL injection, cross-site scripting, and DDoS.

Sanctum's products were widely adopted by enterprises including Yahoo!, Bank of America, and AT&T. Subsequently, Sanctum was acquired by IBM, and its technologies were integrated into the Rational Software portfolio, later sold to HCL Technologies for USD 1.8 billion. These innovations laid the foundation for modern web application security and enterprise cybersecurity frameworks (Roberts, 2003; Shelah, 2006).

Security Doors: Pladelet® by RB-LOCKS

The Israeli security door industry was transformed in the 1970s with the development of the Pladelet® door. In 1972, a customer requested the installation of multiple locks on a residential door in Tel Aviv. Avraham Bahri and his collaborator Moshe Dolev responded by designing a door featuring a multi-bolt locking mechanism, culminating in the founding of Rav-Bariach (RB-LOCKS) in 1973.

The first Pladelet® door, unveiled in 1977, replaced standard wooden doors with a reinforced steel core and a locking system comprising seven bolts that secured the door to its frame. RB-LOCKS became Israel's leading manufacturer of security doors and, eventually, the world's largest producer of high-security doors. Key milestones include the acquisition of its Lock Products Division by Assa Abloy in 2000 for approximately USD 65 million, followed by a 2008 purchase by entrepreneur Shmuel Dornstein, which enabled expansion into international markets and new product lines.

RB-LOCKS has continued to innovate through Master Design Software, a web-based platform for planning organizational access control using mathematically structured Master Key Systems. The company's RB SMART LOCK represents the latest advancement, enabling secure, keyless entry through a smartphone application.

Automotive Safety: Optima Design Automation

Optima Design Automation, founded in 2014 by Jami Mazzawi, focuses on automotive semiconductor safety verification. Mazzawi, with over 25 years of experience in semiconductor and electronic design automation (EDA) industries across Israel, Silicon Valley, and Europe, established the company to address the growing need for fault analysis in high-reliability sectors.

The company has developed proprietary fault analysis algorithms capable of accelerating verification processes by several orders of magnitude, enabling performance improvements up to 1,000 times faster than traditional fault simulation methods. The Optima Safety Platform addresses both hard and soft error analysis, facilitating compliance with the ISO 26262 automotive safety standard. Strategic collaborations with EDA partners, including ANSYS and Mentor (Siemens), provide integrated solutions for semiconductor verification in automotive and other safety-critical industries.

Cyber-Intelligence: NSO Group Technologies

Founded in 2010 by Niv Karmi, Omri Lavie, and Shalev Hulio, NSO Group Technologies is an Israeli cyber-intelligence firm recognized for developing Pegasus, a proprietary spyware platform capable of conducting remote, zero-click surveillance on iOS and Android devices. While marketed for law enforcement and counterterrorism purposes, Pegasus has been used by governments globally for surveillance of journalists, human rights activists, and political dissidents. The sale of Pegasus licenses to foreign entities requires approval from the Israeli Ministry of Defense (Lyngaas, 2019; Kirchgaessner, 2023).

Pegasus exemplifies the dual-use nature of advanced cybersecurity technologies, reflecting both the strategic capabilities and ethical challenges of Israeli cyber-intelligence innovation.

Integration into IVOICs

The technologies described above—spanning telecommunications, cloud computing, data centers, physical security, automotive safety, and cyber-intelligence—represent key domains for integration into Innovative Virtual Open Incubator Clusters (IVOICs). By linking Israeli expertise in these fields with international partners, IVOICs can foster cross-domain innovation, enabling secure, efficient, and intelligent infrastructure solutions in global communications and critical security sectors (Figure 1).

Figure 1. Telecommunication and security IVOICs

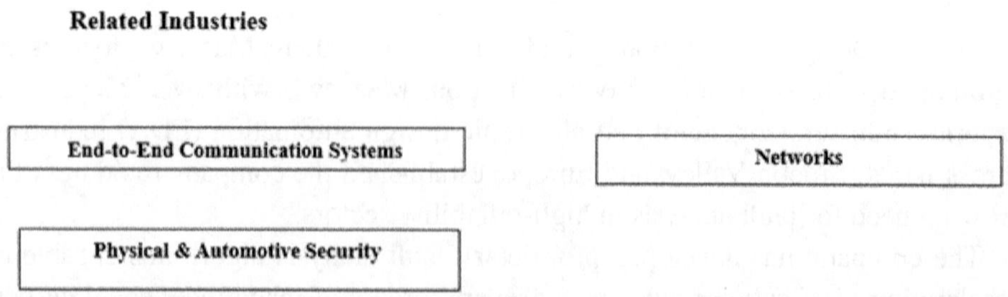

REFERENCES

Bishop, T. (2023). Inside the AI chip race: How a pivotal happy hour changed Amazon's strategy in the cloud. *Geek wire.*

Cohen, D. B. (1974). Toward a theory of dream recall. *Psychological Bulletin*, *81*(2), 138–154. DOI: 10.1037/h0037616 PMID: 4359972

Gilad, A. (2023). Avigdor Willenz breaks his silence. *Globes.*

ISRAEL21c (2004). Israel's Emblaze introduces world's first customized multimedia handset. *ISRAEL21c*, https://www.israel21c.org/israels-emblaze-introduces-worlds-first-customized-multimedia-handset

Kirchgaessner, S. (2023). Washington DC-based group targeted in apparent Pegasus hack. *The Guardian.*

Levine, U. (2011). Was Selling Waze To Google A Good Decision? Founder Of Waze Reflects On The Deal? *Forbes.*

Lock Smith Ledger. (2014). Mul-T-Lock's Evolution: Locksmiths Lead the Revolution. *Lock Smith Ledger.*

Lyngaas, S. (2019). Human rights groups to ask Israeli court to revoke NSO Group's export license. *Cyberscoop.*

Newman, A. (2023). The Evolution of Voice over Internet Protocol: Uncovering the Innovators.*Phone.com.*

Roberts, P. (2003, August 25). Sanctum focuses on quality assurance, Web services. *InfoWorld.*

Shelah, S. (2006). EMC buys nLayers for $50m. *Globes.*

Shulman, S. (2025, April 30). *The 50 most promising Israeli startups - 2025.* Ctech. https://www.calcalistech.com/ctechnews/article/923yvb6hw

Chapter 6
Management Platforms and Tools

ABSTRACT

Israel has developed a robust and interconnected ecosystem of management platforms and operational tools that serve strategic technological sectors, including software development, telecommunications, retail, and cybersecurity. Israeli companies have been at the forefront of video surveillance and analytics, creating systems that extend beyond traditional security monitoring. In the retail sector, Israeli innovators have developed advanced POS management platforms that integrate inventory control, sales analytics, customer relationship management, and payment processing. In software engineering, Israel has emerged as a leader in microservices architecture and DevOps platforms, facilitating the rapid deployment, scaling, and monitoring of distributed applications operations. Israel has also pioneered no-code security automation platforms, which allow enterprises to define and enforce cybersecurity policies without extensive programming expertise.

INTRODUCTION

Israel has developed a robust and interconnected ecosystem of management platforms and operational tools that serve strategic technological sectors, including software development, telecommunications, retail, and cybersecurity.

Israeli companies have been at the forefront of video surveillance and analytics, creating systems that extend beyond traditional security monitoring.

In the retail sector, Israeli innovators have developed advanced POS management platforms that integrate inventory control, sales analytics, customer relationship management, and payment processing.

DOI: 10.4018/979-8-3373-7350-8.ch006

In software engineering, Israel has emerged as a leader in microservices architecture and DevOps platforms, facilitating the rapid deployment, scaling, and monitoring of distributed applications. operations.

Israel has also pioneered no-code security automation platforms, which allow enterprises to define and enforce cybersecurity policies without extensive programming expertise.

MICROSERVICES MANAGEMENT PLATFORM, AMDOCS

Amdocs has developed advanced management platforms to support large-scale digital transformation in telecommunications and enterprise environments. A central component of this effort is amAIz, Amdocs' Generative AI–enabled platform designed to deliver flexibility, security, and regulatory compliance across cloud-native systems. The platform comes preconfigured with a range of generative AI use cases that support standardized, best-practice engineering workflows and accelerate the adoption of AI-driven capabilities within enterprise environments.

In parallel, Amdocs developed a Microservices Management Platform aimed at enabling organizations to transition toward DevOps-oriented operating models. The platform supports the development and delivery of cloud-native software across multiple cloud infrastructures. By automating low-value operational processes, the system minimizes manual intervention, significantly reduces error rates and resolution times, and generates enriched operational data.

This data provides enhanced business intelligence and visibility that was not achievable through traditional monolithic software architectures.

POINT-OF-SALE AND RETAIL MANAGEMENT SOLUTIONS, RETALIX (NCR)

Retalix was founded in 1982 by Barry Shaked and Brian Cooper under the name Point of Sale Ltd., initially focusing on store-level software solutions for grocery retailers. During the late 1990s, the company expanded its product portfolio to include solutions for fuel stations, convenience stores, and chain-level retail management, reflecting the growing complexity of retail operations.

Over time, Retalix became a global provider of software and services for high-volume, high-complexity retail environments, including supermarkets, drugstores, department stores, and fuel retailers. Its solutions enable retailers to optimize operational efficiency, enhance brand differentiation, and strengthen customer loyalty. The company's offerings span point-of-sale systems, in-store and mobile sales channels, e-commerce platforms, customer relationship management, marketing, merchandising, and logistics.

Retalix supported multiple deployment models, including Software-as-a-Service (SaaS), allowing scalability and flexibility across diverse retail environments. Its solutions were deployed in retail operations across more than 50 countries worldwide. In November 2020, NCR Corporation announced a definitive agreement to acquire Retalix Ltd. in a transaction valued at approximately $650 million, integrating Retalix's capabilities into NCR's global retail technology portfolio.

LOGGING, RECORDING, AND ANALYTICS PLATFORMS, NICE SYSTEMS

NICE Systems was established in 1986 and initially focused on developing telecommunications software for defense and government clients. Among its early innovations was a Communications Intelligence (COMINT) system capable of detecting, locating, monitoring, and recording radio transmissions. To support international market expansion, NICE partnered with U.S.-based TRW and later collaborated with Elta Systems, a subsidiary of Israel Aircraft Industries.

Through these partnerships, NICE accelerated its entry into global markets and developed advanced digital communications and electronic information systems. By the end of the 1980s, the United States had become the company's largest revenue market. Over time, NICE evolved into a global leader in multimedia digital recording and analytics solutions.

Today, NICE provides advanced platforms for capturing, managing, and analyzing audio, video, and data across sectors such as public safety, defense, financial services, and customer experience management. Its technologies support large-scale monitoring, compliance, and performance optimization in complex operational environments.

NO-CODE SECURITY AUTOMATION PLATFORMS, TORQ

Founded in 2020, Torq introduced one of the first AI-native autonomous Security Operations (SecOps) platforms with the launch of Torq HyperSOC™. The platform was designed to overcome the limitations of legacy Security Orchestration, Automation, and Response (SOAR) systems, which often require extensive customization and manual oversight.

Torq's platform enables machine-speed security triage, investigation, and remediation through no-code and low-code automation workflows. It integrates seamlessly with an organization's existing technology stack, allowing security teams to orchestrate automated responses across multiple tools and data sources. The system is designed to scale dynamically as organizational needs evolve, enabling faster and more consistent responses to cyber threats through automatically triggered security workflows.

AUTOMATED VEHICLE INSPECTION SYSTEMS, UVEYE

UVeye develops advanced automated vehicle inspection systems designed to enhance security, safety, and operational efficiency. Originally adopted by military and law enforcement organizations, the company's technology is now widely deployed across commercial environments, including vehicle manufacturing lines, new and used car dealerships, auction facilities, large vehicle fleets, and high-security checkpoints.

UVeye's systems significantly improve both the speed and accuracy of vehicle inspections by using computer vision and machine-learning technologies to detect mechanical, structural, and security-related anomalies. In 2023, the company raised an additional $100 million in funding as part of a Series D investment round led by Hanaco Ventures. The capital infusion is intended to support the establishment of manufacturing operations in North America, accelerate sales growth in the United States, and facilitate expansion into new international markets.

MARITIME RISK ANALYTICS PLATFORMS, WINDWARD

Windward is a global leader in maritime risk analytics, providing intelligence solutions to marine insurers, government agencies, law enforcement bodies, and commercial shipping organizations.

Headquartered in Tel Aviv with offices in London, the company specializes in transforming maritime data into actionable insights that enable stakeholders to better assess, monitor, and manage risk at sea.

Windward's platform delivers real-time visibility into vessel behavior and maritime activity, supporting operational decision-making, compliance monitoring, and security risk assessment. The company has attracted investment from prominent global backers, including XL Innovate, Aleph, Horizons Ventures, Marc Benioff, and Lord Browne. In 2024, Windward was acquired for approximately $270 million by the U.S.-based investment firm FTV Capital, underscoring the strategic value of its analytics capabilities within the global maritime sector (Shulman, 2024).

CONTENT DISCOVERY AND RECOMMENDATION PLATFORMS, TABOOLA

Taboola is a leading content discovery and native advertising platform founded by Adam Singolda, who continues to serve as the company's Chief Executive Officer. Drawing on expertise in machine learning and large-scale data analytics. Taboola delivers personalized content recommendations that reach more than one billion users each month.

The platform partners with major publishers, brands, and marketers to drive audience engagement, content monetization, and digital growth. Taboola's proprietary advertising platform, Realize, enables thousands of businesses to advertise directly across premium publisher environments, reaching approximately 600 million daily active users. Prominent media organizations such as NBC News and Yahoo, as well as global original equipment manufacturers (OEMs) including Samsung and Xiaomi, leverage Taboola's technology to expand reach and generate revenue.

Through Realize, Taboola provides advanced recommendation algorithms, real-time optimization tools, and large-scale data insights that allow clients to enhance both user engagement and monetization performance across digital channels.

DIGITAL VIDEO PERSONALIZATION PLATFORMS, EYEVIEW

Eyeview was founded in 2007 by Oren Harnevo (CEO), Tal Riesenfeld (Chief Revenue Officer), and Gal Barnea (Chief Technology Officer). The company is headquartered in New York, with research and development operations based in Tel Aviv. Eyeview's platform integrates dynamic video creation with data-driven creative optimization and audience targeting to improve marketing performance across multiple channels (Lightspeed, 2025).

By combining consumer insights, business intelligence, and one-to-one marketing principles, Eyeview enables advertisers to drive measurable outcomes, including increased online and offline sales, website traffic, in-store visits, and brand engagement. The platform supports deployment through both managed services and self-service interfaces, offering flexibility for organizations with differing operational and campaign management needs.

VIDEO SYNOPSIS AND ANALYTICS TECHNOLOGY, BRIEFCAM

BriefCam pioneered video synopsis technology that enables rapid review and analysis of extensive surveillance footage (BriefCam, 2025). The technology allows users to simultaneously view multiple objects and events that occurred at different times within a condensed video summary, dramatically reducing the time required for forensic analysis, event investigation, and evidence discovery.

With millions of surveillance cameras operating continuously in public and private spaces worldwide, traditional video review processes are often impractical, requiring days or weeks of manual examination. Research originating at the Hebrew University of Jerusalem led to the development of algorithms capable of generating concise video summaries that preserve critical activities captured over extended time periods.

Building on this innovation, the BriefCam Video Analytics Platform provides integrated capabilities for video metadata search, alerting, and visualization. The platform enables organizations of all sizes to extract operational and security value from large-scale video data repositories.

SOFTWARE TESTING, MERCURY INTERACTIVE

Mercury Interactive was a leading provider of software testing and performance management tools before being acquired by Hewlett-Packard in 2006 for approximately $4.5 billion (Hewlett-Packard, 2024). Following the acquisition, Mercury's products were integrated into HP's software portfolio, with many assets later assigned to Hewlett Packard Enterprise after HP's corporate restructuring.

One of Mercury's flagship products, LoadRunner, is a performance testing tool designed to identify and resolve application performance issues prior to deployment. LoadRunner simulates real-world user traffic by generating various users that emulate diverse interaction patterns and workloads (Devex, 2018). This enables organizations to detect performance bottlenecks, assess system scalability, and ensure acceptable response times under peak usage conditions.

LoadRunner is widely used across industries. For example, e-commerce companies employ the tool to simulate high-traffic scenarios during major sales events, such as Black Friday, in order to ensure uninterrupted customer experiences. Similarly, financial institutions use LoadRunner to test online and mobile banking systems, verifying reliability, responsiveness, and transaction integrity during periods of peak demand.

E-Commerce Website

A major e-commerce company might use Mercury LoadRunner to simulate high volume user traffic during a Black Friday sale or other seasonal sales events. By testing their website and applications under such conditions, they can identify bottlenecks, improve the performance of their online store, and ensure smooth and uninterrupted experience for customers.

Banking Application

A financial institution may employ LoadRunner to evaluate the performance of its internet banking system or mobile banking application, ensuring reliability and responsiveness under varying user loads. The tool would help the bank in understanding the system behavior under high load and peak usage hours. This testing process allows the banking institution to ensure secure, reliable, and error-free transaction processing for their customers at all times.

EMBEDDED COMPUTING PLATFORMS: CUBOX, SOLIDRUN

SolidRun was established with the objective of designing and manufacturing hardware components optimized for integration into Internet of Things (IoT) ecosystems (Leichman, 2014). The company's most visible consumer-oriented product line is the CuBox family of ultra-compact mini-computers, which exemplifies the convergence of embedded systems engineering, open-source software, and low-power computing (CuBox, 2024).

The first CuBox model was announced in December 2011, followed by the CuBox-i series in November 2013. These systems were designed to deliver full computing functionality within an extremely small physical footprint. The CuBox-i, measuring approximately 2 × 2 × 2 inches and weighing about 91 grams, integrates processing power, a built-in operating system, wireless connectivity, and support for a wide range of open-source applications. The platform can function as an Android TV device, multimedia streaming system, network-attached storage solution, or compact personal computer.

In December 2014, SolidRun introduced CuBoxTV, a variant tailored specifically for the home entertainment market. In parallel, the company developed the HummingBoard, an uncased single-board computer intended for developers and system integrators seeking an embedded processing module for custom hardware solutions. SolidRun's products are manufactured in Israel by a small engineering team and reflect the company's emphasis on modularity, energy efficiency, and developer-friendly architectures within the embedded computing domain.

HIGH-SPEED DATA TRANSMISSION PLATFORMS, COLORCHIP

ColorChip is a global leader in high-speed optical connectivity solutions for hyperscale data centers and advanced communication infrastructures. The company specializes in single-mode optical transceivers designed to support the rapidly growing demands of data-intensive applications, cloud computing, and large-scale social media platforms.

At the core of ColorChip's innovation is its patented SystemOnGlass™ platform, which enables the integration of optical and electronic components into compact, robust transceiver designs. This technology supports extremely high data transmission rates while maintaining reliability and reducing physical space requirements—an essential factor for modern mega–data centers.

Through vertically integrated, end-to-end production processes, ColorChip delivers scalable solutions that extend the performance limits of existing network infrastructures. Its technologies play a critical role in enabling faster data exchange, supporting cloud expansion, and enhancing global digital connectivity, thereby contributing to the efficiency and resilience of next-generation communication networks.

Figure 1. Platforms management and tools IVOICs

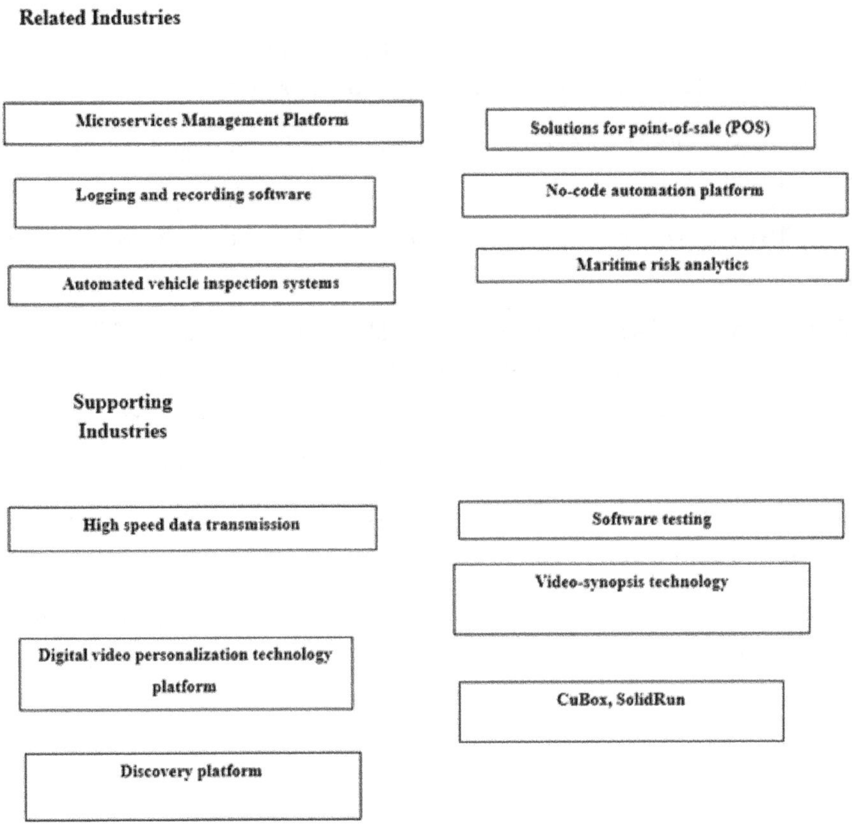

REFERENCES

BreifCam. (2024, September 6). *The BriefCam Solution Ecosystem*. BriefCam. https://www.briefcam.com/the-briefcam-solution-ecosystem/

CuBox. (2024). *Cubox: AI Read-It-Later App. Save Once. Know Forever.* Cubox. https://www.cubox.cc/

Devex. (2018). *Devex International Development.* Devex.com. https://www.devex.com/

Hewlett-Packard. (2024). *Laptop Computers, Desktops, Printers, Ink & Toner.* Www.hp.com. https://www.hp.com/us-en/home.html

Leichman, A. K. (2014, June 18). *A two-inch computer for $55 - ISRAEL21c.* ISRAEL21c. https://archive.israel21c.org/a-two-inch-computer-for-55/

Lightspeed. (2025, October). *Eyeview*. Lightspeed Venture Partners. https://lsvp.com/company/eyeview/

Shulman, S. (2024). Windward acquired for $270M by FTV Capital, doubling its IPO valuation. *Calcalist.*

Chapter 7
Microelectronics

ABSTRACT

Israel has played a formative role in the evolution of modern microelectronics, contributing foundational innovations in memory technologies, digital signal processing (DSP), high-performance data transfer, and semiconductor systems that enable advanced automotive functionalities. Israeli engineers contributed to the development and commercialization of Erasable Programmable Read-Only Memory (EPROM), a type of non-volatile memory (NVM) capable of retaining data without power. Israel contributed to the development of Disc-On-Key (USB flash drives), which provide portable, durable, and high-speed storage solutions for data transfer and backup. Remote Direct Memory Access (RDMA) enables two networked computers to exchange data directly between memory units without CPU intervention. Nitrided Read-Only Memory (NROM) represents another milestone in Israeli semiconductor innovation, storing electrical charge in silicon nitride layers rather than conventional floating gates. DSP Communications Ltd. (DSPC), an Israeli firm, pioneered innovations in digital signal processing.

INTRODUCTION

Israel has played a formative role in the evolution of modern microelectronics, contributing foundational innovations in memory technologies, digital signal processing (DSP), high-performance data transfer, and semiconductor systems that enable advanced automotive functionalities. Israeli research and entrepreneurial activity have significantly shaped the global semiconductor landscape, producing innovations with wide-ranging applications in computing, networking, consumer electronics, and safety-critical systems.

Israeli engineers contributed to the development and commercialization of Erasable Programmable Read-Only Memory (EPROM), a type of non-volatile memory (NVM) capable of retaining data without power. Programmable Read-Only Memory

DOI: 10.4018/979-8-3373-7350-8.ch007

(EEPROM) advanced this paradigm by allowing selective byte-level erasure and programming through electrical signals.

Israel contributed to the development of Disc-On-Key (USB flash drives), which provide portable, durable, and high-speed storage solutions for data transfer and backup. Remote Direct Memory Access (RDMA), enables two networked computers to exchange data directly between memory units without CPU intervention. Nitrided Read-Only Memory (NROM) represents another milestone in Israeli semiconductor innovation, storing electrical charge in silicon nitride layers rather than conventional floating gates. DSP Communications Ltd. (DSPC), an Israeli firm, pioneered innovations in digital signal processing for telecommunications and networking

Israel has become a global hub for automotive semiconductor technologies, particularly in Advanced Driver Assistance Systems (ADAS). Innovations include single-lens camera modules capable of object detection.

EPROM: ERASABLE PROGRAMMABLE READ-ONLY MEMORY

The invention of Erasable Programmable Read-Only Memory (EPROM) represents one of the most influential milestones in semiconductor memory technology. EPROM was invented by Dov Frohman, an early Intel employee and senior researcher who returned to Israel in 1974 to join the Hebrew University of Jerusalem as a professor. Prior to Intel's dominance in microprocessors, the company's primary business focus was memory devices, with EPROM emerging as its most commercially successful product throughout the 1970s and 1980s.

EPROM is a form of non-volatile memory (NVM), meaning it retains stored data even when power is removed. The memory cells are based on floating-gate transistors capable of holding electrical charge. Data erasure is performed by exposing the chip to ultraviolet (UV) radiation, which resets all memory cells simultaneously by discharging the stored electrons. While this process requires physical removal of the chip and global erasure, EPROM's reusability and reliability made it a breakthrough technology during the early era of programmable electronics.

EEPROM: ELECTRICALLY ERASABLE PROGRAMMABLE READ-ONLY MEMORY

Electrically Erasable Programmable Read-Only Memory (EEPROM) advanced non-volatile memory technology by enabling selective, byte-level writing and erasing through electrical signals rather than ultraviolet light. Unlike EPROM or early flash memory, EEPROM allows individual memory locations to be modified without erasing the entire chip, significantly improving flexibility and reliability for embedded applications.

EEPROM typically exhibits longer write times compared to flash memory but offers superior endurance for frequent updates. As a result, it is widely used in embedded microcontrollers, system configuration storage, and BIOS firmware. Special read/write sequences are often implemented to prevent accidental data corruption, making EEPROM particularly suitable for critical system parameters and persistent configuration data.

DISKONKEY, USB FLASH MEMORY

In 1999, the Israeli company M-Systems, led by engineer Dov Moran, introduced the DiskOnKey—widely recognized as the first commercially viable USB flash drive. The device offered 8 MB of storage and utilized the Universal Serial Bus (USB) interface, which was rapidly becoming a standard feature in personal computers. This innovation effectively replaced floppy disks and transformed portable data storage.

The invention of the USB flash drive, however, was marked by overlapping global claims. IBM submitted an invention disclosure through its employee Shimon Shmueli, while Singapore-based Trek 2000 International was the first to commercially market a similar product under the name ThumbDrive. Taiwanese firm Phison Electronics and Chinese company Netac also asserted independent invention claims in the same year. These concurrent developments underscore the highly competitive and international nature of innovation in semiconductor-based storage technologies at the turn of the millennium.

RDMA, REMOTE DIRECT MEMORY ACCESS

Remote Direct Memory Access (RDMA) enables direct data transfer between the main memory of two networked computers without involving the operating systems or central processing units of either system. This architecture dramatically reduces latency and CPU overhead, making RDMA a cornerstone technology in high-performance computing (HPC), cloud data centers, and distributed storage systems.

The conceptual foundations of RDMA trace back to academic research presented in 1995 by Thorsten von Eicken, Anindya Basu, Vineet Buch, and Werner Vogels (von Eicken et al, 1995). Their work demonstrated that high-performance parallel computing could be achieved on commodity servers by bypassing virtualization layers, assigning dedicated processor cores, and mapping network devices directly into user space (Thinking About Distributed Systems).

In modern implementations, RDMA functions as a memory networking protocol that allows one system to read or write memory on another system with minimal software intervention. Similar to local Direct Memory Access (DMA), RDMA frees system resources and improves throughput. As a result, RDMA is widely deployed in cloud infrastructures, distributed databases, and low-latency storage networks.

NROM, NITRIDED READ-ONLY MEMORY

Nitrided Read-Only Memory (NROM) is a non-volatile memory architecture that stores charge in silicon nitride layers rather than a traditional floating gate (Bloom et al, 2001).

This design enables the storage of multiple bits per memory cell—typically two bits per transistor—allowing higher density at lower manufacturing cost.

NROM technology is known for its robustness, resistance to electrical interference, and suitability for embedded systems. It has been widely used in consumer electronics, automotive applications, and industrial systems where durability, reliability, and cost efficiency are critical. The architecture played an important role in the evolution of embedded flash memory solutions.

DSP COMMUNICATIONS LTD. (DSPC)

DSP Communications Ltd. (DSPC) was a pioneering Israeli fabless semiconductor company specializing in Digital Signal Processing (DSP) chipsets for wireless communications. Founded in 1987 by Dr. David (Dadi) Perlmutter and colleagues, DSPC focused on developing DSP-based solutions for second-generation (2G) GSM mobile phones and base stations.

DSPC's innovation lay in its tight integration of hardware and software DSP technologies, enabling efficient signal processing with reduced power consumption. These chipsets contributed directly to the miniaturization of mobile phones and significantly extended battery life—two critical factors in the mass adoption of cellular devices.

In 1999, Intel acquired DSPC for approximately $1.6 billion, marking one of the largest technology exits in Israel at the time. The acquisition allowed Intel to expand into wireless communications by integrating DSPC's GSM expertise into its mobile strategy.

Innovation and Impact

DSPC's chipsets played a key role in miniaturizing mobile phones and enabling longer battery life, thanks to their efficient signal processing algorithms.

Helped establish Israel as a key global player in wireless communications.

Former DSPC engineers went on to launch or join other startups, contributing to the Israeli tech ecosystem.

Legacy

DSPC's success is considered a landmark in Israel's high-tech industry evolution.

Its acquisition by Intel set the stage for Intel's extensive R&D presence in Israel, including facilities in Haifa and Petah Tikva.

DSPs remain at the core of modern smartphones, now integrated within SoCs (System-on-Chips) alongside CPU, GPU, AI engines, and modem components.

DSPs in Cellular Phones

Digital Signal Processors remain central to modern mobile devices, now integrated within complex System-on-Chip (SoC) architectures alongside CPUs, GPUs, AI accelerators, and modem components (Zvonar, 2000). In cellular phones, DSPs are responsible for real-time signal processing tasks, including voice encoding and decoding, echo cancellation, modulation and demodulation, error correction, filtering, audio enhancement, and baseband processing for wireless standards such as GSM, LTE, and 5G.

DRIVER SYSTEMS AND ENABLING MICROELECTRONIC TECHNOLOGIES

Israel's microelectronics expertise also extends to automotive systems, particularly Advanced Driver Assistance Systems (ADAS) (Shah et al, 2025). Innovations in single-lens camera systems, microelectronic sensors, and AI-enabled processing chips have enabled real-time object detection, lane departure warnings, and environmental perception in modern vehicles. These technologies form the foundation for autonomous driving systems and illustrate the convergence of semiconductor design, signal processing, and artificial intelligence within the automotive domain.

Extreme Ultraviolet (EUV) Lithography – L2X Labs

Extreme Ultraviolet (EUV) lithography has become a cornerstone technology for producing semiconductor devices at the cutting edge of miniaturization. Using 13.5 nm wavelength light, EUV lithography enables the fabrication of transistors at 7 nm and below, allowing higher-density integration and improved performance in microchips. L2X Labs has been active in developing tools and processes that support EUV lithography, facilitating precise patterning of nanoscale structures on semiconductor wafers (l2xlabs.com).

Nova Measuring Instruments (Nova)

Nova Measuring Instruments provides advanced metrology solutions that support process control in semiconductor manufacturing. Leveraging X-ray and optical technologies, Nova enables precise measurement of both device dimensions and material properties throughout the fabrication process. Its systems deliver process insight and actionable data, helping semiconductor manufacturers maintain yield, quality, and reliability in high-volume production environments.

Camtek Ltd.

Camtek develops inspection and metrology equipment for semiconductor wafers, with solutions tailored for advanced interconnect packaging, memory, CMOS image sensors, MEMS, and RF components. Its wafer inspection platforms are deployed by Integrated Device Manufacturers (IDMs), Outsourced Semiconductor Assembly and Test (OSAT) providers, and foundries worldwide. Camtek's technologies are compatible with advanced manufacturing processes, including those used in EUV fabs, supporting defect detection, process monitoring, and quality assurance.

Orbotech (a KLA company)

Orbotech is a global leader in automated optical inspection (AOI) and imaging systems for electronics manufacturing. Its tools are applied to bare printed circuit boards (PCBs), flat-panel displays, PCB assemblies, and integrated circuit (IC) packaging. Formed through the merger of Optrotech and Orbot in 1991, Orbotech pioneered the AOI market and continues to dominate, holding approximately 50% of the global market. Orbotech's imaging solutions enhance process reliability, reduce manufacturing defects, and enable precision control in high-volume electronics production.

Tower Semiconductor (Formerly TowerJazz)

Tower Semiconductor has been a leading provider of analog and mixed-signal semiconductor solutions for over three decades. The company offers advanced process technologies for industries such as communications, automotive, consumer electronics, medical devices, industrial applications, and aerospace and defense. Tower Semiconductor collaborates closely with firms utilizing advanced lithography techniques, contributing to the broader semiconductor supply chain and supporting the development of next-generation microelectronic devices.

Single-Lens Camera Systems for ADAS

Modern Advanced Driver Assistance Systems (ADAS) rely heavily on microelectronic sensors and single-lens camera technology to perceive the vehicle's environment. These cameras capture visual data of lane markings, vehicles, pedestrians, obstacles, and traffic signs, which is then processed by embedded AI algorithms to trigger appropriate safety responses, including: Automatic emergency braking; Lane departure warnings; Blind-spot monitoring; Driver alertness detection.

Single-lens camera systems form the foundation for monocular vision-based ADAS, which is essential for higher levels of vehicle automation (SAE levels 4–5). By combining AI-enabled object recognition with real-time sensor processing, these systems allow vehicles to "see" and interpret their surroundings, enabling safer autonomous navigation and advanced driver support features.

Figure 1. Microelectronics IVOICs

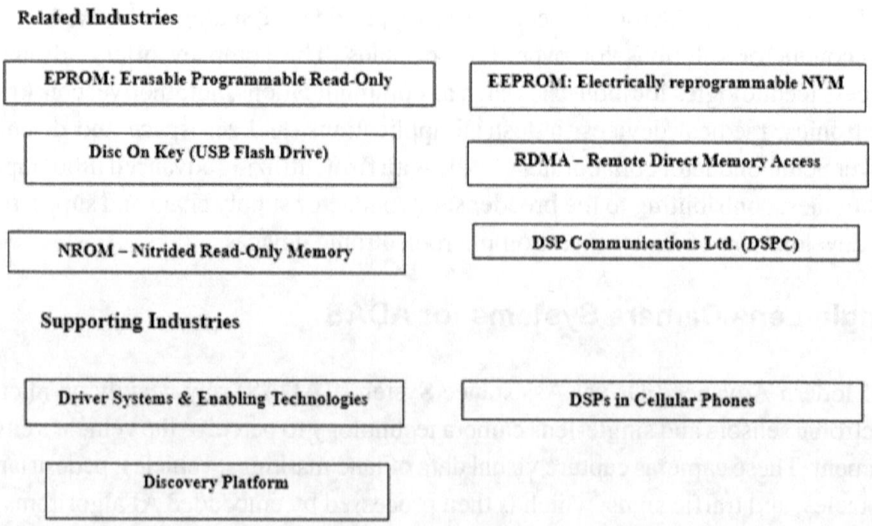

REFERENCES

Bloom, I., Pavan, P., & Eitan, B. (2001, November). NROM™ — a new non-volatile memory technology: From device to products. *Microelectronic Engineering*, *59*(1–4), 213–223. DOI: 10.1016/S0167-9317(01)00625-6

Shah, H., Shah, K., Darji, K., Shah, A., & Shah, M. (2025). Advanced driver assistance system (ADAS) and machine learning (ML): The dynamic duo revolutionizing the automotive industry, *Virtual Reality & Intelligent Hardware,* 7(3) 203-236.

von Eicken, T., Basu, A., Buch, V., & Vogels, W. (1995, December). U-Net: A user-level network interface for parallel and distributed computing (includes URL). *Operating Systems Review*, *29*(5), 40–53. DOI: 10.1145/224057.224061

Zvonar, Z. (2000). DSPs' role in cell phones shifting. *EE Times.*

Chapter 8
Digital Imaging and AI Applications

ABSTRACT

The foundations of this ecosystem were established by Efi Arazi through Scitex, which revolutionized digital prepress and color imaging technologies, embedding computational precision into the global printing industry. Building on this base, Benny Landa advanced digital color printing through Indigo Digital Press, introducing scalable, on-demand production models that disrupted traditional offset printing and integrated Israeli innovation into global markets, notably through acquisition by Hewlett-Packard. Developments such as FreeD by Replay Technologies. Israel's expertise in image processing and signal analysis evolved into a robust AI ecosystem spanning healthcare, agriculture, infrastructure, robotics, and education. In medical diagnostics, firms such as Zebra Medical Vision and Aidoc apply deep learning to radiological imaging. In agriculture, companies like Prospera Technologies integrate computer vision and predictive analytics to optimize crop management and resource efficiency. In autonomous mobility, Mobileye exemplifies Israel's global leadership.

INTRODUCTION

The foundations of this ecosystem were established by Efi Arazi through Scitex, which revolutionized digital prepress and color imaging technologies, embedding computational precision into the global printing industry. This pioneering work not only transformed industrial workflows but also cultivated a generation of engineers who shaped Israel's broader high-technology landscape.

Building on this base, Benny Landa advanced digital color printing through Indigo Digital Press, introducing scalable, on-demand production models that disrupted traditional offset printing and integrated Israeli innovation into global markets, notably through acquisition by Hewlett-Packard. Over time, digital imaging capabilities

DOI: 10.4018/979-8-3373-7350-8.ch008

expanded beyond two-dimensional reproduction into volumetric capture, additive manufacturing, and immersive media technologies. Developments such as FreeD by Replay Technologies—later acquired by Intel—illustrate the transition from static imaging to dynamic, multi-dimensional digital environments.

Israel's expertise in image processing and signal analysis evolved into a robust AI ecosystem spanning healthcare, agriculture, infrastructure, robotics, and education. In medical diagnostics, firms such as Zebra Medical Vision and Aidoc apply deep learning to radiological imaging, enhancing clinical decision-making and advancing precision medicine. In agriculture, companies like Prospera Technologies integrate computer vision and predictive analytics to optimize crop management and resource efficiency. In autonomous mobility, Mobileye exemplifies Israel's global leadership in AI-enabled computer vision systems.

DIGITAL IMAGING, PRINTING, AND VIDEO

Israel's digital imaging sector represents a coherent technological continuum that extends from two-dimensional print innovation to three-dimensional fabrication and immersive video environments. At its core, the field encompasses digital techniques for image acquisition, enhancement, manipulation, and output, whether in printed or video form. Over several decades, Israeli innovation has progressively transformed imaging from a process of visual reproduction into a platform for material fabrication, sustainable manufacturing, and interactive media.

From Digital Print to Nanographic Production

The industrial transformation of printing was significantly shaped by the development of liquid electrophotographic technologies such as ElectroInk, commercialized within the Indigo division of Hewlett-Packard. ElectroInk's microscopic pigment particles suspended in a liquid carrier enable extremely thin, uniform ink layers, producing offset-quality results while retaining the flexibility of digital workflows. This breakthrough allowed short-run, on-demand production across labels, folding cartons, flexible packaging, and high-end photo books. By eliminating the need for mechanical printing plates, digital electrophotography redefined production economics, enabling mass customization and variable data printing.

Building on this foundation, Landa Digital Printing introduced Nanography®, based on nano-sized pigment particles measured in billionths of a meter. These ultra-small pigments function as highly efficient colorants, forming exceptionally thin yet vibrant layers on diverse substrates. Nanographic printing bridges the productivity of offset and flexographic processes with the adaptability of digital systems, offering high-speed, eco-conscious production with reduced material consumption. The integration of nanotechnology into printing exemplifies the convergence of materials science and computational imaging control.

Digital Textile Dyeing and Sustainable Manufacturing

Digital imaging principles have also reshaped textile production. Twine Solutions developed a digital thread-dyeing system that injects dye directly into yarn using waterless inkjet technology prior to or during weaving. Its flagship TS-1800 platform enables real-time color changes, small-batch production, and the elimination of pre-dyed thread inventory. By reducing water usage by up to 90 percent and eliminating industrial dye waste, the technology aligns textile manufacturing with sustainable and just-in-time (JIT) production models. Applications span fashion, sportswear, automotive textiles, footwear, and embroidery. Here, digital control of pigmentation extends imaging logic from flat substrates to fibrous materials, merging sustainability with production agility.

3D PRINTING: MEDICAL, INDUSTRIAL, AND ELECTRONIC DOMAINS

The expansion of digital imaging into additive manufacturing marks a significant conceptual shift from representation to fabrication. Stratasys employs PolyJet and Fused Deposition Modeling (FDM) technologies for medical and dental applications, including prosthetics, orthotics, surgical planning models, and patient-specific devices. These processes enable precise geometric customization and rapid iteration, supporting personalized healthcare solutions.

In high-performance industrial contexts, XJet developed NanoParticle Jetting (NPJ), which facilitates ultra-precise ceramic and metal 3D printing suitable for aerospace and defense applications. Similarly, Nano Dimension applies conductive nano-inks to fabricate multilayer printed circuit boards (PCBs), enabling rapid prototyping and secure, low-volume production for defense, satellite, automotive, and electronics sectors. These technologies illustrate how digital deposition techniques can produce functional, high-performance components with enhanced intellectual property protection and localized manufacturing capability.

Bioprinting and Regenerative Medicine

In the biomedical sphere, additive manufacturing intersects with regenerative science. CollPlant produces plant-derived recombinant human collagen (rhCollagen) used in bio-inks for tissue engineering and organ scaffolding. By enabling scalable production of human-identical collagen, the company supports both therapeutic and aesthetic medical applications.

Matricelf advances patient-specific neural implants derived from induced pluripotent stem cells (iPSCs). Through 3D printing of neuronal constructs designed for spinal cord repair, the firm illustrates the frontier of personalized regenerative therapies. In these contexts, digital imaging models guide cellular placement and scaffold architecture, translating computational precision into biological functionality.

Construction Intelligence and Digital Monitoring

The integration of imaging and artificial intelligence has also transformed construction and architectural management. Buildots combines real-time video capture from wearable cameras with Building Information Modeling (BIM). AI algorithms compare live site imagery with digital blueprints to detect deviations, anticipate delays, and optimize workflow sequences. This application reflects the extension of image analytics into infrastructure management, where visual data becomes a tool for predictive operational control.

Food 3D Printing and Sustainable Protein Production

Digital fabrication has further expanded into food technologies. Redefine Meat employs layered additive manufacturing to replicate the texture and structural complexity of animal muscle using plant-based ingredients. By combining digital modeling with precision extrusion, the company enables scalable, sustainable alternatives to conventional meat production, targeting restaurants and global foodservice markets. This approach exemplifies how imaging-guided deposition can address environmental and supply-chain challenges.

Fashion Innovation and Distributed Production

In fashion, additive manufacturing and digital textile integration have enabled new paradigms of design and distribution. Danit Peleg has pioneered fully 3D-printed garments, demonstrating the feasibility of personalized, on-demand clothing. Her collaborations with Kornit Digital integrate printed textures into conventional fabrics, bridging digital fabrication with textile manufacturing. These innovations support distributed production networks, reduced inventory, and material efficiency, contributing to sustainable fashion ecosystems.

VOLUMETRIC VIDEO AND IMMERSIVE MEDIA

The evolution from print to immersive media is exemplified by FreeD™ (Free Dimensional Video), developed by Replay Technologies and later acquired by Intel. FreeD enables real-time volumetric capture through multi-camera arrays, allowing viewers to dynamically adjust viewing angles during live sports broadcasts. Widely adopted in professional leagues, the technology transforms spectatorship by situating the virtual camera within the scene itself. Through real-time reconstruction and motion tracking, FreeD represents the culmination of digital imaging's shift toward interactive, immersive environments.

Figure 1. Digital imaging IVOICs

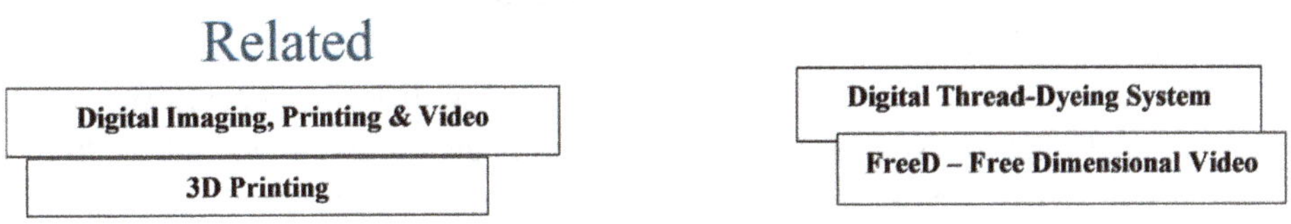

AI MEDIA AND CONTENT CREATION

Israel has emerged as a significant center for AI-driven media technologies, particularly in synthetic media generation, generative AI, automated localization, and immersive volumetric content. These innovations build upon earlier national strengths in computer vision, signal processing, and digital imaging, now enhanced by deep learning architectures and large-scale data modeling.

A leading example is D-ID (founded 2017), which specializes in AI-powered "Live Portrait" and "Talking Head" video generation. Using deep learning and generative adversarial networks (GANs), the platform converts still images and text into lifelike, animated video. Applications include personalized video messaging, digital marketing, educational tools, and historical figure simulations. Strategic collaborations with OpenAI and Microsoft Azure enhance its capabilities in conversational AI presenters and interactive video avatars. Clients such as MyHeritage illustrate the integration of synthetic media into consumer-facing historical storytelling.

Hour One (founded 2019) develops photorealistic AI avatars generated from text input. Supporting more than sixty languages with synchronized facial and vocal synthesis, the platform enables scalable video production for e-learning, corporate training, and AI news broadcasting. Competing globally with Synthesia and Rephrase.ai, Hour One has served clients including Berlitz and NBCUniversal.

In audiovisual localization, DeepDub (founded 2019) applies AI to multilingual dubbing while preserving the original actor's emotional tone and vocal identity. Its technology is used in partnerships with Lionsgate, enabling global streaming platforms to scale content distribution. Competitors include Respeecher and Papercup, underscoring the competitive global market for AI-driven localization.

Speech recognition and captioning are addressed by Verbit (founded 2017), which combines automatic speech recognition (ASR) with human editorial oversight to deliver transcription and subtitling services in more than seventy languages. Following acquisitions such as VITAC and CaptionAccess, Verbit expanded its global footprint, serving clients including CNN and NBC. The company's multibillion-dollar valuation reflects the strategic importance of AI-assisted accessibility and compliance in media and legal sectors.

Automated editing for marketing applications is exemplified by Peech.ai (founded 2020), which leverages NLP and computer vision to generate branded intros, highlights, subtitles, and content segmentation. Competing with Descript and Wisecut, the platform reflects growing demand for scalable video personalization among small and medium-sized enterprises.

Earlier AI-driven text generation efforts include Articoolo (founded 2014), an early automated article-generation system using NLP algorithms. Although subsequently overshadowed by large language model platforms such as ChatGPT, Articoolo illustrates Israel's early engagement with AI-based content automation.

Immersive volumetric media is represented by TetaVi (founded 2016), which develops real-time 3D holographic capture systems for AR/VR, gaming, and virtual events. By enabling AI-enhanced motion capture and interactive holograms, TetaVi extends Israel's digital imaging heritage into metaverse-oriented environments.

Collectively, these companies demonstrate Israel's leadership in synthetic media, AI avatars, localization, automated editing, and volumetric video—fields that redefine authorship, personalization, and global content scalability.

AI MEDICAL AND HEALTHCARE TECHNOLOGIES

Israel has also established itself as a leader in AI-driven healthcare, spanning radiology, predictive diagnostics, quality assurance, precision psychiatry, and biosensing.

Aidoc (established 2016) leverages AI to assist radiologists in detecting acute anomalies in real time, significantly reducing turnaround times and improving diagnostic accuracy. By integrating AI insights into hospital workflows, Aidoc supports data-driven clinical prioritization across large patient populations.

Predictive analytics in oncology and chronic disease management are advanced by Medial EarlySign, which uses machine learning to identify high-risk individuals for cancers, diabetes complications, and kidney disease. By transforming large-scale clinical datasets into actionable risk models, the company enhances early intervention strategies.

In cancer diagnostics, Micromedic Technologies developed the CellDetect® platform, enabling histochemical differentiation between normal and malignant cells across biopsy and cytology samples. Complementary imaging analytics are provided by RSIP Vision, which applies multidisciplinary AI expertise to tumor detection and segmentation tasks.

Radiology quality management is addressed by IMedis, whose cloud-based Duali-Q system detects omissions in CT interpretations, improving identification rates of critical findings. Meanwhile, NanoScent deploys AI-based volatile organic compound (VOC) detection through its VOCID® platform, supporting healthcare diagnostics and environmental monitoring.

Precision psychiatry and neurology are advanced by NeuroKaire (formerly Genetika+), which combines AI analytics with induced pluripotent stem cell (iPSC) modeling to guide individualized treatment decisions.

AI AGRICULTURE AND ENVIRONMENTAL OPTIMIZATION

AI-driven resource management is also central to Israel's agri-environmental innovation. BioFishency developed integrated water-treatment systems for land-based aquaculture, combining AI monitoring, oxygenation control, and filtration to reduce ammonia accumulation and optimize biomass growth. The company's systems improve production while reducing water consumption and energy use.

Aqua Rimat applies IoT-enabled, AI-driven analytics to smart water management, including fish tank biomass prediction and automated feeding optimization. By collecting real-time sensor data on temperature, oxygen, and turbidity, the platform supports predictive operational control in aquaculture and water infrastructure systems.

Environmental Monitoring and Water Quality: AI-Driven Aquatic and Agricultural Intelligence

Israel's innovation ecosystem has long been shaped by structural water scarcity and environmental constraints, conditions that have fostered a distinctive model of technological adaptation. In recent years, artificial intelligence, sensor networks, and advanced aquaculture engineering have converged to produce integrated environmental monitoring systems capable of optimizing water quality, crop performance, and ecological resilience. Companies operating at the intersection of water technology and agri-intelligence illustrate how AI transforms environmental management from reactive mitigation to predictive, data-driven governance.

AI in Aquaculture and Marine Agriculture

A prominent example is Seakura, a producer of nutrient-dense "super seaweed" supplying global retail and food markets. The company cultivates seaweed in proprietary land-based eco-pools designed to eliminate exposure to open-sea pollution. Through multi-crop organic systems and controlled aquaculture environments, Seakura enables year-round cultivation independent of marine weather variability. AI-based monitoring systems optimize microalgae growth, nutrient balance, salinity, and water chemistry, supporting stable biomass yields and consistent product quality. These technologies are adaptable to aquaponics and mariculture, where closed-loop systems integrate biological cultivation with computational oversight to maximize sustainability and minimize ecological risk.

Complementing land-based marine agriculture, BlueGreen Water Technologies (bluegreenwatertech) applies artificial intelligence and advanced environmental surveillance to large-scale water bodies. The company integrates satellite imaging, sensor data, predictive analytics, and its proprietary Lake Guard® formulations to forecast harmful algal blooms (HABs). By predicting when and where blooms are likely to occur, BlueGreen enables targeted and economically efficient interventions at varying scales. Although primarily focused on open freshwater systems, the company's AI modeling frameworks are equally applicable to aquaculture ponds and controlled mariculture environments, where early detection of bloom dynamics is essential for protecting aquatic life and maintaining water quality (Brenckman et al., 2025).

Together, these enterprises exemplify a broader shift toward predictive aquatic ecosystem management, where continuous monitoring and machine learning reduce uncertainty and enhance environmental stability.

Precision Agriculture and Crop Intelligence

In terrestrial agriculture, Israeli startups have deployed AI-driven imaging and analytics platforms to confront persistent threats posed by pests, diseases, nutrient imbalances, and water stress.

Taranis has developed a high-resolution aerial imagery platform that integrates drones, satellites, and aircraft with deep learning algorithms. Its crop intelligence system detects pest infestations, nutrient deficiencies, and weed presence at granular resolution. Insights are delivered through cloud-based dashboards, allowing growers to apply targeted treatments and reduce unnecessary chemical inputs. By replacing periodic manual scouting with continuous computational analysis, Taranis enhances both productivity and environmental efficiency.

Similarly, Prospera Technologies pioneered machine-vision technologies for greenhouse and open-field cultivation. The platform captures multiple layers of plant imagery and climatic data, analyzing growth trajectories, stress indicators, and developmental anomalies in real time. Integrated into pivot irrigation systems and smart greenhouse infrastructures, Prospera's AI-driven dashboards provide actionable recommendations that increase yield stability, improve labor planning, and enhance profitability. The company's acquisition by Valmont reflects the strategic global significance of AI-enabled crop monitoring within irrigation ecosystems.

Cloud-based agronomic intelligence is further advanced by AgroScout which employs drone-based imaging and AI analytics to detect diseases, pests, and nutrient disorders in crops such as potatoes, tomatoes, and soybeans. By automating image analysis and delivering actionable alerts, AgroScout reduces response times and strengthens crop resilience against rapidly evolving biological pressures.

A transformative approach to pesticide application is demonstrated by Greeneye Technology, whose Selective Spraying (SSP) system integrates deep learning with real-time field imaging. Rather than broadcasting agrochemicals uniformly across fields, the system identifies individual weeds and applies targeted treatments. Reported reductions in chemical use—averaging approximately 87 percent—highlight the environmental and economic implications of AI-guided precision spraying, significantly decreasing ecological externalities while maintaining crop protection efficacy.

Plant-Level Water Intelligence

Water optimization at the physiological level is addressed by Saturas, which embeds miniature stem sensors directly into orchard trees. Unlike soil-based moisture sensors, Saturas measures plant water stress internally, providing real-time insights into the tree's actual hydration status. Data are transmitted to cloud-based platforms that translate physiological signals into irrigation recommendations. This approach enhances water-use efficiency, reduces over-irrigation, and aligns agricultural practices with sustainable water management strategies—an especially critical.

AI EDUCATION AND LANGUAGE INTELLIGENCE

A central pillar of Israel's AI innovation is large language model development and enterprise AI platforms.

AI21 Labs is a global leader in foundation model research and enterprise AI applications. The company developed the Jurassic family of large language models, which compete with global LLM ecosystems such as GPT-based and Claude-style architectures. Through products such as Wordtune, AI21 enables intelligent writing assistance including summarization, rewriting, and contextual editing for enterprise and consumer users. Strategic integrations with Amazon Web Services through Amazon Bedrock expand access to foundation models for global developers.

In Hebrew natural language processing, collaborative research between AI21 Labs and academic institutions produced AlephBERT, a transformer-based pre-trained language model designed specifically for Hebrew NLP tasks. The model addresses structural challenges associated with Hebrew language modeling, including limited training datasets and lack of standardized evaluation benchmarks. This research contributes to multilingual AI equity by expanding NLP capabilities beyond English-centric training paradigms.

Enterprise knowledge automation is further advanced by Hebbia, which pioneered production-scale retrieval-augmented generation (RAG) systems. Hebbia's platform applies LLM-based reasoning to legal, financial, and corporate knowledge search, allowing organizations to extract insights from large unstructured document repositories with high precision.

AI for Governance, Enterprise Communication, and Public Intelligence

AI-driven civic analytics represent another major Israeli contribution to applied AI systems. Zencity applies NLP and big data analytics to municipal governance. By aggregating data from social media, surveys, and public service interactions, Zencity enables real-time sentiment and policy feedback analysis across multilingual urban populations. This approach transforms governance from traditional administrative decision-making toward evidence-based, data-informed policy design.

In enterprise customer experience automation, Verint provides AI-powered conversational bots, speech analytics, and intent detection tools for contact centers and security applications. Verint's Open Platform enables organizations to automate customer service workflows while maintaining human oversight in complex service environments.

Cognitive AI and Brain-Inspired Computing

A distinctive research direction in Israeli AI is biologically inspired cognitive computing. Cortica develops neural architectures designed to emulate cortical information processing. Instead of relying on traditional labeled datasets, Cortica systems learn through dynamic environmental interaction and abstract pattern recognition. Their architecture allows multimodal data processing—including audio, visual, radar, and time-series signals—while maintaining computational efficiency on low-power hardware platforms. This research direction supports autonomous intelligence systems capable of operating in resource-constrained environments.

Public Safety, Risk Intelligence, and Social Analytics

AI applications in security intelligence are exemplified by Voyager Labs, which develops AI-based behavioral risk assessment and public safety analytics systems. The platform combines computer vision, network analysis, and natural language understanding to analyze publicly available data for security and law enforcement applications. The company operates globally and serves governmental and commercial clients seeking predictive risk intelligence tools.

Speech Recognition and Inclusive Education Technologies

Speech AI is a particularly strong Israeli domain, especially in accessibility and language learning applications. Amplio develops digital therapeutic platforms for speech and language disorders, using adaptive AI feedback mechanisms to personalize learning interventions.

Voiceitt specializes in recognizing non-standard or impaired speech patterns, improving communication accessibility for individuals with speech disabilities. This technology is increasingly applied in inclusive education environments and assistive communication systems.

Language learning platforms such as SpeakingPal use speech recognition and pronunciation scoring algorithms to provide real-time feedback for language learners. These systems demonstrate the expansion of AI from enterprise environments into personalized education technologies.

AI Infrastructure, Software Automation, and No-Code Intelligence

Israel is also a global center for AI infrastructure development and automated software engineering platforms. BASE44, acquired by Wix.com represents a new generation of no-code AI development environments. The platform enables users to rapidly build software applications by integrating databases, authentication services, analytics engines, and AI capabilities without programming expertise. This model significantly reduces barriers to digital product development and accelerates startup formation (Habib-Valdhorn, 2025).

High-Performance Computing and Scientific AI

Advanced computational infrastructure is essential for modern AI and scientific research. NextSilicon develops intelligent hardware acceleration technologies that optimize computational workloads for scientific discovery. The platform supports research in oncology modeling, astrophysics simulations, and fundamental physics research by reducing hardware bottlenecks through algorithm-aware processing architectures.

Robotics and autonomous logistics represent a rapidly expanding Israeli AI sector. Fabric (formerly CommonSense Robotics) develops micro-fulfillment automation systems for urban e-commerce environments. The company uses robotic picking technologies to enable rapid last-mile delivery.

Similarly, Caja Robotics provides goods-to-person robotic systems that optimize warehouse storage and retrieval operations. These technologies improve supply chain efficiency while reducing reliance on manual labor in high-volume distribution centers.

Figure 2. AI IVOICs

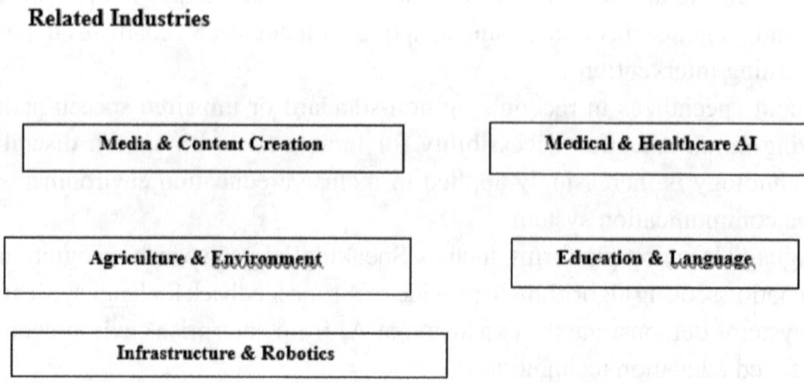

REFERENCES

Brenckman, C. M., Parameswarappa Jayalakshmamma, M., Pennock, W. H., Ashraf, F., & Borgaonkar, A. D. (2025). A Review of Harmful Algal Blooms: Causes, Effects, Monitoring, and Prevention Methods. *Water (Basel)*, *17*(13), 1980. DOI: 10.3390/w17131980

Habib-Valdhorn, S. (2025). Wix acquires Israeli vibe coding co Base44. *Globes.*

Chapter 9
Energy

ABSTRACT

Innovations span the full energy value chain—from production and recovery to storage and distribution—demonstrating a multi-dimensional transformation of modern energy systems. In waste heat recovery, companies such as Brenmiller Energy convert surplus electricity and industrial waste heat into stored thermal energy. Salinity-gradient systems like PRO and RED harness chemical potential differences between freshwater and seawater, while E-TAC hydrogen production enhances the efficiency and safety of green hydrogen generation. Hybrid photovoltaic-thermal systems developed by Tigi Solar increase total energy yield, while robotic cleaning technologies from Ecoppia enhance operational efficiency in utility-scale solar farms. Thermal and cold storage systems such as IceBrick enable demand shifting, while underground compressed-air storage from Augwind provides long-duration capacity. Flexible batteries by Power Paper illustrate the diversification of storage applications beyond grid-scale systems.

INTRODUCTION

The energy applications landscape reflects a systemic shift toward efficiency, decarbonization, and technological integration. Innovations span the full energy value chain—from production and recovery to storage and distribution—demonstrating a multi-dimensional transformation of modern energy systems.

In waste heat recovery, companies such as Brenmiller Energy convert surplus electricity and industrial waste heat into stored thermal energy, enabling electrification of industrial heat and improving energy efficiency. Distributed electrochemical approaches, such as those advanced by HPNow, illustrate how localized production can reduce energy losses associated with transportation and centralized manufacturing.

Energy production technologies increasingly explore alternative renewable sources. Salinity-gradient systems like PRO and RED harness chemical potential

DOI: 10.4018/979-8-3373-7350-8.ch009

differences between freshwater and seawater, while E-TAC hydrogen production enhances the efficiency and safety of green hydrogen generation. Digital optimization tools, including ThermalWatch by Labs, further reduce energy waste through AI-driven monitoring and predictive analytics.

Solar innovation remains central to renewable expansion. Hybrid photovoltaic-thermal systems developed by Tigi Solar increase total energy yield, while robotic cleaning technologies from Ecoppia enhance operational efficiency in utility-scale pter 9solar farms. Flexible and next-generation photovoltaic materials, including those from 3G Solar and Apollo Power, expand integration possibilities across built environments and transportation.

Energy storage solutions support renewable integration and grid stability. Thermal and cold storage systems such as IceBrick enable demand shifting, while underground compressed-air storage from Augwind provides long-duration capacity. Meanwhile, innovations in thin, flexible batteries by Power Paper illustrate the diversification of storage applications beyond grid-scale systems.

Wireless power technologies are redefining energy accessibility. Contributions from Ran Poliakine and charging platforms developed by Powermat highlight the growing importance of cable-free power ecosystems.

Innovations in energy sources supply include waste heat recovery, a smart electronic system that manages solar chips, wireless charging on surfaces, lightweight flexible solar panels, organic photovoltaic cells, batteries 3D Current Collector and a nano-technological coating that cools.

Recent advances in the energy sector are increasingly driven by the need to improve efficiency, reduce emissions, and integrate renewable sources into existing systems. Innovation spans waste heat recovery, novel power generation methods, advanced solar technologies, energy storage solutions, and wireless power transfer. Many of these developments originate from or are strongly connected to Israeli research institutions and technology companies, bridging academic discovery and large-scale industrial implementation.

WASTE HEAT RECOVERY

Waste heat recovery (WHR) technologies capture surplus thermal energy generated by industrial and commercial processes and convert it into usable heat or electricity. By utilizing energy that would otherwise be lost, WHR systems significantly improve overall efficiency without additional fuel consumption (Aresti & Panayiotou, 2025).

Common WHR approaches include thermoelectric generators, Organic Rankine Cycle (ORC) systems, and heat exchangers integrated with thermal energy storage.

These solutions contribute to reduced operational costs and lower greenhouse gas emissions across energy-intensive industries.

Brenmiller Energy

Brenmiller Energy develops thermal energy storage (TES) systems designed to absorb heat from diverse energy sources and discharge it as steam or process heat when required. The technology supports industrial plants, district heating systems, and power generation facilities

Notable installations include the deployment of the bGen™ ZERO TES system at Wolfson Hospital in Holon, where it replaced conventional diesel and natural gas boilers. The project received partial funding from the Israel Innovation Authority. At the Tempo Beverage Plant in Netanya, a bGen™ TES unit delivers up to 14 tons of clean steam per hour with a thermal storage capacity of approximately 35 MWh. This installation is part of a joint venture between Brenmiller Energy and Tempo Beverages Ltd., which produces beverages for brands such as Heineken, Pepsi, and Nestlé.

Brenmiller's system can be charged using electricity from renewable or off-peak sources, biomass, or industrial flue gas, enabling on-demand generation of zero-carbon steam.

HPNow

HPNow doesn't focus on traditional waste-heat-to-energy systems but their HPGen™/GOgen™ on-site hydrogen-peroxide generators are excellent for green oxidation in water and cooling systems, which indirectly reduce energy use and emissions. Here are some notable "waste energy"–related applications.

Cooling Tower Water Treatment

HPNow's GOgen units generate peroxide on-site in cooling loops, replacing traditional chlorine or biocides. Effective bacterial control (solving 100× spikes seen with chlorine).

Safer concentrations (~1%), eliminating risk from hazardous chemicals and reducing corrosion and maintenance. Removal of supply chain dependencies generating oxidant when and where needed.

Energy and Sustainability Credentials

The electrochemical synthesis method consumes only electricity and water, producing no greenhouse gases or toxic waste and breaking H_2O_2 down into oxygen and water . Recognized with the Solar Impulse Efficient Solution label for its positive environmental impact and economic viability. A life-cycle study shows saving up to 3 t CO_2e per ton of H_2O_2 produced versus conventional centralized production.

Geothermal Energy and Industrial Waste Heat, Ormat Technologies

The development of Ormat Technologies represents a significant case study in the commercialization of thermodynamic research into large-scale renewable energy infrastructure. Established in 1965 by Lucien Yehuda Bronicki, the company emerged from patents and scientific research conducted at Israel's National Physical Laboratory under the guidance of Harry Z. Tabor, a leading figure in solar and thermal energy science. This foundational research, centered on applied thermodynamics and energy conversion systems, laid the groundwork for one of the most enduring innovations in renewable energy engineering: the Organic Rankine Cycle (ORC) applied to low- and medium-temperature heat sources.

At the core of Ormat's technological advancement lies the adaptation and industrialization of ORC technology. Unlike conventional steam Rankine cycles, which require high-temperature water or steam, ORC systems utilize organic working fluids characterized by lower boiling points and favorable thermodynamic properties. This allows electricity generation from heat sources that would otherwise be considered too low in temperature for efficient power production. Through this innovation, Ormat enabled the conversion of geothermal heat, industrial waste heat, biomass energy, and solar thermal inputs into reliable electrical output.

The company's Recovered Energy Generation (REG) units exemplify the industrial application of ORC technology. These systems capture residual thermal energy from industrial processes—energy that would otherwise dissipate into the environment—and convert it into electricity for on-site use or grid export. Such systems not only enhance energy efficiency within industrial operations but also directly contribute to carbon emission reduction targets. By improving overall energy utilization rates, ORC-based recovery systems align with global decarbonization strategies and circular energy models.

Beyond waste heat recovery, Ormat has become a global leader in geothermal power development. Its geothermal plants operate across diverse geographies, including Iceland, New Zealand, Hawaii, and Japan, providing stable baseload renewable energy in regions with limited fossil fuel resources. Geothermal energy's inherent capacity for continuous generation distinguishes it from intermittent renewable sources, thereby strengthening grid reliability. To date, the company has constructed over 190 power plants and installed more than 3,200 megawatts (MW) of generating capacity worldwide, positioning it as a major contributor to global geothermal deployment.

Institutionally, Ormat's evolution reflects broader trends in international energy investment. In 2017, ORIX Group, a diversified Japanese corporate group active in finance, infrastructure, and energy sectors, acquired a controlling stake in the company from earlier shareholders, including the founding family and large investment funds. ORIX currently holds approximately 19.7% of Ormat's shares. In parallel, BlackRock increased its participation from 8.3% in April 2022 to approximately 12.5%, becoming the second-largest shareholder after ORIX. This ownership structure underscores the strategic importance of renewable energy assets within global institutional portfolios (ORIX USA, 2026).

Today headquartered in Reno, Nevada, Ormat Technologies operates as an international renewable energy company specializing in geothermal power generation and recovered energy systems. Its trajectory illustrates how early-stage national laboratory research can evolve into globally deployed infrastructure solutions. Through sustained innovation in thermodynamic cycle engineering and strategic integration into global capital markets, Ormat exemplifies the long-term maturation of renewable energy technologies from experimental concepts to cornerstone components of the global energy transition.

ENERGY PRODUCTION TECHNOLOGIES

Pressure Retarded Osmosis (PRO) Producing Power by a Reverse Electrodialysis Heat Engine (RED)

Sidney Loeb immigrated to Israel in 1967 and started teaching RO technology at the Negev Institute, later incorporated into Ben-Gurion University of the Negev (BGU), and over the following 15 years carried out abundant research and taught desalination and membrane processes to generations of young engineers. It was at BGU that Loeb invented Pressure Retarded Osmosis (PRO) (Klaysom & Vankelecom, 2016) and a unique method of producing power by a reverse electrodialysis heat engine (RED) (Tamburini et al, 2017).

The energy generated from the mixing of freshwater and saltwater represents a renewable resource that can be harnessed using pressure-retarded osmosis (PRO).

In PRO, water from a low salinity solution permeates through a membrane into a pressurized, high salinity solution; power is obtained by depressurizing the permeate through a hydro-turbine. The first prototype installation of PRO opened in Norway in late 2009.

The influx of freshwater into the seawater stream increases the pressure in that stream which drives a turbine to generate electricity. PRO, which is used by companies like SaltPower, is predominantly based on osmosis, which is the movement of a solvent (i.e. something that can dissolve other substances) through a semi-permeable membrane from a less concentrated solution to a more concentrated one.

In the case of the PRO process, the solvent is water. To generate electricity from osmosis, a water permeable membrane (i.e. a membrane that allows the passage of water but not salt) is positioned between a stream of fresh water and a stream of seawater. As the stream of seawater has a much higher salt content (so is more concentrated), the fresh water flows into the seawater stream through the membrane via osmosis. SaltPower is the World's first commercial energy production technology based on osmotic energy. Nobian has started a pilot project with SaltPower™ and Dansk Salt at SaltPower's salt mining field in Hvornum, Denmark. The plant, the first of its kind in the world with a capacity of 100 kW, started operating in 2023.

By applying SaltPower to the solution mining process, we can reduce energy demand by injecting diluted salt water back into the cavern. In this way, SaltPower technology can replace the high-pressure pump normally used in solution mining.

Commercial Deployment: SaltPower

SaltPower has commercialized osmotic energy production by exploiting pressure differentials between freshwater and highly concentrated brine. Because brine used in industrial salt production can be significantly more concentrated than seawater, the energy yield and economic feasibility are improved.

In 2023, Nobian launched a 100 kW pilot project with SaltPower and Dansk Salt at a salt mining site in Denmark. The system reduces overall energy consumption by replacing high-pressure pumps traditionally used in solution mining, while simultaneously generating usable power.

E-TAC Hydrogen Production

E-TAC (Electrochemical–Thermally Activated Chemical) hydrogen production represents an alternative to conventional water electrolysis (Dotan et al., 2019). The technology uses electricity to split water into hydrogen and oxygen but separates the two reactions into distinct electrochemical and thermally activated steps.

This design eliminates the need for membranes and precious metal catalysts, enables high-pressure hydrogen output, and improves system safety. Reported efficiencies exceed 95% at the system level, making E-TAC competitive with fossil-fuel-based hydrogen production while maintaining low emissions and high scalability.

SOLAR ENERGY

Solar energy innovation increasingly extends beyond conventional photovoltaic electricity generation to encompass thermal applications, system optimization, advanced materials, and complementary technologies.

Israeli research institutions and companies have played a notable role in advancing solar-thermal systems, smart power electronics, novel photovoltaic architectures, and solar-enabled cooling and laser technologies.

Tigi Solar

Tigi Solar specializes in advanced solar-thermal collectors and integrated heat solutions that combine solar energy with waste heat recovery. Its systems are designed to supply hot water and industrial process heat, particularly for energy-intensive sectors such as commercial laundries, hospitality, and food processing.

Tigi's smart solar-thermal collectors are engineered to maximize heat capture efficiency while integrating seamlessly with existing thermal infrastructure, including boilers and heat pumps. Several installations in Israel demonstrate the commercial viability of these systems.

At Golan Wineries, a 240 m^2 honeycomb-style solar-thermal collector field was installed to support barrel and tank washing operations. The system supplies approximately 12 m^3 of hot water per day at temperatures reaching 85 °C, covering roughly 70% of the winery's annual heat demand and achieving full coverage during summer months, with conventional boilers retained as backup.

A kibbutz laundry facility deployed a 55 m^2 solar hot water system producing approximately 5 m^3 of water per day at 80 °C. The installation delivers annual gas savings of about 70%, with a projected return on investment of four years and an expected operational lifespan of two decades.

At the Unilever plant in Arad, a 25 m^2 roof-mounted solar-thermal array was retrofitted into the existing thermal system. Operational feedback indicates near-total heat coverage during summer months and approximately 75% coverage on an annual basis, highlighting ease of integration and strong economic performance.

In the Of Galil facility in the Upper Galilee, Tigi implemented a hybrid system combining a 720 kW industrial heat pump with thermal energy storage and cloud-based control. The system utilizes waste heat recovered from ammonia chillers to supply hot water at 65 °C for twice-daily cleaning operations, achieving a coefficient of performance (COP) of approximately 4.6.

At the Strauss facility in Karmiel, an integrated solution combining honeycomb solar collectors, waste heat recovery, stratified thermal storage, and cloud-based optimization was completed within three months. The system preheats boiler feed-water to 90 °C, resulting in substantial reductions in LPG consumption.

Robotic Cleaning of Solar Panels, Ecoppia

Founded in 2013, Ecoppia is widely recognized as a global pioneer in autonomous robotic cleaning systems for utility-scale photovoltaic installations. The company's water-free robotic solutions are designed to maximize energy output by maintaining panel cleanliness in large solar fields, particularly in arid and dusty environments.

Ecoppia's platform includes cloud-based monitoring and control, enabling fully autonomous operation across large portfolios of solar assets worldwide. In 2024, Eco-Ops Ltd., a company led by members of Ecoppia's management, acquired the firm and expanded its operational services arm, leveraging over a decade of experience in large-scale solar site maintenance. The company continues to offer one of the most comprehensive portfolios of autonomous robotic cleaning technologies in the global PV market.

Smart Electronic Solar Systems: SolarEdge

SolarEdge was founded in 2006 by Guy Sella together with Lior Handelsman, Galin Meir Adest, and Amir Fishelov. The company emerged from a background in military technology and venture capital, translating advanced power electronics into commercial solar applications.

SolarEdge developed a smart electronic architecture based on module-level power electronics, initially implemented as a chip installed adjacent to each solar panel. This innovation evolved into a DC-optimized inverter system that fundamentally reshaped power generation and management in photovoltaic installations.

The SolarEdge system maximizes energy harvest at the individual module level, improves system reliability, and enables remote monitoring and control via internet connectivity. Since commencing commercial shipments in 2010, SolarEdge has delivered more than 54.5 GW of DC-optimized inverter capacity, with installations spanning approximately 140 countries.

The company attracted early investment from U.S.-based venture capital firms Walden International and Opus Capital Ventures, as well as Israel's Genesis Partners. SolarEdge completed its initial public offering on the Nasdaq in March 2015 at a valuation of approximately USD 620 million. Subsequent strategic acquisitions expanded the application of its power conversion technology beyond the solar sector into broader energy and mobility markets.

Dye-Sensitized Solar Cells (DSC): 3G Solar

Dye-sensitized solar cell (DSC) technology was originally developed by Professor Michael Grätzel and Brian O'Regan at the École Polytechnique Fédérale de Lausanne. Inspired by biological photosynthesis, DSCs generate electricity using organic dye molecules layered with titanium dioxide and an electrolyte.

Unlike conventional silicon photovoltaic cells, DSCs can be manufactured using screen-printing techniques rather than vacuum-based semiconductor fabrication, significantly reducing production complexity, cost, and environmental impact.

Israeli company 3G Solar, led by founder and president Dr. Jonathan Goldstein—an electrochemist with extensive expertise in batteries, fuel cells, and solar materials—has commercialized this technology at scale. The company developed the first commercial-size photovoltaic systems based on colored organic dyes rather than silicon, enabling electricity generation even under low-light or overcast conditions.

Manufacturing costs are estimated at roughly one-fifth of those associated with first- and second-generation silicon or thin-film solar technologies. Production relies on printing-based processes analogous to textile printing, allowing for localized manufacturing and suitability for deployment in regions lacking advanced industrial infrastructure.

DSC technology is widely considered part of third-generation photovoltaics, and recent developments increasingly incorporate hybrid structures, including perovskite materials. In 3G Solar's devices, the electrochemical cell consists of an anode and cathode fabricated on transparent conductive glass substrates, typically coated with fluorine-doped tin oxide (FTO), enabling both optical transparency and efficient charge collection.

In support of its growth, Chinese industrial conglomerate HuaXiang Group invested USD 2.5 million in Jerusalem-based 3G Solar Photovoltaics Ltd.

Lightweight and Flexible Solar Panels, Apollo Power

Apollo Power was founded in 2014 by Eran Maimon and Oded Rozenberg with the objective of developing lightweight, flexible, and durable solar films capable of generating electricity on surfaces unsuitable for traditional glass-based panels.

The company's solar films are designed for deployment on vehicles, rooftops, aircraft, and marine platforms. Each basic unit covers approximately 12 m^2 and weighs around 3 kg per square meter, enabling installation on structures with limited load-bearing capacity.

Apollo Power's technology has been adopted by major global companies, including Amazon, Volkswagen, and Audi, for applications ranging from vehicle-integrated photovoltaics to architectural and aerospace uses. Listed on the Tel Aviv Stock Exchange since 2017, the company has also developed floating solar solutions capable of operating on water surfaces and withstanding wave motion, making them suitable for marine vessels and sail-based platforms.

Organic Photovoltaic Cells

Researchers at the Technion–Israel Institute of Technology, led by Professor Nir Tessler, Director of the Wolfson Microelectronics Center and the Sarah and Moshe Zisapel Nanoelectronics Center, have achieved significant advances in organic photovoltaic (OPV) technology (Tessler et al., 2015).

A patented innovation developed at the Technion increased the power conversion efficiency of organic solar cells by approximately 50%, raising efficiency from around 10% to 15%, a threshold widely regarded as necessary for commercial viability. The research also increased cell voltage by approximately 0.2 volts.

The improvement was achieved by modifying the energy alignment of the electrodes to increase the built-in potential of the device. By addressing electrode pinning effects that limit voltage in organic solar cells, the proposed device architecture enhances both open-circuit voltage and short-circuit current. Detailed modeling suggests that this approach can yield more than a 40% improvement in overall power conversion efficiency.

OPVs offer distinct advantages over silicon-based photovoltaics, including flexibility, low weight, and ease of installation. These characteristics enable deployment on building surfaces in a manner similar to wallpaper, expanding the range of solar-integrated architectural applications.

Advanced Testing of Hematite and Semiconductor Materials

Improving the efficiency of semiconductor materials is critical for advancing photoelectrochemical solar technologies, including water splitting and solar fuel production. Hematite (Fe_2O_3), one of the most abundant and commonly studied semiconductors for these applications, is limited by relatively low efficiency.

A research team led by Professor Avner Rothschild at the Technion, in collaboration with scientists from Ben-Gurion University of the Negev and Helmholtz-Zentrum Berlin, developed a new methodology for evaluating the efficiency of hematite and related semiconductor materials. The technique provides deeper insight into charge transport and loss mechanisms, accelerating the identification of more effective solar-active materials and supporting the development of higher-performance photoelectrochemical cells.

Solar-Pumped Lasers: Weizmann Institute of Science

Israeli leadership in laser research is exemplified by work conducted at the Weizmann Institute of Science. Research into the direct utilization of solar radiation to generate laser beams led to the development of a solid-state, solar-pumped laser by Professor Joseph Shwartz of the Department of Chemical Physics, in collaboration with Dr. Meyer Wechsler from El-Op Ltd.

Experiments with one of the most powerful solar-pumped lasers ever constructed achieved a record output of 100 watts of frequency-pure infrared laser light, representing a significant advance in solar-to-laser energy conversion (Liang et al., 2025).

Solar-pumped lasers hold promise for applications in wireless power transmission, free-space optical communications, photochemical processes, and space-based energy systems. Long-term research goals include solar-driven hydrogen production, solar-heated gas turbines, advanced photovoltaic systems, and the transmission of solar energy collected in high-irradiance regions to distant demand centers.

Outdoor Cooling Coatings, SolCold

Founded in 2016, SolCold is a leading developer of outdoor cooling coatings that actively reduce surface temperatures using solar radiation. The company has developed a patented nanotechnology-based material that converts sunlight and sky radiation into a cooling effect, achieving optimal performance under high solar intensity and elevated ambient temperatures.

SolCold's coatings can be applied to a wide range of surfaces, including buildings, vehicles, shipping containers, textiles, and aircraft. By reducing surface temperatures, the technology lowers cooling and air-conditioning energy demand, contributing to energy savings and greenhouse gas emission reductions.

Following approximately three and a half years of laboratory development, SolCold conducted 25 fully funded pilot projects in 2022 with major partners such as Volkswagen, Hyundai, Elbit Systems, and the Tel Aviv Municipality. The pilots demonstrated strong performance, leading to ongoing negotiations for large-scale commercial deployment.

ENERGY STORAGE SOLUTIONS

Energy storage technologies are essential for enabling large-scale renewable energy integration, stabilizing power systems, and decarbonizing industrial heat and electricity demand. Israeli companies have developed a diverse portfolio of storage solutions, ranging from thermal energy storage and advanced batteries to cold storage, compressed air systems, and wireless power technologies.

Scalable Thermal Energy Storage, Brenmiller Energy

Founded in 1997 by Avi Brenmiller, Brenmiller Energy develops modular thermal energy storage solutions that enable industrial and institutional customers to reduce fossil fuel dependence while improving energy flexibility. The company's patented bGen™ technology stores energy by heating crushed rock to temperatures of up to 650 °C, allowing renewable electricity, biomass, or industrial waste heat to be converted into dispatchable thermal energy.

Similar to electrical batteries, the bGen™ system charges by converting electricity into stored energy, which can be retained for hours or days. During discharge, water is circulated through carbon-steel piping in direct contact with the heated storage medium, generating steam that is delivered to a stabilization tank. The system can provide steam at temperatures of up to 530 °C, as well as hot water or hot air, depending on industrial requirements.

The bGen™ platform is designed for a wide range of applications, including food and beverage processing, plastics manufacturing, paper production, chemical and pharmaceutical industries, and power generation via steam turbines. Its modular architecture consists of standardized prefabricated units known as bCubes™, which are assembled on-site, insulated to minimize thermal losses, and configured to accommodate site-specific footprint constraints.

Recent commercial projects illustrate Brenmiller's growing deployment scale. In Hungary, a 30 MWh bGen™ system was installed for Partner in Pet Food (PPF), reducing natural gas consumption by an estimated 25–30% while supplying low-carbon steam and grid balancing services. In Israel, a 32 MWh installation at Tempo Beverages is projected to generate savings of approximately USD 7.5 million over 15 years and reduce annual carbon emissions by around 6,200 tons. At Wolfson Hospital, a USD 3.55 million project—supported by a USD 450,000 public grant—is expected to produce annual savings of USD 1.3 million while cutting emissions by roughly 3,900 tons.

Advanced Rechargeable Batteries, Addionics

Addionics was founded in 2017 by Dr. Moshiel Biton, Dr. Vladimir Yufit, and Dr. Farid Tariq, and operates development and production facilities in Israel and the United States, with additional sites in the United Kingdom and Germany. The company focuses on improving rechargeable battery performance through fundamental redesign of battery architecture.

At the core of Addionics' technology is a patented, scalable three-dimensional current collector. This 3D structured metal foil increases the effective surface area for electrode coating, strengthens adhesion with active materials, and creates a highly porous structure that enhances ion transport. The result is improved energy density, faster charging, enhanced safety, reduced degradation, and longer battery lifespan.

By minimizing internal resistance and improving thermal and mechanical stability, Addionics addresses key limitations of conventional battery designs. The company's manufacturing process enables precise, cost-effective production of advanced current collectors for electric vehicle and industrial battery applications.

In support of its approach, General Motors Ventures co-led a USD 39 million financing round alongside Deep Insight, with participation from Scania, Union Tech Ventures, Delek Motors, and other strategic investors. Addionics has announced plans to construct a USD 400 million manufacturing facility in the United States to produce copper anodes for electric vehicle batteries beginning in 2027. The facility is planned in three phases and is expected to supply components for approximately one million electric vehicles annually. The company is also undergoing due diligence for up to USD 50 million in grants under the U.S. Inflation Reduction Act to support the first construction phase.

Cold Thermal Energy Storage, IceBrick (Nostromo Energy)

Nostromo Energy was established in 2017 by Yaron Ben Nun and developed the IceBrick™ Energy Storage System, a cold thermal storage solution that avoids the use of toxic or rare materials.

The system stores surplus electrical energy by freezing water during periods of low demand or high renewable generation, typically when electricity prices are lowest.

The stored ice is later used to provide cooling during peak demand hours, reducing electricity consumption at times of grid stress. By shifting cooling loads to off-peak periods, IceBrick™ systems help commercial and industrial buildings lower operating costs, reduce emissions, and function as flexible grid assets.

IceBrick™ units are non-flammable, modular, and compact, allowing for straightforward retrofitting into existing buildings. The technology has been adopted as part of a virtual power plant (VPP) strategy in the United States, where the Department of Energy provided a USD 305 million loan guarantee for Project IceBrick. This initiative will deploy up to 193 cold thermal storage systems across commercial buildings in California.

One notable installation at the Beverly Hilton demonstrates how IceBrick™ shifts cooling demand to hours when solar generation is abundant, thereby alleviating grid congestion and reducing reliance on carbon-intensive electricity during peak periods.

Printed Energy Storage, Power Paper

Power Paper Ltd. was founded in 1997 by Zvi Nitzan and specializes in ultra-thin, printed energy cells. These paper-like power sources are produced using silk-screen printing techniques and can be manufactured in virtually any shape or size to integrate directly into consumer products.

The cells can be laminated, pasted, or printed onto substrates such as paper or plastic, effectively becoming part of the final product. With a shelf life of approximately two and a half years, Power Paper's technology offers an environmentally safer alternative to conventional batteries, particularly for low-power applications in disposable or semi-disposable products.

Compressed Air Energy Storage, Augwind

Augwind develops advanced compression, expansion, and energy storage solutions aimed at improving energy efficiency and enabling renewable integration. The company was founded by Dr. Or Yogev, an energy researcher with a doctorate in mechanical engineering from the California Institute of Technology.

Augwind's core innovation combines underground pressure vessels with a patented liquid piston mechanism that enables near-isothermal compression and expansion of air. This approach significantly improves system efficiency compared to conventional compressed air energy storage technologies.

The company integrates artificial intelligence algorithms with its compressed air systems to optimize performance and support renewable energy storage applications. Augwind's solutions are designed for long-duration energy storage, industrial efficiency improvements, and grid-scale applications.

WIRELESS POWER SOLUTIONS

Ran Poliakine, Powermat

Powermat was founded in 2007 by Ran Poliakine, an Israeli entrepreneur born in Haifa and trained at the Bezalel Academy of Arts and Design in Jerusalem.

The company pioneered wireless charging on surfaces, enabling devices to receive power simply by being placed on a charging-enabled area.

Under Poliakine's leadership until 2014, Powermat experienced rapid growth, reaching a valuation of approximately USD 1.3 billion and annual revenues of around USD 200 million. A major catalyst was a partnership with Starbucks, which launched pilot installations of Powermat charging surfaces in café tabletops in Boston-area locations beginning in 2012. The initiative aligned with Starbucks' sustainability and customer experience goals.

Powermat's technology has been adopted by a wide range of global companies, including General Motors, Procter & Gamble, Duracell, Flextronics, AT&T, and others. Today, Powermat provides Qi-certified and proprietary wireless power solutions for applications spanning IoT, telecommunications, automotive systems, robotics, medical devices, consumer electronics, and industrial equipment.

More than 800 million smartphones, 40 million embedded accessories, and 8 million vehicles worldwide incorporate Powermat technology. In 2023, Powermat partnered with Powercast to integrate Powermat's short-range SmartInductive™ technology with Powercast's long-range radio-frequency wireless power systems. This collaboration enables the delivery of optimized wireless power solutions across both short- and long-range applications.

Powermat also operates a PowerNovelties division, which develops toys, games, gifts, stationery, and promotional products using flat printed power cells. Major retailers, including Hallmark and Marks & Spencer, already commercialize products based on this technology.

Figure 1. Energy IVOICs

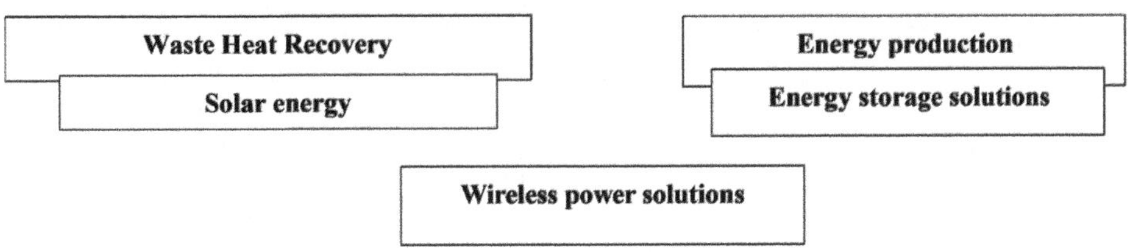

REFERENCES

Aresti, L., & Panayiotou, G. (2025). Applications and new technologies pertaining to waste heat recovery: A vision article. *Energies*, *18*(8), 2086. DOI: 10.3390/en18082086

Dotan, H., Landman, A., Sheehan, S. W., Malviya, K. D., Shter, G. E., Grave, D. A., Arzi, Z., Yehudai, N., Halabi, M., Gal, N., Hadari, N., Cohen, C., Rothschild, A., & Grader, G. S. (2019). Decoupled hydrogen and oxygen evolution by a two-step electrochemical–chemical cycle for efficient overall water splitting. *Nature Energy*, *4*(9), 786–795. DOI: 10.1038/s41560-019-0462-7

Klaysom, C., & Vankelecom, I. (2016). Pressure-Retarded Osmosis. In *Encyclopedia of Membranes*. Springer, Berlin, Heidelberg.

Liang, D., Costa, H., Tibúrcio, B. D., Vistas, C. R., & Almeida, J. (2025). High-efficiency solar-pumped lasers. *Advances in Physics: X*, *10*(1), 2531056. Advance online publication. DOI: 10.1080/23746149.2025.2531056

ORIX USA. (2026, March 30). *Middle Market Asset Management & Lending*. ORIX Group (USA). https://www.orix.com/

Tamburini, A., Tedesco, M., Cipollina, A., Micale, G., Ciofalo, M., Papapetrou, M., Van Baak, W., & Piacentino, A. (2017, November). Reverse electrodialysis heat engine for sustainable power production. *Applied Energy*, *206*(15), 1334–1353. DOI: 10.1016/j.apenergy.2017.10.008

Tessler, Z. D., Vörösmarty, C. J., Grossberg, M., Gladkova, I., Aizenman, H., Syvitski, J. P. M., & Foufoula-Georgiou, E. (2015). Profiling risk and sustainability in coastal deltas of the world. *Science*, *349*(6248), 638–643. DOI: 10.1126/science.aab3574 PMID: 26250684

Chapter 10
Defense

ABSTRACT

Israel's defense innovation ecosystem has developed in response to persistent and complex security challenges, resulting in a technologically integrated framework that combines aerospace systems, missile defense, robotics, precision weaponry, and advanced signal processing. Unmanned systems form a central pillar of this architecture. Companies such as SpearUAV and XTEND develop tactical UAV platforms that enhance intelligence, surveillance, reconnaissance (ISR), and precision engagement capabilities, particularly in urban and GPS-denied environments. The multi-layered framework includes Iron Dome for short-range threats, Arrow for long-range ballistic interception, and the high-energy laser system Iron Beam, firearms and tactical systems developed EMTAN, and breaching technologies from SAN Ltd demonstrate continued innovation in small arms modularity and close-combat capabilities. Odysight.ai AI-driven monitoring platforms and deep-tech communication solutions from R2 Wireless illustrate the convergence of artificial intelligence, optics, and RF systems.

INTRODUCTION

Israel's defense innovation ecosystem has developed in response to persistent and complex security challenges, resulting in a technologically integrated framework that combines aerospace systems, missile defense, robotics, precision weaponry, and advanced signal processing. Unmanned systems form a central pillar of this architecture. Companies such as SpearUAV and XTEND develop tactical UAV platforms that enhance intelligence, surveillance, reconnaissance (ISR), and precision engagement capabilities, particularly in urban and GPS-denied environments. These systems reflect a broader shift toward semi-autonomous and AI-assisted operational models. Missile defense remains a cornerstone of national security. The multi-layered framework includes Iron Dome for short-range threats, Arrow for long-range bal-

DOI: 10.4018/979-8-3373-7350-8.ch010

listic interception, and the high-energy laser system Iron Beam, which introduces directed-energy capabilities with lower per-intercept costs. Together, these systems provide integrated protection for civilian populations and strategic infrastructure.

Ground robotic systems further enhance force protection and reconnaissance, reducing human exposure in hazardous environments. In parallel, firearms and tactical systems developed by manufacturers such as EMTAN and breaching technologies from SAN Ltd demonstrate continued innovation in small arms modularity and close-combat capabilities. Advanced surveillance and signal-processing technologies strengthen operational awareness. AI-driven monitoring platforms such as those developed by Odysight.ai and deep-tech communication solutions from R2 Wireless illustrate the convergence of artificial intelligence, optics, and RF systems within defense applications.

UNMANNED AERIAL VEHICLES (UAVS) AND COMBAT DRONES

Israel's pioneering role in the development of unmanned aerial systems (UAS) reflects a broader pattern within its defense innovation ecosystem: the transformation of strategic necessity into technological leadership. Confronted with complex security threats and limited strategic depth, Israel invested early in force-multiplying technologies capable of enhancing intelligence, surveillance, reconnaissance (ISR), and precision engagement while minimizing risk to personnel. Over time, this emphasis produced foundational contributions to the global UAV sector, influencing both domestic defense capabilities and international aerospace programs.

A central figure in the early evolution of unmanned aviation is Abraham Karem, widely regarded as one of the architects of modern long-endurance UAV design. Born in Baghdad in 1937 and immigrating to Israel in 1951, Karem demonstrated early aptitude in aeronautical engineering. After relocating to the United States, he founded Developmental Sciences Inc. in 1977, where he advanced innovative concepts emphasizing endurance, aerodynamic efficiency, and lightweight composite structures. His work intersected with research programs supported by DARPA, contributing to a new generation of unmanned aircraft optimized for persistent surveillance. Through Karem Aircraft, he later participated in major U.S. Department of Defense initiatives, including the Joint Multi-Role Technology Demonstration and DARPA's VTOL X-Plane program. These efforts underscored the transnational diffusion of UAV innovation and Israel's indirect influence on American aerospace modernization.

Within Israel, institutional progress unfolded in parallel. At Israel Aerospace Industries (IAI), the engineering leadership of David Harari led to the development of the Zahavan ("Scout"), Israel's first operational UAV (Frantzman, 2019). Deployed during the 1982 Lebanon War, the platform provided real-time battlefield reconnaissance, demonstrating the operational effectiveness of unmanned aerial observation in active combat scenarios. The Zahavan's performance validated UAV deployment as a force multiplier and catalyzed further research and procurement efforts.

This early success fostered expanded collaboration between Israeli and American defense industries. A notable outcome was the AAI RQ-2 Pioneer, introduced in 1986 through joint development between IAI's Malat division and U.S. partners. The Pioneer system marked a significant step in bilateral technological integration, reinforcing Israel's position within global UAV supply chains and contributing to doctrinal shifts toward persistent airborne surveillance.

Contemporary Israeli innovation continues to build upon this historical foundation while integrating advanced autonomy, miniaturization, and immersive control systems. SpearUAV, founded in 2017 by Colonel (res.) Gadi Kuperman, exemplifies the evolution toward micro-tactical loitering munitions and compact ISR platforms. Its Ninox family of drones features an encapsulated, capsule-launched configuration enabling deployment from land, air, or maritime platforms. Designed for individual soldier portability or vehicle-mounted integration, these systems unfold mid-air into sensor-equipped structures capable of autonomous navigation and precision engagement. The architecture reflects contemporary operational requirements emphasizing mobility, rapid deployment, and distributed sensing across dynamic environments.

In parallel, advancements in human-machine interfaces are reshaping UAV control paradigms. XTEND, founded by Aviv and Matteo Shapira, applies volumetric imaging and immersive interface technologies to drone operations (Shapira et al., 2020). Building upon prior expertise in commercial volumetric video systems, the company introduced the concept of the "realverse"—an operational environment in which remote systems replicate human sensory perception across distance. Its XOS (XTEND Operating System) platform enables intuitive control of aerial and robotic assets, reducing operator cognitive load while enhancing precision in confined or complex environments. This approach illustrates the convergence of aerospace engineering, extended reality (XR), and artificial intelligence within next-generation defense systems.

MISSILE DEFENSE SYSTEMS

Israel's missile defense and robotic systems illustrate the evolution of a layered security doctrine shaped by persistent rocket and ballistic missile threats, as well as the need to reduce risks to personnel in complex operational environments. These technologies combine automated interception, advanced radar integration, directed-energy systems, and autonomous ground platforms within a unified defensive framework.

Iron Dome: Automated Short-Range Interception

Iron Dome represents the cornerstone of Israel's short-range missile defense architecture. Conceived in the aftermath of rocket attacks during the 2006 Second Lebanon War, the system was developed by Rafael Advanced Defense Systems under the leadership of engineer Daniel Gold, born in Tel Aviv in 1948 to Holocaust survivor parents (Maital & Brazani, 2021).

Iron Dome functions as an automated interception network integrating radar detection, trajectory analysis, and selective engagement algorithms. Its distinguishing feature is discrimination capability: the system calculates projected impact points and intercepts only those projectiles threatening populated areas or strategic assets, while allowing rockets predicted to land in open terrain to fall harmlessly. This selective engagement model optimizes cost-efficiency while maintaining high levels of civilian protection. Operational since 2011, Iron Dome has become a defining element of Israel's defensive resilience and a model for short-range air defense worldwide.

Arrow Missile Defense System: Strategic Ballistic Interception

Complementing short-range interception is the Arrow program, designed to counter long-range ballistic missile threats. Jointly developed by Israel and the United States, the Arrow initiative reflects sustained bilateral cooperation in missile defense technologies.

A key figure in the program's development was Dov Raviv, born in Bucharest in 1937 and later educated at the Technion's Faculty of Aerospace Engineering. Formal U.S.–Israeli collaboration began in 1986, leading to the Arrow-1 technology demonstrator and subsequently the Arrow-2 system, which became operational in 2000.

The evolution continued with Arrow-3, operational since 2017, which provides exo-atmospheric interception capabilities against intercontinental ballistic missiles (ICBMs). By engaging threats outside the Earth's atmosphere, Arrow-3 enhances strategic depth and interception reliability. Its successful employment during the Iranian missile attacks of April 2024 underscored the operational maturity of Israel's upper-tier missile defense layer and demonstrated the viability of space-based interception architecture within active conflict scenarios.

Iron Beam: Directed-Energy Air Defense

The introduction of Iron Beam marks a technological shift toward directed-energy interception. Developed under the leadership of Israel's Ministry of Defense Directorate of Defense Research and Development, with primary industrial partners including Rafael Advanced Defense Systems and Elbit Systems, Iron Beam is a ground-based high-energy laser designed to neutralize rockets, mortars, UAVs, and cruise missiles.

Intended to complement Iron Dome, Iron Beam offers dramatically reduced per-intercept costs compared to kinetic missile systems. By employing concentrated laser energy rather than physical interceptors, it enables rapid engagement cycles and scalable defensive coverage. The integration of directed-energy systems into Israel's air defense network signals a broader transition toward cost-efficient, energy-based countermeasures within layered security frameworks.

MINIATURE CAMERA AND MONITOR COMPONENTS MINIATURE CAMERA, ODYSIGHTAI

Ruggedized Optics and Operator Control Units

Low-light, ruggedized optical systems are increasingly integrated into robots, drones, and soldier-worn equipment. Designed for harsh operational environments, these optics enhance situational awareness in night operations, confined spaces, and adverse weather conditions.

Complementing these systems are ruggedized Operator Control Units (OCUs)—shockproof, field-deployable terminals enabling secure command and control of UAVs and UGVs. Equipped with encrypted communications and hardened casings, these control platforms are engineered for battlefield resilience, ensuring uninterrupted connectivity and secure data transmission in contested electromagnetic environments.

Predictive Maintenance and Visual AI: OdysightAI®

A significant advancement in defense monitoring technologies is represented by Odysight.ai, whose platform builds upon research led by Jacob Bortman, former director of the Israeli Air Force's equipment group and professor at Ben-Gurion University of the Negev.

OdysightAI® operates at the intersection of Predictive Maintenance (PdM) and Condition-Based Monitoring (CBM), leveraging proprietary video-based sensors, embedded software, and AI-driven analytics. The platform provides visibility into inaccessible or harsh operational environments, enabling continuous monitoring of mission-critical systems in aviation, transportation, and energy sectors.

Notably, the system has been embedded within Apache helicopters of the Israeli Air Force and integrated into aircraft systems developed by Elbit Systems. By enabling real-time anomaly detection and predictive diagnostics, the platform enhances operational safety while reducing maintenance costs and downtime.

DEEP-TECH SIGNAL PROCESSING: R2 WIRELESS

Electromagnetic spectrum dominance is an increasingly critical dimension of modern defense strategy. R2 Wireless, founded by Yiftach Richter, advances deep-tech signal processing solutions for wireless threat detection.

Drawing upon expertise in signal processing and wireless communications, R2 Wireless employs proprietary algorithms and artificial intelligence to detect, classify, and geolocate RF-emitting devices across the electromagnetic spectrum. Its technology is object-, network-, frequency-, and protocol-agnostic, enabling comprehensive spectrum defense. By identifying anomalous or hostile transmissions, the company contributes to full-spectrum situational awareness and protection against invisible wireless threats.

PERSONAL AERIAL WEAPON SYSTEMS: SPEAR

SpearUAV has expanded its portfolio with the SPEAR encapsulated aerial weapon system, designed to support maneuvering ground and naval forces. The platform integrates loitering munitions, reconnaissance, electronic warfare (EW), and communication relay functions within a capsule-launched architecture deployable from land vehicles, naval vessels, and unmanned ground systems.

SpearUAV's Multi-Canister Launcher (MCL) has been integrated into Plasan's StormRider armored 4×4 vehicle and the ATeMM (All-Terrain Electric Mission Module) UGV, enhancing mobility and rapid-response capabilities. The encapsulated design enables instant aerial visibility for field commanders, rapid launch with minimal exposure risk, and reduced logistical footprint. The system exemplifies the fusion of aerospace engineering, AI, communications, and modular deployment architecture.

TACTICAL BREACHING SYSTEMS: SAN

For over fifteen years, SAN Ltd has specialized in tactical breaching technologies deployed in more than 40 countries. The company's flagship electro-hydraulic breaching system is designed for single-operator use, enabling rapid, precise, and mobile entry into fortified structures.

By combining mechanical engineering with ergonomic design and reusable training systems, SAN has established new operational standards in speed and safety during urban and counter-terror operations. These technologies reflect the increasing importance of specialized entry tools within asymmetric and urban warfare contexts.

FIREARMS AND PRECISION WEAPON MANUFACTURING: EMTAN

The Israeli small-arms sector is represented prominently by EMTAN, founded in 1977 as Emtan Karmiel Ltd. Under the leadership of CEO Reuven Moshe Zada, the company evolved from producing components for iconic weapons such as the Galil, Jericho, and Uzi into a specialized manufacturer of complete firearms and precision weapon systems.

EMTAN manufactures the MZ rifle family—including the MZ-4, MZ-9, MZ-15, MZ-47, and MZ-300—based on the AR-15 platform and produced according to MIL-SPEC standards. Its product portfolio includes rifles, pistols, submachine guns (SMGs), and suppressors designed for military, police, and security forces worldwide.

Through sustained investment in technological infrastructure and manufacturing precision, EMTAN has established itself as a trusted supplier within global defense markets, emphasizing reliability, modularity, and compliance with stringent operational requirements.

Figure 1. Defense IVOICs

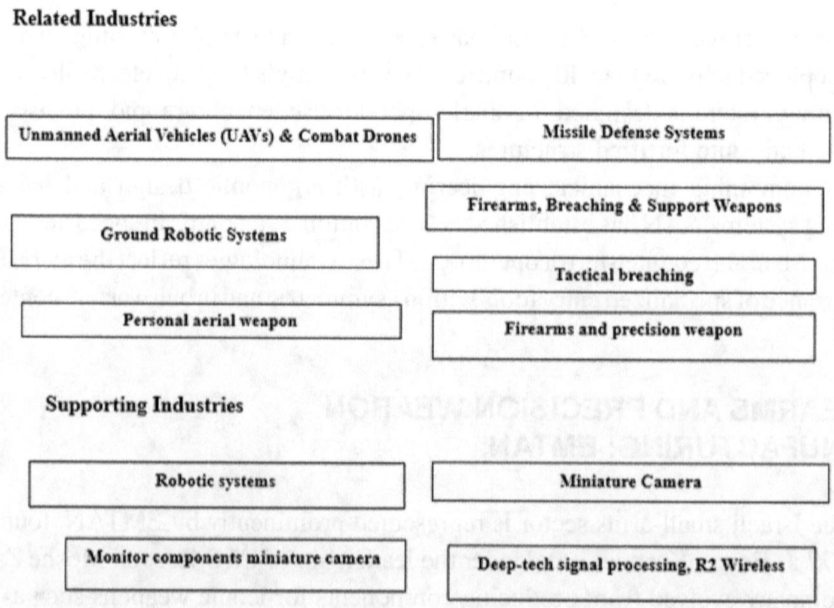

REFERENCES

Frantzman, S. J. (2019). The Fight for ISIS's Old Territory Is Just Beginning. Foreign Policy.

Maital, S., & Barzani, E. (2021). The economic impact of the Abraham Accords after one year: Passions vs. interests. Samuel Neaman Institute for National Policy Research.

Shapira, A., Noor, N., Oved, H., & Dvir, T. (2020). Transparent support media for high resolution 3D printing of volumetric cell-containing ECM structures. Biomedical Materials (Bristol).

Chapter 11
The Open Incubators Cluster Model for Discontinuous and Disruptive Innovations

ABSTRACT

Israel's innovation ecosystem is largely shaped by the Law for the Encouragement of Industrial Research and Development, which established state-supported R&D incentives aimed at strengthening export-oriented high-tech industries. The policy is implemented by the Israel Innovation Authority, which provides funding and support through a flexible, project-based evaluation model that has helped develop a globally competitive startup ecosystem across sectors such as cybersecurity, AI, health technologies, and clean energy. While this bottom-up approach has encouraged entrepreneurial diversity and rapid technological commercialization, it also limits large-scale strategic knowledge integration. Future policy development could involve greater use of data-driven planning to identify emerging technology clusters and align innovation investment with national priorities such as climate resilience, healthcare, food security, and sustainable resource management.

INTRODUCTION

Israel's innovation ecosystem is largely shaped by the Law for the Encouragement of Industrial Research and Development, which established state-supported R&D incentives aimed at strengthening export-oriented high-tech industries. The policy is implemented by the Israel Innovation Authority, which provides funding and support through a flexible, project-based evaluation model that has helped develop

DOI: 10.4018/979-8-3373-7350-8.ch011

a globally competitive startup ecosystem across sectors such as cybersecurity, AI, health technologies, and clean energy.

While this bottom-up approach has encouraged entrepreneurial diversity and rapid technological commercialization, it also limits large-scale strategic knowledge integration. Future policy development could involve greater use of data-driven planning to identify emerging technology clusters and align innovation investment with national priorities such as climate resilience, healthcare, food security, and sustainable resource management.

INNOVATION TYPES

Innovation can be classified across several dimensions, ranging from resource-constrained creativity to transformative technological breakthroughs:

Frugal Innovation

Frugal innovation emphasizes simplicity, cost-effectiveness, and accessibility (Escudero-Cipriani et al, 2024).

It involves devising practical solutions under constraints, often serving low-income or resource-limited populations. Despite its capacity to stimulate local economies and support underserved markets, frugal innovation aimed at domestic markets currently receives limited backing from the Israel Innovation Authority (IIA).

Inclusive Innovation

Inclusive innovation focuses on creating affordable, high-quality solutions for broad, low-income markets, fostering both social equity and sustainable economic growth (World Bank, 2013). It addresses the needs of consumers whose purchasing decisions are constrained by economic limitations. While promising for grassroots development, inclusive innovation targeted at local markets is not currently prioritized by the IIA.

Radical Innovation

Radical innovation is defined as the introduction of products or technologies that are fundamentally different from existing solutions and that address core customer needs more effectively (Chandy & Tellis, 1998).

Such innovations often give rise to entirely new platforms, targeting emerging needs in previously untapped markets through transformative approaches. Typically driven by scientific and technological breakthroughs, radical innovation can substantially enhance economic value, fostering growth and competitiveness in both local and global markets. In Israel, such innovations are primarily supported at the academic level by the Ministry of Education and by domain-specific ministries such as Agriculture and Energy.

The Israel Innovation Authority (IIA) generally does not support radical innovations unless they are linked to export-oriented firms. However, fostering collaboration between scientific innovators and export-capable companies could open a path for IIA involvement—bridging fundamental research with commercial application and market scaling.

Discontinuous Innovation

Discontinuous innovation creates new technological or market trajectories, often requiring firms to move beyond existing capabilities (Tripsas & Gavetti, 2000; Hodgkinson & Sparrow, 2002). These innovations target potential customer segments where demand is nascent, necessitating exploration of new competitive landscapes (Picaud, 2013). The IIA currently prioritizes discontinuous innovation only when it targets international markets, underutilizing its potential for domestic economic development.

Disruptive Innovation

Disruptive innovation introduces new technologies that meet the needs of underserved or emerging market segments (Di Minin & Corsi, 2011). Typically, it addresses two main customer groups:

Users willing to pay for premium value.

Cost-sensitive customers seeking "good enough" solutions at lower price points (Govindarajan, 2013).

Disruptive innovations require a combination of intensive R&D and strategic market engagement to achieve commercial viability. While they are increasingly supported by the IIA, the focus remains largely on export-oriented applications, limiting their potential impact on local markets.

SAMPLE ANALYSIS

This study examines a total of 229 high-impact innovations supported by the Israel Innovation Authority (IIA) within the industrial sector, distinguishing between discontinuous and disruptive forms of innovation. Of these, 94 are classified as discontinuous innovations, primarily distributed across agriculture, energy, healthcare, and telecommunications (see Appendix I). These innovations reflect significant technological advances that reshape existing processes and capabilities, particularly in sectors where scientific knowledge and applied research play a central role.

In contrast, 135 innovations are identified as disruptive, spanning a broader and more digitally intensive set of domains, including agriculture, healthcare, energy, digital platforms, imaging technologies, education, and defense (see Appendix II). These innovations are characterized not only by technological novelty but also by their capacity to transform market structures, introduce new business models, and redefine value chains.

Collectively, the distribution of these innovations underscores their cross-sectoral nature, with strong representation in healthcare, energy, agriculture, defense, and digital technologies. This breadth highlights the systemic role of innovation in driving industrial transformation, as well as the increasing convergence between traditionally distinct sectors through digitalization and advanced technological integration.

Discontinuous Innovations analysis

An analysis of innovation patterns reveals a clear distinction between discontinuous and disruptive innovations across sectoral domains, highlighting differences in technological trajectories, market impact, and systemic transformation.

Discontinuous innovations, totaling 94 cases, are unevenly distributed across industries, with a strong concentration in healthcare (30) and agriculture (16). This distribution suggests that sectors characterized by complex biological systems and evolving societal needs tend to generate innovations that significantly alter existing technological paradigms without necessarily overturning market structures. In healthcare, discontinuous innovation often emerges through breakthroughs in diagnostics, treatment methodologies, and biomedical technologies, reshaping clinical practices while remaining embedded within established institutional frameworks. Similarly, agriculture (16) and healthy food (15) sectors exhibit notable activity, reflecting growing pressures related to food security, sustainability, and nutritional transitions. These innovations frequently involve novel inputs, precision techniques, or bio-based solutions that redefine production processes.

Digital imaging (13) and telecommunication and security (8) also demonstrate meaningful levels of discontinuous innovation, indicating incremental yet substantial shifts in data capture, processing, and transmission technologies. Energy (8) and cosmetics (4), by contrast, show relatively lower levels, suggesting either technological maturity or slower rates of paradigm-shifting developments within these fields.

In contrast, disruptive innovations—accounting for a larger total of 135 cases—are more strongly associated with sectors undergoing rapid digital transformation and platform-based restructuring. Telecommunication (33), AI platforms (23), and hardware/software platforms (21) dominate this category, underscoring the centrality of digital ecosystems in redefining market boundaries and competitive dynamics. These innovations typically introduce new business models, displace incumbent firms, and create entirely new value networks. The prominence of AI platforms highlights the increasing role of algorithmic intelligence and data-driven architectures as foundational infrastructures for disruption across industries.

Healthcare (17) and agriculture and water treatment (19) also feature within disruptive innovation, though to a lesser extent than in the discontinuous category. This suggests that while these sectors experience significant technological breakthroughs, only a subset fundamentally transforms market structures or access models. Microelectronics (9) and defense (9) indicate moderate disruptive activity, often linked to advancements in miniaturization, embedded systems, and strategic technologies.

Notably, energy (2) and digital imaging (2) exhibit minimal disruptive innovation, which may reflect high capital intensity, regulatory constraints, or entrenched infrastructure systems that limit rapid market displacement despite ongoing technological change.

AGRICULTURE AND WATER TREATMENT IVOICS OF DISCONTINUOUS INNOVATIONS

The portfolio of innovations reflects a strong orientation toward advanced agricultural biotechnology, precision farming, and biosecurity, illustrating the convergence between life sciences and digital technologies in contemporary agri-industrial systems.

At the molecular level, the use of microRNA (miRNA) as a genome regulator in plants represents a significant discontinuous innovation in plant biotechnology. miRNAs function as key post-transcriptional regulators, enabling precise control over gene expression associated with plant growth, stress responses, and disease resistance. Their application enhances the ability to engineer crops with improved resilience and productivity, marking a shift toward highly targeted and efficient genetic modulation techniques.

This molecular approach is complemented by crop-specific innovations such as research on the Hibiscus cannabinus (kenaf plant), a fast-growing fiber crop with applications in sustainable materials, bio-composites, and environmental remediation. Advances in kenaf cultivation and genetic improvement underscore the growing importance of alternative crops in circular and bio-based economies.

Digital and platform-based innovations further reinforce this transformation. Systems designed to monitor pollinators introduce new capabilities for tracking ecosystem health and biodiversity, addressing critical concerns related to pollination decline and its implications for agricultural productivity. Similarly, real-time crop monitoring platforms—such as Croptune—leverage sensors, data analytics, and remote sensing technologies to provide continuous insights into crop development, enabling precision agriculture practices and data-driven decision-making.

Technologies like NOF Cooling contribute to post-harvest innovation by optimizing cooling processes to extend shelf life and reduce food loss. These solutions are particularly significant in supply chain efficiency, linking production with distribution while maintaining product quality.

In parallel, hydroponic systems represent a transformative approach to cultivation, allowing crops to be grown in controlled, soil-less environments with optimized nutrient delivery. This method enhances resource efficiency—particularly water use—and supports urban and vertical farming models, thereby contributing to sustainable intensification of agriculture.

Finally, innovations targeting biological threats, such as solutions developed against the H5N1 avian influenza virus, highlight the intersection of agriculture and biosecurity. Addressing highly pathogenic avian influenza is critical not only for livestock health but also for global food security and public health, emphasizing the role of technological innovation in mitigating systemic risks.

Figure 1. Agro business and water treatment IVOICs of discontinuous innovations

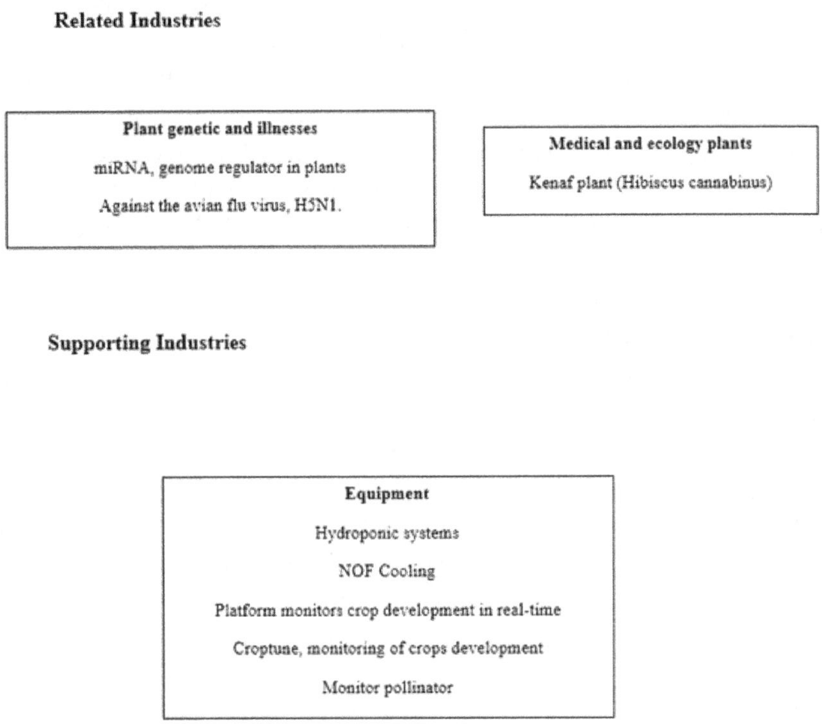

AGRICULTURE AND WATER TREATMENT IVOICS OF DISRUPTIVE INNOVATIONS

A central feature of agricultural IVOICs is the integration of intelligent digital platforms with biological innovation. For instance, N-Drip Connect represents a shift toward data-driven irrigation management, optimizing water delivery through real-time analytics and precision control. Similarly, innovations such as Supree's self-drying cherry tomatoes—semi-dried produce developed at the cultivation stage—demonstrate how value addition is increasingly embedded directly within primary production processes, thereby altering traditional post-harvest value chains.

Biotechnological disruption is particularly evident in genetic and reproductive innovations. The development of gene-edited female-only eggs by Golda Hen introduces a transformative solution to ethical and economic challenges in poultry production by eliminating the need for male chick culling. In parallel, Soos Technology advances acoustic sex determination and reversal technologies, further enhancing efficiency and sustainability in hatchery operations. These approaches reflect a broader shift toward precision breeding and reproductive control.

At the genomic level, next-generation gene-editing platforms are central to the IVOIC model. Technologies such as CRISPR-based systems—developed through initiatives led by Evogene and applied by firms like CanBreed—enable precise modification of plant and animal genomes to enhance yield, resilience, and nutritional value. Complementary tools such as Cas-CLOVER, developed by Demeetra Biotech, expand the gene-editing toolkit, offering high specificity and reduced off-target effects. These innovations extend across multiple applications, including cannabis genomics (in collaboration with ToolGen and Plant ArcBio) and soybean improvement projects, illustrating the scalability of genome engineering within agricultural systems.

Water treatment IVOICs similarly demonstrate disruptive transformation through the convergence of advanced desalination, purification, and resource-generation technologies. Reverse osmosis (RO), a foundational technology in modern desalination, is being continuously enhanced by organizations such as IDE Technologies, Mekorot, and Aqwise. These advancements improve efficiency, reduce energy consumption, and expand applicability across industrial and municipal contexts.

Emerging technologies further redefine water production paradigms. Vacuum Freezing Vapor Compression (VFVC), pioneered by IDE Technologies, introduces an alternative desalination process with potential energy advantages. Atmospheric water generation technologies developed by Watergen and H2OLL represent a radical departure from conventional water sourcing by extracting potable water directly from air.

In addition, Closed-Circuit Desalination (CCD) technology—advanced by IDE Technologies, ROTec, and Negev Eco Desal—demonstrates how system-level innovation can significantly increase water recovery rates while minimizing brine discharge and environmental impact.

Figure 2. Agro business and water treatment IVOICs of discontinuous innovations

Related Industries

Plant genetic and illnesses

Supree – Self-Drying Cherry Tomatoes. Semi-dried cherry

Gene-editing tool. Cas-CLOVER (Demeetra Biotech); CRISPR-IL

Consortium Led by Evogene; CanBreed: CRISPR-Edited Livestock; Cannabis Plant ArcBio & ToolGen ; Soybean Project.

Animal genetic

Golda Hen – Gene-Edited Female-Only Eggs.

Soos Technology – Acoustic Sex Reversal

Supporting Industries

Equipment

N-Drip Connect. An intelligent digital platform

Reverse osmosis (RO). IDE Technologies; Mekorot; Aqwise WFI group

Vacuum Freezing Vapor Compression (VFVC). IDE Technologies

Water from air. Watergen and H2OLL

Closed-Circuit Desalination (CCD) technology. IDE Technologies; ROTec (Reverse Osmosis Technologies); Negev Eco Desal

HEALTHY FOOD IVOICS OF DISCONTINUOUS INNOVATIONS

A central pillar of this transformation is cellular agriculture technology, which enables the production of food components without reliance on conventional livestock systems. Animal-free production methods—ranging from cultured ingredients to fermentation-derived compounds—are redefining the boundaries of food manufacturing by decoupling protein production from land- and resource-intensive animal agriculture. In parallel, natural flavor solutions are being developed through biotechnological processes, allowing manufacturers to replicate or enhance sensory profiles without synthetic additives, thereby aligning with clean-label consumer demands.

Plant-based innovation constitutes another major axis of disruption. Companies such as InnovoPro are advancing proteins derived from chickpeas, with applications including dairy-free yogurts and other alternative dairy products. These developments highlight the increasing functional sophistication of plant proteins, which are being engineered to match the texture, taste, and nutritional properties of traditional animal-derived products. Similarly, the production of proteins from microalgae and other plant sources introduces highly efficient and scalable alternatives, leveraging organisms with rapid growth cycles and minimal environmental footprints.

Product innovation is also evident in the development of plant-based fish fillets and other analogues designed to replicate the sensory and nutritional attributes of seafood. These offerings address both sustainability concerns—such as overfishing—and shifting consumer preferences. At the same time, novel food formats such as meal pods represent a reconfiguration of food consumption patterns, emphasizing convenience, personalization, and integration with automated preparation systems.

Automation and robotics further enhance this ecosystem. SavorEat exemplifies this trend through its development of automated robot chefs capable of preparing customized plant-based meals on demand. This innovation not only transforms food service operations but also integrates digital control with food production, enabling real-time adaptation to consumer preferences.

Complementing production and preparation technologies are innovations in quality assurance and packaging. Advanced analytical monitoring systems for heat-sealed packages ensure product integrity, safety, and shelf life by detecting defects and maintaining optimal storage conditions. These systems are critical in supporting the scalability of alternative protein products, particularly in global distribution networks.

Figure 3. Healthy food IVOICs of discontinuous innovations

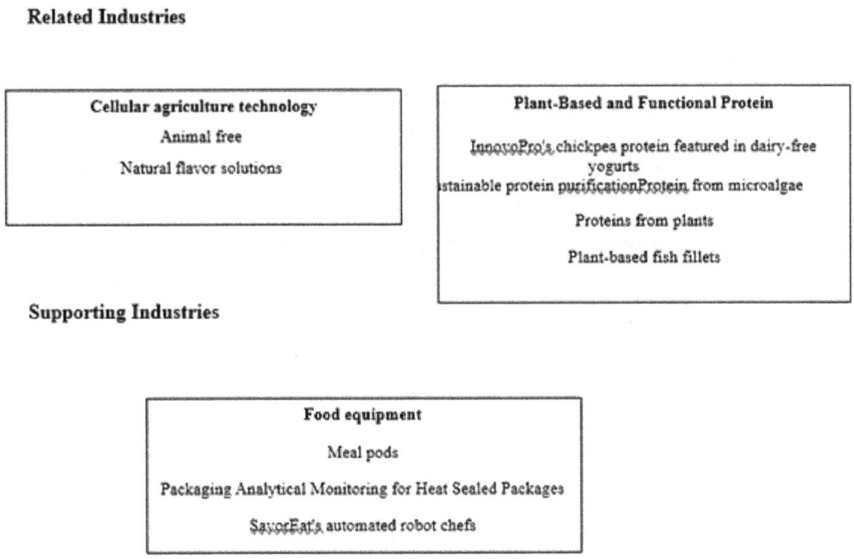

HEALTHCARE IVOICS OF DISCONTINUOUS INNOVATIONS

Within the IVOIC framework, discontinuous innovations in healthcare are characterized by significant technological breakthroughs that reshape clinical capabilities, therapeutic approaches, and patient management systems without fully displacing existing institutional structures. These innovations span diagnostics, therapeutics, medical devices, and digital health, reflecting the increasing convergence of engineering, life sciences, and data-driven technologies.

Advanced medical imaging technologies, including computed tomography and magnetic resonance breast imaging, exemplify discontinuous progress in diagnostic precision. These modalities enhance early detection and characterization of complex conditions, particularly in oncology, by improving spatial resolution and tissue differentiation. Their integration into clinical workflows strengthens diagnostic accuracy while remaining embedded within established healthcare systems.

Surgical innovation is similarly evident in robotic brain surgery, where high-precision robotic systems enable minimally invasive procedures with enhanced accuracy and reduced risk. These technologies augment surgical capabilities rather than replace traditional practices, illustrating the nature of discontinuous advancement.

In the domain of connected care, devices such as the Avoset™ infusion pump developed by Eitan Medical represent a shift toward home-based treatment. This connected home platform enables remote monitoring and controlled drug delivery, supporting the decentralization of healthcare while maintaining clinical oversight. Likewise, wearable solutions from Biobeat enable continuous, non-invasive blood pressure monitoring, enhancing preventive care and real-time health tracking.

Therapeutic innovations further illustrate discontinuity across multiple domains. Portable hyperbaric oxygen therapy (HBOT) systems expand access to oxygen-based treatments beyond hospital settings, while novel drug therapies for acute bleeding conditions improve emergency response and patient outcomes. Advances in the treatment of complex conditions such as endometriosis highlight the role of targeted technologies in addressing previously underdiagnosed or inadequately treated diseases.

Mobility and rehabilitation technologies, including wheeled motorized devices, enhance patient independence and quality of life, particularly for individuals with physical impairments. At the cellular level, innovations utilizing the cell membrane of mesenchymal stem cells (MSCs) introduce new therapeutic pathways in regenerative medicine, leveraging the biological properties of stem cells without requiring full cell transplantation.

Oncology-focused platforms for cancer treatment, alongside regenerative medicine platforms targeting spinal cord injuries, represent significant advances in addressing high-burden conditions. These platforms integrate biological insights with engineering solutions to promote tissue repair, immune modulation, and targeted therapy delivery.

Additional innovations include localized fat reduction technologies, which combine medical and aesthetic applications, and novel treatments for glaucoma, addressing chronic eye conditions through improved pharmacological or device-based interventions. The emergence of nano-drugs further underscores the shift toward precision medicine, enabling targeted drug delivery at the molecular level to enhance efficacy and reduce side effects.

Figure 4. Healthcare IVOICs of discontinuous innovations

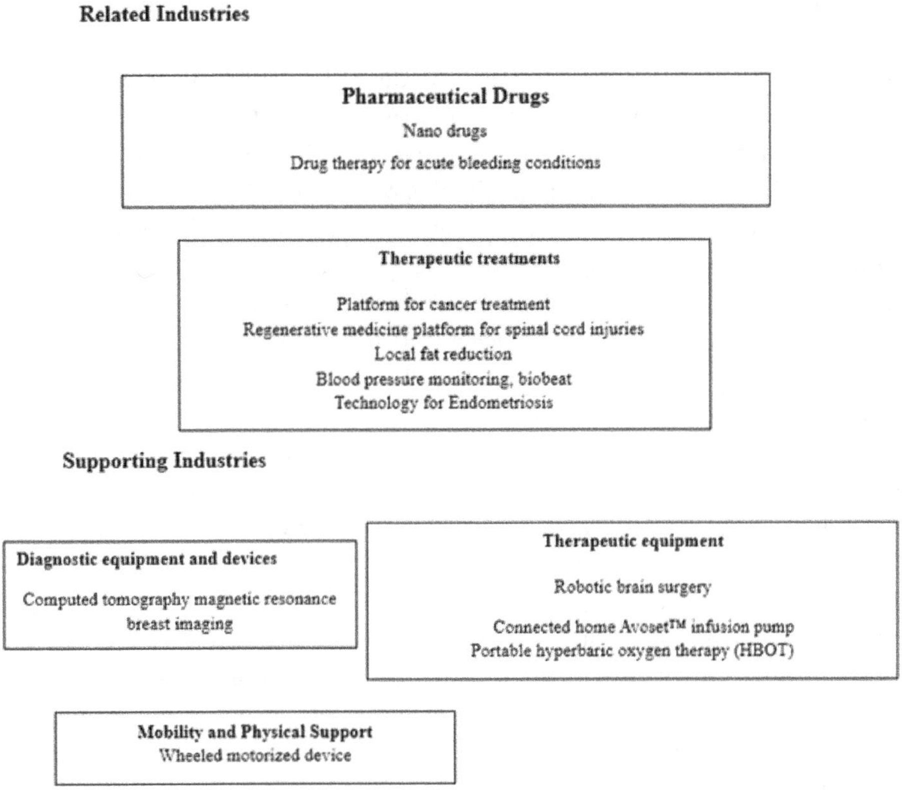

HEALTHCARE IVOICS OF DISRUPTIVE INNOVATIONS

Within the IVOIC framework, discontinuous innovations in healthcare are further exemplified by a set of advanced technologies and platforms that significantly enhance diagnostic precision, therapeutic capability, and personalized medicine, while remaining embedded within existing clinical and institutional systems. These innovations demonstrate the depth and diversity of Israel's health-tech ecosystem, spanning medical devices, digital health, biotechnology, and regenerative medicine.

A critical dimension of healthcare innovation is improved access and affordability. The Hematology Oncology Paediatric Excellence (HOPE) initiative, led by Teva Pharmaceutical Industries, focuses on the provision of high-quality generic drugs for Sub-Saharan Africa, addressing disparities in pediatric oncology treatment and strengthening global health equity.

In interventional cardiology, Medinol stands out as a leading manufacturer of advanced stents, contributing significantly to minimally invasive cardiovascular treatments. Complementing this, Corindus has pioneered robotic-assisted percutaneous coronary intervention (PCI), enhancing procedural precision and reducing operator risk. Innovations such as Tryton bifurcation stents further address complex coronary anatomies, improving outcomes in patients with multi-branch arterial disease.

Diagnostic innovation is prominently illustrated by the PillCam SB capsule, developed by Given Imaging, which revolutionized gastrointestinal diagnostics through non-invasive capsule endoscopy. This technology enables the detection of conditions such as obscure gastrointestinal bleeding, Crohn's disease, and small-bowel tumors. Similarly, the nano-artificial nose developed by NanoScent introduces a novel diagnostic paradigm, capable of detecting multiple cancers and neurodegenerative diseases through volatile biomarker analysis.

The expansion of home-based and digital health solutions is reflected in devices such as the HeraBEAT fetal monitor by HeraMED, which enables remote monitoring of fetal heart rates via smartphone integration. Non-invasive glucose monitoring technologies further exemplify this trend. OrSense has developed wearable ring-based systems using optical spectroscopy, while GlucoTrack and HAGAR employ multi-sensor and radiofrequency-based approaches, respectively. Additionally, Gili Medical focuses on hypoglycemia detection, particularly during sleep, addressing a critical risk for individuals with Type 1 diabetes.

Early detection technologies extend beyond metabolic monitoring. SensPD leverages modified oto-acoustic emission (OAE) technology to enable early identification of autism during routine newborn hearing tests, illustrating how existing screening infrastructures can be enhanced through innovation.

In regenerative medicine and bioengineering, Matricelf has pioneered 3D bioprinting of human tissues, including cardiac constructs and spinal implants, based on patient-specific cells. These efforts are complemented by the development of miniature 3D brain replicas—organoids incorporating vascular systems and tumor models—facilitating advanced research in oncology and neurology.

Innovations at the frontier of reproductive and biological engineering are also emerging. Research led by Mahmoud Huleihel explores the creation of sperm in vitro אב microfluidic systems using polydimethylsiloxane (PDMS), representing a potential breakthrough in fertility science.

Neurological therapies are advancing through established yet continuously evolving techniques such as deep brain stimulation (DBS), which is widely used to treat Parkinson's disease, dystonia, and essential tremor, with expanding applications in psychiatric disorders. Complementary to this, innovations in visual and cognitive interfaces—such as Virtual Retinal Display (VRD) systems and eye-tracking technologies developed by EyeJets—are redefining human-machine interaction in both clinical and assistive contexts.

Additional discontinuous innovations highlight the breadth of the ecosystem. Lumenis has advanced Intense Pulsed Light (IPL) technologies, expanding applications across dermatology, ophthalmology, and cosmetic medicine. Meanwhile, novel bio-inspired systems such as the "Like a Fish" wearable device—developed by Alon Bodner—explore unconventional approaches to oxygen extraction, illustrating the experimental edge of health-related innovation.

Figure 5. Healthcare IVOICs of disruptive innovations

Related Industries

Pharmaceutical Drugs

Hematology Oncology Paediatric Excellence (HOPE) generic drugs

Therapeutic treatments

Platform for cancer treatment
Regenerative medicine platform for spinal cord injuries
Local fat reduction
Blood pressure monitoring, biobeat
Technology for Endometriosis
Intense Pulsed Light (IPL)
Deep Brain Stimulation (DBS)

Supporting Industries

Diagnostic equipment and devices

PillCam SB capsule
Nano-artificial nose
Home pregnancy monitor HeraMED
OrSense
GlucoTrack
HAGAR GWave
Gili Medical
Hypoglycemia
SensPD

Therapeutic tools

Medinol is the standout Israeli stent manufacturer
Corindus (robotic PCI)
Tryton bifurcation stents
Like-a-Fish
Matricelf
Creating sperm

TELECOMMUNICATION AND SECURITY IVOICS OF DISCONTINUOUS INNOVATIONS

Within the IVOIC framework, cloud infrastructure represents a critical layer of discontinuous innovation, enabling scalable computing, data sovereignty, and hybrid digital ecosystems. The Israeli cloud landscape illustrates how localized infrastructure, advanced data management, and hybrid deployment models are reshaping enterprise IT architectures without fully displacing existing systems.

A key trend is the localization of cloud services to meet regulatory, linguistic, and performance requirements. Nebius Israel exemplifies this shift by offering compute, storage, and virtual private cloud services from multiple domestic data centers. Its localized Hebrew/English support and compliance with national regulations position it as a strategic solution for organizations requiring data residency and low-latency services.

Global providers are also embedding themselves within the local ecosystem. Vultr entered the Israeli market through a Tel Aviv data center in partnership with Bezeq, delivering cost-effective cloud compute, Kubernetes, and bare-metal services. Similarly, Acronis established a local data center to support managed service providers (MSPs), focusing on integrated cyber protection and backup solutions—an increasingly critical component of cloud adoption.

Infrastructure specialization is another defining feature. Anan Data Centers operates high-security underground facilities designed for high-performance computing (HPC) and AI workloads. With substantial power capacity, these facilities cater to data-intensive applications, reflecting the growing demand for compute infrastructure optimized for artificial intelligence and advanced analytics.

Hybrid and edge-cloud architectures are also gaining prominence. ASOCS provides on-premises and virtual private cloud solutions leveraging virtualized radio access network (vRAN) technologies, supporting industries such as telecommunications and smart venues. This approach enables flexible deployment models that bridge centralized cloud and edge environments.

Data storage and management innovations further reinforce this ecosystem. Infinidat focuses on high-performance, enterprise-grade storage systems, supporting large-scale data operations and global expansion strategies. Meanwhile, CTERA Networks delivers cloud storage gateways and distributed file systems, facilitating secure hybrid-cloud integration in collaboration with major global partners such as Amazon Web Services, Hewlett Packard Enterprise, IBM, and Deutsche Telekom.

At the data orchestration layer, K2view introduces real-time data integration and synthetic data generation capabilities, which are particularly valuable in hybrid and multi-cloud environments. These tools enable enterprises to manage distributed data assets efficiently while maintaining compliance and supporting advanced analytics use cases.

Figure 6. Telecommunication and security IVOICs of discontinuous innovations

Related Industries

Cloud servers

Nebius Israel (by Aman)
Vultr
Acronis
Anan Data Centers
ASOCS
Infinidat
CTERA Networks

TELECOMMUNICATION AND SECURITY IVOICS OF DISRUPTIVE INNOVATIONS

Within the IVOIC framework, the domains of telecommunications, automotive safety, and cybersecurity illustrate a dense concentration of both discontinuous and disruptive innovations. These sectors are unified by their reliance on digital infrastructure, real-time data processing, and platform-based architectures, which collectively enable systemic transformation across industries.

End-to-End Communication and Telecom Platforms

A defining feature of telecom IVOICs is the development of integrated, end-to-end communication solutions that combine hardware, software, and cloud-native architectures. AudioCodes exemplifies this approach by delivering comprehensive VoIP ecosystems, including session border controllers, IP phones, and media gateways. These systems form the backbone of enterprise and carrier-grade communications.

Cloud-native disruption is further advanced by DriveNets, which provides a network operating system that enables telecom operators to run disaggregated routing on white-box hardware, reducing costs and increasing scalability. Similarly, Gilat Satellite Networks offers end-to-end VSAT systems, extending connectivity to remote and underserved regions.

Enterprise communication platforms—such as Voicenter, Bynet, myTnet, and Voipe—demonstrate the integration of PBX and cloud VoIP functionalities, including voicemail-to-email, IVR, and intelligent call routing.

These solutions are supported by backend technology providers like VocalTec, Tadiran Telecom, Mind CTI, and CALLUP, which collectively sustain the telecom infrastructure layer.

At the consumer level, Viber represents a major disruptive innovation. Founded by Talmon Marco and Igor Magazinnik, and later acquired by Rakuten, Viber introduced cross-platform messaging and VoIP services with end-to-end encryption, reshaping global communication practices.

Automotive Safety and Intelligent Mobility

The automotive sector is undergoing rapid transformation through advanced sensing, AI, and connectivity technologies. Mobileye is a global leader in camera-based ADAS systems, with its EyeQ processors, REM mapping, and autonomous driving platforms embedded in hundreds of millions of vehicles worldwide.

Complementing vision-based systems, Arbe Robotics delivers ultra-high-resolution radar capable of precise object detection under challenging conditions. Opsys Tech enhances perception through windshield-integrated sensors, while RFISee develops compact 3D radar systems for real-time environmental mapping.

Connectivity innovations are equally critical. Autotalks leads in vehicle-to-everything (V2X) communication, enabling seamless interaction between vehicles, infrastructure, and other road users. This capability is foundational for the development of cooperative, autonomous mobility ecosystems.

Cybersecurity and Cyber-Intelligence Platforms

Cybersecurity IVOICs represent one of the most globally influential domains, spanning both defensive and offensive technologies. On the controversial end of the spectrum, firms such as NSO Group, Candiru, Cytrox, and Quadream have developed advanced spyware platforms capable of zero-click intrusion into smartphones and other devices. These technologies, while technically sophisticated, raise significant ethical and regulatory concerns regarding privacy and human rights.

In contrast, defensive cybersecurity innovations are driving major disruption in enterprise and cloud security. Wiz has emerged as a leader in agentless cloud security posture management, achieving global prominence through its acquisition by Google. Cato Networks pioneered the Secure Access Service Edge (SASE) model, integrating networking and security into a unified cloud-native platform.

Established players such as Check Point Software Technologies and CyberArk continue to lead in areas such as firewall protection and privileged access management (PAM), respectively. Emerging firms—including Ermetic, Akeyless, Laminar, Cyera, Perimeter 81, and Lightspin—are advancing cloud-native security, data protection, and zero-trust architectures.

Web application firewalls and data security posture management (DSPM) solutions further reinforce this ecosystem, addressing vulnerabilities in increasingly distributed and cloud-based environments.

Figure 7. Telecommunication and Security IVOICs of disruptive innovations

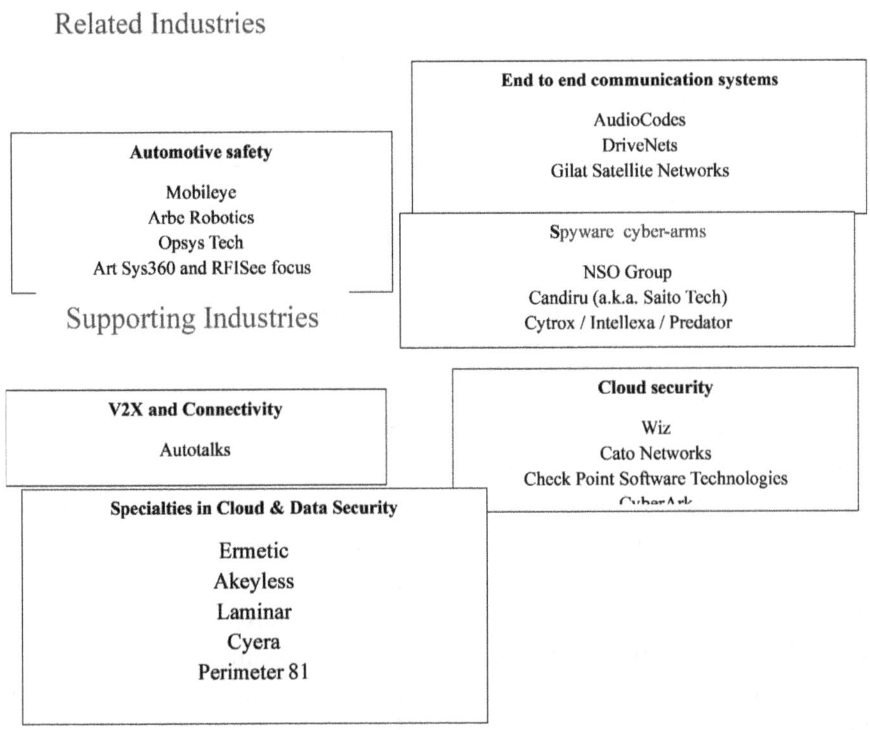

MANAGEMENT PLATFORMS AND TOOLS IVOICS OF DISRUPTIVE INNOVATIONS

Within the IVOIC framework, software platforms, testing systems, data logging technologies, and AI-driven content ecosystems represent a dense layer of both discontinuous and disruptive innovations. These systems form the digital backbone of modern industries, enabling scalable architectures, automation, and real-time intelligence across sectors.

Microservices Management and Cloud-Native Architectures

The transition toward microservices and cloud-native systems is a defining feature of contemporary digital infrastructure. Platforms such as Kong provide API gateways and microservices management tools that handle authentication, traffic control, and service orchestration. These capabilities are essential for managing distributed applications at scale.

Similarly, Solo.io advances service mesh and API management, enabling secure and efficient communication between microservices. Security and governance are further strengthened by Tufin, which automates policy enforcement across hybrid cloud environments, and SpectralOps, which focuses on scanning infrastructure-as-code and identifying vulnerabilities early in the development lifecycle.

Operational resilience is enhanced by StackPulse, which provides continuous monitoring and automated incident remediation. Together, these platforms illustrate a shift toward self-healing, policy-driven, and highly distributed software ecosystems.

Software Testing and Quality Assurance Platforms

Discontinuous innovation in software testing has evolved from manual processes to AI-driven automation. Mercury Interactive pioneered the field of testing and quality assurance tools, laying the foundation for modern DevOps practices.

Building on this legacy, Testim leverages machine learning to create and maintain automated UI tests with reduced instability. Applitools introduces visual AI validation, enabling detection of UI regressions that traditional testing methods often miss. Meanwhile, Qyrus integrates functional and performance testing into DevOps pipelines, supporting web, mobile, and API environments.

These innovations collectively reduce development cycles, improve software reliability, and enable continuous delivery in complex digital ecosystems.

Logging, Monitoring, and Digital Forensics

Data capture and analysis platforms play a critical role in compliance, performance optimization, and security. Globitel offers the SpeechLog call recorder, a widely used solution for voice logging in call centers. Complementary platforms such as Avdor CIS and Lanonyx extend these capabilities to multi-channel recording, analytics, and reporting.

Advanced voice logging systems developed by Acmatel provide real-time monitoring and integration with enterprise systems. At the user experience layer, Glassbox captures session-level behavioral data across web and mobile platforms, enabling organizations to optimize user journeys and diagnose friction points.

In the domain of digital forensics, Cellebrite is a global leader, providing tools for data extraction and analysis used by law enforcement and enterprises. These technologies highlight the increasing importance of data traceability and evidentiary integrity in digital environments.

Edge Computing and Embedded Systems

Hardware-software convergence is reflected in compact, energy-efficient computing platforms such as the CuBox series developed by SolidRun. These miniature systems support applications ranging from IoT to home streaming, demonstrating how edge computing complements centralized cloud infrastructure.

AI-Driven Discovery and Innovation Platforms

A key example of collaborative innovation is AION Labs, a consortium-backed platform involving major pharmaceutical firms such as Pfizer, AstraZeneca, Merck KGaA, Teva Pharmaceutical Industries, and Amazon Web Services. This venture studio model accelerates AI-driven drug discovery and biomedical innovation, illustrating the role of IVOICs in orchestrating multi-stakeholder collaboration.

AI-Powered Content Personalization and Media Platforms

Disruptive innovation is particularly visible in AI-driven content generation and personalization. Companies such as Treepodia, Promo.com, Lightricks, Idomoo, and Gan.ai enable automated creation and customization of video assets at scale. These platforms transform marketing, communication, and user engagement by leveraging AI to tailor content in real time.

Autonomous Systems and Drone Technologies

The transformation of off-the-shelf drones into autonomous systems highlights the integration of AI, software, and robotics. High Lander provides software enabling full autonomy and fleet coordination, while Xtend combines AI and virtual reality interfaces for enhanced control in complex environments. These innovations extend drone capabilities across defense, logistics, and industrial applications.

Advanced Manufacturing and 3D Innovation Ecosystems

Finally, research-driven IVOICs such as the Technion Additive Manufacturing Center and the Tel Aviv University 3D Printing Center illustrate the role of academic-industry collaboration in advancing 3D printing, additive manufacturing, and digital fabrication technologies. These platforms support innovation in materials science, biomedical engineering, and industrial design.

Figure 8. Management platforms and tools IVOICs of disruptive innovations

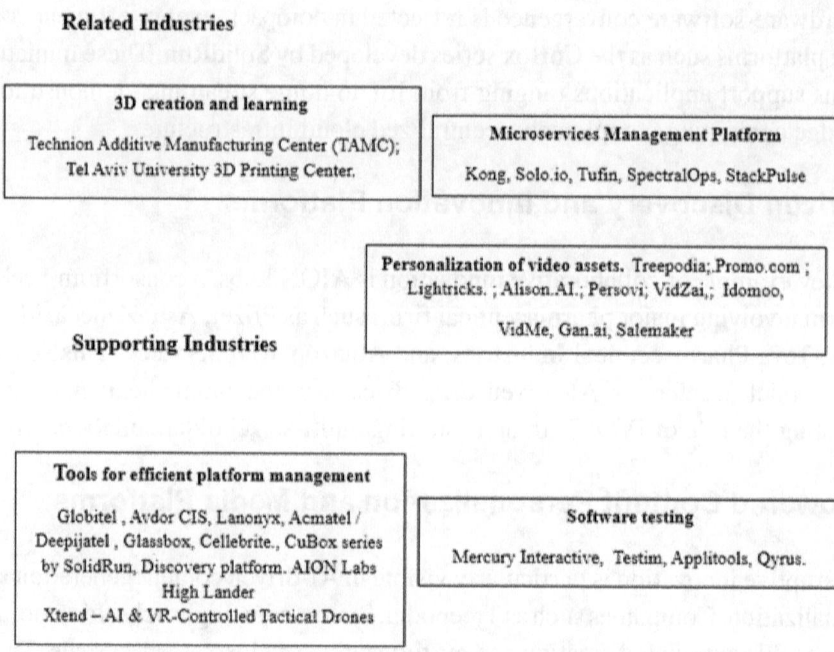

ENERGY IVOICS DISCONTINUOUS INNOVATIONS

Within the IVOIC framework, renewable energy technologies illustrate both discontinuous and disruptive innovation, particularly in the areas of solar power, energy storage, and green hydrogen production. These innovations enhance efficiency, scalability, and sustainability while enabling integration with existing energy infrastructures.

Advanced Photovoltaic Technologies

Lightweight and flexible solar panels exemplify discontinuous innovations that expand the applications of solar energy beyond traditional rigid panels. Their portability, adaptability to curved surfaces, and reduced structural requirements enable deployment in urban, transportation, and off-grid contexts.

Organic photovoltaic cells (OPCs) further represent a transformative innovation in solar energy. By using organic semiconducting materials, OPCs offer lightweight, semi-transparent, and low-cost solar solutions suitable for integration into building materials, wearable devices, and flexible electronics. Their development signals a shift toward multifunctional energy-generating surfaces, combining aesthetics and utility.

Energy Storage and Battery Innovation

Advances in battery manufacturing, such as the 3D Current Collector technology, improve the energy density, charging speed, and longevity of electrochemical storage systems.

These discontinuous innovations enhance performance while maintaining compatibility with existing battery architectures, supporting applications from electric vehicles to grid-scale energy storage.

The IceBrick energy storage system represents a modular and scalable approach to thermal and electrical energy storage. By combining thermal management with conventional storage methods, such systems increase efficiency, resilience, and adaptability in decentralized energy networks.

Green Hydrogen Production

The Electrochemical–Thermally Activated Chemical (E TAC) method is a disruptive innovation for producing green hydrogen. By coupling electrochemical processes with thermally activated reactions, this approach reduces energy consumption, eliminates the need for expensive catalysts, and enables large-scale sustainable hydrogen production. As hydrogen becomes a critical energy vector for decarbonization, technologies like E TAC are poised to transform industrial processes, power generation, and transportation fuels.

Figure 9. Energy IVOICs of discontinuous innovations

Related Industries

Solar Energy

Solar converter's technology
Lightweight flexible solar panels
Organic photovoltaic cells (OPC)

Supporting Industries

Energy storage

Batteries 3D Current Collector manufacturing
IceBrick energy storage system
E-TAC (Electrochemical–Thermally Activated Chemical) method for producing green hydrogen

ENERGY IVOICS DISRUPTIVE INNOVATIONS

Within the IVOIC framework, energy generation and resource management demonstrate innovative approaches that merge renewable energy, water technology, and automation. These technologies exemplify both discontinuous innovations—improving efficiency or enabling new operational models—and disruptive breakthroughs that could transform energy and water sectors.

Pressure Retarded Osmosis (PRO) and Reverse Electrodialysis (RED)

Sidney Loeb pioneered the concept of Pressure Retarded Osmosis (PRO), which generates power by exploiting the osmotic pressure difference between freshwater and seawater or brine. PRO can be combined with a Reverse Electrodialysis (RED) heat engine to convert salinity gradients into electricity efficiently.

This technology represents a discontinuous innovation in renewable energy because it leverages natural gradients rather than fossil fuels, while maintaining compatibility with conventional energy infrastructure. Its application is particularly relevant in coastal and brackish water environments, offering sustainable power generation with minimal environmental impact.

Robotic and Automated Solar Maintenance

Ecoppia has developed robotic cleaning systems for solar panels that use micro-fiber brushes and airflow to remove dust and debris without water. These robots are powered by solar energy and operate via a cloud-based management platform.

This technology exemplifies a discontinuous innovation that enhances solar panel efficiency and reduces maintenance costs, particularly in arid regions where water scarcity limits traditional cleaning methods. By integrating automation, renewable power, and cloud connectivity, it also demonstrates an emerging convergence of energy technology, robotics, and IoT management platforms.

Figure 10. Energy IVOICs of disruptive innovations

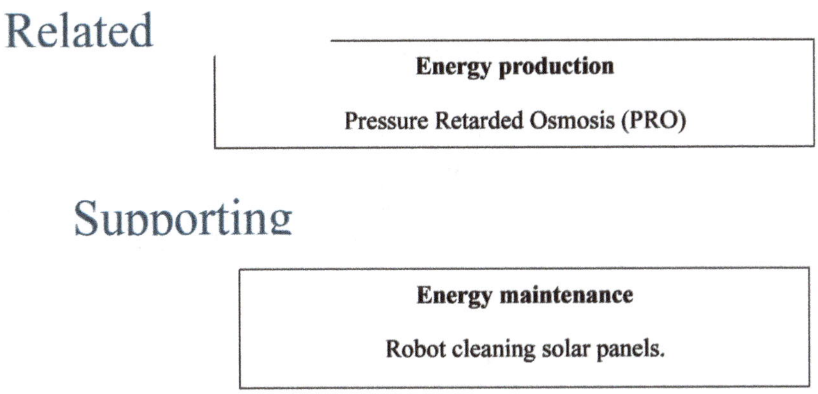

DIGITAL IMAGING IVOICS OF DISCONTINUOUS INNOVATIONS

Within the IVOIC framework, 3D printing and associated digital fabrication technologies represent a broad spectrum of discontinuous and disruptive innovations. They span industrial production, biomedical applications, food technology, consumer products, and creative industries, demonstrating how additive manufacturing and AI-driven design are reshaping production, personalization, and creative expression.

Industrial and Construction 3D Printing

Industrial and construction 3D printing platforms enable the fabrication of large-scale components and structures with reduced material waste and accelerated production cycles. By integrating additive manufacturing with advanced materials, these technologies enhance efficiency in construction, aerospace, and automotive sectors. They represent a discontinuous innovation that complements existing manufacturing workflows while introducing new design flexibility and scalability.

Bioprinting and Food Technology

In the biomedical domain, bioprinting enables the layer-by-layer construction of tissues and organ analogues using living cells. Applications include regenerative medicine, organoid research, and surgical training. Food-tech 3D printing leverages similar principles to produce customized, nutritionally optimized meals, plant-based alternatives, and alternative protein products. Both areas illustrate discontinuous innovations that enhance personalization and functionality while maintaining compatibility with existing clinical or culinary systems.

Medical and Surgical Applications

3D printing in medicine allows for patient-specific implants, prosthetics, and surgical models. These technologies reduce procedural risk, improve outcomes, and shorten production lead times for highly customized medical devices. They exemplify discontinuous innovations that integrate seamlessly into established healthcare infrastructures.

Consumer and Fashion 3D Printing

Consumer-focused 3D printing platforms support bespoke product creation, from footwear to jewelry and electronics. In fashion, digital thread-dyeing systems and additive fabrication enable highly personalized garments and patterns. These technologies exemplify the convergence of manufacturing, design, and digital creativity, offering new business models in retail and consumer personalization.

AI-Enhanced Visual and Media Platforms

AI-driven tools that "automagically" transform images and videos represent a disruptive layer of innovation in media and content creation. Platforms such as FreeD enable interactive, multi-angle replay and virtual scene reconstruction, enhancing sports analytics, entertainment, and immersive experiences. Combined with AI-powered image transformation, these tools accelerate the production of creative assets and democratize content creation.

Figure 11. Digital imaging IVOICs of discontinuous innovations

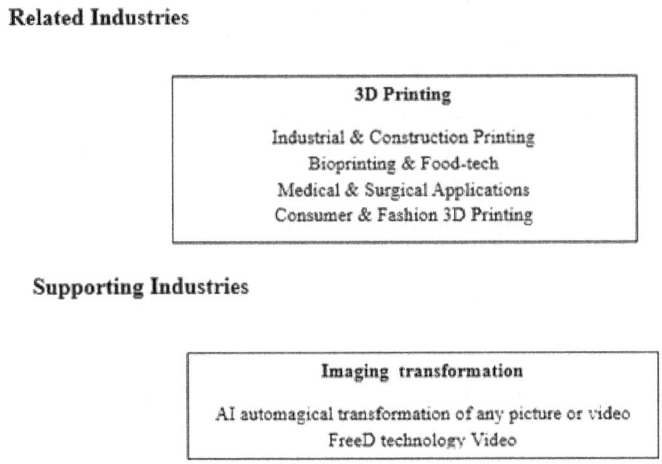

DIGITAL IMAGING IVOICS OF DISRUPTIVE INNOVATIONS

Within the IVOIC framework, nanographic printing and printed electronics technologies exemplify both discontinuous and disruptive innovations, bridging materials science, additive manufacturing, and digital fabrication. These innovations enable precision printing, functional materials integration, and high-performance electronics production, transforming conventional manufacturing and electronics industries.

Nanographic Printing Platforms

Landa Nanographic Printing leverages Nanographic Printing technology combined with proprietary NanoInk to produce high-resolution, fast-drying, and cost-efficient prints for commercial and packaging applications. Similarly, HP Indigo utilizes ElectroInk technology to achieve precise, vibrant, and scalable digital printing outputs.

These platforms represent discontinuous innovations by enhancing existing printing processes with higher resolution, faster turnaround, and lower environmental impact, while maintaining compatibility with traditional printing supply chains.

Conductive Nano-Inks for Electronics

PV Nano Cell specializes in silver, carbon, dielectric, and gold nano-inks for inkjet-printed resistors, capacitors, and sensors. By enabling high-performance printed electronics, these materials facilitate lightweight, flexible, and low-cost electronic components, essential for IoT, wearable devices, and embedded sensors.

Nano Dimension, in partnership with XTPL, develops high-performance conductive nanoinks for additive manufacturing of electronics (AME). This collaboration enhances 3D-printed circuits, functional devices, and rapid prototyping, allowing for disruptive innovation in electronics manufacturing by reducing production cycles and enabling complex geometries unattainable with traditional PCB fabrication.

Figure 12. Digital imaging IVOICs of disruptive innovations

Related Industries

ElectroInk

HP, Indigo

Nanographic

Landa

PV Nano Cell

MICRO ELECTRONICS IVOICS OF DISRUPTIVE INNOVATIONS

Within the IVOIC framework, semiconductor devices, memory technologies, and nanoelectronics illustrate a rich interplay of discontinuous and disruptive innovations. These technologies underpin digital transformation across computing, communications, and electronics, enabling higher performance, miniaturization, and novel functionalities.

Memory and Storage Innovations

Early breakthroughs in non-volatile memory exemplify discontinuous innovation by enhancing storage density, speed, and reliability:

Intel developed EPROM technology, enabling electrically erasable programmable read-only memory for reprogrammable digital storage.

M-Systems introduced the Disc On Key, pioneering portable USB flash drives and revolutionizing data portability.

SanDisk advanced EEPROM and flash memory technologies for consumer and enterprise applications, supporting increasingly compact and durable storage solutions.

Saifun Semiconductors developed NROM (Nitride Read-Only Memory) for enhanced density and endurance in embedded memory applications.

These memory innovations reflect discontinuous innovation, improving performance while remaining compatible with existing computing and storage architectures.

High-Performance Computing and Networking

Innovations in semiconductor and interconnect technologies enable faster, lower-latency data transfer and computing efficiency:

Mellanox developed RDMA (Remote Direct Memory Access) technologies, reducing CPU overhead and enabling low-latency, high-bandwidth networking for data centers and HPC clusters.

DSP Group produced DSP-DSPC technologies, enhancing real-time signal processing for communications and multimedia applications.

Advanced Fabrication and Nanoelectronics

Pioneering work in lithography and nanoscale structures supports the next generation of microchips and electronic devices:

L2X Labs contributed EUV (Extreme Ultraviolet) lithography techniques, allowing fabrication of sub-10 nm transistors and high-density integrated circuits.

Applied Materials Precision 5000 device enables precision deposition and etching for semiconductor manufacturing, critical for next-gen chip scaling. Dr. Mokari developed novel nanostructures that enhance electronic, photonic, and quantum device performance. These represent both discontinuous and disruptive innovations, as they enable previously impossible device architectures, higher integration density, and the emergence of new computing paradigms, including quantum and neuromorphic computing.

Figure 13. Micro electronics IVOICs of disruptive innovations

Related Industries

Memory technologies

Intel EPROM; M-Systems Disc On Key; Mellanox RDMA; SanDisk EEPROM;

Supporting Industries

Driver Systems & Enabling Technologies

Saifun Semiconductors, NROM; DSP group DSP-DSPC; L2X Labs; EUV lithography; Applied Materials Precision 5000 device; Dr. Mokari' Novel nano structure.

AI IVOICS OF DISRUPTIVE INNOVATIONS

Within the IVOIC framework, developer-centric platforms, MLOps systems, and AI infrastructure represent a convergence of discontinuous and disruptive innovations, enabling scalable AI deployment, real-time decision-making, and enterprise automation across multiple sectors. These innovations bridge software development, operational management, and domain-specific intelligence.

AI Development, Testing, and Observability

Platforms designed for AI lifecycle management improve code integrity, model monitoring, and infrastructure utilization:

Qodo (formerly CodiumAI) leverages AI to automatically test and validate software code, enhancing reliability and reducing human error.

Aporia provides anomaly detection and continuous model monitoring, ensuring AI systems operate reliably in production (Goldberg, 2024).

Run:AI virtualizes GPU infrastructure, optimizing utilization for large-scale AI and deep learning training workloads.

Pinecone offers vector database solutions for similarity search, recommendation systems, and large language model (LLM) applications, enabling high-performance AI queries.

These platforms exemplify discontinuous innovations that improve existing workflows, scalability, and reliability for AI engineers and DevOps teams.

Domain-Specific AI Assistants and Automation Tools

Disruptive AI applications are emerging across healthcare, finance, agriculture, and enterprise operations:

Healthcare: Navina integrates with EHRs to detect medication conflicts, extract clinical insights, and support ambient scribing. MedyMatch focuses on stroke and trauma detection, collaborating with Samsung and IBM.

Finance: FundGuard and EverC provide real-time cloud-native AI for operational efficiency and risk management.

Agriculture: Croptimus detects crop pests and diseases, optimizing yield and reducing chemical usage.

Enterprise & Transport: Optibus improves public transport scheduling and resource allocation.

These systems illustrate disruptive innovations that reshape sectoral operations by automating complex decisions, increasing efficiency, and generating new data-driven insights.

AI-Enhanced Content, Media, and Computer Vision

Advanced AI platforms are transforming content creation, media personalization, and visual perception:

Visual & Video AI: Bria AI and D ID generate photorealistic images and videos for marketing and enterprise applications.

Low-light and enhanced vision: Visionary.ai improves low-light video and image capture, collaborating with Qualcomm, NVIDIA, and CEVA.

Conversational & Emotion AI: aiOla enables speech recognition across 120+ languages, while Beyond Verbal infers sentiment and health markers from voice.

Computer Vision: Cortica provides real-time AI recognition for smart cities, autonomous vehicles, and industrial applications.

These innovations combine AI, computer vision, and human-computer interaction to create entirely new modalities for content production, situational awareness, and real-time analytics, representing disruptive change in media, security, and operational intelligence.

AI Operations, Cybersecurity, and Monitoring Platforms

Ensuring reliability, security, and optimization in AI deployments is critical:

Logz.io enables real-time monitoring of cloud and DevOps systems.

Robust Intelligence validates and sanitizes AI model inputs to prevent erroneous or malicious predictions.

Optimization: Finout monitors and optimizes cloud infrastructure expenses.

These platforms are discontinuous innovations, enhancing operational safety, reliability, and cost-efficiency in complex AI ecosystems.

Figure 14. AI IVOICs of disruptive innovations

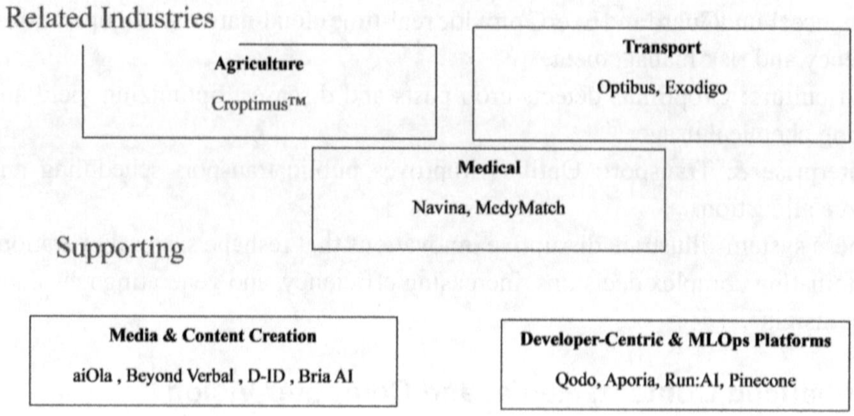

Defense IVOICs of Disruptive Innovations

Within the IVOIC framework, defense and homeland security technologies demonstrate a convergence of discontinuous and disruptive innovations, particularly in UAVs, missile defense, laser systems, and robotic platforms. These innovations enhance situational awareness, operational precision, and autonomous capabilities while integrating advanced sensing, AI, and signal-processing technologies.

Unmanned Aerial Vehicles (UAVs) and Drone Technologies

Albatros UAV produces UAVs for reconnaissance, surveillance, and tactical operations, emphasizing autonomous navigation and payload flexibility.

Spear UAV develops drones with realverse technology for dynamic mission adaptation.

Platforms such as XTEND and Reply Technologies integrate advanced autonomy, AI-driven decision-making, and secure communication links for complex operational environments.

These UAV platforms represent discontinuous innovations, improving existing drone capabilities in endurance, payload versatility, and real-time operational control.

Missile Defense and Tactical Systems

Arrow Antimissile System and Iron Dome provide active interception of incoming projectiles, protecting civilian and military assets.

Iron Beam demonstrates a tactical laser platform capable of intercepting short-range threats with precision, reducing dependency on conventional munitions.

These systems exemplify disruptive innovations in missile defense, combining sensor fusion, AI targeting, and rapid-response automation to redefine threat neutralization strategies.

Robotics, Miniaturized Sensors, and Signal Processing

Roboteam develops autonomous ground robots for reconnaissance, bomb disposal, and battlefield support.

Miniature sensor components, such as cameras by Odysight, enhance situational awareness in compact form factors for UAVs and robotic platforms.

Advanced signal-processing capabilities from R2 Wireless enable real-time communication, threat detection, and decision-making in complex operational theaters.

These innovations represent discontinuous enhancements to sensor integration, autonomous systems, and real-time command capabilities, improving operational efficiency while enabling new mission profiles.

Figure 15. Defense IVOICs of disruptive innovations

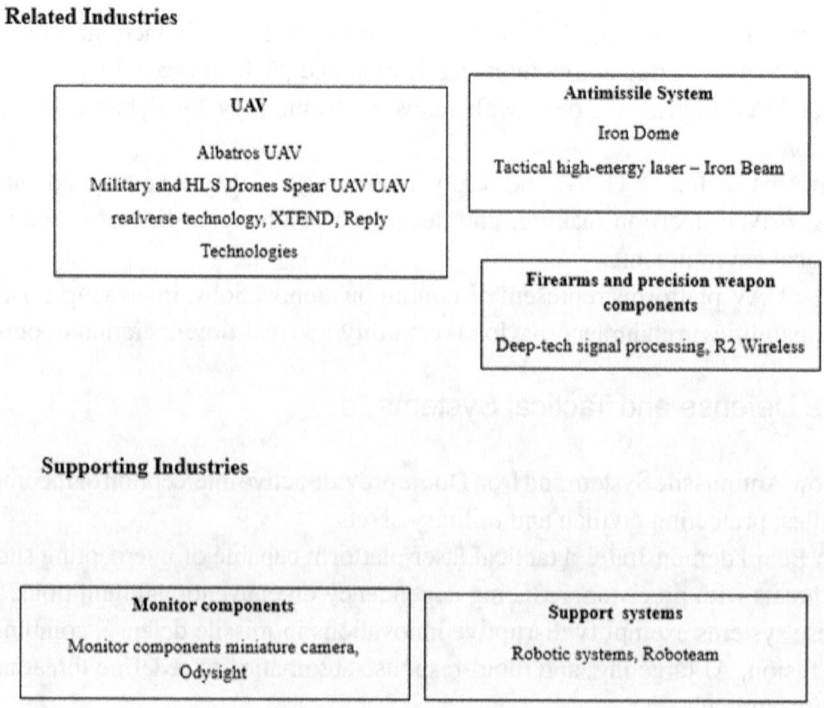

REFERENCES

Chandy, R. K., & Tellis, G. J. (1998). Organizing for radical product innovation: The overlooked role of willingness to cannibalize. *JMR, Journal of Marketing Research, 35*(4), 474–487. DOI: 10.1177/002224379803500406

Di Minin, A., & Corsi, S. (2011). Extending the Uppsala model: Disruptive innovation from a Chinese evolved subsidiary [Paper presentation]. *71st Annual Meeting of the Academy of Management*, San Antonio, TX, United States.

Escudero-Cipriani, C., García-del Junco, J., Chafloque-Céspedes, R., & Alvarez-Risco, A. (2024). Frugal innovation in the business environment: A literature review and future perspectives. *Frontiers in Artificial Intelligence, 7*, 1385522. Advance online publication. DOI: 10.3389/frai.2024.1385522 PMID: 39712468

Goldberg, N. (2024, December 24). Coralogix acquires AI monitoring platform Aporia to strengthen ML observability solutions. *Jewish Business News*. https://jewishbusinessnews.com/2024/12/24/coralogix-acquires-ai-monitoring-platform-aporia-to-strengthen-ml-observability-solutions

Govindarajan, V. (2013, November 18). Reverse innovation starts with education. *Harvard Business Review*. https://hbr.org/2013/11/reverse-innovation-starts-with-education

Hodgkinson, G. P., & Sparrow, P. R. (2002). *The competent organization: A psychological analysis of the strategic management process*. Open University Press.

Picaud, K. (2013). Discontinuous innovation (DI): A review of definitions, theoretical perspectives, and measures – Towards an empirical study of the role of the purchasing department in DI [Conference paper]. https://www.researchgate.net/publication/270744949_Discontinuous_Innovation_DI_A_review_of_definitions_theoretical_perspectives_and_measures

Tripsas, M., & Gavetti, G. (2000). Capabilities, cognition, and inertia: Evidence from digital imaging. *Strategic Management Journal, 21*(10–11), 1147–1161. DOI: 10.1002/1097-0266(200010/11)21:10/11<1147::AID-SMJ128>3.0.CO;2-R

World Bank. (2013). *Barriers to access to payment systems and proposed actions: Special-purpose*. http://hdl.handle.net/10986/21532

Chapter 12
Domains of Potential Regional Cooperation of MNCs in the Middle East

ABSTRACT

Water, energy, food, and ecosystem security cooperation between Egypt, Jordan, and Israel reflects broader geopolitical strategies to address climate vulnerability and population growth pressures. Under the Water-Energy-Food-Ecosystems (WEFE) Nexus framework, large-scale infrastructure projects have become central policy instruments for sustainable development and regional stability. Energy cooperation has expanded through natural gas trade networks involving Chevron Corporation-operated regional extraction and export systems. Gas flows from Eastern Mediterranean offshore fields are transported Israel to Egypt and Jordan. Digital infrastructure development further accelerates regional integration through subsea telecommunications cable systems linking Mediterranean, Red Sea, and global cloud computing hubs. AI ecosystems are emerging as strategic economic enablers. G42 (Group 42) develops sector-specific AI applications across healthcare, energy optimization, and public administration, while maintaining global cloud and AI partnerships with Microsoft Corporation.

INTRODUCTION

Water, energy, food, and ecosystem security cooperation between Egypt, Jordan and Israel reflects broader geopolitical strategies to address climate vulnerability and population growth pressures. Under the Water-Energy-Food-Ecosystems (WEFE)

DOI: 10.4018/979-8-3373-7350-8.ch012

Nexus framework, large-scale infrastructure projects have become central policy instruments for sustainable development and regional stability.

Energy cooperation has expanded through natural gas trade networks involving Chevron Corporation-operated regional extraction and export systems. Gas flows from Eastern Mediterranean offshore fields are transported Israel to Egypt and Jordan, reinforcing electricity generation capacity and industrial energy security while promoting regional market interdependence.

Digital infrastructure development further accelerates regional integration through subsea telecommunications cable systems linking Mediterranean, Red Sea, and global cloud computing hubs. AI ecosystems are emerging as strategic economic enablers. G42 (Group 42) develops sector-specific AI applications across healthcare, energy optimization, and public administration, while maintaining global cloud and AI partnerships with Microsoft Corporation.

MNCS AND AGRI-TECH

The Middle East and North Africa are facing interconnected challenges of food insecurity, water scarcity, and climate volatility. These pressures have accelerated the adoption of innovative agri-tech solutions, including high-tech greenhouses, solar-powered irrigation systems, and climate-resilient crops, transforming the region into a laboratory for agricultural innovation under extreme conditions.

United Arab Emirates

Bustanica – The world's largest vertical farm, integrating hydroponic cultivation with artificial intelligence to reduce water consumption while improving yield efficiency.

International Center for Biosaline Agriculture (ICBA) – Conducts research on salt-tolerant crops suitable for arid and saline soils.

Agrico (Qatar) – Utilizes solar-powered hydroponic greenhouses for year-round fresh produce.

Pure Harvest Smart Farms – Expands desert-adapted agricultural solutions internationally, including operations in Asia.

Saudi Arabia

Saudi Arabia exemplifies a state-led approach to agricultural innovation through public-private partnerships.

Notable initiatives include the collaboration between the Public Investment Fund and AeroFarms, which has established one of the largest vertical farms globally in Riyadh, supported by the Agricultural Development Fund. These projects aim to transform arid landscapes into productive agricultural zones, combining technology and sustainable development.

Egypt

Al Dahra – Employs water-efficient irrigation systems such as drip irrigation and no-till practices, improving both soil health and biodiversity.

Collaborations with Syngenta – Enable the development of advanced Farm Management Systems, modernizing large-scale desert agriculture through technological integration.

Israel

Israel's agricultural innovation ecosystem, often referred to as "Silicon Wadi," attracts substantial investment from multinational corporations and supports research in precision irrigation, seed improvement, biopesticides, and water management:

Netafim – A global leader in drip irrigation technologies, optimizing water use and crop yields.

Syngenta, Bayer Crop Science, Corteva Agriscience – Conduct joint research in sustainable farming and crop protection.

ADM (Archer Daniels Midland) – Partners with Israeli startups to develop sustainable food technologies, including alternative proteins and food additives.

MNCS AND WATER SUPPLY COOPERATION

Egypt-Jordan Water Cooperation

Egypt and Jordan are collaborating on water, energy, and food security through frameworks like the "Water-Energy-Food-Ecosystems (WEFE) Nexus" to combat scarcity. While not sharing a direct water border, they discuss joint projects and desalination initiatives.

Egypt is positioning itself as a regional hub for water management, establishing an Islamic Network on Water Resources Development and Management (INWRDAM) office to enhance regional cooperation and climate adaptation.

Jordan is one of the most water-scarce countries in the world, with its population relying on severely limited resources, including water from the Jordan and Yarmouk rivers that is often controlled or contested by upstream neighbours like Syria and Israel (The New Arab Staff & Agencies, 2025). Jordan receives 55 million cubic meters of water annually from Israel as part of their 1994 peace treaty.

Egypt and Jordan are active in the Islamic Network on Water Resources Development and Management (INWRDAM), which facilitates research and policy innovation.

Aqaba Amman project

French infrastructure specialists Meridiam lead the project in partnership with SUEZ, Orascom Construction and VINCI Construction Grands Projets.

The project would supply more than 300 million cubic metres of drinking water to Amman and Aqaba, serving in excess of three million people.

The Aqaba Amman project is expected to cost more than $5bn and will take about four years to complete.

This project will increase the total annual available domestic water supply by almost 60 percent" for households and will also include about 445 kilometres of pipelines to transport the desalinated water from the Red Sea. The European Investment Bank, has lent $200m towards the construction cost of the scheme.

Agricultural wastewater treatment projects

Egypt's flagship agricultural wastewater treatment projects, including the New Delta, Bahr El-Baqar, and Al-Mahsama plants, which are expected to contribute around 5 billion cubic meters of treated water annually by 2026 (Daily News Egypt, 2025).

Transboundary Water Cooperation

Transboundary Water Cooperation includes the lower part of the Jordan River Basin (Yasuda et al., 2017). In the 1970s, it took three to four times its share from the Yarmouk River—as delineated by the Johnston Plan of 1955—and blocked

Jordan from carrying out projects using the river, like the Maqarin (or Wehda) Dam (Bargash, 2025).

After normalization, Jordan's share of the Yarmouk River fell sharply—from an average of 125 million cubic meters between 1961 and 1999 to just 71.5 million cubic meters between 1999 and 2018. This decline followed the construction of the Adassiyeh Weir, which diverted flows in line with the 1994 treaty's water annex. The agreement thus became a pivotal mechanism for institutionalizing unequal access to both the Yarmouk and Jordan Rivers. Post-treaty infrastructure, such as the Adassiyeh Weir and canal diversions, consolidated Israel's upstream control while constraining Jordan's ability to secure even its allocated shares.

With the 2024 collapse of Syrian President Bashar al-Asad's regime and Israeli military expansion into southern Syria, Israel controls most of the water that flows into the Jordan and Yarmouk river basins.

Leading Water Technology Multinationals

A number of multinational corporations provide critical technologies for desalination, wastewater treatment, and water management across the Middle East:

Veolia is a major player in water technology and services, supplying desalination and wastewater treatment solutions to large-scale projects across the Middle East, such as

Hassyan desalination plants in the UAE, Hamriyah desalination plants in Saudi Arabia and Sur Plant in Oman, Sadara-Marafiq plant in Saudi Arabia

Veolia is supplying its cutting-edge technologies to the Hassyan desalination plant (United Arab Emirates), the second largest in the world, supplying water to 2 million people; to the Hamriyah plant, supplying drinking water to 1.4 million people; and to the Mirfa 2 plant, supplying drinking water to 210,000 households in the United Arab Emirates. The Group also equips the Sur plant in Oman with its reverse osmosis technologies, and the Sadara-Marafiq plant in Saudi Arabia, which has been operating since 2016 to supply industrial water to the Jubail petrochemical complex.

Modern Water Solutions (MWS) is an environmental and water treatment company with a strong presence in the Middle East, MWS provides a range of services including wastewater treatment systems and water treatment for various applications.

Pall Corporation is a global leader in filtration, separation, and purification technologies (6W Research, 2025). With operations in over 40 countries, the company serves critical industries such as biotechnology, pharmaceuticals, food and beverage, energy, aerospace, and microelectronics. Its membrane filtration solutions help industries ensure product purity, enhance efficiency, and meet stringent regulatory standards.

Suez Water Technologies & provides innovative water purification technologies, including membrane filtration solutions for municipal and industrial applications. Its services include desalination, wastewater treatment, and advanced purification processes.

Dow Chemical Company offers specialized membranes used in water purification, food processing, pharmaceuticals, and industrial applications. Its FILMTEC™ reverse osmosis membranes are widely recognized for their efficiency and durability.

Koch Membrane Systems, a subsidiary of Koch Industries, Koch Membrane Systems (KMS) designs and manufactures advanced membranes for water treatment, food and beverage processing, and industrial separation processes. Its products include ultrafiltration, microfiltration, and reverse osmosis systems.

Toray Industries is a leading provider of membrane filtration technologies, including reverse osmosis (RO), ultrafiltration (UF), nanofiltration (NF), and microfiltration (MF). Its membranes are used extensively in desalination, wastewater treatment, and industrial water recycling.

Pentair membrane filtration technologies are used in residential, commercial, and industrial applications, including drinking water purification, wastewater treatment, and food and beverage processing.

Evoqua Water Technologies offers a broad range of membrane filtration products, including reverse osmosis (RO), ultrafiltration (UF), nanofiltration (NF), and microfiltration (MF).

Alfa Laval offers membrane filtration solutions for water purification, food and beverage processing, and industrial separation processes. Its product range includes spiral-wound, hollow fiber, and ceramic membranes.

3M Purification‘s membrane filtration products are used in industries such as healthcare, food and beverage, and residential water treatment. Its product portfolio includes reverse osmosis and ultrafiltration membranes designed for high efficiency and long-lasting performance.

MNCS, AI AND TELECOMMUNICATIONS COOPERATION

Artificial intelligence and advanced analytics technologies further reinforce regional transformation through private-sector innovation ecosystems. G42 (Group 42) has emerged as a major provider of AI-driven solutions in healthcare analytics, energy optimization, and public service automation. The company maintains strategic global technological partnerships with Microsoft Corporation, enabling scalable cloud-based AI deployment across regional markets. Additionally, Presight AI specializes in integrating Internet of Things (IoT) sensor data with satellite-based geospatial intelligence to support smart city governance, public safety management, and urban infrastructure planning.

The telecommunications sector represents another strategic domain of cooperation, particularly through investments in subsea fiber-optic cable infrastructure linking regional digital economies to global data networks. Subsea cable systems traversing Mediterranean and Red Sea corridors enhance bandwidth capacity, improve latency performance, and enable cloud computing and digital commerce expansion across North Africa and the Middle East. These developments are critical for supporting emerging knowledge economies and digital financial ecosystems.

Submarine Fiber-Optic Cables

Egypt's strategic location has historically made it a critical transit hub linking Asia, Europe, and Africa via dense submarine cable corridors. However, this advantage faces increasing challenges from regional instability, geopolitical competition, and emerging alternative routes. Scholars such as Murphy and Bryja (2025) emphasize that protection of subsea cables is now both a national security and economic priority.

Sustaining Egypt's role as a digital gateway requires coordinated national strategy, including institutional coordination, regulatory clarity, maritime surveillance, cybersecurity enhancement, and trusted international partnerships. The SEA-ME-WE-6 submarine cable system, connecting Asia, the Middle East, and Europe, illustrates Egypt's ongoing relevance, with Telecom Egypt as a major global stakeholder.

Data Centers

Significant capital is being invested in hyperscale data centers, particularly in Saudi Arabia, where national strategies focus on cloud sovereignty, AI readiness, and digital industrialization. Global technology firms such as Huawei and Microsoft, alongside regional players including Center3 and Tonomus, are establishing large-scale facilities for cloud computing, AI training, and government digital services. These investments align closely with economic diversification and digital transformation objectives.

5G and 5G-Advanced Deployment

The Middle East is a global leader in 5G deployment. Operators including stc, e&, Ooredoo, and Zain are advancing toward 5G-Advanced, enabling next-generation applications such as augmented/extended reality, autonomous mobility, industrial automation, and smart energy grids. Strong state support and strategic telecommunications planning have positioned the region as a hub for innovation-led growth.

Smart City Ecosystems

Smart city initiatives are major drivers of regional digital infrastructure investment. Over USD 100 billion has been allocated to flagship projects such as NEOM and Oxagon in Saudi Arabia, and Lusail in Qatar. Telecommunications operators act as system integrators, providing IoT connectivity, edge computing, and data platforms essential for urban management, mobility, utilities, and public services. These initiatives demonstrate the integration of telecom, urban planning, and digital governance.

AI and Telco-Led Digital Transformation

Telecommunications operators are increasingly evolving from connectivity providers to digital orchestrators, embedding AI, cloud computing, and IoT solutions across sectors such as healthcare, tourism, logistics, and energy. Regional MNCs and firms deploy AI to enhance network efficiency, automate operations, develop digital services, and support data-driven public sector transformation.

Key Industry MNC Actors

Middle East:

e& (formerly Etisalat): Emirati state-owned group with a growing global footprint and active technology acquisition strategy.

stc (Saudi Telecom Company): Largest telecom operator in MENA, central to infrastructure and giga-projects.

- Ooredoo: Qatar-based operator emphasizing digital health, cloud services, and regional expansion.
- Zain: Kuwait-based multinational operator with diversified infrastructure and regional reach.
- Huawei and Ericsson: Leading global vendors supplying 5G and core network technologies.
- Microsoft and Google: Major investors in regional cloud and AI ecosystems.

Israel:

Israel functions as a regional ICT hub, hosting R&D centers of global MNCs such as Huawei, Cisco, Nokia, Ericsson, Qualcomm, Google, Microsoft, Intel, IBM, and Apple. These centers focus on advanced domains including cloud computing, AI, IoT, cybersecurity, and next-generation communications. Specialized firms such as Gilat (satellite communications) and Siklu (millimeter-wave wireless) further strengthen Israel's position in next-generation telecom infrastructure.

MNCS AND ENERGY COOPERATION

Natural gas trade flows originating from Eastern Mediterranean offshore reserves have become an important component of regional energy security. Trade and transport systems involving Chevron Corporation-associated extraction operations facilitate gas transfers from Israeli offshore fields to Egypt and Jordan, where the resources are utilized for domestic electricity generation and industrial consumption. Such arrangements contribute to energy market stabilization, reduce reliance on imported fuels, and support regional economic interdependence through cross-border energy trade networks.

Oil and Gas: Continuity and Transformation

Despite diversification, hydrocarbons remain foundational to the regional economy. National oil companies (NOCs) such as Saudi Aramco, ADNOC, and QatarEnergy dominate upstream investment, while MNCs are embedded through joint ventures, EPC contracts, technology provision, and downstream partnerships. Key projects include:

Fadhili Gas Expansion (Saudi Arabia): Natural gas processing project led by Saudi Aramco with international EPC contractors.

North Field Expansion (Qatar): One of the largest LNG expansions globally, nearly doubling liquefaction capacity.

New Refinery Capacity (2024): Projects such as Al-Zour (Kuwait), Duqm (Oman), and Jizan (Saudi Arabia) highlight MNC involvement in downstream value-chain development.

These investments maintain the strategic relevance of oil and gas while enabling cleaner fuels, higher efficiency, and export flexibility.

Renewable Energy and Green Hydrogen

Global decarbonization and climate pressures are accelerating renewable energy and green hydrogen adoption in the region. MNCs play key roles in financing, construction, and technology deployment via public-private partnerships and Independent Power Producer (IPP) models:

NEOM Green Hydrogen Project (Saudi Arabia): USD 5 billion JV between NEOM, Air Products, and ACWA Power, aiming to become the world's largest commercial green hydrogen facility.

Mohammed bin Rashid Al Maktoum Solar Park (Dubai, UAE): World's largest single-site solar park, targeting 5,000 MW by 2030 through IPP phases with international consortia.

Al Dhafra Solar PV Project (Abu Dhabi, UAE): 2 GW facility delivering record-low tariffs, developed by Masdar and global investors.

Gulf of Suez Wind Power Project (Egypt): 1.1 GW onshore wind farm led by ACWA Power, supplying over one million households.

MNCs also introduce advanced technologies such as AI-enabled energy management systems, digital twins, and carbon capture, utilization, and storage (CCUS).

Israeli Natural Gas

MNCs have been instrumental in developing Israel's offshore gas reserves, including Tamar, Leviathan, and Karish fields. Key players include Chevron (acquired Noble Energy) and Energean. Their involvement has enabled Israel to transition from an energy importer to a self-sufficient natural gas producer and exporter.

In 2016, Jordan's National Electric Power Company (NEPCO) signed a long-term gas purchase agreement with Israel, supplied via NBL Jordan Marketing Limited (Noble Energy), supporting regional energy interdependence. Following recent military escalations, Israel temporarily suspended gas exports on 13 June 2025, halting production at Leviathan (Chevron) and Karish (Energean) fields, while the Tamar field continued supplying domestic demand (Pipeline and Gas Journal, 2025).

Energy Management in the Middle East

The Middle East has become a strategic hub for digital transformation in energy management and industrial automation. This shift is largely driven by national initiatives such as Saudi Vision 2030 and the UAE Net Zero 2050 strategy, which prioritize autonomous operations, artificial intelligence (AI), energy efficiency, and emission reduction. These programs aim not only to modernize industrial operations but also to optimize energy usage across generation, transmission, and consumption networks.

Recent studies (2025) highlight the increasing involvement of both multinational corporations (MNCs) and regional technology firms in deploying cutting-edge digital technologies across the energy value chain.

These include smart grids, predictive maintenance, AI-enabled monitoring systems, industrial IoT (IIoT) integration, and advanced energy analytics platforms.

TRENDS AND INNOVATIONS IN THE MIDDLE EAST

The Middle East energy sector demonstrates a strong presence of multinational corporations (MNCs) delivering energy management solutions, industrial automation, and digital transformation platforms. These companies are driving the digitalization of energy generation, distribution, and industrial processes across the region.

Table 1.

Company	Headquarters	Key Capabilities / Regional Activities
Schneider Electric SE	France	EcoStruxure™ platform enabling AI-driven autonomous operations; pilot projects with ADNOC Refining (Abu Dhabi)
Honeywell International Inc.	USA	Energy management systems, building automation, and industrial control solutions
Siemens AG	Germany	Advanced distribution management systems, industrial process automation, and digital transformation solutions
ABB Ltd.	Switzerland	Grid automation, energy management systems, industrial automation solutions
Rockwell Automation Inc.	USA	Industrial automation, AI integration for manufacturing and energy operations
Emerson Electric Co.	USA	Industrial process automation, control systems, and digital optimization
Wood	UK	Digital and AI Hub in the Middle East; advisory services and technology partnerships for digital transformation and net-zero initiatives

Key Trends in Energy Management

AI-Driven Autonomy

Deployment of artificial intelligence platforms to optimize energy consumption, reduce operational costs, and enhance predictive maintenance capabilities.

Integration of Energy Management Systems (EMS)

Adoption of connected systems for real-time monitoring, analytics, and efficiency optimization across industrial facilities.

Industrial Automation Expansion

Increased use of robotics, IoT-enabled process control, and automation in refineries, manufacturing plants, and utilities.

Net-Zero Alignment

Implementation of technologies supporting energy decarbonization, renewable energy integration, and sustainability reporting.

Digital Ecosystem Partnerships

Collaboration between multinational corporations, regional utilities, and governments to accelerate technology adoption, transfer knowledge, and build local capacity.

The Middle East is actively advancing toward autonomous and AI-driven energy management, with MNCs playing a central role in deploying advanced digital solutions. Companies such as Schneider Electric, Honeywell, Siemens, ABB, Rockwell Automation, Emerson, and Wood exemplify how digitalization, AI integration, and industrial automation are transforming the region's energy and manufacturing sectors, improving efficiency, sustainability, and operational resilience.

Trends and Innovations in Israel

Israel's energy technology ecosystem comprises over 350 companies specializing in digital transformation, energy management, and industrial automation. This sector leverages cutting-edge technologies—including artificial intelligence (AI), big data analytics, fiber-optic sensing, and advanced control systems—to address challenges such as grid efficiency, distributed energy resource integration, electric vehicle (EV) deployment, and operational technology (OT) cybersecurity.

The ecosystem is characterized by a dynamic mix of innovative local startups and global industry leaders, creating a fertile environment for collaboration, technology transfer, and rapid commercialization. Key players and their focus areas include:

Table 2.

Company	Focus Area	Key Capabilities
SolarEdge Technologies	Solar PV electronics	Advanced energy management systems for residential, commercial, and industrial applications
Ormat Technologies	Geothermal energy	Renewable energy generation; investment in energy storage startups
mPrest	Smart grids	Mission-critical monitoring and control systems; AI and big data applications derived from defense technologies
Driivz	EV charging management	End-to-end smart energy management software; optimization of local grid capacity
Prisma Photonics	Grid monitoring	Fiber-optic sensing and AI for real-time grid monitoring and optimization
Augury	Industrial energy efficiency	AI-driven predictive maintenance and machine health solutions
Soltell Systems	Decentralized energy	Solar performance analytics and industrial automation tools (solar PV, storage, EV charging)

continued on following page

Table 2. Continued

Company	Focus Area	Key Capabilities
Powercom	Utilities management	Smart metering, load management, real-time energy loss detection
Ardan Control Tech (Ludan-Tech)	Energy efficiency projects	Integration of advanced monitoring and control systems for industrial energy optimization
Claroty & SaiFlow	Cybersecurity	Protection of operational technology networks and distributed energy resources from cyber threats

Israel's energy tech ecosystem also attracts major multinational corporations (MNCs), which establish local operations to collaborate with startups, scout emerging technologies, and co-develop solutions. Notable MNCs operating in Israel include:

Schneider Electric – energy management and automation solutions

Siemens Energy – industrial automation, smart grids, and renewable integration

ABB – grid automation and distributed energy management

Enel – renewable energy and digital transformation projects

EDF Renewables – solar, wind, and storage integration with advanced digital platforms

These collaborations accelerate technology adoption, foster cross-sector innovation, and position Israel as a regional hub for intelligent energy systems, smart grid solutions, and industrial automation technologies.

MNCS AND THE MEDICAL SECTOR

Middle East

Multinational corporations (MNCs) maintain a dominant position in the Middle East pharmaceutical and medical technology sectors, with particularly strong growth in Saudi Arabia, the United Arab Emirates (UAE), and Egypt. Regulatory modernization, population growth, and increased healthcare spending have attracted sustained foreign direct investment. Parallel expansion is occurring in the medical devices sector, supported by government-led industrial strategies.

Governments across the Gulf Cooperation Council (GCC) are prioritizing domestic manufacturing to enhance supply chain resilience and reduce import dependence. Key developments include:

Saudi Arabia: MS Pharma launched the country's first biologics manufacturing facility.

UAE: A large-scale biopharmaceutical campus established through a partnership between G42 and Mubadala.

The UAE has also accelerated adoption of AI-driven healthcare solutions, spanning diagnostic imaging, predictive analytics, and personalized medicine. Global medical technology firms—Philips, GE HealthCare, Medtronic—are positioning the region as a deployment and innovation hub. Collaborative initiatives, such as oncology trials at the King Faisal Specialist Hospital & Research Centre with U.S. partners in 2025, illustrate MNC-public cooperation to expand regional R&D capacity.

Companies such as Novo Nordisk and Hikma Pharmaceuticals focus on developing and localizing diabetes and weight-management treatments, including generics to improve affordability and accessibility.

Israel

MNCs hold a significant operational presence in Israel's healthcare ecosystem, leveraging the country's innovation capacity rather than merely accessing local markets. Key activities include:

Early-stage startup scouting and venture investment

Advanced clinical collaborations with hospitals and academic research centers

R&D partnerships integrating digital and biological technologies

Global firms—Pfizer, Johnson & Johnson, Merck KGaA, AbbVie, Philips, Microsoft, Google (Verily)—engage in co-development and pilot deployments. Research focuses include:

AI-driven diagnostics

Natural language processing for clinical and administrative data

Precision and regenerative medicine

Next-generation medical devices

Israel's strengths in data science, cybersecurity, and software engineering give MNCs a comparative advantage in accelerating digital health innovation in regulated clinical environments.

Recent M&A activity underscores the strategic value of Israeli medical innovation:

Johnson & Johnson acquired V-Wave for approximately USD 600 million

Insightec raised USD 150 million, reflecting growing integration of Israeli medtech into global value chains

MNCS AND ADVANCED HALAL AND KOSHER ECOSYSTEMS

The globalization of dietary and pharmaceutical markets highlights the strategic importance of Halal and Kosher products, governed by Shariah and Jewish dietary law (Halacha), respectively. Compliance affects raw materials, processing, and certification, impacting food, pharmaceuticals, and medical devices.

Halal Market

The Middle East's Halal ecosystem remains constrained by shortages of compliant raw materials, limiting industry growth. Fully integrated Halal supply chains are critical for: Enhancing production efficiency, Promoting exports and Generating value-chain synergies.

The Halal food market exhibits a diverse competitive landscape, encompassing global MNCs and regional specialists across food, beverages, and cosmetics. Key players include:

Table 3.

Company	Headquarters	Market Focus / Capabilities
Nestlé S.A.	Switzerland	Global reach; diversified portfolio for Muslim consumers
Cargill, Inc.	USA	Large-scale production; sustainable supply chain; wide range of Halal products
Unilever PLC	UK/ Netherlands	Extensive distribution; brand loyalty; focus on health and sustainability
BRF S.A. (Sadia)	Brazil	Halal meat processing; strong Middle East presence
Al Islami Foods	UAE	Authentic Halal meat; quality control; frozen and ready-to-eat products
Kawan Food Berhad	Malaysia	Convenience and marine-based Halal products; Asia-Pacific focus
Saffron Road	USA	Premium, ethically sourced Halal products; North American market

Halal Medical Market

MNC engagement in halal medical research is driven by market expansion, regulatory harmonization, and trust-based healthcare delivery. Key focuses include:

Alternatives to porcine-derived gelatin, alcohol-based solvents, and non-halal cell lines

Synthetic biology, plant-based excipients, and recombinant technologies for halal-compliant formulations

Vaccine development addressing stabilizers, growth media, and inputs

Notable MNCs and regional players: CCM Pharmaceuticals, Pharmaniaga, Rosemont Pharmaceuticals, Simpor Pharma, Bosch Pharmaceuticals, NOOR Vitamins

Halal research also extends to medical devices and digital health technologies, emphasizing ethical governance, data privacy, and clinical alignment. AI-driven healthcare solutions increasingly adopt halal-by-design principles, including culturally sensitive datasets, inclusive clinical trials, and governance frameworks aligned with Islamic bioethics.

Kosher Market

The Kosher market is increasingly integrating technological innovation to improve certification efficiency, traceability, and quality control. Multinational corporations (MNCs) actively collaborate with Israeli food technology startups and research institutions to develop new kosher-compliant ingredients and production processes.

Major MNC participants in the Kosher market include:

Table 4.

Company	Key Contributions
Nestlé S.A.	Global kosher-certified product lines
General Mills, Inc.	Kosher cereals and snack products
PepsiCo, Inc. (Sabra brand)	Kosher-certified dips and spreads
Conagra Brands, Inc.	Kosher packaged foods and snacks
Kellogg Company	Kosher cereals and processed foods
Kraft Heinz Company	Kosher sauces and packaged foods
Cargill, Inc. / ADM	Kosher-compliant ingredient supply

Emerging technologies such as AI, robotics, and blockchain are increasingly deployed to strengthen compliance, optimize production, and ensure global traceability in both food and medical Kosher supply chains.

KEY REGIONAL AI MNCS IN THE MIDDLE EAST

Several home-grown AI companies in the Middle East have grown into regional and global leaders, often backed by sovereign wealth funds such as Saudi Arabia's Public Investment Fund (PIF) and Abu Dhabi's Advanced Technology Research Council.

Major AI Players

Several home-grown companies in the Middle East have grown into major regional or global players, often backed by sovereign wealth funds like Saudi Arabia's Public Investment Fund (PIF) or Abu Dhabi's Advanced Technology Research Council (Trigui et al, 2024).

G42

Headquartered in Abu Dhabi, G42 is a technology holding group that operates some of the region's most powerful AI computing resources and has developed industry-specific solutions in healthcare, energy, and public services. They have a major global partnership with Microsoft.

AIQ AI

AIQ AI for energy is a joint venture between the Abu Dhabi National Oil Company (ADNOC) and G42, focused on applying AI to the energy sector to optimize drilling operations, reduce emissions, and improve asset maintenance.

AIQ accelerates the digital transformation of the global energy sector. A joint venture between Presight and ADNOC, the company brings advanced AI to the heart of energy operations — solving complex challenges and driving a more sustainable future. Proudly rooted in the UAE, AIQ supports the nation's ambition to lead on the global AI stage.

Astra Tech is simplifying how people connect and manage their finances. Technology designed for your convenience.is simplifying how people connect and manage their finances. Technology designed for your convenience.

CORE42

CORE42 is the powerhouse behind enterprise and sovereign AI. With deep expertise in cloud and infrastructure, it delivers the backbone that transforms bold ideas into nation-shaping outcomes.

CPXX

CPXX provides cutting-edge cybersecurity solutions that protect people, governments, and organizations — helping build a society that's ready, resilient, and confidently digital.

Inseption

Inseption is the region's leading innovator of AI-powered domain-specific as well as industry-agnostic products, built on a rich heritage of research and development. Within the G42 ecosystem, Inception functions as the core intelligence layer, transforming data and compute infrastructure into real-world, applied AI solutions.

Khazna Data Centers

Khazna Data Centers is the largest data center platform in the UAE and the Middle East, holding over 70% market share. It provides secure, scalable infrastructure that powers cloud, AI, and enterprise innovation — from the ground up.

M42

M42 is an Abu Dhabi-based, tech-enabled healthcare company focused on transforming global care. It combines technology and clinical expertise to address the world's most urgent health and diagnostic challenges.

Presight

Presight combines AI with powerful analytics to tackle challenges at scale. Its omni-analytics platform, TAQ, enables clients to make sense of complex data — and act on it with confidence. Presight AI provides AI-powered analytics for public safety, national security, and urban planning, integrating IoT data and satellite imagery to support smart city initiatives. It is a publicly listed company on the Abu Dhabi Securities Exchange.

Space42

Space42 is a UAE-based SpaceTech company applying AI beyond Earth. Listed on the Abu Dhabi Securities Exchange, it operates globally — helping partners navigate, observe, and innovate from orbit.

HUMAN

HUMAN is a global AI company based in Saudi Arabia, developing full-stack AI capabilities, including data centers, infrastructure, and advanced Arabic Large Language Models (LLMs). HUMAIN has formed significant global partnerships with companies like Adobe, Qualcomm, and Nvidia.

Lucidya

A leader in customer experience management tailored to Arabic-speaking markets, utilizing proprietary analytics engines that understand sentiment across 15 Arabic dialects.

DataToBiz

DataToBiz offers various services, such as: Artificial intelligence and machine learning; Big data analytics and business intelligence; Data engineering an harmonization; Natural language processing and vision analytics; Power BI and Tableau implementation (Roy, 2023).

Accubits Technologies

The company's AI services include generative AI development and integration, automation, computer vision, and consultancy services to help various organizations benefit from using artificial intelligence for day-to-day work. Accubits also provides business intelligence solutions to drive accurate insights for decision-making.

The company offers the following services: AI development; Robotic process; Automation; Enterprise solutions; Product development; Blockchain development.

Silwana Infotech

Silwana Infotech is a software development and AI company in UAE offering transformative and technology-driven solutions to clients from several industries.

Silwana Infotech offers the below services: Cloud integration; Mobile and web development; AR/ VR development ; Artificial intelligence ; Digital transformation ; Business intelligence; Enterprise mobility and IoT.

Citrus Consulting Services

The company is a hybrid cloud expert and also specializes in information and cybersecurity system implementation and development.

It works with businesses from the Middle East and African regions and India in assisting enterprises through their digital transformation journey.

Citrus Consulting Company provides the following services: Enterprise and big data management; Advanced analytics; Business intelligence; Data center modernization; Security architecture and consulting; Managed support services.

Codeflash Infotech

Codeflash Infotech specialises in AI and aims to make the UAE a global AI centre; it is one of Dubai's top artificial intelligence development companies, offering tailor-made services (Codflash Infotec, 2025). They offer machine learning solutions like SME packages for UAE companies, predictive analytics, AI-based chatbots, and corporate automation.

Intuz

Intuz is one of the top-rated AI companies in the UAE. It provides AI-based applications to verticals including healthcare, logistics, and fintech. They specialize in creating intelligent automation solutions, AI chatbots & mobile-first AI-based solutions for Dubai companies.

Vegavid Technology

Vegavid is one of the most thought-leading AI companies in Dubai with a principal focus on enterprise-level AI, blockchain, and Web3 integrations. Their team is currently working on intelligent automation projects aligned with Dubai Smart City AI firms' efforts, enabling the evolution of customer and government services across the public and private sectors.

Emirates AI

Emirates AI itself is headquartered in the UAE, but this only adds more benefits, as the experience of Dubai AI companies has been used to maintain the same high level of performance on the local market.

The company offers predictive analytics, computer vision, and NLP automation services that are targeted at the Middle East, and it closely follows government-led initiatives and regional laws. That is why the companies seeking enterprise AI solutions in Dubai may trust this provider.

TekRevol

It is the industry leader in artificial intelligence development in Dubai and remains committed to creating disruptive AI technologies for mobile applications, enterprise software, and digital products.

They specialize in collaborating with user-driven design and AI-fueled features to create a simple, entertaining experience. Their team is building predictive engines, chatbots, and automation tools for businesses to scale with.

Hyperlink InfoSystem

Hyperlink InfoSystem is one of the oldest international tech companies that established a presence in Dubai. They offer AI apps, predictive modeling, and bespoke AI services.

Appinventiv

Appinventiv deploys enterprise AI solutions in Dubai with a consultative approach. They specialize in AI-enabled analytics, predictive engines, and intelligent automation for retail, health care, and logistics. It is their fluency in the two custom AI applications, UAE, and strategy and implementation that separates them.

GCC Marketing

GCC Marketing in Dubai has AI, automation & digital transformation services. They are also among the most SME-friendly media agencies and AI software companies in Dubai, and have endless budget-chopping testimonials for our affordable, effective AI-driven apps, powered by process automation and chatbots.

Flynava Technologies

Flynava's AI product is focused on the aviation, travel & logistics industries. Among their machine learning portfolio is also the Dubai-based chart-topping companies – predictive pricing engines, demand prediction tools, and AI-driven automation software for airline operators.

InnovationM Middle East

InnovationM has established a fast-growing footprint in Dubai as an AI & digital transformation company. Their specialities include custom AI solutions for UAE-based projects such as chatbots, dashboards, and computer vision.

GLOBAL MNC PRESENCE AND PARTNERSHIPS

Microsoft has a strong alliance with the UAE, including a $1.5 billion investment in G42, to expand its reach and reinforce data residency compliance.

Nvidia & Amazon haave landed significant AI deals in the Middle East, including plans with Khazna to build AI factories in the MEA region.

Qualcomm & Adobe are collaborating with the Saudi-backed HUMAIN to deploy data center AI solutions and develop culturally intelligent generative AI for Arabic-speaking markets.

Huawei & Ericsson are involved in regional telecommunications and smart utility deals, providing AI-powered intelligent operations and infrastructure.

Google has partnered with entities like the Saudi Ministry of Culture to use AI in preserving and presenting cultural heritage.

Global MNC Partnerships

Microsoft: $1.5 billion investment in G42 for AI expansion and data residency compliance

Nvidia & Amazon: Regional AI infrastructure projects, including AI factories with Khazna

Qualcomm & Adobe: Collaborations with HUMAIN for culturally intelligent generative AI

Huawei & Ericsson: AI-enabled telecom and smart utility infrastructure

Google: AI projects in cultural heritage preservation in Saudi Arabia

Key AI Applications by Industry

Healthcare AI is being used for diagnostic imaging analysis, telemedicine, and even detecting vocal biomarkers for mental health conditions.

Energy and Sustainability AI applications optimize drilling operations, manage smart energy grids, and enhance the efficiency of solar projects and water conservation.

Finance (Fintech) has a rapidly growing fintech sector using AI for investment platforms, anti-money laundering tools, and personalized banking services.

Logistics and Smart Cities AI is applied in route optimization, intelligent traffic management systems, and urban planning in futuristic cities like Saudi Arabia's NEOM and Dubai's smart city initiatives.

ISRAEL'S AI ECOSYSTEM

By 2025, multinational corporations (MNCs) significantly intensified their engagement with Israel's artificial intelligence (AI) sector, reinforcing the country as a critical node in the global innovation system.

This engagement has been characterized by: Expanded R&D operations; Record merger and acquisition (M&A) activity; Sustained long-term investment commitments in AI-driven technologies; Cybersecurity Leadership.

Israel's prominence in cybersecurity is particularly notable. Seven of the world's ten leading cybersecurity firms maintain R&D operations in Israel.

AI is increasingly embedded in threat detection, automation, and resilience strategies

Israel commands over 20% of global deep-tech investment in cybersecurity, reflecting its global strategic importance.

M&A and Investment Trends

The year 2025 marked a historic peak in Israeli AI M&A activity, signaling both market maturity and strategic value to global technology leaders:

Google acquired Wiz for ~$32 billion, the largest transaction in Israeli high-tech history

Nvidia and SAP made additional strategic acquisitions in semiconductors, enterprise AI, and data infrastructure

M&A trends emphasize capability-driven integration rather than purely market entry

Public Policy Support

The Israel Innovation Authority has played a pivotal role in enabling international collaboration:

Grants and support programs actively promote global R&D partnerships

Policies aim to integrate Israeli innovation into global value chains

Collaboration between military R&D, academia, and private sector firms accelerates dual-use technology development.

Key Domains of AI Innovation

Cybersecurity

AI-powered threat detection, automation, and resilience

Integration of deep-tech solutions into enterprise and government infrastructure

Medical Devices & Biotech

AI-enabled diagnostics, drug discovery, and precision medicine

MNCs collaborate with Israeli startups to accelerate innovation

PropTech (Property Technology)

AI applications in market analysis, underwriting, and operational efficiencies

Adoption of smart-building and predictive analytics solutions

Dual-Use Innovation

Technologies with military origins adapted for civilian applications

Examples include smart city systems, infrastructure monitoring, and energy management

REFERENCES

Bargash, M. (2025). Energy, Water and the Cost of Jordan's Dependence on Israel. Merip.

Codflash Infotec. (2025). Top 10 AI Development Companies in Dubai, UAE | Expert Guide. Codflash Infotec.

Daily News Egypt. (2025). Egypt, Jordan explore joint projects in water, food, and energy sectors. *Daily News Egypt.*

Murphy, E. L., & Bryja, T. (2025). *The Strategic Future of Subsea Cables: Egypt Case Study*. Csis.org. https://www.csis.org/analysis/strategic-future-subsea-cables-egypt-case-study

6W. Research. (2025). Leading Companies in the Middle East Membrane Filtration Market. 6W Research.

Roy, K. (2023). 7 Top Artificial Intelligence Companies in UAE. *Medium.*

The New Arab Staff & Agencies. (2025). *French-led group signs Jordan's 'biggest-ever infrastructure project' for desalination plant.* The New Arab Staff & Agencies.

Trigui, H., Guerfa, F., Harigua-Souiai, E., Qasrawi, R., Atri, Ch., Salem Sokhn, E., El Morr, C., Hammami, K., Souiai, O., Wu, J., Dzevela Kong, J., Rousseau, J.J., & Znaidi, S. (2024). Exploring AI governance in the Middle East and North Africa (MENA) region: gaps, efforts, and initiatives. Data & Policy, 6, e83. DOI: 10.1017/dap.2024.85

Yasuda, Y., Schillinger, J., Huntjens, P., & Alofs, Ch. (2017). *Transboundary Water Cooperation over the lower part of the Jordan River Basin.* Stockholm International Water Institute (SIWI).

Chapter 13
Multinational Corporations and Innovation Ecosystems in the Middle East

ABSTRACT

This overview highlights the role of leading multinational corporations (MNCs) and strategic institutions in driving technological innovation, digital transformation, energy transition, and industrial modernization across United Arab Emirates, Egypt, Israel, Turkey, and Saudi Arabia. In the UAE, companies such as Etisalat anchor digital infrastructure and smart connectivity. Egypt's ecosystem includes firms in outsourcing, engineering, and industrial technologies that support manufacturing and digital services expansion. Israel contributes globally competitive expertise in energy, cybersecurity, software, and autonomous mobility through corporations such as Check Point Software Technologies and Mobileye. Turkey combines heavy industry and advanced manufacturing with diversified conglomerates and digital enterprises. Saudi Arabia's transformation is driven by major entities including Saudi Aramco, NEOM, and ACWA Power, supporting diversification into energy transition, smart infrastructure, and industrial development.

INTRODUCTION

This overview highlights the role of leading multinational corporations (MNCs) and strategic institutions in driving technological innovation, digital transformation,

DOI: 10.4018/979-8-3373-7350-8.ch013

energy transition, and industrial modernization across the United Arab Emirates, Egypt, Israel, Turkey, and Saudi Arabia.

In the UAE, firms such as e& anchor digital infrastructure and smart connectivity, supporting the country's transition toward a knowledge-based economy (GSMA, 2023; World Bank, 2022). Egypt's ecosystem includes firms in outsourcing, engineering, and industrial technologies that underpin manufacturing expansion and digital services growth (UNCTAD, 2022). Israel contributes globally competitive expertise in energy, cybersecurity, software, and autonomous mobility through corporations such as Check Point Software Technologies and Mobileye, reflecting its advanced innovation system (Senor & Singer, 2009; OECD, 2023). Turkey combines heavy industry with advanced manufacturing and diversified conglomerates (OECD, 2022). Saudi Arabia's transformation is driven by entities including Saudi Aramco, NEOM, and ACWA Power, supporting diversification into energy transition and smart infrastructure (Vision 2030, 2016; International Energy Agency, 2023).

UNITED ARAB EMIRATES (UAE)

Emirates serves as a strategic connector linking the UAE to global markets. Its hub-and-spoke model centered in Dubai enhances trade, tourism, and global value chain integration (ICAO, 2022; Krane, 2015).

e&

e& (formerly Etisalat) represents a central actor in regional digital infrastructure. Founded in Abu Dhabi, it has evolved into a diversified technology group operating in over 30 countries, with activities spanning AI, cloud computing, cybersecurity, fintech, and IoT platforms (GSMA, 2023; e&, 2023). Its five-pillar organizational structure reflects a platform-based approach to digital ecosystems and innovation.

In Egypt, e& operates customer service and operational centers, contributing to employment generation and digital capacity building (UNCTAD, 2022). In Israel, cooperation has expanded following normalization agreements, including content distribution (e.g., i24NEWS), cybersecurity partnerships (e.g., Cyberint), and telecommunications integration (World Bank, 2022).

Abu Dhabi National Oil Company (ADNOC)

Abu Dhabi National Oil Company is a fully integrated energy company operating across exploration, production, refining, and distribution. ADNOC plays a central role in global energy markets while investing in carbon management, hydrogen, and digital optimization technologies (IEA, 2023; ADNOC, 2022). Its partnerships with international oil companies reflect hybrid governance models combining state ownership with global capital and expertise (Hertog, 2010).

Abu Dhabi National Energy Company (TAQA)

Abu Dhabi National Energy Company operates across power generation, water desalination, and energy infrastructure. The firm is increasingly involved in renewable energy and international infrastructure projects, aligning with global decarbonization trends (International Energy Agency, 2023).

Majid Al Futtaim

Majid Al Futtaim exemplifies the role of consumption-driven conglomerates in regional economic diversification. Its operations across retail, leisure, and hospitality contribute to urban development and service-sector expansion (World Bank, 2022).

Emaar Properties

Emaar Properties is globally recognized for flagship developments such as the Burj Khalifa and Dubai Mall. These projects illustrate the integration of real estate, tourism, and global investment strategies in national development models (Krane, 2015).

Landmark Group and Al-Futtaim Group

These conglomerates operate extensive retail and distribution networks across multiple sectors, reinforcing the UAE's role as a regional trade and logistics hub (World Bank, 2022).

EGYPT

Egypt's innovation ecosystem is increasingly shaped by business process outsourcing (BPO), industrial automation, and digitally enabled service platforms, positioning the country as a regional hub for cost-effective, technology-driven services (UNCTAD, 2022; World Bank, 2022).

Xceed

Xceed represents one of Egypt's leading outsourcing providers, delivering customer support, technical helpdesk, and back-office services alongside advanced solutions such as recruitment process outsourcing (RPO) and finance and accounting outsourcing (FAO). Operating across multiple regions—including North Africa and the Gulf—it integrates artificial intelligence, robotic process automation (RPA), and data analytics to enhance service efficiency and customer engagement (UNCTAD, 2022). Strategic collaboration with e& illustrates growing regional convergence between telecommunications infrastructure and digital service ecosystems.

Egyptian Industrial Technology Firms

A growing cohort of Egyptian firms contributes to Industry 4.0 adoption through automation, IoT integration, and localized manufacturing innovation:

Egyptian Modern Technology develops factory automation and industrial software, including IoT-enabled dashboards that optimize energy consumption and production efficiency.

Black and Romans Machinery specializes in FMCG packaging technologies, integrating global manufacturing standards into local production systems.

Sants Group operates across renewable energy, lighting, and industrial systems, often collaborating with state-linked entities.

MAG Group Egypt focuses on climate-adapted LED manufacturing supported by internal R&D.

Innovation Platform Solutions

Innovation Platform Solutions delivers integrated IT, automation, and smart infrastructure solutions, including AI-enabled resource optimization systems for workspace and asset management. These platforms reflect Egypt's shift toward smart environments and digitally managed infrastructure (World Bank, 2022).

Key Egyptian Multinationals by Sector

Financial Services: EFG Holding; Banque Misr; Commercial International Bank; QNB Al Ahli

Telecom & IT: Telecom Egypt; Orange Egypt; Raya Holding; e-finance

Construction & Real Estate: Orascom Construction; Talaat Moustafa Group; Emaar Misr; SODIC

These firms collectively support Egypt's transition toward a diversified, digitally enabled economy (UNCTAD, 2022).

ISRAEL

Israel's innovation ecosystem is characterized by high R&D intensity, strong university–industry linkages, and the presence of globally competitive firms in cybersecurity, pharmaceuticals, energy, and digital technologies (OECD, 2023; Senor & Singer, 2009).

Teva Pharmaceutical Industries

Teva Pharmaceutical Industries is a global leader in generic and specialty pharmaceuticals, with R&D focused on neuroscience, immunology, and respiratory therapeutics. Its dual emphasis on innovation and generics contributes to global pharmaceutical accessibility (OECD, 2023).

ICL Group

ICL Group operates in specialty chemicals and advanced materials, with innovation spanning fertilizers, food technologies, and circular economy solutions. Its integration of digital agriculture and IoT-based systems reflects convergence between traditional industries and advanced technologies (OECD, 2023).

NewMed Energy and Enlight Renewable Energy

These firms represent Israel's dual energy strategy: natural gas export (e.g., Leviathan field) and renewable energy expansion. Their cross-border partnerships, including exports to Egypt, position energy as a vector for regional integration (International Energy Agency, 2023).

Amdocs

Amdocs leads in telecom software and AI-enabled customer experience platforms. Its R&D focuses on cloud-native architectures, 5G monetization, and generative AI integration, supporting global telecom operators' digital transformation (OECD, 2023).

Check Point Software Technologies

Check Point Software Technologies is a global cybersecurity leader, with research spanning threat intelligence, zero-trust architectures, and AI-enhanced security analytics, reflecting Israel's dominance in cyber defense technologies (OECD, 2023).

Mobileye

Mobileye develops advanced driver assistance systems (ADAS) and autonomous mobility platforms, integrating sensor fusion, mapping technologies, and AI-driven perception systems. Its innovations contribute to global smart mobility and urban transport systems (Intel, 2023).

TURKEY

Turkey's industrial ecosystem combines traditional heavy industry with emerging digital transformation capabilities, supported by diversified conglomerates and export-oriented manufacturing (OECD, 2022).

Erdemir focuses on advanced steel production, energy efficiency, and emissions reduction.

Ford Otosan operates major R&D centers supporting vehicle engineering and global automotive exports.

Koç Holding integrates AI, IoT, and digital twin technologies through KoçDigital.

Sabancı Holding invests in climate technologies and advanced materials via corporate innovation platforms.

Arçelik emphasizes smart and energy-efficient appliances.

ASELSAN leads in defense technologies and advanced systems.

Turkish Airlines leverages digital platforms and analytics to manage global operations.

Additionally, platforms such as Udemy support regional workforce upskilling through digital education ecosystems.

SAUDI ARABIA

Saudi Arabia's innovation ecosystem is driven by large-scale state-led initiatives under Saudi Vision 2030, emphasizing diversification, sustainability, and technological localization (Vision 2030, 2016; International Energy Agency, 2023).

Saudi Aramco

Saudi Aramco is a global leader in energy R&D, investing in AI, hydrogen, and decarbonization technologies, with a substantial patent portfolio (International Energy Agency, 2023).

SABIC

SABIC operates a global innovation network focused on advanced materials, nanotechnology, and low-carbon petrochemicals.

SAMI Advanced Electronics Company

SAMI Advanced Electronics Company integrates AI, IoT, and defense technologies while promoting localization and innovation through structured internal programs.

Saudi Electricity Company and Saline Water Conversion Corporation

These entities form the backbone of Saudi infrastructure innovation, applying AI and digital systems to energy and water management (International Energy Agency, 2023).

ACWA Power

ACWA Power leads renewable energy and green hydrogen projects across multiple countries, contributing to global energy transition efforts.

NEOM

NEOM represents a large-scale experimental ecosystem integrating AI, renewable energy, smart infrastructure, and digital governance, positioning Saudi Arabia as a global innovation hub.

REFERENCES

ADNOC. (2022). *ADNOC annual report*. Abu Dhabi National Oil Company.

e&. (2023). *Annual report and corporate overview*. Emirates Telecommunications Group.

GSMA. (2023). *The mobile economy: Middle East and North Africa*. GSMA Intelligence.

Hertog, S. (2010). *Princes, brokers, and bureaucrats: Oil and the state in Saudi Arabia*. Cornell University Press.

ICAO. (2022). *Air transport statistics*. International Civil Aviation Organization.

Intel. (2023). *Mobileye technology overview*. Intel Corporation.

International Energy Agency. (2023). *World energy outlook 2023*.

Krane, J. (2015). *City of gold: Dubai and the dream of capitalism*. St. Martin's Press.

OECD. (2022). *Economic surveys*. OECD Publishing.

OECD. (2023). *Israel innovation policy review*. OECD Publishing.

Saudi Vision 2030. (2016). *Vision 2030 document*. Government of Saudi Arabia.

Senor, D., & Singer, S. (2009). *Start-up nation: The story of Israel's economic miracle*. Twelve.

UNCTAD. (2022). *World investment report 2022. United Nations Conference on Trade and Development.*

World Bank. (2022). *Digital development overview: Middle East and North Africa*.

Chapter 14
Innovative Activities of Multinational Corporations in the Middle East

ABSTRACT

Multinational corporations (MNCs) are key drivers of innovation and technological transformation in the Middle East, particularly in United Arab Emirates, Saudi Arabia, and Israel. These countries have leveraged national economic transformation strategies and digitalization agendas to attract global technology investments and integrate into the global knowledge economy. In the UAE, innovation is driven by public-private partnerships and smart city, AI, and cloud computing initiatives. In Saudi Arabia, diversification programs emphasize advanced manufacturing, renewable energy, and digital industrial systems. In Israel, a globally competitive startup and research-driven ecosystem supports breakthroughs in cybersecurity, artificial intelligence, and advanced software technologies. Collectively, MNC participation accelerates technology transfer, workforce development, and regional economic diversification.

INTRODUCTION

Strategic partnerships between global technology firms and sovereign actors are reshaping the region's digital infrastructure. Microsoft has engaged in partnerships with MGX and BlackRock to develop large-scale data centers, positioning the UAE as a global AI hub. Similarly, Google Cloud has partnered with Saudi Arabia's Public Investment Fund to develop a USD 10 billion cloud and AI hub, while Am-

DOI: 10.4018/979-8-3373-7350-8.ch014

azon Web Services has committed USD 5 billion to an "AI Zone" in Saudi Arabia (International Energy Agency, 2023; World Bank, 2022).

Beyond digital transformation, MNCs also contribute to sustainability and clean energy transitions. For example, JinkoSolar participates in large-scale renewable projects such as the Mohammed bin Rashid Al Maktoum Solar Park, one of the largest solar energy installations globally (International Renewable Energy Agency, 2023).

INTEL

Intel plays a strategic role in advancing semiconductors, AI, and smart infrastructure across the Middle East.

UAE: Collaboration with Dubai Silicon Oasis Authority led to the establishment of an innovation center focused on IoT, AI, and cloud technologies.

Saudi Arabia: Intel contributes to NEOM and collaborates with Saudi Aramco on Open RAN and digital infrastructure (International Energy Agency, 2023).

Egypt: Partnerships with Telecom Egypt support Open RAN deployment and telecom virtualization.

Israel: Intel's largest R&D base outside the U.S. operates in Haifa, Petah Tikva, and Jerusalem, contributing to processor design and AI innovation (OECD, 2023).

VALEO

Valeo exemplifies automotive innovation through AI-driven mobility solutions.

Egypt: Its Cairo R&D center is a major global hub for automotive software engineering and AI applications.

Saudi Arabia & UAE: Partnerships support localization of EV and autonomous vehicle technologies.

Israel: Collaboration with Mobileye and startups enhances ADAS and imaging radar systems (OECD, 2023).

DELL TECHNOLOGIES

Dell Technologies contributes to enterprise IT modernization and cloud ecosystems.

Egypt: The Egypt Center of Excellence supports AI, blockchain, and digital skills development.

Saudi Arabia: Manufacturing and data infrastructure investments support localization and workforce training.

Israel: R&D centers in Herzliya and Haifa focus on cybersecurity and storage technologies.

CONCENTRIX

Concentrix operates major outsourcing hubs across the region.

Egypt: A leading global delivery hub with tens of thousands of employees and major investment expansion supported by Information Technology Industry Development Agency.

Israel: AI-driven CX platforms and cybersecurity services reflect integration with advanced digital ecosystems.

GENERAL MOTORS

General Motors positions the Middle East as a testbed for EVs and autonomous mobility.

Israel: The GM Technical Center develops AI-based autonomous driving systems and battery analytics (OECD, 2023).

Regional: Deployment of smart mobility technologies and workforce training initiatives.

PROCTER & GAMBLE (P&G)

Procter & Gamble integrates global R&D with regional manufacturing.

UAE: The i Dubai Center focuses on consumer insights and retail innovation.

Israel: Open innovation through partnerships with Hebrew University of Jerusalem enables technology transfer via startups and academia.

AMAZON (AWS)

Amazon and Amazon Web Services drive digital infrastructure and e-commerce integration.

Egypt: Expansion through Souq.com acquisition and Amazon.eg platform (UNCTAD, 2022).

Israel: R&D centers contribute to AI, cloud computing, and semiconductor innovation.

Jordan: AWS enabled national e-learning platforms during COVID-19.

MICROSOFT

Microsoft is a major driver of AI and cloud innovation.

UAE & Saudi Arabia: Investments in AI infrastructure and sovereign cloud partnerships.

Israel: Advanced R&D across cybersecurity, AI, and cloud platforms, supported by acquisitions such as CyberX and Adallom (OECD, 2023).

NVIDIA

NVIDIA drives AI computing and data center innovation.

Saudi Arabia: Partnerships support AI factories and large-scale computing infrastructure aligned with Vision 2030.

Israel: Investment in AI supercomputing infrastructure strengthens global AI leadership.

SIEMENS

Siemens supports Industry 4.0 transformation.

Egypt: Smart manufacturing and high-speed rail development.

UAE & Saudi Arabia: IoT, AI, and healthcare digitalization initiatives.

Israel: Digital twin and industrial software innovation.

REFERENCES

International Energy Agency. (2023). *World energy outlook 2023.*

International Renewable Energy Agency. (2023). *Renewable energy market analysis: MENA.*

OECD. (2023). *Israel innovation policy review.* OECD Publishing.

Saudi Vision 2030. (2016). *Vision 2030 document.* Government of Saudi Arabia.

Senor, D., & Singer, S. (2009). *Start-up nation.* Twelve.

UNCTAD. (2022). *World investment report 2022.* United Nations.

World Bank. (2022). *Digital development in the Middle East and North Africa.*

Chapter 15
MNCs and Innovative Virtual Open Incubators Cluster

ABSTRACT

The Middle East is increasingly positioning itself as a global center for innovation and entrepreneurship, with major urban hubs such as Dubai and Riyadh driving regional transformation. These cities are not only advancing digitalization and technological development but are also strengthening intellectual property (IP) governance frameworks to attract multinational corporations (MNCs), global talent, and foreign direct investment. Riyadh's transition from an oil-dependent economy toward a knowledge-based model reflects broader structural reforms within Saudi Arabia. Strategic initiatives such as NEOM, Saudi Venture Capital Company, and the Saudi Authority for Intellectual Property strengthen entrepreneurial ecosystems, enhance regulatory capacity, and promote innovation-driven growth. These reforms contribute to a more favorable investment climate and reinforce the region's appeal to innovative global firms.

INTRODUCTION

The Middle East is increasingly emerging as a global hub for innovation and entrepreneurship, with cities such as Dubai and Riyadh at the forefront of this transformation (Al-Nasser, 2025). These urban centers are not only fostering creativity and technological advancement, but are also addressing complex intellectual property (IP) governance challenges in order to attract global talent, multinational corporations, and foreign direct investment. Riyadh, in particular, is undergoing a strategic transition from an oil-dependent economy toward a knowledge-based

DOI: 10.4018/979-8-3373-7350-8.ch015

economic model. Flagship initiatives such as NEOM, the Saudi Venture Capital Company (SVC), and the Saudi Authority for Intellectual Property (SAIP) play a central role in this shift by strengthening innovation ecosystems, supporting entrepreneurship, and enhancing IP regulation and enforcement. These developments have contributed to the growing attractiveness of the region for innovative multinational corporations (MNCs), supported by an increasingly favorable regulatory and investment environment.

The Abraham Accords is an enabling framework for innovation-driven economic diplomacy, providing political legitimacy and institutional space for multilateral collaboration beyond traditional trade and security domains. The establishment of MNC-centered VIOICs could operationalize innovation cooperation at the regional level. Accordingly, this chapter proposes a set of potential MNC VIOICs, drawing on the existing innovative activities, technological competencies, and regional presence of multinational corporations currently operating in the Middle East.

The companies examined throughout this chapter constitute high-impact multinational corporations (MNCs) and Innovation-Driven Virtual Open Incubators Clusters (IVOICs) with significant potential to foster economic interdependence, accelerate technological diffusion, and promote sustainable development across the Middle East. Through their innovation-oriented activities, these actors provide a concrete and operational foundation for economic peace, grounded in principles of shared value creation, collaborative innovation, and long-term regional integration. By embedding cross-border cooperation within innovation ecosystems, these MNCs and IVOICs contribute to the institutionalization of mutual economic interests that can support enduring regional stability and development.

INTEL

Egypt UAE

IoT, cloud computing, AI and video analytics.
software and hardware tools for the oil and gas industry.
Open RAN (radio access network)
City infrastructure, traffic management systems, and green data centers

Israel

processors and AI
communication and AI solutions
cybersecurity

Herewith Intel Middle East IVOIC (Figure 1)

Figure 1. Intel Middle East IVOIC

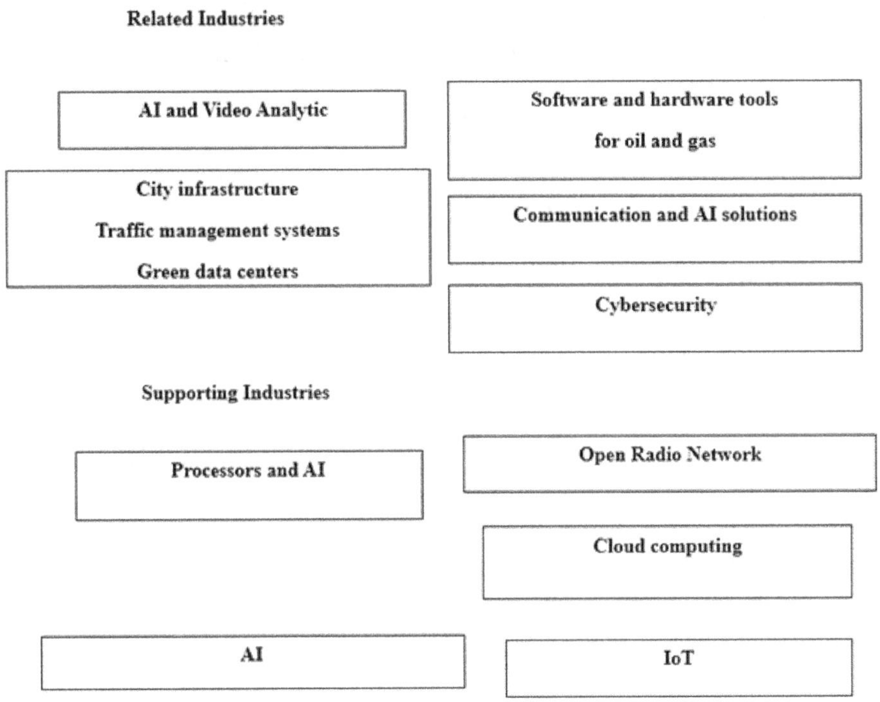

VALEO

Egypt

AI, computer vision, and machine learning for automotive applications.
Autonomous driving, electric vehicles
Automated parking
Software Integration & Validation; Neural Networks & Deep Learning; Cyber Security; System Architecture and Simulation; Advanced Driving Assistance Systems (ADAS)

Israel

Modify: Masks the perception of foul smells in cars

Mobileye: autonomous driving systems. World-Class Imaging Radars

antenna design, a high-end radio frequency design

vital sign detector that can evaluate a patient's health risks based on Valeo's Driver Monitoring System (DMS)

Herewith Valeo Middle East IVOIC (Figure 2).

Figure 2. Valeo Middle East IVOIC

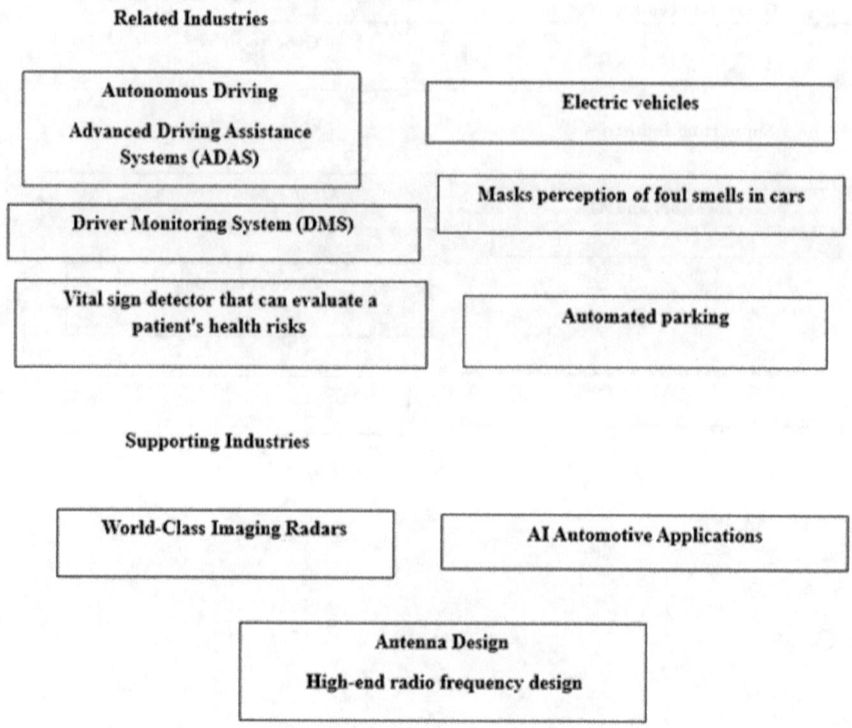

DELL TECHNOLOGIES

Egypt

AI and blockchain.
IT training

Israel

PowerFlex software
flash storage, data protection, and information security.
Herewith Dell Technologies Middle East IVOIC (Figure 3).

Figure 3. Dell Technologies Middle East IVOIC

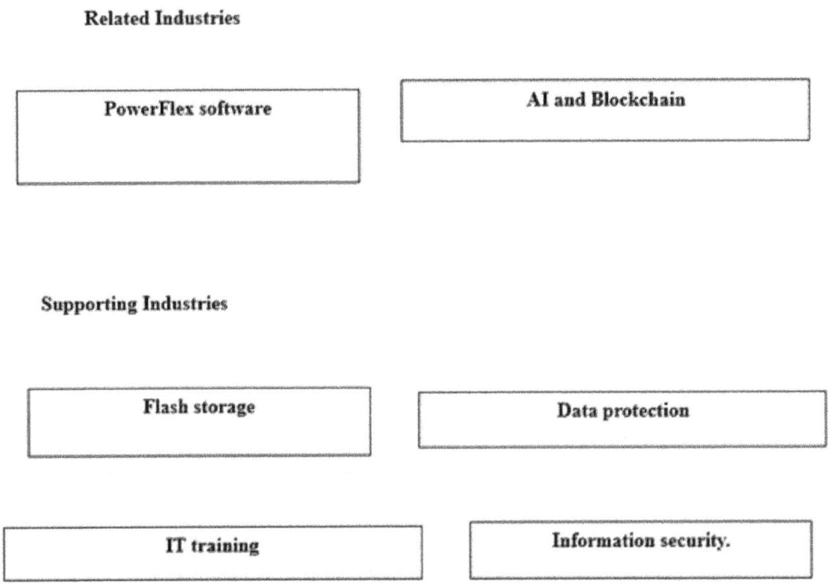

CONCENTRIX

Egypt Israel

iX Hero AI-powered application

customer experience (CX) solutions government, banking, real estate, fintech, healthcare, crypto, travel, retail and e-commerce, media and communication, insurance, and telecom

CyberProtect.

Herewith Concentrix Middle East IVOIC (Figure 4)

Figure 4. Concentrix Middle East IVOIC

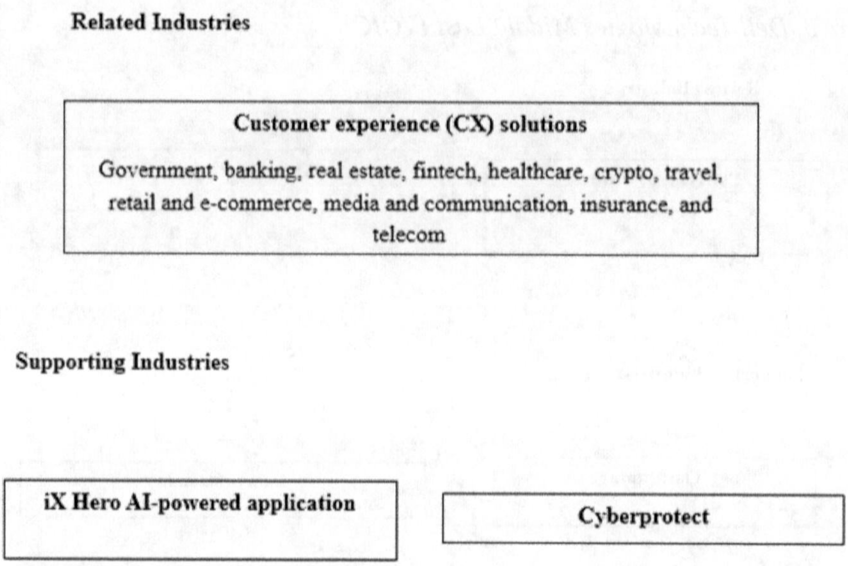

GENERAL MOTORS

Middle East

Ultium battery technology

Super Cruise, enabled by OnStar offers hands-free driving, automatic lane changes, and trailering support.

Israel

Powermat, wireless charging technologies

Sital Technology, locating damaged or torn cables inside a vehicle.

Herewith General Motors Middle East IVOIC (Figure 5).

Figure 5. General Motors Middle East IVOIC

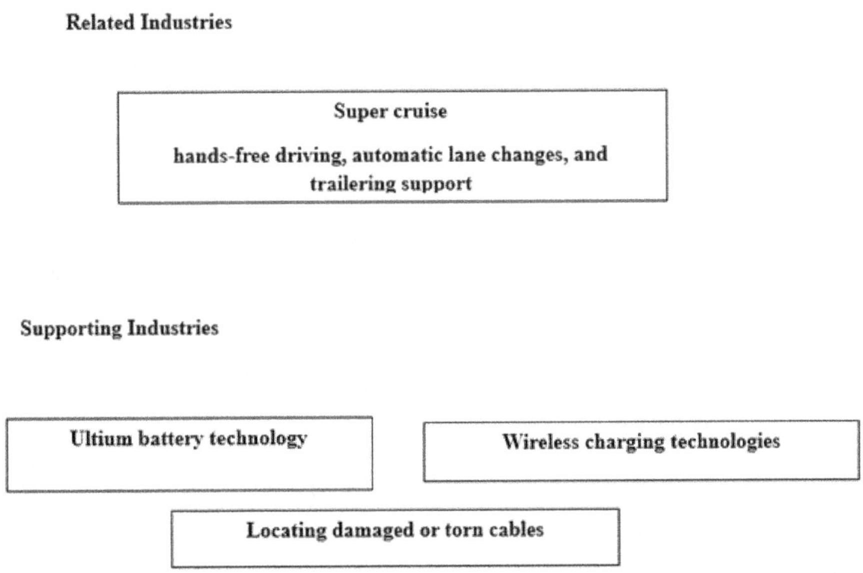

NESTLÉ

Middle East

Coffee, infant nutrition, dairy

Israel

Israeli cultured meat startup Future Meat Technologies
a new pea-based dairy-free milk line, Wunda
Herewith Nestlé Middle East IVOIC (Figure 6)

Figure 6. Nestlé Middle East IVOIC

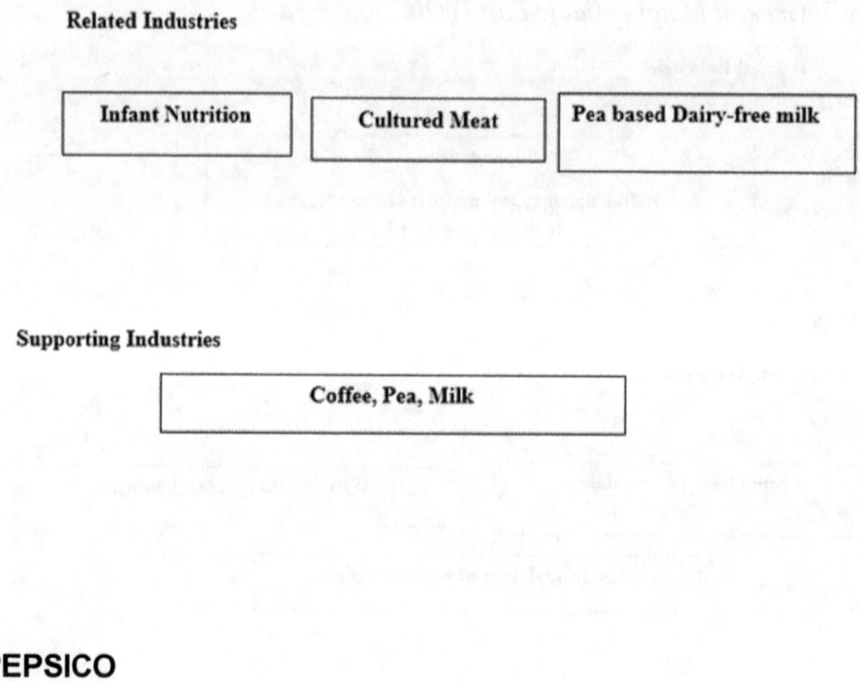

PEPSICO

Middle East

Water conservation, Waste management

Israel

Refrigerated Dips & Spreads
Sabra's salad
SodaStream
Herewith Pepsico Middle East IVOIC (Figure 7).

Figure 7. Pepsico Middle East IVOIC

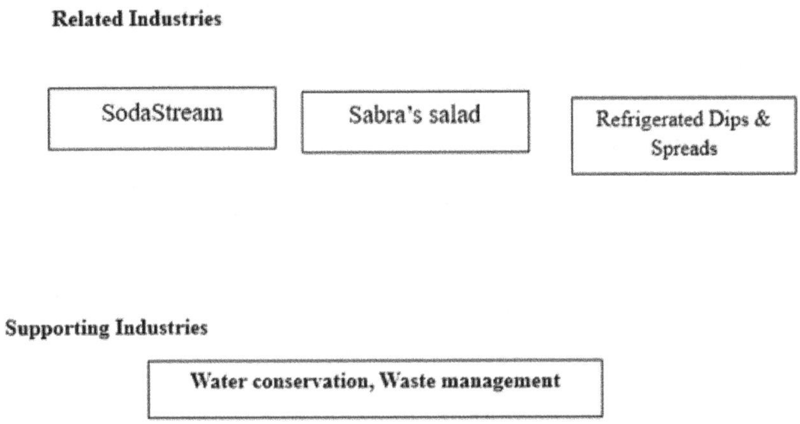

SCHNEIDER ELECTRIC

ADNOC pilot AI-driven autonomous operations EcoStruxure™
cyber company Claroty
EnStorage large energy storage
Herewith Schneider Electric Middle East IVOIC (Figure 8).

Figure 8. Schneider Electric Middle East IVOIC

Related Industries

AI-driven autonomous operations

EnStorage large energy storage

Supporting Industries

Cybersecurity Solutions

Claroty

PFIZER

Egypt

Sickle Cell Disease (SCD) and thalassemia

IUdo, in Egypt, Qatar and Lebanon to enhance the patient experience for those accessing their medicines through their affordability programmes.

Israel

CytoReason's digital models of the human immune system and diseases

Herewith Pfizer Middle East IVOIC (Figure 9)

Figure 9. Pfizer Middle East IVOIC

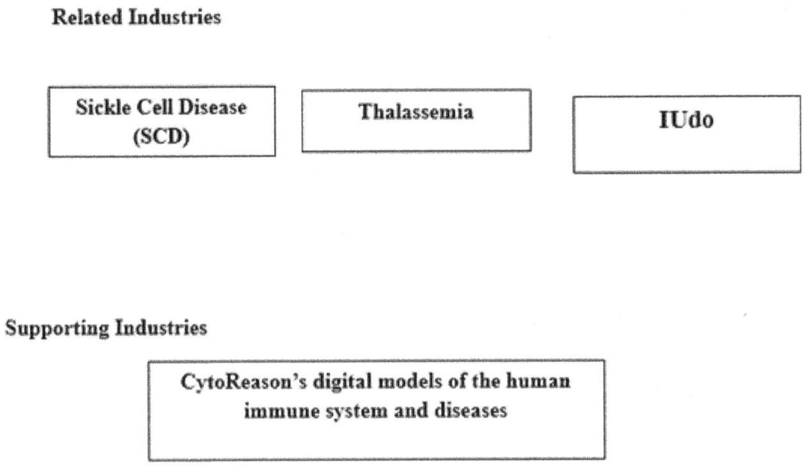

AMAZON

Middle East

Amazon Payment
Souq.com online retail platforms

Turkey

Türkiye's e-commerce platform Trendyol.com

UAE

Amazon. ae marketplace in the UAE

Saudi Arab

Amazon.sa

Jordan

darsak.gov.jo e-learning platform

Israel

Amazon Lab126
Annapurna Lab
Herewith Amazon Middle East IVOIC (Figure 10)

Figure 10. Amazon Middle East IVOIC

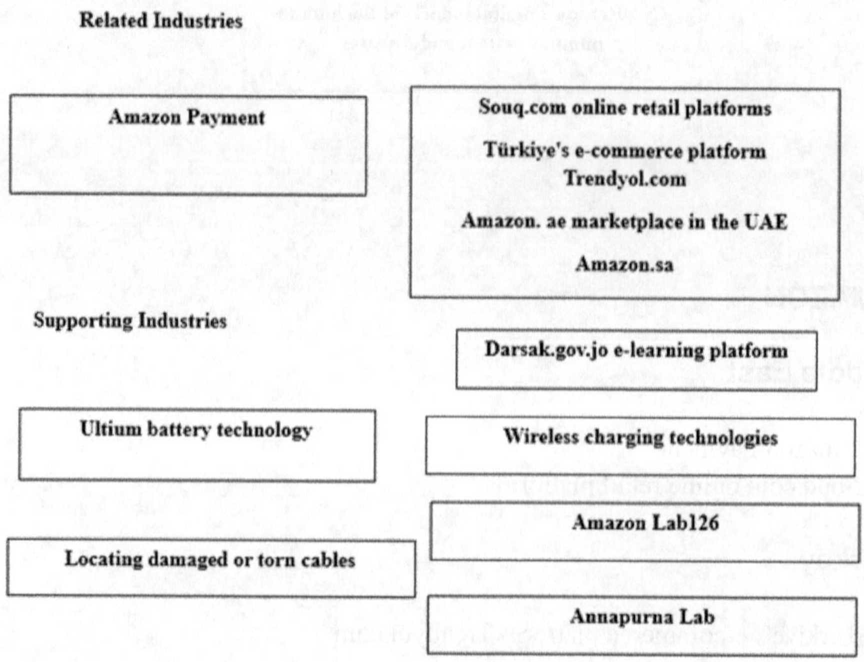

IBM

With AWS to Fuel Innovation and Cloud Adoption Across the Middle East. IBM, Sep 29, 2025.

Saudi Arabia

Cloud adoption and digital transformation

Egypt

IBM stepped up their game big time, partnering with major Egyptian banks like FABMISR and CIB to completely transform digital banking.

Israel

FDPR-Pro. Optimization problems, both in compilers and post-link optimization tools

This technology proved itself in a variety of market segments such as database engines, embedded software components.

Herewith IBM Middle East IVOIC (Figure 11)

Figure 11. IBM Middle East IVOIC

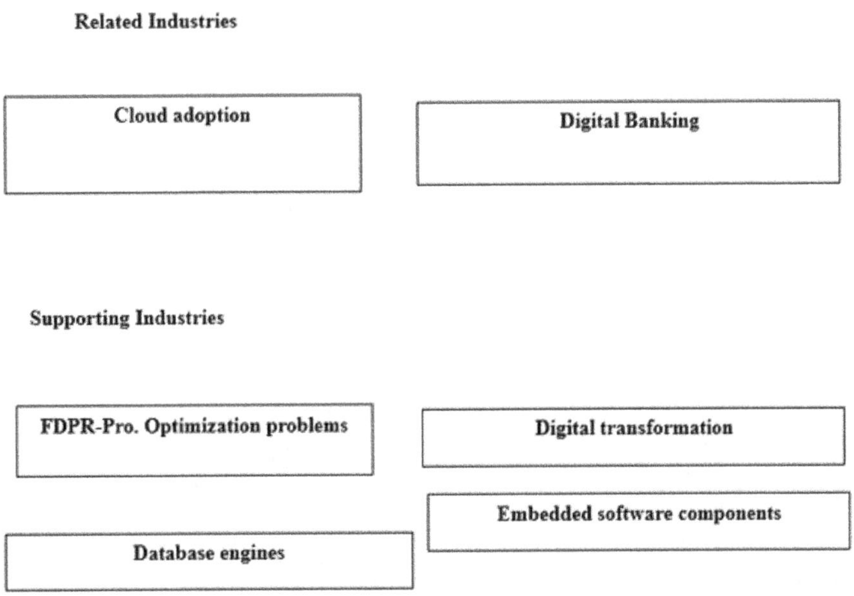

Jordan

Oracle Hospitality solutions

Israel

Cloud Infrastructure & AI
AI Development Platforms
AI Life Sciences and Industry Solutions.
Herewith Oracle Middle East IVOIC (Figure 12).

Figure 12. Oracle Middle East IVOIC

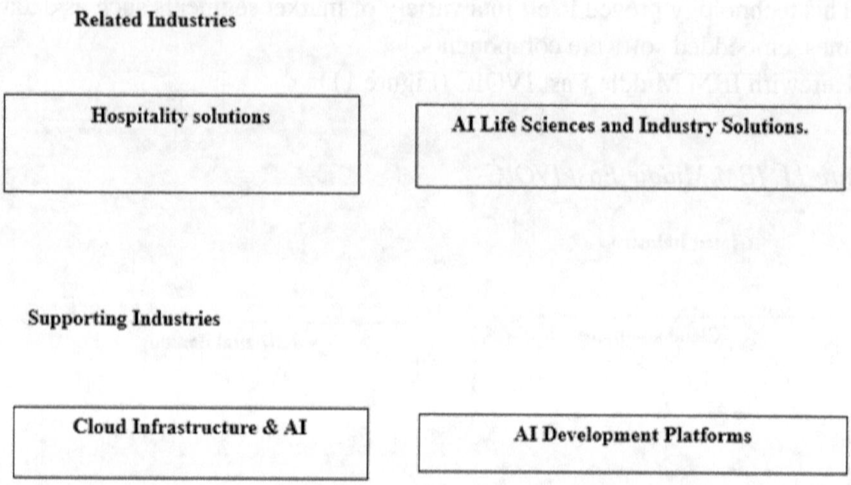

CISCO

Middle East

Digital transformation, AI, infrastructure development and cybersecurity
AI-native communication systems
Advanced edge infrastructure for Industry 5.0, autonomous mobility, and AI use cases in sectors like energy, health, and water.

Israel

Wireless & mobility, cloud application security, data centers, analytics, and Internet of Things (IoT).

Herewith CISCO Middle East IVOIC (Figure 13).

Figure 13. CISCO Middle East IVOIC

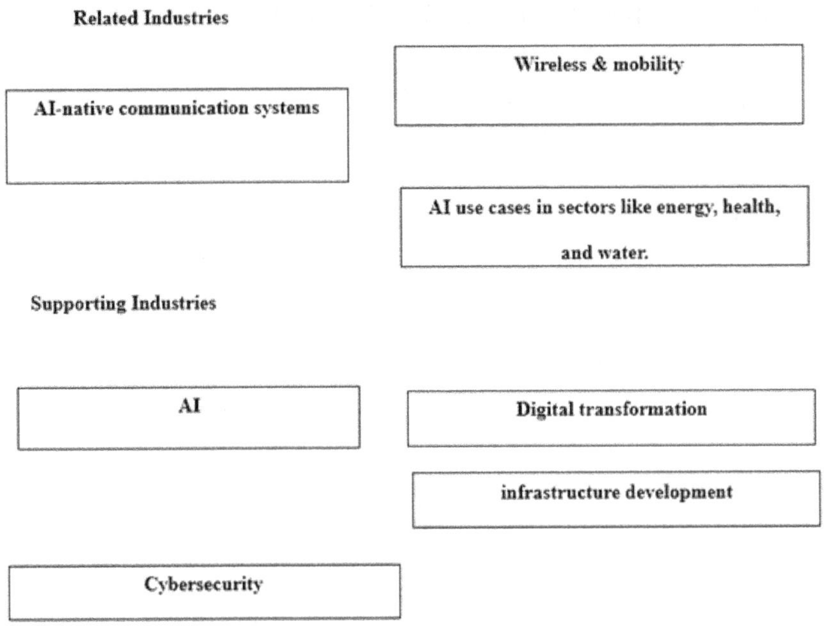

MICROSOFT

Middle East

Cyber Security; Business Analytics; Artificial Intelligence; Computer Vision
AI innovations, cloud technologies and advanced cybersecurity solutions.

Israel

Security; Digital Transformation Platforms; Experiences & Devices; Cloud & AI Platform.

adaptive cloud AI service for video analysis.

Microsoft Defender for CloudApps (MDA) is a comprehensive security solution that protects organizations from cyber threats associated with the use of SaaS applications.

Herewith Microsoft Middle East IVOIC (Figure 14).

Figure 14. Microsoft Middle East IVOIC

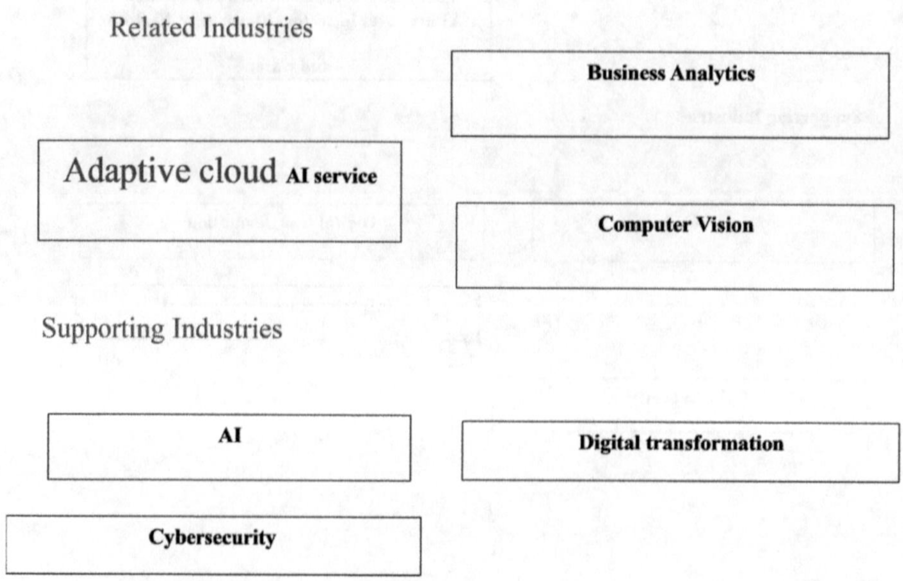

REFERENCES

Al-Nasser, A. (2025). The Rise of Innovation Hubs in the Middle East. Abu-Ghazaleh Intellectual Property.

Chapter 16
The Resource Curse Debate and Rent Capture

ABSTRACT

The African continent is endowed with extensive natural resources, including hydrocarbons, precious metals, and strategic minerals such as cobalt, copper, and rare earth elements. Several countries occupy pivotal positions in global commodity supply chains. Nigeria remains a major exporter of crude oil; the Democratic Republic of the Congo accounts for a dominant share of global cobalt production while also possessing significant copper reserves; South Africa has long been a leading producer of gold and platinum-group metals; and Botswana's economic trajectory has been closely tied to diamond extraction. Paradoxically, this substantial resource endowment has not consistently translated into broad-based economic development. Many resource-rich African states continue to experience high levels of poverty, inequality, and limited structural transformation. This apparent contradiction—where natural wealth coexists with underdevelopment—has generated extensive scholarly discussion under what is commonly termed the resource curse.

INTRODUCTION

The African continent is endowed with extensive natural resources, including hydrocarbons, precious metals, and strategic minerals such as cobalt, copper, and rare earth elements. Several countries occupy pivotal positions in global commodity supply chains. Nigeria remains a major exporter of crude oil; the Democratic Republic of the Congo accounts for a dominant share of global cobalt production while also possessing significant copper reserves; South Africa has long been a leading

DOI: 10.4018/979-8-3373-7350-8.ch016

producer of gold and platinum-group metals; and Botswana's economic trajectory has been closely tied to diamond extraction.

Paradoxically, this substantial resource endowment has not consistently translated into broad-based economic development. Many resource-rich African states continue to experience high levels of poverty, inequality, and limited structural transformation. This apparent contradiction—where natural wealth coexists with underdevelopment—has generated extensive scholarly discussion under what is commonly termed the resource curse.

The concept gained prominence through the work of Richard Auty (1993) in the early 1990s and was later reinforced by empirical studies such as those of Sachs and Warner (1995), which identified a negative relationship between resource dependence and long-term economic growth. This body of literature highlights several mechanisms through which resource abundance may hinder development, including exposure to volatile commodity prices, the emergence of rent-seeking behavior, and the weakening of institutional quality.

Historical factors also play a significant role in shaping these outcomes. During the colonial period, many African economies were structured around extractive activities designed to serve external markets. Infrastructure systems—such as railways and ports—were primarily oriented toward the export of raw materials rather than fostering domestic industrialization or regional economic integration. Following independence, many states inherited administrative systems that were not well-suited to managing complex, diversified economies, reinforcing dependence on primary commodity exports.

KEY DRIVERS OF THE RESOURCE CURSE

A central feature of resource-dependent economies is the *rentier effect*, whereby governments derive a substantial portion of their revenues from natural resource rents rather than taxation. This reduces the fiscal reliance of the state on its citizens, often weakening mechanisms of accountability and democratic oversight. In such contexts, political elites may have limited incentives to strengthen institutions, promote transparency, or pursue inclusive development strategies.

Resource wealth can also interact with political dynamics in ways that heighten instability. In environments characterized by weak governance, competition over resource revenues may intensify political rivalries, contribute to corruption, and, in some cases, finance armed conflict or reinforce authoritarian rule. As a result, rather than serving as a foundation for development, natural resources may exacerbate existing governance challenges.

Another important mechanism is the phenomenon known as *Dutch Disease*, first identified following the Netherlands' natural gas boom in the 1960s (Whittaker, 2026). Large inflows of foreign exchange from resource exports can lead to currency appreciation, making non-resource sectors such as manufacturing and agriculture less competitive internationally. This dynamic can crowd out productive sectors, limiting diversification and increasing economic dependence on a narrow range of commodities.

More recently, the debate has expanded to include so-called *critical minerals*—including cobalt, lithium, and rare earth elements—which are essential inputs for emerging technologies such as electric vehicles, renewable energy infrastructure, and advanced electronics. While demand for these resources presents new economic opportunities for African producers, it also raises concerns about intensified rent capture, governance challenges, and unequal distribution of benefits.

In many cases, the concentration of resource revenues within a narrow political and economic elite has been associated with weak public investment in key sectors such as education and infrastructure. This has contributed to persistent inequality and has limited the capacity of resource wealth to generate inclusive and sustainable development outcomes.

THE CONCEPT OF THE RESOURCE CURSE

The paradox of resource abundance alongside weak development outcomes is commonly analyzed through the Resource Curse Hypothesis (RCH). This framework posits that countries endowed with significant natural resources may, under certain conditions, experience slower economic growth, institutional fragility, and heightened exposure to economic volatility compared to less resource-dependent economies (Hannan and Mohsin, 2015). Rather than serving as a guaranteed pathway to prosperity, resource wealth can introduce structural distortions that complicate long-term development trajectories.

Empirical evidence suggests that the impact of resource dependence is not uniform across countries. Some states have demonstrated relatively stable or positive outcomes in managing resource revenues, while others exhibit repeated episodes of economic disruption linked to fluctuations in commodity rents. For example, countries such as Qatar, Indonesia, and Egypt have, at times, shown more favorable performance patterns, whereas Algeria, Malaysia, and Saudi Arabia have experienced more frequent adverse cycles. Others, including Kuwait and Oman, display relatively neutral trends, suggesting a degree of insulation from rent volatility (Pehlivan, 2026). These variations highlight the importance of domestic policy choices and institutional frameworks in shaping development outcomes.

While natural resources can generate substantial fiscal revenues, their developmental impact depends critically on how these revenues are governed and utilized. Strong institutions, effective regulatory frameworks, and integration into global value chains (GVCs) can enable resource wealth to support diversification and industrial upgrading. Conversely, weak governance structures often lead to rent-seeking behavior, patronage networks, and inefficient allocation of public resources, undermining the potential benefits of resource endowments (Anser et al., 2025).

In many African economies, the challenge is not the absence of resource wealth but the limited degree of domestic value addition. Natural resources are frequently exported in raw or minimally processed forms, while higher-value activities—such as refining, advanced manufacturing, and technological innovation—are conducted elsewhere. This pattern constrains local industrial development and reduces the potential for job creation, technological learning, and broader economic transformation. As a result, the gains from resource extraction are often unevenly distributed and insufficient to drive inclusive growth.

Recent empirical research further underscores these structural constraints. Ado et al. (2025) identify four major categories of barriers limiting participation in and upgrading within global value chains in countries such as Côte d'Ivoire, the Democratic Republic of the Congo, Ghana, and Nigeria, particularly in sectors like cocoa, cobalt, and petroleum. These constraints include institutional weaknesses, infrastructure deficits, limited technological capabilities, and unfavorable trade and investment conditions. At the same time, the study highlights cases such as Chad and Niger, where targeted policy interventions and governance improvements have contributed to more successful GVC upgrading, illustrating that the adverse effects of resource dependence are not inevitable but can be mitigated through effective policy design and institutional strengthening.

POLITICAL ELITES, RENT CAPTURE, AND MULTINATIONAL MINING CORPORATIONS

The relationship between political elites and multinational mining corporations (MNCs) is a central feature of resource governance in many African economies. Rather than operating independently, corruption and corporate activity are often deeply intertwined within broader political–economic systems that regulate access to and control over mineral wealth. As argued in the political economy literature (Acemoglu & Robinson, 2012), the structure of institutions plays a decisive role in determining whether resource wealth is broadly distributed or captured by narrow elite groups.

At the heart of this dynamic lies the control of resource rents. In mineral-rich countries such as the Democratic Republic of the Congo, Angola, and Guinea, governments derive a large share of revenue from extractive industries. This creates strong incentives for political elites to dominate licensing processes, contract negotiations, and revenue flows. MNCs seeking secure access to high-value deposits may engage—directly or indirectly—in practices that enable elite rent capture, including opaque contractual arrangements, aggressive tax planning, and, in some cases, informal payments. In such contexts, corruption becomes a mechanism for allocating access to lucrative natural resources rather than an aberration from the system (Gereffi et al., 2005; Soros, 2007; Kaplinsky, 2005).

Major firms operating in these environments—including Glencore in the DRC and Rusal in Guinea—often navigate institutional landscapes characterized by weak regulatory enforcement and limited transparency. These conditions can reduce compliance costs in the short term but contribute to long-term governance challenges by reinforcing opaque and discretionary decision-making processes.

Governance Implications of Rent Capture

The consequences of this interaction between political elites and MNCs are far-reaching. First, it weakens the state's ability to secure an equitable share of resource revenues. Funds that could support infrastructure development, education systems, or industrial policy are frequently lost through unfavorable contracts or diverted through illicit channels. Second, regulatory oversight is often compromised, allowing environmental degradation and labor violations to persist. Third, public policy may become oriented toward short-term revenue maximization rather than long-term economic diversification and structural transformation.

Efforts to address these challenges have included global transparency initiatives such as the Extractive Industries Transparency Initiative (EITI), which promotes disclosure of resource revenues. However, scholars such as Kolstad and Wiig (2009) argue that transparency alone is insufficient. While revenue disclosure improves information availability, it does not necessarily ensure accountability or effective public spending. A narrow focus on revenues—without equal attention to how those revenues are allocated—limits the ability of such initiatives to fully address the structural drivers of the resource curse.

Implications for Knowledge Transfer and Innovation

Rent capture also has significant implications for knowledge transfer and technological development. In environments where access to resources is shaped by political connections rather than competitive or developmental criteria, MNCs face limited incentives to invest in local capacity-building. Instead of fostering local supplier networks, research partnerships, or skills development, firms may rely heavily on imported technologies and expatriate labor.

This pattern is evident in regions such as the Copperbelt in the Democratic Republic of the Congo and Zambia, where strong MNC presence has not consistently translated into deep integration with domestic firms or universities. Similarly, in Guinea's bauxite sector, continued reliance on raw material exports reflects limited progress in downstream processing and industrial upgrading. These dynamics reinforce enclave-style production systems, where extraction occurs with minimal linkages to the broader domestic economy.

A comparable pattern can be observed in the oil sector of Nigeria. Despite decades of substantial petroleum revenues, governance challenges have constrained the translation of resource wealth into inclusive economic development, illustrating that the interaction between corruption and extractive industries is not limited to mining alone (Standing, 2007).

Comparative Governance: The Case of Botswana

Not all resource-rich countries follow this trajectory. Botswana provides an important counterexample, demonstrating how stronger institutional frameworks can mitigate rent capture. The partnership between Debswana and De Beers has been characterized by relatively transparent agreements, effective regulation, and sustained state capacity. This has enabled a more effective channeling of resource revenues into national development, including public investment and economic planning.

Political Leadership and Elite Capture

Individual political leadership has also played a critical role in shaping patterns of rent capture (Table 1). In Angola, José Eduardo dos Santos presided over decades of oil- and diamond-driven growth that disproportionately benefited a narrow elite. Control over state-owned enterprises such as Sonangol and Endiama enabled the concentration of wealth within politically connected networks, reinforcing patronage systems and limiting broader socio-economic gains (Dinika, 2025).

In the Democratic Republic of the Congo, Joseph Kabila oversaw a resource-rich but institutionally fragile system in which mining concessions were frequently allocated through opaque processes. Rent capture in this context intersected with conflict dynamics, as resource revenues flowed through informal channels that supported both elite networks and, at times, armed groups (Pepe et al., 2014).

Similarly, in Guinea, Alpha Condé presided over a period in which mining contracts and concessions were often linked to political alliances and patronage networks. Despite vast bauxite reserves, the broader developmental impact remained limited due to the concentration of benefits among elite actors (Majumder, 2021).

In South Africa, the tenure of Mosebenzi Zwane illustrates that rent capture dynamics can also emerge in more diversified and middle-income economies. Allegations of irregular licensing decisions and preferential treatment for politically connected firms highlight how governance weaknesses can distort resource allocation even within relatively advanced institutional settings.

Nigeria: Presidential Control and Rent Capture in the Oil Economy

The cases of Olusegun Obasanjo and Goodluck Jonathan illustrate how presidential authority over resource sectors can shape the dynamics of rent capture in resource-dependent states. In Nigeria, where oil revenues have historically dominated public finances, control over extraction, licensing, and revenue allocation has provided political leaders with significant leverage to consolidate power and distribute economic benefits through patronage networks.

Olusegun Obasanjo (1999–2007): Democratization and Centralized Rent Control

Obasanjo's presidency coincided with Nigeria's transition from military rule to civilian governance, a period marked by high expectations for institutional reform. Despite these expectations, the oil sector remained highly centralized, with the Nigerian National Petroleum Corporation (NNPC) serving as the primary channel through which oil revenues were managed and distributed. Under presidential and ministerial oversight, decisions regarding joint ventures, export arrangements, and contract allocations enabled politically connected actors to secure preferential access to lucrative opportunities.

Although oil dominated the economy, the administration also influenced the allocation of mining licenses for resources such as tin and gold. The discretionary nature of licensing processes created additional avenues for elite rent capture beyond the petroleum sector. In this context, resource revenues were not only an economic asset but also a political tool, used to finance electoral campaigns, reinforce regional alliances, and sustain elite networks across both public institutions and private industry.

Goodluck Jonathan (2010–2015): Rent Distribution and Political Stabilization

The presidency of Goodluck Jonathan reflects a continuation—and in some respects, intensification—of centralized control over resource rents. Government authority over licensing, joint ventures, and foreign partnerships remained a key mechanism through which economic advantages were distributed to politically aligned firms and individuals.

Beyond direct control of oil production, resource rents were increasingly channeled through state-linked infrastructure and energy projects. Public contracts became an important vehicle for rent allocation, with politically connected contractors gaining access to high-value projects often mediated through ministerial discretion. This blurred the boundary between public investment and patronage, reinforcing elite capture within broader development initiatives.

The dynamics of rent capture were also closely tied to regional politics, particularly in the Niger Delta. Long-standing tensions over the distribution of oil revenues contributed to conflict and instability in the region. In response, Jonathan's administration deployed resource revenues to fund both security operations and development programs aimed at consolidating support among local elites. While these measures contributed to short-term political stabilization, they also embedded rent distribution within conflict management strategies, reinforcing the structural link between resource wealth, political loyalty, and governance outcomes.

THE MINING INDUSTRY AND AFRICA'S RESEARCH ECOSYSTEM

Despite notable progress in expanding research capacity across Africa, the mining sector remains only weakly integrated into the continent's broader knowledge and innovation systems. Over the past two decades, African governments, universities, and international partners have increased investments in scientific research, higher education, and technological infrastructure. These efforts reflect a growing recognition that sustainable development depends not only on resource extraction but also on the ability to generate, adapt, and apply knowledge locally.

Continental-Level Initiatives and Institutional Gaps

At the continental scale, the African Union has assumed a leading role in coordinating science and innovation policy (African Union, 2025), Its flagship framework, the Science, Technology and Innovation Strategy for Africa, seeks to promote research capacity, technological advancement, and knowledge-driven economic transformation. Complementary institutions—including the African Academy of Sciences, the African Institute for Mathematical Sciences, and the African Agricultural Technology Foundation—have contributed to strengthening scientific excellence, fostering collaborative research networks, and advancing innovation in fields such as agriculture, mathematics, artificial intelligence, and public health.

However, a critical gap persists: the relative marginalization of the mining sector within continental research and innovation agendas. While extractive industries remain central to many African economies, they are not systematically embedded within major science and technology policy frameworks. Compared to sectors such as agriculture, health, or digital technologies, mining receives limited attention as a domain for research collaboration, technological upgrading, or knowledge-intensive industrial development. This omission is particularly significant given the strategic importance of minerals—especially critical minerals—in global value chains.

Structural Disconnect Between Mining and Knowledge Systems

This disconnect reflects deeper structural dynamics. Mining in Africa has historically operated as an enclave sector, characterized by weak linkages to domestic economies and limited integration with local research institutions. As a result, universities and public research centers often play only a marginal role in extractive value chains, with minimal involvement in areas such as geological research, mineral processing technologies, environmental management, or mining engineering innovation.

At the same time, multinational corporations (MNCs) dominate large-scale mining operations across the continent. These firms typically operate within global production networks that prioritize efficiency, cost control, and proprietary technology protection. As a result, they tend to limit the scope and depth of knowledge transfer to host economies. This pattern is not incidental but reflects strategic considerations: maintaining technological advantages, protecting intellectual property, and minimizing the risks associated with building local competitors.

Constraints on Knowledge Transfer

The weak integration of the mining sector into Africa's research ecosystem is shaped by the interaction of firm-level strategies, global production structures, and domestic institutional conditions. These factors operate simultaneously, reinforcing a pattern in which knowledge remains concentrated outside host economies rather than diffusing into local innovation systems.

At the firm level, multinational corporations (MNCs) typically prioritize efficiency, cost control, and the protection of proprietary technologies. As a result, they rely heavily on imported equipment, expatriate expertise, and established global supplier networks. Local engagement is often limited to operational training rather than deeper forms of knowledge exchange, such as collaborative research or technological co-development. This reflects strategic considerations linked to maintaining competitive advantage, where core technological capabilities are retained within the firm.

At the level of global production structures, mining value chains are highly centralized and hierarchically organized. High-value activities—including advanced mineral processing, engineering design, and research and development—are concentrated in industrialized economies where firms' headquarters and innovation hubs are located. African operations are therefore typically positioned at the lower end of the value chain, focused on extraction and primary processing. This structural positioning limits opportunities for technological upgrading and reduces the scope for domestic firms and institutions to participate in knowledge-intensive segments.

Institutional conditions within host countries further reinforce these constraints. In many cases, regulatory frameworks governing local content, technology transfer, and research collaboration remain underdeveloped or weakly enforced. At the same time, universities and public research institutions often face funding limitations, skills gaps, and insufficient linkages with industry. Together, these factors reduce the incentives—and in some cases the capacity—for MNCs to engage in meaningful knowledge transfer or long-term capability-building.

Implications for Innovation and Development

The absence of strong linkages between mining activities and domestic research ecosystems has significant consequences for long-term development. Without sustained interaction between industry and academia, opportunities for technological learning and innovation remain limited. This constrains the ability of resource-rich economies to move beyond extractive activities toward higher-value functions such as mineral beneficiation, advanced manufacturing, and the development of mining-related technologies.

In addition, the marginalization of mining within broader science and innovation strategies weakens the capacity of African economies to respond effectively to shifts in global demand. The accelerating transition toward low-carbon energy systems has increased the strategic importance of minerals such as cobalt, lithium, and rare earth elements. However, without local technological capabilities, African countries risk remaining suppliers of raw materials rather than active participants in emerging high-value industries linked to clean energy and advanced manufacturing.

Toward Integration

Bridging this gap requires a more deliberate alignment between resource extraction and innovation policy. This includes integrating mining into national and continental science and technology strategies, strengthening university–industry collaboration, and designing regulatory frameworks that incentivize local research and development. Policies such as local content requirements, joint research initiatives, and innovation funds can play a role in encouraging deeper engagement between MNCs and domestic institutions.

Equally important is the development of absorptive capacity within local economies. This involves sustained investment in higher education, technical training, and research infrastructure, enabling domestic actors to effectively utilize and build upon external knowledge. Without such capacity, even well-designed knowledge transfer policies are unlikely to generate meaningful outcomes.

Case Illustration: The Copper–Cobalt Cluster

The dynamics described above are particularly evident in the Copperbelt region spanning the Democratic Republic of the Congo and Zambia. This region hosts one of the world's most significant concentrations of copper and cobalt resources, forming a critical node in global supply chains for energy transition technologies.

Major firms such as Glencore and China Molybdenum have introduced advanced extraction and processing technologies in their operations. However, the transfer of knowledge associated with these technologies tends to remain limited in scope. Local workers are typically trained in operational tasks—such as equipment use and routine maintenance—while higher-order capabilities, including geological modeling, process optimization, and digital mine management, remain concentrated within corporate headquarters or global technical centers.

Diamond Sector: Partial Upgrading in Botswana

The diamond industry in Botswana provides a contrasting—yet still constrained—example of knowledge transfer within Africa's extractive sectors. Through its joint venture, Debswana, with De Beers, Botswana has achieved a relatively higher level of domestic participation in the value chain. Activities such as sorting, valuation, and aggregation have been localized, reflecting deliberate state policies aimed at capturing greater value from diamond extraction and strengthening domestic capabilities.

However, this progress remains partial. The most profitable and knowledge-intensive segments of the global diamond value chain—such as branding, global pricing strategies, and advanced cutting and polishing technologies—continue to be controlled by the multinational partner. This demonstrates that even under conditions of comparatively strong governance and institutional capacity, MNCs selectively transfer knowledge in ways that preserve their competitive advantage. Botswana thus represents a case of partial upgrading, where meaningful gains in local participation coexist with structural limits on deeper technological and strategic capabilities.

Bauxite Sector: Enclave Extraction in Guinea

A more constrained pattern is evident in the bauxite industry of the Boké region in Guinea. Multinational corporations such as Rusal and Chalco focus primarily on the extraction and export of raw bauxite. The technologically advanced stages of the value chain—particularly refining into alumina and smelting into aluminum—are conducted outside the host economy.

As a result, local economic participation is largely limited to low- and medium-skill activities, with minimal development of domestic processing capabilities. Structural constraints—including inadequate energy infrastructure, limited industrial capacity, and weak policy incentives—further restrict opportunities for upgrading. In this context, knowledge flows largely bypass the domestic economy, producing a classic enclave model characterized by extraction without significant learning or technological accumulation.

Oil Sector: Technological Concentration in Angola

A similar dynamic can be observed in the oil sector of Angola, where major firms such as TotalEnergies and Chevron dominate offshore exploration and production. The technological complexity of deepwater drilling, combined with the strategic importance of proprietary exploration and extraction techniques, results in a high concentration of knowledge within multinational firms.

Local participation tends to be confined to supporting services—such as logistics, maintenance, and basic operations—while core engineering, geophysical analysis, and advanced technological functions remain externalized. This reinforces a pattern in which substantial resource revenues coexist with limited domestic capability development and weak technological spillovers.

Research Activity and Institutional Capacity Across Africa

Natural resource research constitutes a critical domain for Africa's long-term development, given the continent's extensive mineral wealth. However, research capacity in mining-related fields remains uneven and geographically concentrated.

In Southern Africa, institutions such as the University of the Witwatersrand and the University of Pretoria have developed relatively strong capabilities in mining engineering, geology, and mineral processing. Similarly, in West Africa, the Université Gamal Abdel Nasser de Conakry has established programs with Guinea's mining sector. In East Africa, the University of Dar es Salaam has developed expertise in petroleum engineering and mineral processing, reflecting the region's growing resource base.

Despite these developments, much of the research conducted within African universities remains oriented toward applied problem-solving and operational efficiency rather than frontier innovation. This reflects both funding constraints—often linked to immediate industry needs—and the continued dominance of MNCs in setting technological agendas.

Moreover, the overall scale and impact of research activity are limited by structural challenges, including insufficient funding, weak laboratory infrastructure, and limited integration with industrial actors. As a result, knowledge generated within academic institutions is rarely translated into commercial or industrial applications, reinforcing the disconnect between research systems and extractive industries.

Botswana: A More Integrated Approach

Botswana again provides a relatively more coordinated model. The University of Botswana has been incorporated into national strategies aimed at leveraging diamond resources for human capital development. Collaborative initiatives with industry actors, including Debswana, have supported training in geology, mining engineering, and mineral economics.

While this approach has contributed to a stronger base of local expertise, it remains constrained by the global structure of the diamond industry. High-value knowledge—particularly in branding, marketing, and advanced processing—continues to reside within multinational firms such as De Beers.

REFERENCES

Acemoglu, D., & Robinson, J. (2012). *Why Nations Fail: The Origins of Power*. Prosperity, and Poverty.

Ado, A., Osabutey Ellis, L. C., Sinha, P., & Adeola, O. (2025). Africa's international trade paradox, technology transfer, and value chain upgrade. *Technological Forecasting and Social Change*, 213.

African Union. (2025). Driving African Future. the Science, Technology and Innovation Strategy for Africa (STISA 2034). https://au.int/sites/default/files/documents/45087-doc-AU_STISA_2025-2034_Strategy_ENGLISH.pdf

Anser, M. K., Nazir, M., Nassani, A. A., Al-Aiban, K. M., Zaman, K., & Haffar, M. (2025, September). Rethinking Economic Policies: Diversification and Governance Strategies to Address the Resource Curse in Mineral-Rich Economies. *Natural Resource Modeling*, *38*(4), 14. DOI: 10.1111/nrm.70011

Auty, R. (1993) Sustaining Development in Mineral Economies: The Resource Curse Thesis. Routledge.

Dinika, A. A. (2025). Angola and the Isabel Dos Santos web, Good Governance Africa, Jun 6, 2025 https://gga.org/angola-and-the-isabel-dos-santos-web

Gereffi, G., Humphrey, J., & Sturgeon, T. (2005). The governance of global value chains. *Review of International Political Economy*, *12*(1), 78–104. DOI: 10.1080/09692290500049805

Hannan, A., & Mohsin, H. M. (2015). Regional Analysis of Resource Curse Hypothesis: Evidence from Panel Data. *Pakistan Journal of Applied Economics*, *25*(1), 45–66.

Kaplinsky, R. (2005). *Globalization, poverty and inequality: between a rock and a hard place*. Polity.

Kolstad, I., & Wiig, A. (2009). Is Transparency the Key to Reducing Corruption in Resource-Rich Countries? *World Development*, *37*(3), 521–532. DOI: 10.1016/j.worlddev.2008.07.002

Majumder, R. (2021). Corruption on exploitation of Bauxite in Guinea, investigation filed against President Alpha Condé and others. *Al Circle*.

Pehlivan, M. (2026). Is the resource curse persistent? Dynamic causality evidence from resource-dependent economies. *Resources Policy*, *113*(C).

Pepe, C., Mushagalusa Nshombo, J.M., & Risso, M. (2014). Preventing Corruption in Africa: Emerging Challenges in the Mining Sector of the Democratic Republic of Congo. *SYMPHONYA Emerging Issues in Management.*

Sachs, J. D., & Warner, A. (1995). Natural resource abundance and economic growth.

Soros, G. (2007). *Escaping the Resource Curse* (Humphreys, M., Sachs, J. D., & Stiglitz, J. E., Eds.). Columbia University Press.

Standing, A (2007). Corruption and the extractive industries in Africa Can combatting corruption cure the resource curse? Institute of Security Studies, ISS Paper 153.

Whittaker, M. (2026). Dutch disease and the resource curse: Paradoxes of plenty. *Encyclopedia Britannica.* https://www.britannica.com/money/Dutch-disease

Chapter 17
Leading Mining MNCs in Africa

ABSTRACT

Multinational mining corporations (MNCs) play a pivotal role in structuring Africa's extractive sectors, influencing how production is organized, how value is distributed, and how knowledge circulates across the continent. Their prominence stems from the capital-intensive and technologically sophisticated nature of mining activities. However, this dominance also situates African resource economies within asymmetrical global production networks, where control over high-value segments remains largely external. Across Africa, a relatively small number of globally diversified mining firms exercise considerable influence over resource extraction.

INTRODUCTION

Multinational mining corporations (MNCs) play a pivotal role in structuring Africa's extractive sectors, influencing how production is organized, how value is distributed, and how knowledge circulates across the continent. Their prominence stems from the capital-intensive and technologically sophisticated nature of mining activities. However, this dominance also situates African resource economies within asymmetrical global production networks, where control over high-value segments remains largely external.

Across Africa, a relatively small number of globally diversified mining firms exercise considerable influence over resource extraction.

DOI: 10.4018/979-8-3373-7350-8.ch017

MNCS ACROSS KEY COMMODITY DOMAINS

In the copper–cobalt belt spanning the Democratic Republic of the Congo and Zambia, multinational firms control some of the world's most strategically significant reserves, particularly in the context of rising demand linked to the global energy transition. In recent years, Chinese corporations such as China Molybdenum and Zijin Mining have expanded their presence, often through investments tied to state-supported resource-for-infrastructure agreements.

Within the gold sector, leading firms including Barrick Gold and Newmont maintain dominant positions in West and East Africa, especially in countries such as Ghana and Tanzania. While these companies introduce advanced exploration and extraction technologies, their operations are typically structured around export-oriented models with limited downstream processing within host economies.

The diamond industry presents a similar pattern of concentration, largely shaped by De Beers. Its long-standing operations in Botswana, Namibia, and South Africa have created a highly integrated global value chain, in which mining, sorting, and marketing functions are closely coordinated at the international level.

In West Africa's bauxite sector, particularly in Guinea, companies such as Rusal and Chalco dominate extraction activities. The bulk of processing, however, takes place in the continent, illustrating a broader structural pattern in which African economies remain positioned at the lower end of global value chains.

A comparable concentration is evident in Southern Africa's platinum group metals (PGMs) industry. Firms such as Anglo American Platinum and Sibanye-Stillwater control production within the Bushveld Complex, the largest known global reserve of PGMs.

GOVERNANCE, VALUE CAPTURE, AND KNOWLEDGE DYNAMICS

MNCs generally maintain control over high-value functions, including exploration technologies, advanced processing capabilities, and international marketing networks. In contrast, host countries primarily contribute access to mineral resources and labor. This arrangement reflects the governance structure of global value chains, where lead firms coordinate geographically dispersed production while retaining a disproportionate share of economic value.

The strategic behavior of MNCs also shapes the scope and depth of knowledge transfer within African economies. Although firms invest in workforce training and operational improvements, they tend to limit the diffusion of proprietary knowledge that could undermine their competitive position. Consequently, domestic capabilities are often restricted to routine or operational activities, with limited advancement toward innovation-driven functions. This pattern reinforces enclave-type production systems, particularly in contexts characterized by weaker institutional capacity.

Nevertheless, outcomes vary across countries. In Botswana, for example, stronger state institutions and negotiated partnerships have enabled greater local participation in segments of the mining value chain. Even in such cases, however, the most profitable and knowledge-intensive activities remain largely externally controlled. By contrast, in countries with less robust institutional frameworks, MNC dominance is more frequently associated with weak local linkages and constrained industrial development.

CONTRIBUTION TO THE LOCAL ECONOMY

Multinational corporations (MNCs) occupy a dominant position within Africa's extractive industries, overseeing large-scale operations in key minerals such as copper, cobalt, diamonds, gold, bauxite, and platinum. Their presence introduces significant capital investment, advanced technologies, and integration into global markets. At the same time, however, their activities reveal persistent structural imbalances in the control of knowledge and the distribution of value across global production systems (Gereffi, Humphrey, & Sturgeon, 2005; Kaplinsky, 2000).

MNCs operating in African mining sectors tend to carefully manage the extent of knowledge transfer in order to safeguard proprietary technologies and sustain their competitive advantages. In the Copperbelt region, encompassing the Democratic Republic of the Congo and Zambia, firms such as Glencore and China Molybdenum deploy sophisticated extraction and processing systems. Despite this, the transfer of knowledge is typically restricted to operational competencies, including equipment handling and routine maintenance. More advanced capabilities—such as geological data modelling, process optimization, and digital mine management—remain concentrated within corporate headquarters (Morris, Kaplinsky, & Kaplan, 2012; Farole & Winkler, 2014).

This approach aligns with the Knowledge-Based View of the firm, which emphasizes the strategic importance of retaining core knowledge internally. Furthermore, the ability of host economies to absorb and utilize transferred knowledge depends heavily on local absorptive capacity, shaped by the strength of universities, technical training institutions, and research systems (Cohen & Levinthal, 1990).

A contrasting example can be observed in Botswana's diamond industry. Through the Debswana joint venture with De Beers, a greater degree of knowledge transfer has occurred, particularly in midstream activities such as diamond sorting, valuation, and aggregation. Collaboration between the industry and domestic educational institutions has supported skills development in these areas. Nevertheless, high-value functions—including branding, global pricing strategies, and advanced cutting technologies—remain firmly under the control of De Beers. This case illustrates that knowledge transfer outcomes depend not only on foreign investment but also on state capacity and the effectiveness of negotiated arrangements (Taylor, 2006; Acemoglu, Johnson, & Robinson, 2003).

In Guinea's bauxite sector, particularly in the Boké Region, where firms such as Rusal and Chalco dominate extraction, knowledge transfer remains limited. Mining activities are largely confined to basic extraction processes, while refining and smelting are conducted the continent. Weak institutional capacity, underdeveloped infrastructure, and the absence of supporting industries constrain the development of local absorptive capacity, reinforcing an enclave-style economic structure (Auty, 2001; World Bank, 2020).

ECONOMIC IMPACT

Despite these constraints, MNCs make measurable contributions to domestic economies through employment generation, local procurement, infrastructure investment, and corporate social responsibility initiatives.

Employment and Skills Development

Mining operations create both direct and indirect employment opportunities. Direct jobs are concentrated in extraction, maintenance, and administrative functions, while indirect employment emerges in sectors such as transport, construction, and service provision. In regions such as the Copperbelt, mining remains a major employer, while Botswana's diamond sector plays a central role in national labor markets. Training programs, often implemented in collaboration with technical institutions, enhance workforce capabilities, although they are generally limited to operational rather than innovation-intensive skills (UNCTAD, 2007).

Local Procurement and SME Linkages

MNCs can stimulate domestic economic activity through procurement of goods and services. In Zambia and the DRC, local firms supplying construction, transportation, and equipment maintenance benefit from mining-related demand, fostering localized supply chains. Botswana provides a stronger example, where procurement policies linked to Debswana support the development of small and medium-sized enterprises (SMEs). In contrast, Guinea's mining sector remains heavily dependent on imported inputs, limiting the growth of domestic supplier industries (World Bank, 2020).

Infrastructure and Community Development

Investment in infrastructure constitutes another important channel of economic contribution. Mining companies often develop transport corridors, energy systems, and port facilities necessary for their operations. In Botswana, such investments have supported broader economic linkages and beneficiation efforts. Conversely, in Guinea and parts of the Copperbelt, infrastructure development is frequently oriented toward facilitating raw material exports rather than enabling diversified economic growth.

Corporate social responsibility (CSR) programs further contribute to community development, including initiatives in education, healthcare, and technical training. While these efforts can enhance human capital and social welfare, their scope and sustainability are often shaped by corporate priorities and project lifecycles (ICMM, 2015).

Universities and Innovation Ecosystems

Universities and research institutions serve as key intermediaries in linking MNC activity with domestic knowledge systems. Institutions such as the University of the Witwatersrand and the University of Botswana offer specialized training in mining engineering, geology, and mineral economics. These programs contribute to the development of skilled labor and support applied research relevant to the mining sector (Cloete, Maassen, & Bailey, 2015).

However, the scope of innovation remains relatively constrained. Research activities tend to focus on incremental improvements in operational efficiency rather than the development of transformative technologies. This reflects both limited funding environments and the dominant influence of MNC-driven technological priorities (Lorentzen, 2005).

The extent to which universities are integrated into broader innovation ecosystems varies across countries. Botswana represents a relatively more advanced case, where collaboration between government, industry, and academia has fostered an emerging innovation cluster linked to the diamond sector (Taylor, 2006). In contrast, universities in the Copperbelt and Guinea remain more peripheral to global knowledge networks, limiting their ability to drive technological upgrading or support industrial diversification (UNCTAD, 2018).

REFERENCES

Acemoglu, D., Johnson, S., & Robinson, J. A. (2003). An African success story: Botswana. In Rodrik, D. (Ed.), *In search of prosperity: Analytic narratives on economic growth* (pp. 80–119). Princeton University Press.

Auty, R. M. (2001). *Resource abundance and economic development*. Oxford University Press.

Cloete, N., Maassen, P., & Bailey, T. (2015). *Knowledge production and contradictory functions in African higher education*. African Minds. DOI: 10.47622/9781920677855

Cohen, W. M., & Levinthal, D. A. (1990). Absorptive capacity: A new perspective on learning and innovation. *Administrative Science Quarterly*, *35*(1), 128–152. DOI: 10.2307/2393553

Farole, T., & Winkler, D. (2014). *Making foreign direct investment work for sub-Saharan Africa: Local spillovers and competitiveness in global value chains*. World Bank.

Gereffi, G., Humphrey, J., & Sturgeon, T. (2005). The governance of global value chains. *Review of International Political Economy*, *12*(1), 78–104. DOI: 10.1080/09692290500049805

Grant, R. M. (1996). Toward a knowledge-based theory of the firm. *Strategic Management Journal*, *17*(S2), 109–122. DOI: 10.1002/smj.4250171110

ICMM (International Council on Mining and Metals). (2015). *The role of mining in national economies* (2nd ed.).

Kaplinsky, R. (2000). Globalisation and unequalisation: What can be learned from value chain analysis? *The Journal of Development Studies*, *37*(2), 117–146. DOI: 10.1080/713600071

Lorentzen, J. (2005). The absorptive capacities of South African automotive component suppliers. *World Development*, *33*(7), 1153–1182. DOI: 10.1016/j.worlddev.2005.04.006

Morris, M., Kaplinsky, R., & Kaplan, D. (2012). "One thing leads to another" – Commodities, linkages and industrial development. *Resources Policy*, *37*(4), 408–416. DOI: 10.1016/j.resourpol.2012.06.008

Taylor, I. (2006). *China and Africa: Engagement and compromise*. Routledge.

UNCTAD. (2007). *World investment report: Transnational corporations, extractive industries and development*. United Nations.

UNCTAD. (2018). *Economic development in Africa report: Migration for structural transformation*. United Nations.

World Bank. (2020). Guinea: Country economic memorandum. World Bank.

Chapter 18
Chinese Companies in Africa's Extractive Industries

ABSTRACT

The expansion of Chinese companies into Africa's extractive industries has significantly reshaped the governance of natural resources across the continent. Since the early 2000s, China has emerged as Africa's largest trading partner and a major investor in strategic sectors including oil, copper, cobalt, and infrastructure. This growing presence is closely associated with the Belt and Road Initiative (BRI), which integrates infrastructure financing with long-term trade and resource access agreements. This chapter examines Chinese corporate engagement through selected cases in the Democratic Republic of the Congo, Angola, and Zambia, with a focus on governance implications, knowledge transfer, and development outcomes.

INTRODUCTION

The expansion of Chinese companies into Africa's extractive industries has significantly reshaped the governance of natural resources across the continent. Since the early 2000s, China has emerged as Africa's largest trading partner and a major investor in strategic sectors including oil, copper, cobalt, and infrastructure (Brautigam, 2009; UNCTAD, 2023). This growing presence is closely associated with the Belt and Road Initiative (BRI), which integrates infrastructure financing with long-term trade and resource access agreements (Hillman, 2018).

This section examines Chinese corporate engagement through selected cases in the Democratic Republic of the Congo, Angola, and Zambia, with a focus on governance implications, knowledge transfer, and development outcomes.

DOI: 10.4018/979-8-3373-7350-8.ch018

HUAYOU COBALT

Huayou Cobalt has established a vertically integrated presence in the Katanga region, encompassing mining, processing, and trading activities. Through its subsidiary Congo Dongfang International Mining, the firm sources cobalt from both industrial and artisanal producers, processes it locally, and exports intermediate products for refining and battery manufacturing in China (Amnesty International, 2016).

The company holds significant interests in assets such as the Luiswishi Mine and the Kolwezi Copper Cobalt Mine, the latter in partnership with the state-owned Gécamines. These operations are integrated into broader transnational supply chains supplying cobalt for lithium-ion batteries.

A central component of Chinese engagement in the DRC is the Sicomines Agreement, established in 2008 between Gécamines and a consortium of Chinese firms including China Railway Group and Sinohydro. Under this arrangement, infrastructure financing—initially valued at approximately $3 billion and later expanded—was exchanged for mining rights.

While such agreements have accelerated infrastructure development, they have also raised concerns regarding transparency, debt sustainability, and governance oversight (Brautigam, 2011; IMF, 2021).

Technologically, Huayou has introduced advanced hydrometallurgical processes, including solvent extraction and electro-winning systems. However, these capabilities are typically embedded within firm-controlled operations, limiting broader knowledge diffusion into the domestic economy (Morris et al., 2012).

CHINA MOLYBDENUM (CMOC)

China Molybdenum controls major assets in the DRC's copper–cobalt belt, including Tenke Fungurume Mine and Kisanfu Mine. These mines are among the largest global producers of cobalt, a critical input for electric vehicle batteries (IEA, 2022).

The Tenke Fungurume operation has received The Copper Mark, reflecting compliance with international sustainability standards. CMOC has invested in process optimization technologies, improved ore recovery systems, and energy infrastructure, including hydroelectric power sourcing, to stabilize production and reduce operational risks.

Despite these advancements, technological knowledge remains largely internalized, with limited spillovers to local firms or institutions. This reflects broader patterns in global value chains, where lead firms retain control over high-value knowledge assets (Gereffi et al., 2005).

WANBAO MINING

Wanbao Mining participates in copper and cobalt processing through investments such as the Feza Mining Smelter. While these operations contribute to regional metallurgical capacity, they remain integrated into externally oriented processing systems.

In Zambia, collaboration between Chinese firms and local universities, such as the University of Zambia and Copperbelt University, remains limited in scale. This weakens the potential for knowledge spillovers and local innovation system development (UNCTAD, 2018).

SINOPEC

Sinopec has expanded its footprint across Africa's oil and gas sector, particularly in Angola, Nigeria, and Gabon. In Angola, Sinopec operates through joint ventures with Sonangol in offshore oil blocks, contributing to deepwater exploration and production (Corkin, 2013).

In Nigeria, Sinopec expanded its presence through the acquisition of Addax Petroleum, gaining access to offshore reserves in the Gulf of Guinea. Similar investments in Gabon reflect a strategy of portfolio diversification across multiple hydrocarbon producers.

However, Sinopec's engagement in local research and development remains limited. Unlike some Western firms, it has not extensively developed partnerships with African universities, instead concentrating R&D activities within China. This model prioritizes resource extraction and infrastructure delivery over local innovation system development (Kaplinsky & Morris, 2016).

CHINA NONFERROUS METAL MINING GROUP

China Nonferrous Metal Mining Group (CNMC) has developed one of the most integrated mining-industrial ecosystems in Africa. In Zambia, its operations include the Chambishi Copper Mine, the Chambishi Smelter, and the Chambishi Multi-Facility Economic Zone.

This vertically integrated model combines extraction, processing, and manufacturing, contributing to local industrial capacity and infrastructure development. Similarly, in the DRC, CNMC's involvement in projects such as Deziwa Project integrates mining with hydrometallurgical processing.

These investments support industrialization but also reinforce China's strategic control over critical mineral supply chains, particularly for battery and renewable energy technologies (IEA, 2022).

ZIJIN MINING

Zijin Mining has evolved into a major global mining company through acquisitions and technological innovation. Its African portfolio includes assets such as the Kolwezi Copper Mine, the Bisha Mine, and the Akyem Gold Mine.

The company has also entered the lithium sector through the Manono Lithium Project, reflecting the growing importance of critical minerals in the global energy transition. These investments illustrate how Chinese firms are increasingly embedded across multiple stages of global mineral value chains.

While such expansion contributes to production capacity and export revenues, it also raises questions regarding governance, environmental standards, and the extent of local economic integration (UNCTAD, 2023).

Governance Implications and Development Outcomes

Chinese engagement in Africa's extractive industries presents a complex mix of opportunities and challenges. On one hand, investments have accelerated infrastructure development, expanded production capacity, and integrated African economies into global supply chains. On the other hand, concerns persist regarding transparency, debt dependency, environmental management, and limited knowledge transfer.

The predominance of resource-for-infrastructure agreements and vertically integrated supply chains suggests that Chinese firms, like other MNCs, prioritize control over high-value activities. As a result, local economies often remain concentrated in lower value-added segments, with limited progression toward innovation-driven industrialization (Kaplinsky & Morris, 2016; Morris et al., 2012).

REFERENCES

Amnesty International. (2016). *This is what we die for: Human rights abuses in the Democratic Republic of the Congo power the global trade in cobalt.*

Brautigam, D. (2009). *The dragon's gift: The real story of China in Africa.* Oxford University Press.

Brautigam, D. (2011). Aid 'with Chinese characteristics': Chinese foreign aid and development finance meet the OECD-DAC aid regime. *Journal of International Development, 23*(5), 752–764. DOI: 10.1002/jid.1798

Corkin, L. (2013). *Uncovering African agency: Angola's management of China's credit lines.* Ashgate.

Farole, T., & Winkler, D. (2014). *Making foreign direct investment work for sub-Saharan Africa.* World Bank.

Gereffi, G., Humphrey, J., & Sturgeon, T. (2005). The governance of global value chains. *Review of International Political Economy, 12*(1), 78–104. DOI: 10.1080/09692290500049805

Hillman, J. E. (2018). *China's Belt and Road Initiative: Five years later.* Center for Strategic and International Studies.

IEA. (2022). *The role of critical minerals in clean energy transitions.* International Energy Agency.

IMF. (2021). *Democratic Republic of the Congo: Staff report.*

Kaplinsky, R., & Morris, M. (2016). Thinning and thickening: Productive sector policies in the era of global value chains. *European Journal of Development Research, 28*(4), 625–645. DOI: 10.1057/ejdr.2015.29

Morris, M., Kaplinsky, R., & Kaplan, D. (2012). Commodities and linkages in Africa. *Resources Policy, 37*(4), 408–416. DOI: 10.1016/j.resourpol.2012.06.008

UNCTAD. (2023). *World investment report 2023.* United Nations.

Chapter 19
Indian and Japanese Companies in Africa's Extractive Industries

ABSTRACT

The engagement of Indian and Japanese firms in Africa's extractive industries reflects distinct strategic approaches compared to Western and Chinese multinational corporations. While Indian firms tend to pursue asset ownership and operational control such as Vedanta Resources and Tata Steel, Japanese corporations, Mitsubishi Corporation, Marubeni Corporation, often adopt partnership-based models that prioritize supply security while minimizing direct operational exposure. These differing strategies shape patterns of investment, knowledge transfer, and integration into local economies.

INTRODUCTION

The engagement of Indian and Japanese firms in Africa's extractive industries reflects distinct strategic approaches compared to Western and Chinese multinational corporations. While Indian firms tend to pursue asset ownership and operational control, Japanese corporations often adopt partnership-based models that prioritize supply security while minimizing direct operational exposure (UNCTAD, 2023; Japan Oil, Gas and Metals National Corporation, 2020). These differing strategies shape patterns of investment, knowledge transfer, and integration into local economies.

DOI: 10.4018/979-8-3373-7350-8.ch019

INDIAN COMPANIES

Vedanta Resources

Vedanta Resources plays a significant role in Zambia's copper sector through its majority ownership of Konkola Copper Mines (KCM). Following a protracted dispute with the Zambian government, Vedanta regained control of KCM in 2023, holding approximately 79–80% of the operation, with the state-owned ZCCM Investments Holdings retaining a minority stake.

A key asset within KCM is the Nchanga Mine, one of the largest integrated copper and cobalt mining operations in Africa. The mine combines open-pit and underground extraction methods, utilizing mechanized drilling systems, electric shovels, and high-capacity haulage equipment. These technologies require a technically skilled workforce and advanced maintenance systems, contributing to localized skills development (ICMM, 2015).

KCM has also upgraded its metallurgical infrastructure, including concentrators, flash smelters, and tailings leach facilities, incorporating advanced processing technologies to improve recovery rates and efficiency. More recently, the company has moved toward "smart mining" systems, including sensor-based ore sorting, artificial intelligence (AI)-driven optimization, real-time monitoring through Internet of Things (IoT) systems, and the use of drone and satellite-based geospatial analysis.

Academic and Research Linkages

A notable feature of Vedanta's operations is its interaction with local academic and research institutions. The Copperbelt University (CBU), particularly its School of Mines and Mineral Sciences, serves as a key provider of technical skills and applied research.

CBU hosts the Africa Centre of Excellence for Sustainable Mining, a World Bank-supported initiative focusing on mining-related challenges such as environmental management, occupational health, energy efficiency, and post-mining land restoration (World Bank, 2020). These programs contribute to building absorptive capacity and supporting incremental innovation within the mining sector.

Collaborative initiatives further strengthen these linkages. For example, partnerships involving the University of Zambia and CBU have supported applied training in mineral exploration, while international collaborations—such as the Mine Water Atlas of the Zambian Copperbelt—integrate geospatial analysis and environmental monitoring (BGS, 2018).

Vedanta itself is increasingly investing in digital transformation, including AI-driven exploration tools and predictive maintenance systems. Its establishment of

CopperTech Metals Inc. reflects a strategy aimed at mobilizing capital for technological upgrading and modernization. Despite these advancements, high-level research and proprietary innovation largely remain concentrated outside Africa, limiting deeper technological spillovers (Morris et al., 2012).

Tata Steel (Africa Operations)

Tata Steel has a more limited but regionally significant presence in Africa, particularly in South Africa. Its activities focus on iron ore supply chains and logistics, including linkages between mining operations and export infrastructure.

Compared to Vedanta, Tata Steel's role in upstream mining is less dominant, with a stronger emphasis on integration into global steel production networks. This reflects a strategy centered on securing raw material inputs rather than developing extensive local extraction ecosystems (UNCTAD, 2023).

JAPANESE COMPANIES

Mitsubishi Corporation

Mitsubishi Corporation represents a typical Japanese approach to resource investment in Africa. Rather than direct operational control, Mitsubishi emphasizes joint ventures, minority equity stakes, and long-term partnerships with both governments and private firms.

This model reduces operational risk while ensuring stable access to strategic resources. It also reflects broader Japanese industrial policy, which prioritizes supply chain security for manufacturing sectors such as automotive and electronics (Japan Oil, Gas and Metals National Corporation, 2020).

Marubeni Corporation

Similarly, Marubeni Corporation participates in African mining projects through partnerships and consortium arrangements. Its investments are concentrated in base metals and industrial minerals critical for global manufacturing and energy transition technologies.

Marubeni's strategy focuses on ensuring reliable supply chains rather than direct extraction. As a result, its involvement in local production systems is often indirect, with limited engagement in domestic value addition or technological development.

COMPARATIVE INSIGHTS: INDIAN VS JAPANESE APPROACHES

The contrasting strategies of Indian and Japanese firms highlight different models of engagement in Africa's extractive industries:

Indian firms (e.g., Vedanta) emphasize ownership and operational control, leading to deeper involvement in extraction and processing activities. This can generate stronger local employment and infrastructure linkages but does not necessarily translate into high-level knowledge transfer.

Japanese firms (e.g., Mitsubishi, Marubeni) prioritize partnership-based investment and supply security, resulting in lower operational risk but also weaker direct contributions to local industrial development.

In both cases, knowledge transfer remains selective and often limited to operational or incremental improvements. Advanced technological capabilities and strategic decision-making functions continue to be retained at the corporate level, reinforcing existing asymmetries in global value chains (Gereffi et al., 2005; Kaplinsky & Morris, 2016).

REFERENCES

British Geological Survey (BGS). (2018). *Mine water and environmental monitoring in the Zambian Copperbelt.*

Gereffi, G., Humphrey, J., & Sturgeon, T. (2005). The governance of global value chains. *Review of International Political Economy, 12*(1), 78–104. DOI: 10.1080/09692290500049805

ICMM (International Council on Mining and Metals). (2015). *The role of mining in national economies.*

Kaplinsky, R., & Morris, M. (2016). Thinning and thickening: Productive sector policies in the era of global value chains. *European Journal of Development Research, 28*(4), 625–645. DOI: 10.1057/ejdr.2015.29

Morris, M., Kaplinsky, R., & Kaplan, D. (2012). Commodities and linkages in Africa. *Resources Policy, 37*(4), 408–416. DOI: 10.1016/j.resourpol.2012.06.008

Japan Oil, Gas and Metals National Corporation. (2020). *Japan's resource strategy and overseas investments.*

UNCTAD. (2023). *World investment report 2023.* United Nations.

World Bank. (2020). *Africa Centres of Excellence project report.*

Chapter 20
European Companies in Africa's Extractive Industries

ABSTRACT

European multinational corporations (MNCs) have maintained a long-standing presence in Africa's extractive sectors, reflecting historical ties rooted in colonial-era resource exploitation as well as continued economic engagement in global energy and mineral markets. Firms from countries such as the United Kingdom, France, Germany, and Netherlands play dominant roles in oil, gas, mining, and energy infrastructure across key resource-producing countries including Nigeria, Angola, and the Democratic Republic of the Congo. European engagement offers an important analytical contrast to American and Chinese investment models, particularly in terms of governance structures, regulatory compliance, and environmental and social standards. While European firms often emphasize corporate governance and sustainability frameworks, their operations continue to reflect global value chain asymmetries in which high-value functions remain externally controlled.

INTRODUCTION

European multinational corporations (MNCs) have maintained a long-standing presence in Africa's extractive sectors, reflecting historical ties rooted in colonial-era resource exploitation as well as continued economic engagement in global energy and mineral markets. Firms from countries such as the United Kingdom, France, Germany, and Netherlands play dominant roles in oil, gas, mining, and energy

DOI: 10.4018/979-8-3373-7350-8.ch020

infrastructure across key resource-producing countries including Nigeria, Angola, and the Democratic Republic of the Congo.

European engagement offers an important analytical contrast to American and Chinese investment models, particularly in terms of governance structures, regulatory compliance, and environmental and social standards. While European firms often emphasize corporate governance and sustainability frameworks, their operations continue to reflect global value chain asymmetries in which high-value functions remain externally controlled (Gereffi et al., 2005; UNCTAD, 2023).

SHELL PLC

Shell plc has a long-established presence in Africa, particularly in Nigeria, where it operates through joint ventures with the Nigerian National Petroleum Company Limited. Its activities span upstream exploration, oil production, refining, and gas commercialization, especially in the Niger Delta region (Watts, 2004).

Shell's operations have contributed significantly to government revenues and export earnings. However, they have also been associated with environmental degradation, oil spills, and community conflict, highlighting the governance challenges associated with resource extraction in weak institutional contexts (Watts, 2004; Ross, 2012).

TOTAL ENERGIES

TotalEnergies maintains extensive operations across West and Central Africa, including in Nigeria, Angola, Gabon, and the Republic of the Congo. Its portfolio spans upstream oil and gas production, liquefied natural gas (LNG) infrastructure, and renewable energy projects.

The company has increasingly diversified into solar and gas-to-power initiatives, reflecting a broader strategy aligned with the global energy transition. Through partnerships with national oil companies and governments, TotalEnergies contributes to infrastructure development that links resource extraction with domestic energy systems (IEA, 2022). Nevertheless, core technological and strategic capabilities remain centralized within the firm's global operations.

BP PLC

BP plc operates major upstream projects in Angola, Egypt, Algeria, and Libya. Its strategy focuses on oil and gas exploration, deepwater drilling, and gas commercialization, often through joint ventures with national oil companies.

BP has also invested in natural gas value chains and emerging renewable energy projects, reflecting a dual strategy of maximizing hydrocarbon revenues while positioning for long-term energy transition pathways (IEA, 2022). Its gas monetization projects play a role in linking resource extraction to industrial development and electricity generation in host economies.

UMICORE

Umicore represents a different segment of the value chain, focusing on advanced materials, battery technologies, and recycling. The company sources cobalt, nickel, and other critical minerals from African producers, particularly in the Democratic Republic of the Congo, which accounts for a majority of global cobalt production (IEA, 2022).

Umicore emphasizes responsible sourcing and traceability, participating in initiatives such as the RelSource blockchain platform, which tracks cobalt from mine to end-use markets. This reflects increasing global pressure to ensure environmental, social, and governance (ESG) compliance in mineral supply chains (UNCTAD, 2023).

Despite these initiatives, much of the high-value processing—such as refining germanium and battery-grade materials—takes place in Belgium and other industrialized economies. This reinforces the structural separation between African extraction and global high-value manufacturing.

SOCIÉTÉ DE TRAITEMENT DE LUBUMBASHI

Société de Traitement de Lubumbashi (STL) plays a key midstream role in the DRC's copper–cobalt sector. Based in Lubumbashi, STL processes concentrates from industrial and artisanal sources using hydrometallurgical techniques such as leaching and precipitation.

By producing intermediate products such as cobalt hydroxide and copper cathodes, STL contributes to domestic beneficiation and partially offsets the export of raw materials. However, final-stage refining and manufacturing remain largely external, limiting full value capture within the domestic economy (Morris et al., 2012).

AMIRA GLOBAL

Amira Global represents a collaborative model of research and innovation in the mining sector. Through partnerships with companies, universities, and governments, it facilitates knowledge sharing, technological development, and skills training across multiple regions, including Africa.

Such initiatives contribute to capacity building and incremental innovation, although their impact depends on the extent to which local institutions are integrated into global research networks (Cloete et al., 2015).

GLENCORE

Glencore is one of the most prominent European mining firms operating in Africa, particularly in the DRC and South Africa. Its operations include large copper and cobalt assets such as the Kamoto Copper Company.

Glencore has introduced digital technologies—including artificial intelligence, automation systems, and advanced mineral processing techniques—to improve operational efficiency and recovery rates. Its internal R&D arm, Glencore Technology, develops proprietary metallurgical processes used globally.

In addition to production activities, Glencore engages in skills development through training programs, apprenticeships, and educational initiatives, including projects promoting digital and technical skills in local communities. The company has also begun integrating renewable energy solutions into its operations, reflecting growing environmental pressures and sustainability commitments.

GOVERNANCE AND DEVELOPMENT IMPLICATIONS

European companies contribute significantly to African economies through investment, employment, infrastructure, and fiscal revenues. Their operations are often embedded within more formalized regulatory and ESG frameworks compared to other actors. However, this does not fundamentally alter the structural dynamics of global value chains.

High-value activities—including advanced R&D, financial control, and global marketing—remain concentrated in corporate headquarters located outside Africa. As a result, African economies continue to participate primarily in lower value-added stages of production, limiting opportunities for technological upgrading and industrial diversification (Gereffi et al., 2005; Kaplinsky & Morris, 2016).

At the same time, European firms' emphasis on sustainability, transparency, and governance standards may contribute to improved regulatory practices and environmental management, particularly in countries with stronger institutional capacity (UNCTAD, 2023).

REFERENCES

Cloete, N., Maassen, P., & Bailey, T. (2015). *Knowledge production and higher education in Africa*. African Minds.

Gereffi, G., Humphrey, J., & Sturgeon, T. (2005). The governance of global value chains. *Review of International Political Economy*, *12*(1), 78–104. DOI: 10.1080/09692290500049805

IEA. (2022). *The role of critical minerals in clean energy transitions*. International Energy Agency.

Kaplinsky, R., & Morris, M. (2016). Thinning and thickening: Productive sector policies in the era of global value chains. *European Journal of Development Research*, *28*(4), 625–645. DOI: 10.1057/ejdr.2015.29

Morris, M., Kaplinsky, R., & Kaplan, D. (2012). Commodities and linkages in Africa. *Resources Policy*, *37*(4), 408–416. DOI: 10.1016/j.resourpol.2012.06.008

Ross, M. L. (2012). *The oil curse: How petroleum wealth shapes the development of nations*. Princeton University Press. DOI: 10.1515/9781400841929

UNCTAD. (2023). *World investment report 2023*. United Nations.

Watts, M. (2004). Resource curse? Governmentality, oil and power in the Niger Delta. *Geopolitics*, *9*(1), 50–80. DOI: 10.1080/14650040412331307832

Chapter 21
North American Companies in Africa's Extractive Industries

ABSTRACT

North American multinational corporations (MNCs) have played a central role in Africa's extractive industries since the mid-twentieth century, particularly in oil, gas, and mining. Their investments have significantly influenced patterns of economic development, state revenue generation, and resource governance across the continent. In countries such as Nigeria and Angola, major U.S. firms including ExxonMobil, Chevron Corporation, and ConocoPhillips have long been involved in offshore oil production. Similarly, Kosmos Energy played a key role in offshore oil discoveries in Ghana. Compared to other global actors, North American firms often combine large-scale capital investment with advanced technological capabilities and structured training programs. However, as with other MNCs, high-value knowledge and strategic decision-making functions remain largely externalized, limiting deeper industrial transformation in host economies.

INTRODUCTION

North American multinational corporations (MNCs) have played a central role in Africa's extractive industries since the mid-twentieth century, particularly in oil, gas, and mining. Their investments have significantly influenced patterns of economic development, state revenue generation, and resource governance across the continent. In countries such as Nigeria and Angola, major U.S. firms including ExxonMobil, Chevron Corporation, and ConocoPhillips have long been involved

DOI: 10.4018/979-8-3373-7350-8.ch021

in offshore oil production. Similarly, Kosmos Energy played a key role in offshore oil discoveries in Ghana (Ross, 2012; UNCTAD, 2023).

Compared to other global actors, North American firms often combine large-scale capital investment with advanced technological capabilities and structured training programs. However, as with other MNCs, high-value knowledge and strategic decision-making functions remain largely externalized, limiting deeper industrial transformation in host economies (Gereffi et al., 2005).

IVANHOE MINES

Ivanhoe Mines has established a major presence in Africa through large-scale projects in the Democratic Republic of the Congo and South Africa. Its flagship project, the Kamoa-Kakula Copper Complex, is one of the world's highest-grade copper developments and operates through a joint venture involving Zijin Mining and the Congolese state.

A notable feature of Ivanhoe's operations is its emphasis on workforce development and local capacity building. The Kansoko Training Centre provides practical training in mining operations, metallurgical processing, and safety systems. In 2024 alone, thousands of trainees participated in programs combining classroom instruction with hands-on technical experience.

The planned Kamoa Centre of Excellence further extends this approach by offering accredited programs in engineering, geosciences, and mining management. These initiatives contribute to strengthening local human capital and enhancing absorptive capacity, although advanced technological knowledge remains embedded within corporate systems (Cohen & Levinthal, 1990).

Technologically, Kamoa-Kakula incorporates advanced underground mining systems, modern concentrators, and a direct-to-blister smelter designed to improve efficiency and reduce emissions. Approximately 85% of the workforce is locally sourced, with structured pathways for advancement into supervisory and managerial roles.

Beyond copper, Ivanhoe is developing the Platreef Project in South Africa's Bushveld Complex and the Kipushi Mine, which includes a modern concentrator facility using advanced processing technologies. Exploration activities such as the Western Forelands project further illustrate the company's long-term investment strategy in African mineral resources.

BARRICK GOLD

Barrick Gold is one of the largest gold producers globally, with extensive operations across Africa, including in Tanzania, Mali, and the Democratic Republic of the Congo.

Its flagship African asset, the Kibali Gold Mine, operates as a joint venture with AngloGold Ashanti and the state-owned SOKIMO. Kibali integrates renewable energy solutions, including a solar power plant with battery storage, reducing reliance on diesel and improving environmental sustainability (IEA, 2022).

In Tanzania, operations such as the Bulyanhulu Gold Mine and North Mara Gold Mine incorporate advanced mineral analysis technologies such as PhotonAssay, which enhances efficiency and reduces environmental impact.

Barrick also operates the Loulo-Gounkoto Complex, a major contributor to national export revenues. The company has introduced innovations such as cyanide recovery systems and biodiversity assessment tools to improve environmental performance.

The Barrick Academy further supports workforce development by providing training in leadership, safety, and technical skills. While such programs enhance local capacity, they primarily support operational efficiency rather than independent innovation systems (UNCTAD, 2007).

FIRST QUANTUM MINERALS

First Quantum Minerals is a major copper producer with significant operations in Zambia. Key assets include the Kansanshi Mine and the Sentinel Mine, both large-scale open-pit operations with extensive processing facilities.

These projects have expanded Zambia's copper production capacity and contributed to export revenues, infrastructure development, and employment. However, as with other MNC-led projects, downstream processing and high-value activities remain limited (Morris et al., 2012).

Additional Canadian firms, including Allied Gold and IAMGOLD, have contributed to the expansion of gold mining in West Africa. Projects such as the Sadiola Gold Mine and Essakane Gold Mine generate government revenues, employment, and infrastructure development.

At the same time, corporate restructuring and asset divestment strategies highlight the volatility of foreign investment and its dependence on global commodity cycles.

NEWMONT CORPORATION

Newmont Corporation is a major actor in Ghana's gold sector. Its flagship Ahafo Mine represents a large-scale open-pit operation contributing significantly to national export revenues.

The company previously operated the Akyem Mine, illustrating the role of U.S. firms in developing Ghana's modern gold industry. These investments have supported economic growth but also reflect broader patterns of external control over high-value activities (Ross, 2012).

ALLIED GOLD CORPORATION

Allied Gold Corporation is an emerging Canadian gold producer headquartered in Toronto, with a growing operational footprint in West Africa. The region has become a major center of global gold production, attracting international mining firms due to its favorable geology, relatively underexplored deposits, and improving regulatory frameworks (Hilson, 2019; World Bank, 2020).

The company's activities are concentrated in Mali and Côte d'Ivoire, where it operates both producing mines and development-stage projects. One of its most significant assets is the Sadiola Gold Mine, a historically important gold operation in western Mali. Originally developed by other multinational firms, the mine was later acquired and redeveloped by Allied Gold as part of a broader strategy to revitalize mature assets.

Allied Gold has implemented modernization and expansion programs at Sadiola aimed at extending the mine's operational lifespan and increasing production capacity. These efforts include upgrading processing facilities, improving recovery rates, and optimizing extraction techniques. In addition, the company is advancing nearby exploration projects such as the Korali-Sud Project, which forms part of a wider strategy to expand the resource base within the Sadiola mining district.

In Côte d'Ivoire, Allied Gold is pursuing exploration and development initiatives designed to establish new production hubs. The country has emerged as one of the most attractive destinations for mining investment in West Africa, supported by relative political stability, improved mining legislation, and increasing geological exploration activity (UNCTAD, 2023).

IAMGOLD CORPORATION

IAMGOLD Corporation has played a significant role in the development of the gold mining sector in West Africa. Headquartered in Toronto, the company has historically maintained a diversified portfolio of producing assets and exploration projects across the region.

Its principal African operation is the Essakane Gold Mine, located in northeastern Burkina Faso. Developed as a large-scale open-pit mine, Essakane began commercial production in 2010 and has since become one of the country's most important gold producers. The project operates under a joint ownership structure that includes a minority equity stake held by the Burkinabè government, reflecting a common model of state participation in mining ventures across Africa (ICMM, 2015).

The Essakane mine has contributed significantly to the national economy through tax revenues, royalties, and dividends, while also generating employment and supporting infrastructure development in a remote Sahelian region. These contributions illustrate the role of large-scale mining projects in regional economic development, particularly in resource-dependent economies (Ross, 2012).

Beyond Burkina Faso, IAMGOLD previously held a range of exploration and development assets across West Africa. Among the most notable was the Boto Gold Project in southeastern Senegal, located along the Senegal–Mali shear zone, a geologically significant gold-bearing corridor. The company also maintained interests in projects such as the Diakha-Siribaya Project and the Karita Project.

However, as part of a broader corporate restructuring strategy in the early 2020s, IAMGOLD divested several of its West African assets. This strategic shift was aimed at concentrating financial and operational resources on core producing assets and large-scale development projects, particularly in North America. Such restructuring highlights the volatility of foreign investment in extractive industries and its sensitivity to global market conditions and corporate priorities (Morris et al., 2012).

RESEARCH, INNOVATION, AND INSTITUTIONAL LINKAGES

North American firms are often associated with structured training programs, research collaborations, and technological innovation. In South Africa, collaboration between mining companies and institutions such as the University of the Witwatersrand and Mintek supports research in metallurgy, digital mining, and environmental management (Cloete et al., 2015).

These partnerships contribute to incremental innovation and skills development. However, they rarely result in the full localization of advanced research and development, as core innovation activities remain concentrated in corporate headquarters and global research centers.

GOVERNANCE AND DEVELOPMENT IMPLICATIONS

North American MNCs contribute significantly to African economies through investment, employment, infrastructure development, and fiscal revenues. Their operations are often associated with higher technological sophistication and structured governance frameworks.

However, similar to other global actors, these firms retain control over high-value segments of the value chain, including advanced R&D, financial management, and global marketing. As a result, African economies continue to participate primarily in lower value-added activities, limiting opportunities for industrial upgrading and economic diversification (Gereffi et al., 2005; Kaplinsky & Morris, 2016).

At the same time, initiatives in training, renewable energy integration, and environmental management suggest that North American firms may play a role in supporting more sustainable and technologically advanced extractive sectors, particularly where host country institutions are strong.

REFERENCES

Cloete, N., Maassen, P., & Bailey, T. (2015). *Knowledge production and higher education in Africa.* African Minds.

Cohen, W. M., & Levinthal, D. A. (1990). Absorptive capacity: A new perspective on learning and innovation. *Administrative Science Quarterly, 35*(1), 128–152. DOI: 10.2307/2393553

Gereffi, G., Humphrey, J., & Sturgeon, T. (2005). The governance of global value chains. *Review of International Political Economy, 12*(1), 78–104. DOI: 10.1080/09692290500049805

Hilson, G. (2019). Why is there a large-scale mining "bias" in sub-Saharan Africa? *Land Use Policy, 81*, 352–362. DOI: 10.1016/j.landusepol.2017.02.013

ICMM (International Council on Mining and Metals). (2015). *The role of mining in national economies.*

IEA. (2022). *The role of critical minerals in clean energy transitions.* International Energy Agency.

Kaplinsky, R., & Morris, M. (2016). Thinning and thickening: Productive sector policies in the era of global value chains. *European Journal of Development Research, 28*(4), 625–645. DOI: 10.1057/ejdr.2015.29

Morris, M., Kaplinsky, R., & Kaplan, D. (2012). Commodities and linkages in Africa. *Resources Policy, 37*(4), 408–416. DOI: 10.1016/j.resourpol.2012.06.008

Ross, M. L. (2012). *The oil curse: How petroleum wealth shapes the development of nations.* Princeton University Press. DOI: 10.1515/9781400841929

UNCTAD. (2007). *World investment report.* United Nations.

UNCTAD. (2023). *World investment report 2023.* United Nations.

World Bank. (2020). *Mining sector development in West Africa.* World Bank.

Chapter 22
Brazilian in Africa's Extractive and Energy Sectors

ABSTRACT

Brazil's engagement in Africa's extractive and energy sectors has been characterized by an emphasis on technical cooperation, long-term partnerships, and integrated value chains. Brazilian companies in Africa illustrate a hybrid model of engagement characterized by Integration of extraction with infrastructure development (e.g., Vale); transfer of specialized technical expertise in offshore energy (e.g., Petrobras, Forship); expansion into renewable energy and agro-industrial systems (e.g., Raízen, Cosan). This approach contrasts with Western shareholder-driven extractive models and Chinese state-backed infrastructure-for-resources strategies, reflecting a broader South–South cooperation framework.

INTRODUCTION

Brazil's engagement in Africa's extractive and energy sectors has been characterized by an emphasis on technical cooperation, long-term partnerships, and integrated value chains. This approach contrasts with Western shareholder-driven extractive models and Chinese state-backed infrastructure-for-resources strategies, reflecting a broader South–South cooperation framework (Alden & Alves, 2009; UNCTAD, 2013).

DOI: 10.4018/979-8-3373-7350-8.ch022

VALE S.A.

Vale S.A., headquartered in Rio de Janeiro, expanded into Africa during the early 2000s as part of a strategy to diversify its global resource base and access new mining frontiers. Its most significant investment was the Moatize Coal Mine, located in Tete Province, Mozambique, which the company acquired in 2004.

The Moatize project focused on the extraction of high-grade metallurgical coal used in global steel production. To support the operation, Vale undertook extensive infrastructure investments, including the rehabilitation of the Sena Railway and the development of export capacity at the Port of Nacala. These projects formed part of the broader Nacala Logistics Corridor, designed to link inland mining operations to international shipping routes.

This integrated infrastructure-mining model reflects a more holistic approach to resource development, combining extraction with transport and logistics systems. However, in 2021, Vale divested its Moatize operations and associated logistics assets to Vulcan International as part of a strategic shift away from coal and toward core commodities such as iron ore and energy transition minerals. This move aligns with broader global trends toward decarbonization and sustainability in the mining sector (IEA, 2022).

PETROBRAS

Petrobras, established in 1953, developed into one of the world's leading firms in deep-water oil exploration. The company expanded into several African energy-producing countries, including Angola, Nigeria, Tanzania, and Namibia.

In Angola, Petrobras participated in offshore exploration projects in partnership with Sonangol. The geological similarities between Angola's offshore basins—particularly the Lower Congo Basin—and Brazil's Santos Basin enhanced the relevance of Petrobras' technical expertise. In Nigeria, the company also held stakes in offshore oil blocks and collaborated with both local and international partners.

In East Africa, Petrobras engaged in offshore exploration in Tanzania, particularly in the Rovuma Basin, where major natural gas discoveries attracted global investment. The company also explored opportunities along the Atlantic margin of Namibia.

However, following financial pressures linked to declining oil prices and domestic political challenges, Petrobras adopted a strategy of asset divestment and refocused on its core offshore assets in Brazil, particularly pre-salt reserves. Consequently, the company reduced its direct operational presence in Africa (Alden & Alves, 2009).

FORSHIP ENGENHARIA

Forship Engenharia is a Brazilian engineering and maritime services firm that has supported offshore oil and gas operations in African markets, particularly in Angola and Nigeria.

Operating within the Gulf of Guinea, the company provides technical services for offshore exploration and production. Brazilian firms such as Forship have leveraged their expertise in deep-water environments—developed in Brazil's offshore basins—to support energy operations in geologically comparable African regions. This reflects a form of South–South technological transfer, although such contributions are typically confined to service provision rather than long-term industrial development.

BIOENERGY AND AGRO-INDUSTRIAL ACTORS

Brazilian involvement in Africa extends beyond extractive industries into renewable energy and agro-industrial systems, particularly biofuels.

Raízen, a joint venture between Cosan S.A. and Shell plc, is the world's largest producer of sugarcane ethanol. Its expertise in large-scale ethanol production and bioenergy infrastructure provides a model for renewable energy development in African economies.

Cosan S.A. plays a central role in Brazil's sugar and ethanol industries, supplying feedstock and supporting integrated energy production systems.

UNICA represents the collective interests of Brazil's sugar and ethanol producers and has been actively involved in technical cooperation and knowledge-sharing initiatives with developing countries.

These actors highlight the potential for transferring bioenergy technologies and production models to African contexts, particularly in countries seeking to diversify their energy mix and promote sustainable development (World Bank, 2020).

ANALYTICAL PERSPECTIVE

Brazilian companies in Africa illustrate a hybrid model of engagement characterized by:

Integration of extraction with infrastructure development (e.g., Vale)

Transfer of specialized technical expertise in offshore energy (e.g., Petrobras, Forship)

Expansion into renewable energy and agro-industrial systems (e.g., Raízen, Cosan)

While this approach differs from both Western and Chinese models, it remains subject to similar structural constraints. High-value activities—such as advanced research, financial control, and global marketing—are largely retained outside host economies. Moreover, the withdrawal of firms such as Vale and Petrobras from African assets underscores the vulnerability of such partnerships to global market dynamics and domestic corporate priorities (Gereffi et al., 2005; UNCTAD, 2013).

REFERENCES

Alden, C., & Alves, A. C. (2009). China and Brazil in Africa: Emerging partners or competitors? *The Journal of Modern African Studies*, *47*(4), 563–586.

Gereffi, G., Humphrey, J., & Sturgeon, T. (2005). The governance of global value chains. *Review of International Political Economy*, *12*(1), 78–104. DOI: 10.1080/09692290500049805

IEA. (2022). *The role of critical minerals in clean energy transitions*. International Energy Agency.

UNCTAD. (2013). *Economic development in Africa report*. United Nations.

World Bank. (2020). *Africa mining vision and development frameworks*. World Bank.

Chapter 23
African Companies in Mining and Energy Sectors

ABSTRACT

African-owned and state-affiliated companies play a crucial role in shaping the continent's extractive industries, combining local knowledge with strategic resource management. Firms such as Seplat Petroleum, headquartered in Lagos, Nigeria; Debswana in Botswana; Sibanye Stillwater, headquartered in Johannesburg, South Africa; Gécamines, headquartered in Lubumbashi, Democratic Republic of Congo (DRC), operate across diverse sectors, from hydrocarbons to precious metals (platinum, palladium, and rhodium), which are critical for automotive catalytic converters, and diamonds, reflecting a range of corporate models and governance approaches.

INTRODUCTION

African-owned and state-affiliated companies play a crucial role in shaping the continent's extractive industries, combining local knowledge with strategic resource management. These firms operate across diverse sectors, from hydrocarbons to precious metals and diamonds, reflecting a range of corporate models and governance approaches.

SEPLAT PETROLEUM

Seplat Petroleum, headquartered in Lagos, was founded in 2009 and has grown into one of Nigeria's largest indigenous energy producers. Its core operations are

DOI: 10.4018/979-8-3373-7350-8.ch023

concentrated in the onshore Niger Delta, one of Africa's most significant hydrocarbon basins. Seplat holds interests in multiple oil mining leases and operates several fields through joint ventures with the state-owned Nigerian National Petroleum Company Limited.

A central aspect of Seplat's strategy is natural gas development to support domestic energy supply. The company operates the Oben Gas Plant, one of the largest gas processing facilities in Nigeria, supplying the national grid for electricity generation and industrial use. Seplat further expanded its footprint by acquiring shallow-water onshore assets from ExxonMobil through Mobil Producing Nigeria Unlimited, increasing offshore production capacity and solidifying its position as a leading local energy company (Obi, 2010).

DEBSWANA

Debswana operates several large-scale diamond mines, including the Jwaneng Mine, Orapa Mine, and Letlhakane Mine. Jwaneng is widely regarded as the world's richest diamond mine by value, producing high-quality diamonds for global markets.

Botswana has strategically promoted downstream beneficiation to increase local value capture. Notable initiatives include relocating diamond sorting and trading operations from London to Gaborone and developing local cutting and polishing industries. This approach integrates resource extraction with domestic industrial and skills development, illustrating a state-led, long-term strategy for value addition (Hilson, 2006).

SIBANYE STILLWATER

Sibanye Stillwater, headquartered in Johannesburg, is one of the world's largest producers of platinum group metals (PGMs), as well as gold and associated minerals. Formed through the 2017 merger of Sibanye Gold and Stillwater Mining Company, its operations are concentrated in South Africa, exploiting both deep-level gold reefs and shallow-to-medium PGM deposits.

Key assets include the Kloof and Driefontein gold mines and the Rustenburg PGM operations. These mines supply global markets with platinum, palladium, and rhodium, which are critical for automotive catalytic converters, jewelry, and industrial applications. Sibanye Stillwater emphasizes operational efficiency, safety, and sustainability, while investing in local skills development, employment, and community initiatives (Sibanye Stillwater, 2023).

GÉCAMINES

Gécamines, formally La Générale des Carrières et des Mines, was established in 1966 after the nationalization of colonial mining assets in the Democratic Republic of the Congo. Headquartered in Lubumbashi, the company manages, explores, and produces copper and cobalt in the mineral-rich Katanga (now Haut-Katanga) province.

Historically, Gécamines operated large-scale facilities such as the Kamoto Copper Company and the Luilu Metallurgical Plant. Since the 2000s, it has entered joint ventures with international companies, including Glencore and Huayou Cobalt, to modernize operations and increase output of metals critical to global industrial and energy transition markets. This model illustrates a state-led approach to resource management that combines sovereignty over resources with selective international collaboration (Humphreys, 2010).

REFERENCES

Hilson, G. (2006). Sustainable development in the African mining sector: Experiences and prospects. *Journal of Cleaner Production*, *14*(3–4), 305–314.

Humphreys, D. (2010). Extractive industries and poverty: A review of recent findings and linkages. *The Journal of Development Studies*, *46*(4), 517–538.

Obi, C. (2010). The changing face of energy governance in Nigeria: Seplat and the Nigerian energy transition. *African Affairs*, *109*(436), 407–426.

Sibanye Stillwater. (2023). *Sustainability and corporate responsibility report*. Sibanye Stillwater Ltd.

Chapter 24
Australian Companies in Africa

ABSTRACT

Firms such as Resolute Mining and Perseus Mining have developed large-scale gold operations in West Africa, while companies like Syrah Resources and AVZ Minerals are actively involved in graphite and lithium projects that are critical to global energy transitions. These investments are not limited to extraction; rather, they are embedded within a broader ecosystem of Australian mining services, including engineering consultancy, equipment supply, and geoscientific analysis. As a result, Australian engagement often entails the transfer of operational practices and technical systems that shape local mining industries.

INTRODUCTION

Australian mining companies play a significant role in Africa's extractive industries, particularly in gold, graphite, lithium, and base metals. Firms such as Resolute Mining and Perseus Mining have developed large-scale gold operations in West Africa, while companies like Syrah Resources and AVZ Minerals are actively involved in graphite and lithium projects critical to global energy transitions (International Energy Agency, 2023; World Bank, 2020).

These investments extend beyond extraction, forming part of a broader ecosystem of Australian mining services, including engineering consultancy, equipment supply, and geoscientific analysis. Consequently, Australian engagement often facilitates the transfer of operational practices, technical expertise, and management systems that shape local mining industries and contribute to capacity building (OECD, 2018; UNCTAD, 2022).

DOI: 10.4018/979-8-3373-7350-8.ch024

PERSEUS MINING

Perseus Mining is a prominent Australian gold producer with operations across multiple African jurisdictions. Its portfolio includes the Edikan Gold Mine in Ghana and the Sissingué Gold Mine and Yaouré Gold Mine in Côte d'Ivoire, alongside the Meyas Sand Gold Project in Sudan.

These operations reflect a strategy of geographic diversification and risk distribution across resource-rich regions. Perseus integrates modern mining technologies, operational efficiency systems, and environmental management practices, contributing to local employment and infrastructure development (UNCTAD, 2022).

ANGLOGOLD ASHANTI

AngloGold Ashanti is a major global gold producer with extensive operations across Africa, including the Democratic Republic of the Congo, Ghana, Guinea, Tanzania, and Egypt.

The company integrates advanced technologies such as automation, data analytics, and digital mine management systems to enhance productivity, safety, and environmental performance. Its collaboration with Amira Global supports applied research in mining science, including geospatial technologies and process optimization (OECD, 2018).

BLACK ROCK MINING

Black Rock Mining focuses on graphite development through the Mahenge Graphite Project in Tanzania.

The project is strategically positioned within global lithium-ion battery supply chains, particularly for graphite anodes. It operates under a joint ownership model that includes a free-carried interest for the Tanzanian government, reflecting evolving resource governance frameworks in Africa (World Bank, 2020).

SYRAH RESOURCES AND AVZ MINERALS

These firms are central to Africa's integration into global clean energy value chains. Their investments in graphite and lithium extraction support the production of electric vehicle batteries and energy storage systems, aligning African mineral resources with global decarbonization efforts (International Energy Agency, 2023).

METALSGROVE MINING

MetalsGrove Mining is engaged in gold exploration along the Birimian greenstone belts in West Africa. Its Central West Gold Project and joint venture with Aucrest SARL across the Zuénoula permit in Côte d'Ivoire form a contiguous exploration corridor targeting orogenic gold deposits.

This region is globally recognized for high-grade gold mineralization, attracting sustained exploration investment and reinforcing West Africa's position as a leading gold-producing region (USGS, 2022).

ORION MINERALS

Orion Minerals focuses on base-metal redevelopment in Southern Africa. Its flagship Prieska Copper-Zinc Project involves the rehabilitation of a historic underground mine in South Africa.

Additional projects, including the Okiep Copper Project and Jacomynspan Project, target minerals critical to battery technologies and renewable energy systems (International Energy Agency, 2023).

NORONEX

Noronex explores copper resources along the Kalahari Copper Belt, with projects such as Humpback–Damara and Powerline. The company has established partnerships with South32 to support exploration financing.

It is also advancing uranium exploration through the Etango North Uranium Project in Namibia, contributing to nuclear energy supply chains (World Nuclear Association, 2022).

SOUTH32

South32 operates significant mining and processing assets in Southern Africa. Its manganese operations in the Kalahari Basin in South Africa produce material essential for steelmaking and increasingly relevant for battery technologies.

The company also operates the Hillside Aluminium Smelter, illustrating integration between mining and downstream processing within regional industrial ecosystems (OECD, 2018).

REFERENCES

International Energy Agency. (2023). *World energy outlook 2023.*

OECD. (2018). *Enhancing the contribution of mining to sustainable development.* OECD Publishing.

UNCTAD. (2022). *World investment report 2022*. United Nations.

USGS. (2022). *Mineral commodity summaries: Gold.* U.S. Geological Survey.

World Bank. (2020). *Minerals for climate action: The mineral intensity of the clean energy transition.* World Bank.

World Nuclear Association. (2022). *Uranium resources and nuclear fuel cycle.*

Chapter 25
Main African Mines

ABSTRACT

State-owned enterprises remain among the most prominent African operators in the mining sector. In Botswana, the joint venture between the government and De Beers—Debswana—illustrates how state participation can enhance domestic value capture through involvement in diamond sorting, valuation, and aggregation. Similarly, entities such as Gécamines in the Democratic Republic of Congo have historically played central roles in managing copper and cobalt resources, although their effectiveness has fluctuated due to governance and financial constraints. These examples highlight both the potential and limitations of state-led mining models in Africa. From an analytical perspective, the growth of African mining operators reflects an ongoing reconfiguration of the extractive sector, in which control over natural resources is becoming more contested and diversified.

INTRODUCTION

State-owned enterprises remain among the most prominent African operators in the mining sector. In Botswana, the joint venture between the government and De Beers—Debswana—illustrates how state participation can enhance domestic value capture through involvement in diamond sorting, valuation, and aggregation. Similarly, entities such as Gécamines in the Democratic Republic of Congo have historically played central roles in managing copper and cobalt resources, although their effectiveness has fluctuated due to governance and financial constraints. These examples highlight both the potential and limitations of state-led mining models in Africa.

From an analytical perspective, the growth of African mining operators reflects an ongoing reconfiguration of the extractive sector, in which control over natural resources is becoming more contested and diversified.

DOI: 10.4018/979-8-3373-7350-8.ch025

DEMOCRATIC REPUBLIC OF THE CONGO

The Democratic Republic of the Congo (DRC) is the world's dominant source of cobalt, a mineral critical for lithium-ion batteries used in electric vehicles, consumer electronics, and energy storage technologies. The country's Central African Copperbelt also produces large quantities of copper, another key metal in electrification and renewable infrastructure (Umicore, 2026; MiningSEE, 2026).

Despite this strategic importance, the DRC captures only a limited share of total value created in the battery ecosystem. Cobalt and copper are typically exported as intermediates (e.g., cobalt hydroxide, copper concentrates), with refining and battery-grade chemical production located largely outside the country—especially in China and Europe—where advanced refining infrastructure and chemical production facilities exist. This reflects the segmented nature of global value chains: upstream extraction is concentrated in resource-rich economies like the DRC, while higher value-added processing and manufacturing remain anchored in industrialized economies.

Tenke Fungurume Mine — Copper & Cobalt

The Tenke Fungurume Mine is among the most significant copper and cobalt mining complexes in the world. Located in Lualaba Province within the Central African Copperbelt, it produces copper concentrate and cobalt hydroxide, which are essential inputs for global battery and electronics industries. The mine is majority-owned by China Molybdenum (CMOC Group) (80%) with the remainder held by the state mining enterprise Gécamines.

Tenke Fungurume has also been central to global commodity trading dynamics, with major traders like Glencore, Mercuria, and Trafigura securing sales agreements for its copper output, underscoring the mine's integration into international supply networks.

Kamoa-Kakula Copper Complex

The Kamoa-Kakula Copper Complex is a world-class high-grade copper project on the western edge of the Central African Copperbelt. Developed as a joint venture involving Ivanhoe Mines, Zijin Mining, and Gécamines, it is rapidly becoming one of the largest copper producers globally, with output exceeding 400,000 tonnes and ongoing expansion plans for deepening underground operations.

The project also includes a direct-to-blister flash smelter—expected to produce up to 500,000 tonnes per year of high-purity copper anodes—illustrating a move toward partial downstream integration within the country, though final refining remains abroad.

Kamoto Copper Company Mine (KCC)

The Kamoto Copper Company Mine is a key integrated copper and cobalt operation near Kolwezi in Lualaba Province. Operated by Glencore (75%) in partnership with Gécamines (25%), Kamoto includes underground mining, concentrators, and hydrometallurgical facilities, contributing significantly to national mineral output.

Mutanda Mine — Cobalt

The Mutanda Mine is widely recognized as one of the largest cobalt mines in the world. Located in Lualaba Province, it is wholly owned by Glencore and produces both copper and cobalt, with cobalt accounting for a significant portion of its output. The mine's production levels have made it a cornerstone of global cobalt supply and underscore the DRC's strategic position within critical mineral value chains.

Pumpi Mine — Copper & Cobalt

The Pumpi Mine, an open-pit operation near Kolwezi, is operated by Comika Mining. Ownership is shared among Wanbao Mining (75%), Morocco's Managem (20%), and Gécamines (5%). The mine uses conventional methods (crushing, grinding, acid leaching, CCD, SX-EW) to produce copper cathode and cobalt hydroxide, integrating established processing technologies in the region.

Etoile Mine — Copper & Cobalt

The Etoile Mine, licensed to Chemaf SA (95% owned by Shalina Resources, 5% by the DRC government), produces copper and cobalt and operates a modern solvent extraction–electrowinning (SX-EW) plant commissioned in 2016. Subsequent expansion phases include additional flotation and roasting circuits to broaden processing capabilities, reflecting technology integration beyond basic SX-EW.

In 2022, Chemaf secured significant project financing and marketing support from global trader Trafigura, illustrating the interconnection between mineral production and international commodity markets.

Local Value Addition and Research Constraints

Despite its dominant role in cobalt supply, the DRC's local participation in value-added processing remains limited. Most cobalt and copper intermediates are exported for refining and battery-grade chemical synthesis abroad. This pattern partly reflects deficiencies in domestic applied research infrastructure, including limited funding for industrial chemistry and metallurgical engineering, weak university–industry linkages, and underdeveloped laboratory and pilot facilities. These structural constraints inhibit the emergence of competitive, locally based materials processing industries within the DRC.

SOUTH AFRICA

Prieska and Phalaborwa Mines, Copper and Zinc

The Prieska Copper-Zinc Mine is located within the Proterozoic volcanic sequences of the Namaqua–Natal Metamorphic Belt. It is classified as a volcanogenic massive sulfide (VMS) deposit, formed through hydrothermal activity linked to ancient submarine volcanism. This process resulted in stratiform accumulations of copper, zinc, and other base metals, distinguishing Prieska geologically from the sediment-hosted copper deposits of the Central African Copperbelt (Miller et al., 2018).

In contrast, the Phalaborwa Mine, operated by the Palabora Mining Company, exploits one of South Africa's largest copper deposits, hosted within a carbonatite intrusive complex. This orebody not only contains copper but also by-products such as magnetite, vermiculite, and rare earth elements. Phalaborwa transitioned from open-pit to underground block-caving operations as surface resources were depleted. Its integrated metallurgical complex, including concentrators and smelting facilities, enables the production of copper cathodes and contributes substantially to local industrial development and urban growth (van Zyl, 2020).

Both Prieska and Phalaborwa exemplify the geological diversity of South Africa's base-metal sector and illustrate the potential for these operations to contribute to global supply chains, particularly as demand for copper and zinc grows in the context of electrification and renewable energy development (Miller et al., 2018; van Zyl, 2020).

Hillside Aluminium Smelter, Aluminium

Hillside Aluminium, located near Richards Bay in KwaZulu-Natal, is among South Africa's largest aluminum smelting operations. Managed by South32 (formerly part of BHP Billiton), the smelter forms a critical link in the domestic aluminum value chain, supporting downstream sectors including automotive manufacturing, packaging, construction, and engineering. The facility relies on bauxite and alumina supplies, historically sourced both domestically and through global imports, and produces high-quality aluminum for industrial applications (South32, 2023).

Mogalakwena, Platreef, and Other Limpopo Operations, Platinum Group Metals

South Africa dominates global platinum group metals (PGM) production, which are essential for automotive emissions control, petrochemical catalysis, and emerging hydrogen technologies. The sector is characterized by vertically integrated mining corporations such as Anglo American Platinum and Impala Platinum, which operate extraction, smelting, and refining facilities, capturing greater value than raw ore exports alone (Mudd, 2015).

The Mogalakwena Mine, operated by Anglo American Platinum near Mokopane, is the world's largest open-pit platinum mine. It produces platinum, palladium, rhodium, and gold from complex ore bodies within the Bushveld Igneous Complex. Its mechanized large-scale open-pit operation distinguishes it from other South African PGM mines, which are often deep underground (Anglo American Platinum, 2022).

The Platreef Mine, developed by Ivanhoe Mines, is an underground operation on the northern limb of the Bushveld Complex targeting platinum, palladium, rhodium, nickel, and copper. It is designed to become one of the largest and lowest-cost PGM mines globally once fully operational. Other important Limpopo mines include Modikwa (Anglo American Platinum and African Rainbow Minerals joint venture) and Marula (Impala Platinum), which exploit high-grade PGM deposits and contribute significantly to South Africa's mining exports and industrial ecosystems (Ivanhoe Mines, 2023).

Gauteng and the Bushveld Complex, Gold and Platinum

The Bushveld Igneous Complex, extending across Limpopo, North West, and Mpumalanga provinces, is among the world's most important mineral-producing regions. Together with Gauteng's goldfields, these regions support South Africa's dominant position in global precious metal production. Major operators such as Anglo American Platinum, Impala Platinum, and Sibanye-Stillwater exploit large-scale platinum deposits, cementing the country's central role in global PGM supply chains (Sibanye-Stillwater, 2023; Mudd, 2015).

ZAMBIA

Copper and the Challenge of Industrial Linkages

Copper remains the central pillar of Zambia's economy, with the country's fiscal revenues, employment, and industrial activity heavily dependent on the sector. The industry is largely dominated by multinational corporations (MNCs) that control capital-intensive mining technologies and global marketing networks. Prominent operators include Glencore and Vedanta Resources, both of which have historically held major mining assets in Zambia's Copperbelt (Fraser & Lungu, 2007).

The technological evolution of copper extraction in Zambia has progressed from traditional open-pit methods toward more mechanized operations incorporating modern processing, smelting, and refining techniques. Despite this industrial sophistication, the domestic knowledge production system remains primarily anchored in public universities, which provide essential engineering and scientific training rather than large-scale applied research or industrial innovation (Situmbeko & Tembo, 2019). Leading institutions include the University of Zambia and Copperbelt University, which supply graduates to the sector but have limited integration with high-value activities such as semiconductor materials, electric vehicle components, and precision manufacturing (Yambayamba, 2021). Consequently, the highest-value segments of the copper value chain continue to depend on foreign expertise and technology.

Konkola Copper Mines (KCM)

The Konkola Copper Mines (KCM) represents one of Zambia's most significant copper operations, situated in the northern sector of the Central African Copperbelt. KCM operates both the Konkola Mine and the Nchanga Mine, located near Chililabombwe and Chingola, respectively. In 2004, Vedanta Resources acquired a majority stake in KCM, introducing new capital and modern mining technologies. However, the company experienced disputes over investment obligations, environmental compliance, and financial performance, leading the Government of Zambia to place KCM under provisional liquidation in 2019. Subsequent negotiations have aimed to restructure ownership and ensure stable operations, illustrating the complex interplay between multinational investors and host states in resource-dependent economies (Banda, 2020).

KCM's operations encompass the entire copper value chain, from extraction to integrated smelting and refining, including the Nchanga Smelter, which produces both copper concentrate and refined cathodes for export. Copper from KCM contributes substantially to national export earnings and fiscal revenues, reinforcing its status as Zambia's economic cornerstone.

Other Major Copper Producers in Zambia

In addition to KCM, several other multinational and foreign-invested firms play a central role in Zambia's copper industry:

First Quantum Minerals operates the Kansanshi Mine and the Sentinel Mine in Northwestern Province, both among Zambia's largest copper producers (First Quantum Minerals, 2022).

Glencore previously managed the Mopani Copper Mines, an integrated underground and smelting operation near Kitwe, before restructuring and divestment (Glencore, 2021).

While these operations are technologically advanced, they remain largely enclave-based, with limited integration into domestic innovation ecosystems. This highlights the persistent challenge of developing local industrial linkages capable of moving Zambia beyond extractive dependency toward higher-value copper processing and manufacturing (Situmbeko & Tembo, 2019).

BOTSWANA, ANGOLA AND GUINA

Botswana: Diamond Mining and Economic Development

Botswana's diamond sector is globally recognized for its high-quality gem production and significant contributions to national revenue. The Jwaneng Mine, located in the southern region of the country, is widely regarded as the world's richest diamond mine by value. Operating as a large open-pit mine, Jwaneng has sustained high-quality diamond production since 1982 through continuous investment in pit deepening and processing capacity expansion. The mine has been a major driver of export earnings and government revenue (Debswana, 2023).

In northern Botswana, the Orapa Mine represents one of the largest diamond deposits by area and was the country's first major kimberlite discovery. Together with the Letlhakane and Damtshaa deposits, Orapa forms a regional diamond cluster that has been operational since the early 1970s. The integrated operations of these mines have facilitated employment generation, infrastructure development, and fiscal revenues, underpinning Botswana's transformation into one of Africa's most stable resource-based economies (Debswana, 2023; Humphreys, 2005).

Angola: Copper Diversification with Tetelo Mine

The Tetelo Copper Mine, situated near Maquela do Zombo in Uíge Province, is Angola's first modern large-scale copper mining project since independence, reflecting efforts to diversify the national economy beyond oil dependency. The mine is developed by Shining Star Icarus (SSI), SU Limitada, a joint venture between the Angolan company Sociedade Mineira de Cobre de Angola and China's Shining Star International Group.

Construction of the Tetelo Mine required a capital investment of approximately US $305 million. Early operations focus on open-pit mining, processing roughly 4,000 tonnes of ore per day with a recovery rate of around 92%, producing an estimated 25,000 tonnes of copper concentrate annually. Plans to transition to underground mining by late 2026 aim to extend operational capacity and ensure a long-term copper supply over an expected mine life of approximately 14 years. The project has already generated employment for over 1,800 workers, approximately 70% of whom are Angolan nationals, with projections of surpassing 3,000 direct and indirect jobs as operations expand (Angola Ministry of Minerals, 2024).

Guinea: Bauxite and Alumina Production

Guinea hosts some of the world's richest bauxite reserves, supporting both mining and alumina processing projects.

Sangaredi Mine, located in western Guinea, is operated by Compagnie des Bauxites de Guinée (CBG), a consortium comprising Rio Tinto, Alcoa, and Dadco Investments Limited. Ownership is split 49% by the Guinean government and 51% by Halco Mining Inc., highlighting a public-private partnership model. The mine produces high-quality bauxite for global markets, primarily serving alumina refineries in Asia and Europe (CBG, 2022).

Alufer Mining Limited, an independent Guinean producer, operates the Bel Air and Labé projects in the Boké Bauxite Belt. The Bel Air Project, discovered in 2011 and operational since 2018, produces direct shipping ore (DSO) bauxite with low impurities, supporting efficient processing at international alumina plants. Alufer has developed integrated haulage and port infrastructure at Cap Verga, facilitating cost-competitive exports (Alufer Mining, 2023).

The Boffa region is another key bauxite hub. The Boffa Mine, operated by Chalco Guinea Co., Ltd. (85% Chinalco, 15% Guinea government), produces between 12–20 million tonnes of bauxite annually, primarily for export to China. A Chinese-backed alumina refinery is under construction, aiming to expand domestic value addition. Meanwhile, the Fria Alumina Refinery, operated by RUSAL since its 2006 privatization, produces alumina rather than raw bauxite, contributing to Guinea's emerging downstream processing capabilities (RUSAL, 2024; Chalco, 2025).

Collectively, these projects illustrate Guinea's role as a globally strategic supplier of high-grade bauxite and its gradual shift toward integrated mining and processing operations that enhance economic value domestically.

REFERENCES

Alufer Mining. (2023). *Bel Air and Labé projects overview*. Alufer Mining Limited.

Anglo American Platinum. (2022). *Mogalakwena mine overview*. Retrieved from https://www.angloamericanplatinum.com

Angola Ministry of Minerals. (2024). *Tetelo Copper Mine project report*. Government of Angola.

Banda, F. (2020). Zambia's copper sector: Investment challenges and industrial linkages. *Journal of African Economies, 29*(3), 255–275.

CBG. (2022). *Sangaredi Mine annual report*. Compagnie des Bauxites de Guinée.

Chalco Guinea Co. Ltd. (2025). *Boffa mining and alumina expansion project*. Beijing: Chalco Group.

Debswana. (2023). *Botswana diamond operations: Jwaneng and Orapa*. Gaborone: Debswana Diamond Company.

First Quantum Minerals. (2022). *Kansanshi and Sentinel mines: Overview*. Retrieved from https://www.first-quantum.com

Fraser, A., & Lungu, J. (2007). *For Whom the Windfalls? Winners and losers in the privatisation of Zambia's copper mines*. Civil Society Trade Network.

Glencore. (2021). *Mopani Copper Mines: Operations overview*. Retrieved from https://www.glencore.com

Humphreys, D. (2005). *Natural resources, governance and development: Botswana diamonds in comparative perspective*. Oxford University Press.

Ivanhoe Mines. (2023). *Platreef project: Mineral resources and development*. Retrieved from https://www.ivanhoemines.com

Kamoa Copper S.A. (2025). *Operations overview*. Retrieved from company materials.
Congo Mining Network. (2025). *Trafigura financing for Kamoa-Kakula copper flow*.

Miller, R., Smith, J., & van der Walt, L. (2018). Geology and mining of South Africa's base-metal deposits. *Journal of African Earth Sciences, 145*, 345–362.

MiningSEE. (2026). *Cobalt in 2026: Global supply chains, DRC dominance, Chinese refining power, and the future of battery metals*.

Mudd, G. (2015). Sustainable mining in South Africa: Platinum and gold industry insights. *Resources Policy, 45*, 90–99.

RUSAL. (2024). *Fria Alumina Refinery operational report.* United Company RUSAL.

Sibanye-Stillwater. (2023). *Annual report: South African PGM operations.* Retrieved from https://www.sibanyestillwater.com

Situmbeko, T., & Tembo, M. (2019). University-industry linkages in Zambia's mining sector. *African Journal of Science, Technology, Innovation and Development, 11*(6), 737–749.

South32. (2023). *Hillside Aluminium: Smelter operations and industrial contributions.* Retrieved from https://www.south32.net

Umicore. (2026). *Responsible sourcing of cobalt.* Retrieved from https://www.umicore.com/en/media/responsible-sourcing-of-cobalt/

van Zyl, P. (2020). Phalaborwa: Carbonatite-hosted copper mining in South Africa. *Mineral Economics, 33*(2), 167–181.

Wikipedia contributors. (2024). Tenke Fungurume Mine. In Wikipedia, The Free Encyclopedia.

Wikipedia contributors. (2024). Pumpi Mine. In Wikipedia, The Free Encyclopedia.

Wikipedia contributors. (2024). *Etoile mine.* In Wikipedia, The Free Encyclopedia.

Wikipedia contributors. (2024). *Kamoto mine.* In Wikipedia, The Free Encyclopedia.

Wikipedia contributors. (2024). *Mutanda mine.* In Wikipedia, The Free Encyclopedia.

Yambayamba, B. (2021). Human capital and technological capacity in Zambia's Copperbelt. *Mining Research Review, 15*(2), 48–67.

Chapter 26
The Innovative Virtual Open Incubators Cluster (IVOIC) Adaptation to African Mining

ABSTRACT

The Innovative Virtual Open Incubators Cluster (IVOIC) framework represents a novel approach to fostering technological development and innovation in resource-based economies, with a particular focus on the mining sector. Unlike traditional industrial clusters, which rely heavily on geographic proximity, the IVOIC model leverages virtual platforms to enable collaboration between firms, universities, and research institutions across spatial boundaries. At its core, the IVOIC framework seeks to transform mineral-based economies from extractive production systems into innovation-oriented industrial ecosystems. By linking mining companies, technology providers, research institutions, and government agencies, the model promotes the circulation of technological knowledge, supporting the development of new capabilities in areas such as mineral processing, battery materials, digital mining systems, and clean energy technologies.

INTRODUCTION

The Innovative Virtual Open Incubators Cluster (IVOIC) framework represents a novel approach to fostering technological development and innovation in resource-based economies, with a particular focus on the mining sector (Bijaoui, 2025, 2026). Unlike traditional industrial clusters, which rely heavily on geographic proximity, the IVOIC model leverages virtual platforms to enable collaboration between

DOI: 10.4018/979-8-3373-7350-8.ch026

firms, universities, and research institutions across spatial boundaries. This hybrid approach allows remote mining regions to access global knowledge networks while simultaneously enhancing local innovation capacity.

At its core, the IVOIC framework seeks to transform mineral-based economies from extractive production systems into innovation-oriented industrial ecosystems. By linking mining companies, technology providers, research institutions, and government agencies, the model promotes the circulation of technological knowledge, supporting the development of new capabilities in areas such as mineral processing, battery materials, digital mining systems, and clean energy technologies. This approach is particularly relevant in the African context, where mining operations are often located in regions with limited industrial infrastructure and weak connections to research institutions.

STRUCTURAL COMPONENTS OF THE IVOIC MODEL

Innovation Clusters

Innovation clusters refer to the geographic concentration of firms, research institutions, and supporting industries around specific economic activities. In African mining regions, these clusters typically include mining operators, equipment suppliers, geological research institutions, mineral processing facilities, and specialized service providers. Examples include the Copperbelt in the Democratic Republic of the Congo and Zambia, the Bushveld Complex in South Africa, and the diamond mining sector in Botswana. These clusters form the industrial foundation upon which innovation ecosystems can develop (Bijaoui, 2025).

Virtual Open Innovation Incubators

The IVOIC model incorporates virtual incubators across supporting industries and services. These platforms facilitate innovation activities such as remote geological analysis, AI-driven exploration modelling, mineral processing simulations, and collaborative engineering design. By transcending geographic constraints, virtual incubators enable joint innovation among multinational corporations, universities, startups, technology firms, and venture capital investors. Open innovation networks within mining facilitate access to expertise in areas including advanced mineral processing, battery materials, digital mining automation, and environmental monitoring technologies.

Operational Structure

The operational framework of IVOIC is conceptualized as a multilayered system comprising five interacting components:

Resource Base: The foundation of the cluster, consisting of natural mineral endowments such as copper and cobalt in the DRC and Zambia, platinum-group metals in South Africa, and diamonds in Botswana.

Industrial Core: Large multinational mining firms provide capital, operational expertise, and access to global markets. Examples include Anglo American, Sibanye-Stillwater, South32, and Zijin Mining, which influence local supply chains and technological innovation.

Virtual Innovation Platforms: Universities, research laboratories, and engineering institutes generate scientific knowledge, conduct applied research, and train skilled personnel. In Africa, institutions such as the Council for Scientific and Industrial Research and the University of the Witwatersrand contribute significantly to mining engineering, mineral processing, and environmental management research.

Local Related and Supporting Industries: Industries that develop around the mines, enhancing regional value addition through mineral processing, equipment supply, and services.

Policy and Governance Framework: Governments shape the innovation ecosystem through regulations, research funding, local content requirements, and industrial development strategies. Regional coordination is facilitated by organizations such as the African Minerals Development Centre, which supports policy harmonization and knowledge exchange.

Together, these layers form an integrated system linking resource extraction to technological capability development. By combining physical clusters with virtual innovation networks, IVOIC allows African mining regions to overcome geographic isolation and institutional fragmentation. This framework supports higher value-added activities in mineral processing, advanced materials manufacturing, and clean energy technologies, aligning with growing global demand for critical minerals in electric vehicles, renewable energy, and electronics (Bijaoui, 2026).

ADVANTAGES OF THE IVOIC MODEL

Accelerated Knowledge Transfer: Virtual platforms reduce geographic barriers, enabling rapid exchange of geological data, mineral processing research, and technological solutions. This is particularly valuable in geographically dispersed mining regions such as the Copperbelt in the DRC and Zambia.

Industrial Diversification: By integrating research institutions, technology developers, and digital incubators into mining clusters, the framework supports downstream activities including mineral processing, battery materials production, and advanced manufacturing. The Bushveld Complex platinum ecosystem exemplifies how mining regions can evolve toward higher-value industrial activities.

Enhanced Innovation Capacity: Open collaboration networks encourage experimentation with new mining technologies, environmental management systems, and energy-efficient solutions, facilitating local capability development.

IVOIC model provides a conceptual framework for transforming resource-based mining regions into innovation-driven industrial ecosystems. By integrating digital collaboration networks, research institutions, and industrial actors, IVOIC facilitates technological upgrading, knowledge diffusion, and economic diversification in regions historically dependent on extractive activities (Bijaoui, 2025; 2026). Several African mining regions already possess the structural foundations required for such transformation, including substantial mineral reserves, established mining companies, and emerging research capabilities.

THE COPPERBELT: TRANSFORMING A RESOURCE CLUSTER

The Copperbelt region, spanning the Democratic Republic of the Congo (DRC) and Zambia, exemplifies the potential application of the IVOIC model. The region contains one of the world's largest concentrations of sediment-hosted copper and cobalt deposits, forming the backbone of mining industries in both countries and supplying critical minerals to global markets. Within the IVOIC framework, these mineral-rich clusters can evolve from primarily extractive zones into innovation-driven ecosystems through:

Digital collaboration platforms that connect geographically dispersed stakeholders.

Partnerships between multinational mining corporations, local state-owned enterprises, and universities.

Development of downstream industries and advanced processing capabilities.

Key Mines and Resource Base

The Copperbelt hosts several high-profile mining operations central to the IVOIC framework:

Democratic Republic of the Congo (DRC):

Tenke Fungurume Mine – Copper & Cobalt
Kamoa-Kakula Mine – Copper
Kamoto Mine – Copper & Cobalt
Mutanda Mine – Cobalt
Pumpi Mine (Comika) – Copper & Cobalt
Etoile Mine – Copper & Cobalt
Zambia:
Kansanshi Mine – Copper
Sentinel Mine – Copper
Mopani Copper Mines – Copper

These operations provide the natural resource base around which mining clusters and related industries can coalesce.

Related Industries and Potential Innovation Fields

The IVOIC model emphasizes development in core beneficiation and advanced processing, including:

Hydrometallurgical processing of copper and cobalt ores.

Battery materials production, particularly cathode materials for lithium-ion batteries.

Integration into renewable energy and electric vehicle supply chains, leveraging minerals as inputs for global energy transition technologies.

Supporting industries include:

Mining Equipment and Engineering Services: Provision and maintenance of drilling machinery, haul trucks, and mineral processing equipment.

Metallurgical Processing and Smelting: Copper smelting, refining, and cobalt processing. Smelting facilities are concentrated near Kitwe and Ndola in Zambia, and Lubumbashi and Kolwezi in the DRC.

Chemical and Mineral Processing: Production of reagents, solvents, and industrial chemicals used in flotation, leaching, and purification processes.

Infrastructure and Governance

Effective IVOIC implementation depends on robust infrastructure and supportive governance frameworks:

Governance: Coordination through the African Union, alongside national authorities in the DRC and Zambia.

Transport and Logistics: Rail networks, trucking services, and export terminals linking mining hubs to southern African ports and Atlantic trade routes. Logistics companies handle movement of heavy equipment, ores, and refined metals.

Energy and Power: Large hydropower plants along the Zambezi and Congo rivers supply electricity to mining and processing facilities. Grid operators provide distribution, maintenance, and backup power infrastructure.

Academic and Research Cooperation

The Copperbelt IVOIC model integrates local and international research institutions to enhance technological capabilities:

Université de Kolwezi (UNIKOL) – DRC

Collaborations with University of Mons (Belgium) and Copperbelt University (Zambia)

Joint research in mining engineering, mineral processing, and environmental monitoring

Student and faculty exchange programs focusing on hydrometallurgy, geotechnical studies, and digital mining systems

University of Lubumbashi (UNILU) – DRC

Partnerships with Free University of Brussels (Belgium) and University of Mons

Research collaborations with French and Canadian institutions in geosciences, hydrology, and sustainable mining practices

Focus areas include tailings management, groundwater impact studies, and environmentally responsible mining operations

These academic and research partnerships enhance the flow of technological knowledge, train skilled personnel, and enable the development of innovation-driven clusters.

Figure 1. The Copperbelt Innovative Virtual Open Incubators Cluster (IVOIC) Model

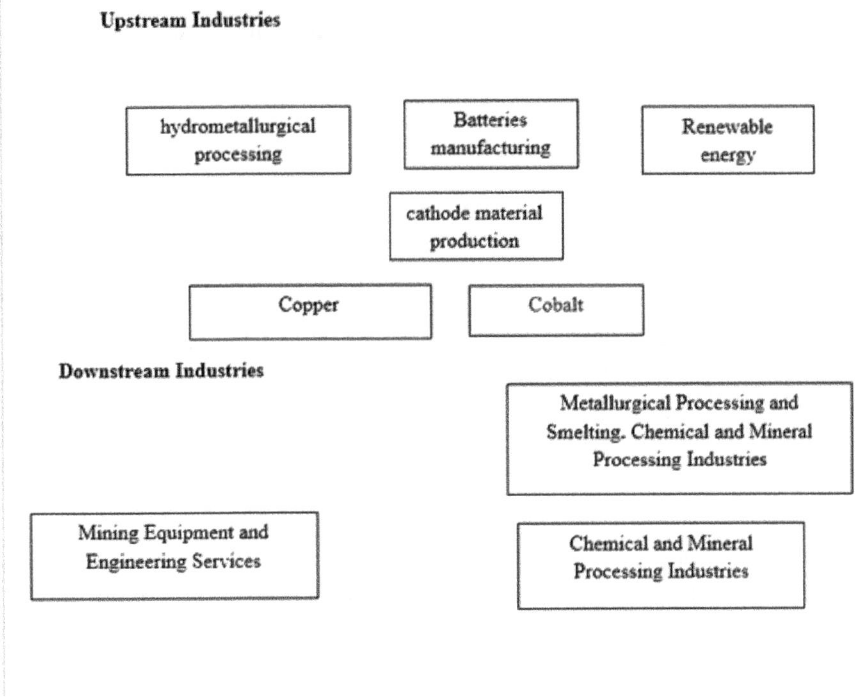

First Layer: The Resource Base

DRC:Tenke Fungurume Mine, Copper & Cobalt; Kamoa-Kakula Mine, Copper; Kamoto Mine, Copper & Cobalt; Mutanda Mine, cobalt; Pumpi Mine (Comika); Etoile Mine

Zambia: Kansanshi Mine ; Sentinel Mine ; Mopani Copper Mines

Second Layer: The Industrial Core

Glencore (Swiss) Crystal River Global (China) CMOC Group (China) Ivanhoe Mines (US), Zijin Mining (China) Gécamines (DRC). Wanbao Mining (China) ; Managem (Morocco); Shalina (UAE)

Third Layer: Virtual Innovative Open Incubators

Advanced hydrometallurgical processing, battery manufacturing, cathode material production, and renewable energy.

Figure 2.

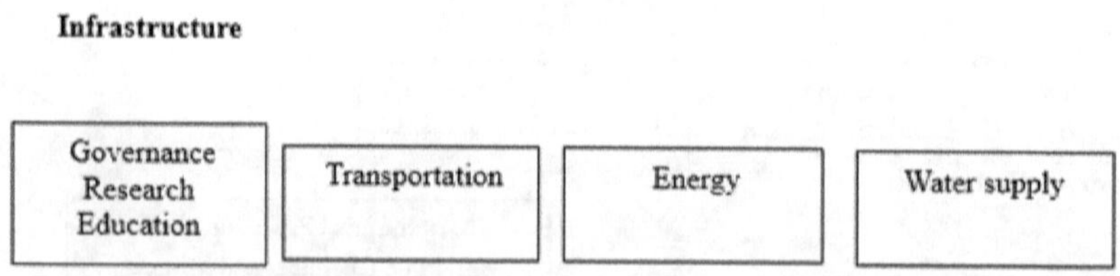

Potential innovation fields include advanced hydrometallurgical processing, battery cathode material production, and integration into electric vehicle supply chains. The development of such capabilities would enable local economies to move beyond the export of raw or intermediate mineral products toward higher value-added activities within global battery manufacturing networks. Key actors in this ecosystem include national mining companies such as Gécamines, along with international mining corporations and research institutions that contribute technological expertise and capital investment.

Platinum-Group Metals Cluster in the Bushveld Complex, South Africa

The Bushveld Complex in South Africa is home to the majority of the world's known reserves of platinum-group metals (PGMs), including platinum, palladium, and rhodium. These metals are critical for automotive catalytic converters, fuel cell technologies, and emerging hydrogen energy systems. Within the IVOIC (Innovative Virtual Open Incubators Cluster) framework, the Bushveld region has the potential to evolve into a global innovation hub for green hydrogen production, advanced catalytic materials, and fuel cell technologies, leveraging integrated networks of mining companies, engineering firms, and research institutions (Bijaoui, 2025; 2026).

Major mining corporations, such as Sibanye-Stillwater, play a central role in this ecosystem by providing capital, operational expertise, and access to international markets.

Key Mines and Ownership

The Bushveld PGM cluster encompasses numerous major mines across Rustenburg, Limpopo, and North West provinces:

Impala Rustenburg Mine – Operated by Impala Platinum (Implats)

Rustenburg Platinum Mines – Operated by Anglo American Platinum

Marikana Mine – Operated by Sibanye-Stillwater

Kroondal Mine – Previously operated jointly by Sibanye-Stillwater and Anglo American Platinum

Mototolo Mine – Operated by Anglo American Platinum

Two Rivers Mine – Joint venture between African Rainbow Minerals and Impala Platinum

Modikwa Mine – Joint venture between Anglo American Platinum and African Rainbow Minerals

Mogalakwena Mine – Largest open-pit PGM mine globally, operated by Anglo American Platinum

Platreef Mine – New underground development by Ivanhoe Mines

These mines collectively produce the majority of South Africa's PGMs and serve as the industrial backbone for both domestic supply chains and global export markets.

Related Industries and Innovation Applications

The Bushveld Complex's PGMs support a range of industrial and technological applications, including:

Hydrogen fuel cell technologies
Advanced catalytic materials
Green hydrogen production systems
Automotive catalytic converter manufacturing
Jewelry fabrication
Electronics and sensor components
Chemical catalysts and industrial processing

Major Companies

Major companies operating across this cluster include Anglo American Platinum, Impala Platinum Holdings, Sibanye-Stillwater, Northam Platinum, and Royal Bafokeng Platinum. These firms operate integrated mining, concentration, smelting, and refining facilities, transforming PGM ores into high-purity metals for industrial, automotive, and energy applications.

Supporting Industries

Supporting industries in the Bushveld PGM cluster provide essential services, technologies, and equipment:

Mining Equipment and Engineering Services:
Sandvik: Underground mining equipment
Epiroc: Drilling and rock excavation systems
Metso: Mineral processing technology
FLSmidth: Smelting and processing systems

Additional support includes ventilation systems, conveyors, drilling rigs, and mine safety equipment

Metallurgical and Refining Industries:
Johnson Matthey: Catalyst and PGM refining technologies

Heraeus: Precious metals processing and industrial applications

Catalytic and Hydrogen Technology Firms:
BASF – Industrial chemical catalysts
Ballard Power Systems – Fuel cell development

Infrastructure and Cluster Support Systems

Effective operation of the PGM cluster relies on robust infrastructure and service networks:

Transport and Logistics: Rail networks connecting mines to industrial centers and export ports (e.g., Richards Bay, Durban), specialized bulk transport services for minerals.

Energy Supply: Electricity provision primarily by Eskom, supporting both mining operations and downstream processing.

Research and Innovation Institutions:
Council for Scientific and Industrial Research (CSIR)
Mintek – Advanced metallurgy and mineral technology
University of the Witwatersrand – Mining engineering and geosciences
University of Pretoria – Materials science and catalysis research

Integration of these research and industrial capabilities within the IVOIC framework enables virtual collaboration, accelerates knowledge transfer, and supports technological innovation in PGMs for energy transition and industrial applications.

Figure 3. The platinum-group metals cluster associated with the Bushveld Complex in South Africa Virtual Open Incubators Cluster (IVOIC) model

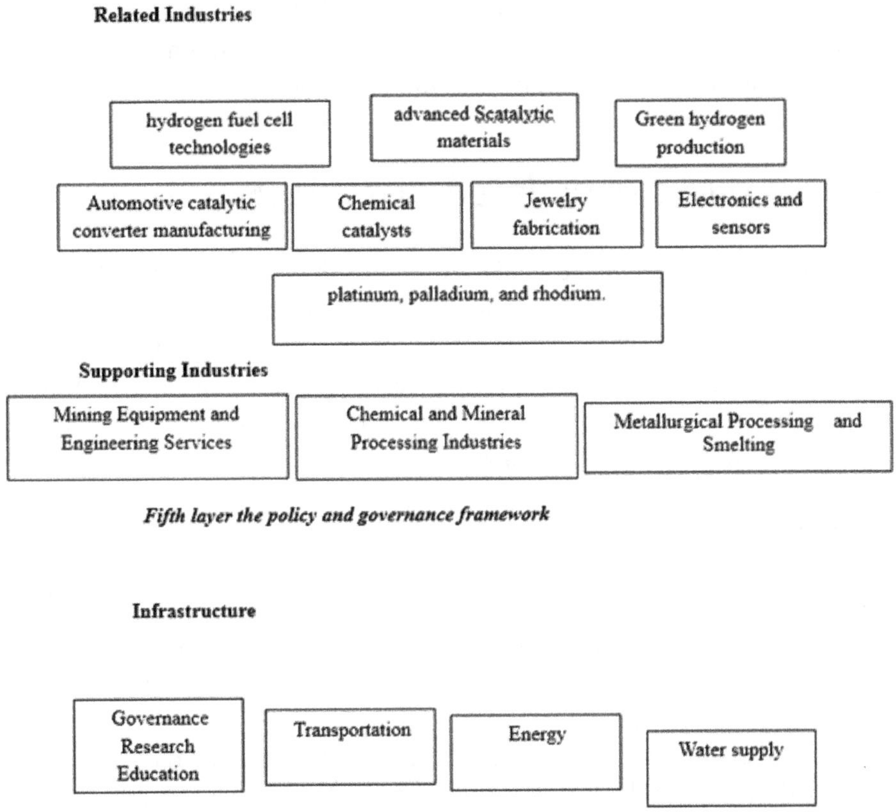

First Layer: The Resource Base

Impala Rustenburg Mine; Gauteng and the Bushveld Complex;Rustenburg Platinum Mines ; Marikana Mine; Impala Rustenburg Mine; Kroondal Mine; Mototolo Mine; Two Rivers Mine; Modikwa Mine ; Mogalakwena Mine ; Platreef Mine.

Second Layer: The Industrial Core

Anglo American Platinum Sibanye-Stillwater Sibanye-Stillwater African Rainbow Minerals and Impala Platinum African Rainbow Minerals; Ivanhoe Mines.

Third Layer: Virtual Innovative Open Incubators

Platinum, palladium, and rhodium. hydrogen fuel cell technologies, advanced Scatalytic materials, green hydrogen production systems; Automotive catalytic converter manufacturing; Jewelry; Electronics and sensors; Chemical catalysts

DEBSWANA DIAMOND CLUSTER, BOTSWANA

The Debswana joint venture, established between the Government of Botswana and the global diamond company De Beers, has been instrumental in developing domestic capabilities in diamond extraction, processing, and trading (Bijaoui, 2025; 2026). This partnership has created a robust diamond mining and innovation cluster, integrating mining operations, valuation services, polishing industries, and specialized skills development programs.

Key Mines

Jwaneng Mine – Located in southern Botswana, Jwaneng is one of the world's richest diamond mines by value, operating as a large open-pit mine. It produces high-quality gem diamonds that feed both domestic and international processing industries.

Orapa Mine – Situated in northern Botswana, Orapa is among the largest diamond mines globally by area and represents the country's first major kimberlite discovery.

Cluster Extensions – Surrounding Orapa, the Letlhakane and Damtshaa deposits form a regional mining hub that supports a network of processing, trading, and logistical infrastructure.

RELATED INDUSTRIES

The Debswana cluster supports several downstream industries that enhance value addition:

Diamond Sorting, Valuation, and Trading

Conducted in collaboration with De Beers, these processes ensure high-quality diamonds are prepared for global markets.

International partners include HB Antwerp and Leo Schachter Diamonds, specializing in transforming rough stones into polished diamonds for jewelry.

Jewelry Manufacturing and Retail

Includes design workshops and artisanal manufacturing units, providing products for domestic and export markets.

Gemological Certification Services

Supports quality assurance and global market credibility for Botswana diamonds.

Supporting Industries

Supporting industries provide essential services to maintain operational efficiency across the cluster:

Mining Equipment and Engineering Services

Sandvik – Underground and surface mining machinery

Epiroc – Drilling, excavation, and rock handling technologies

Caterpillar – Heavy-duty mining trucks and loaders

Diamond Cutting and Polishing Industry

Facilities equipped with advanced polishing machinery, gemological tools, and workforce training programs to maximize value addition.

Infrastructure and Logistics

Efficient infrastructure underpins the Debswana cluster's performance:

Transport and Logistics

Regional road corridors linking mines to trading hubs and ports in South Africa and Namibia.

Air cargo services through Sir Seretse Khama International Airport ensure secure transport of high-value diamonds.

Specialized logistics providers handle secure and compliant movement of rough and polished stones.

Energy and Utilities

Stable electricity supply is provided by Botswana Power Corporation.

Industrial water supply systems support both mining operations and processing facilities.

Figure 4. The joint venture Debswana—formed between the Government of Botswana and the global diamond company De Beers

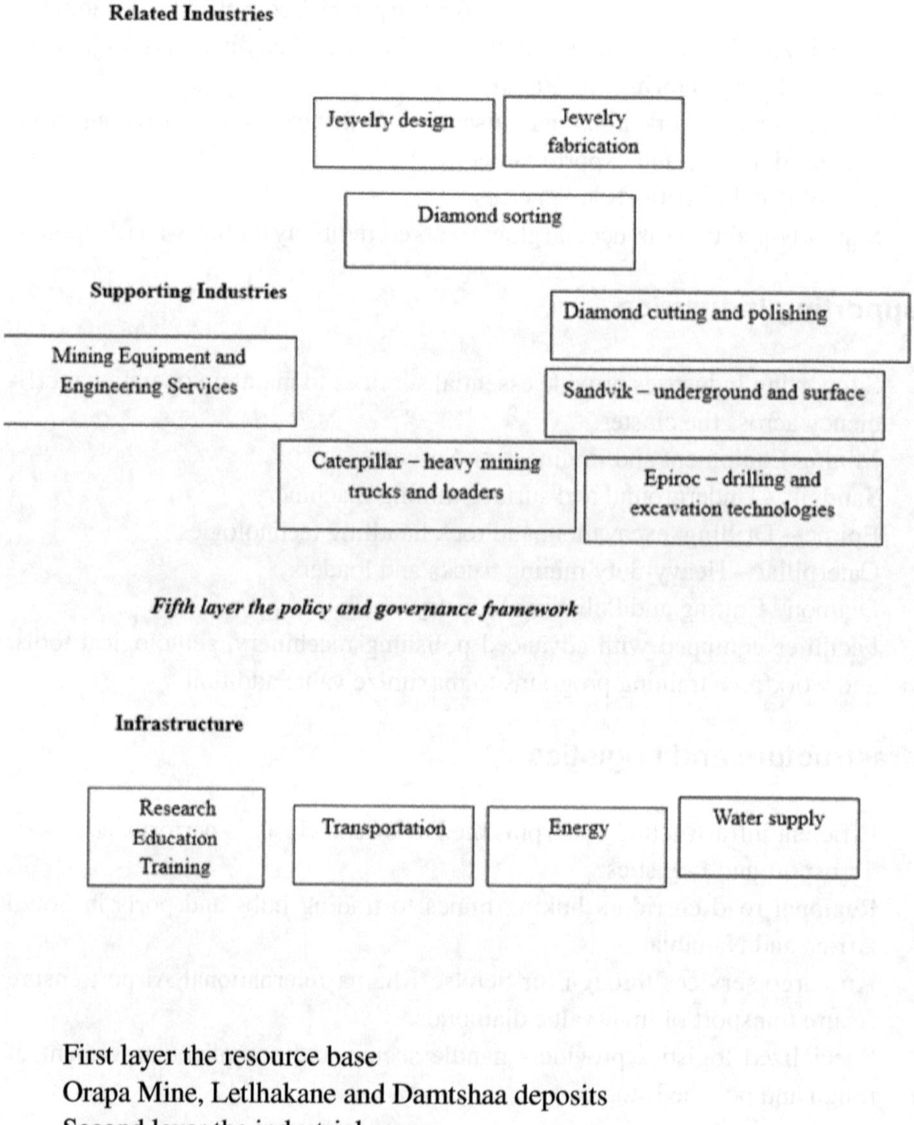

First layer the resource base
Orapa Mine, Letlhakane and Damtshaa deposits
Second layer the industrial core
De Beersl HB Antwerp; Leo Schachter Diamonds
Third layer virtual innovative Open Incubators
Diamond Sorting, Valuation Jewelry Manufacturing and Retail

Boké Bauxite Cluster, Guinea

The Boké Region in northwestern Guinea constitutes the heart of the country's bauxite industry and one of the most significant aluminum raw-material provinces globally. Guinea possesses the largest known bauxite reserves in the world, a substantial proportion of which are concentrated within the Boké bauxite belt along the Atlantic coast (Bijaoui, 2025; 2026).

Industrial-scale mining in the Boké region began in the early 1970s with the establishment of the Compagnie des Bauxites de Guinée (CBG), which developed the Sangarédi mining complex and a dedicated rail corridor linking the mines to the export port of Kamsar. Supported by international aluminum producers such as Alcoa and Rio Tinto, CBG's operations laid the foundational infrastructure and institutional frameworks that underpin Guinea's modern bauxite sector.

Main Mines

Since the mid-2010s, the Boké region has witnessed rapid expansion driven by growing demand from Chinese aluminum smelters. Key developments include:

Société Minière de Boké (SMB) – A consortium comprising Winning International Group and China Hongqiao Group, SMB operates multiple open-pit mines along the Boké–Boffa corridor and has developed integrated transport and port infrastructure to facilitate bauxite exports.

Guinea Alumina Corporation (GAC) – A subsidiary of Emirates Global Aluminium (EGA), GAC represents one of the largest greenfield mining projects in West Africa. It includes open-pit mining operations, dedicated rail and road networks, and export facilities on the Atlantic coast.

Fria Mine (ACG–Fria / Friguia) – Operated by United Company RUSAL, this mine combines bauxite extraction with alumina refining, demonstrating the potential for domestic value-added processing.

Other notable mining operations in the region include Boffa Bauxite Mine (Chalco), Bel Air Mine (Alufer Mining Ltd + Guinean government), and additional SMB-associated deposits (Dabiss, Malapouya, Santou, Houda).

Related Industries

The Boké bauxite cluster supports industries that enhance value addition and processing capacity:

Alumina Refining and Mineral Processing

Bauxite washing and beneficiation

Alumina production using the Bayer process

Chemical processing to produce aluminum feedstock
Potential Industrial Expansion
Downstream aluminum smelting and alloy production
Production of high-value chemicals for industrial applications

Supporting Industries

Several industries support the operational and technological efficiency of the Boké cluster:

Heavy mining machinery supply (excavators, haul trucks, drilling rigs)
Maintenance and repair services for industrial equipment
Geological surveying, mine planning, and exploration services
Industrial automation and digital mine management systems
Bulk material handling facilities and port storage terminals
Environmental impact assessment, climate, and biodiversity monitoring technologies
Industrial construction, steel fabrication, and urban development for mining communities

Infrastructure

Robust infrastructure is essential for the extraction, processing, and export of bauxite:

Transport – Road and rail corridors (notably the Boké–Kamsar corridor) connecting mines to export ports

Energy – Power generation and transmission networks supporting industrial operations

Water – Industrial water supply, treatment systems, and land rehabilitation programs

Maritime Logistics – Port infrastructure and freight handling facilities for bulk bauxite shipments

Academic and Research Institutions

Human capital development and research are crucial for sustaining technological innovation and operational efficiency in the bauxite sector:

Université Gamal Abdel Nasser de Conakry – Faculties of Sciences and Engineering

Institut Supérieur des Mines et Géologie de Boké – Mining engineering, mineral processing, geological exploration, environmental management

Université Kofi Annan de Guinée – Industrial management, environmental studies, applied technology programs

Université Julius Nyerere de Kankan – Geography, geology, environmental science, and regional development

Figure 5. Boké Region, Guinea

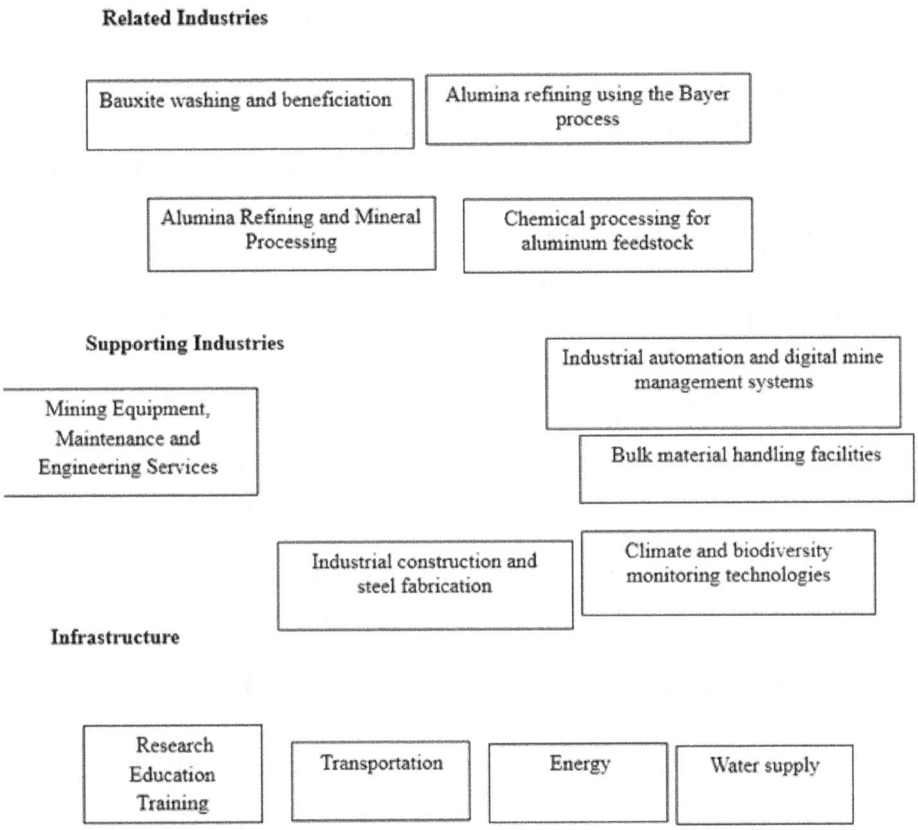

First Layer: The Resource Base

Fria Mine (ACG–Fria / Friguia); Société Minière de Boké (SMB); United Mining Supply (UMS); Compagnie des Bauxites de Guinée (CBG) (Sangarédi mines); Guinea Alumina Corporation (GAC) Mine; Boffa Bauxite Mine; Bel Air Mine

Second Layer: The Industrial Core

Alcoa; Rio Tinto; Emirates Global Aluminium (EGA) ; SMB-Winning consortium Chalco / Hongqiao

Third Layer: Virtual Innovative Open Incubators

Alumina Refining and Mineral Processing; Alumina refining using the Bayer process; Chemical processing for aluminum feedstock

Fourth layer local creation of related and supporting industries based on the minerals of the mines

The Mahenge Graphite Project, located in the Morogoro region of Tanzania and developed by Black Rock Mining, represents one of the largest undeveloped graphite deposits globally (Bijaoui, 2025; 2026). The project's scale, high-quality flake graphite, and long projected mine life position it as a strategic asset within the emerging global supply chain for battery materials, particularly for electric vehicles (EVs) and energy storage systems.

The project illustrates a transition from a traditional extractive enclave toward a resource-based innovation cluster, highlighting the potential for downstream value addition. The involvement of POSCO, a leading South Korean industrial conglomerate, signals a deliberate strategy to develop battery-grade anode materials, linking raw graphite extraction to high-value industrial applications.

Main Mines / Deposits

The Mahenge Graphite Project consists of a multi-deposit mining complex, including:

Ulanzi Deposit
Cascade Deposit
Ownership Structure:
Black Rock Mining – 84% (indirect)
Faru Graphite Corporation – equity partner
Government of Tanzania – 16%

Related Industries

Graphite from Mahenge has applications across several high-value sectors:

Battery and Energy Storage Industry – Lithium-ion battery anodes, EV supply chains

Advanced Materials – Graphene and carbon-based nanomaterials
Industrial Materials – Refractories, lubricants, steel additives

Supporting Industries

Supporting industries are crucial for operational efficiency and value addition:

Mining Engineering and Technical Services – Drilling, blasting, mine planning, and geological surveying

Metallurgical Testing and Laboratory Services – Mineral characterization and quality control

Equipment and Machinery Supply – Earth-moving machinery, crushers, grinding systems, and processing plant infrastructure

Midstream Industries (Processing and Beneficiation)

Processing infrastructure enables the transformation of raw graphite into high-value products:

Mineral processing: crushing, flotation, and purification of graphite concentrate

Chemical processing and materials refinement: thermal and chemical purification, shaping (spheronization) for battery-grade applications

Infrastructure

Key infrastructure supports extraction, processing, and export:

Transport and Logistics – Road networks connecting Ulanga to Dar es Salaam port, freight logistics for export

Energy Supply – Initially diesel-based, with potential for renewable energy integration

Water Management and Environmental Services – Water treatment, recycling systems, tailings management, and environmental monitoring

Universities and Research Institutions Involved

University of Dar es Salaam – Provides upstream expertise in economic geology, mineral resource assessment, and environmental impact analysis. The university supports fundamental understanding of graphite mineralization across Tanzania's Neoproterozoic belts.

Nelson Mandela African Institution of Science and Technology (NM-AIST) – Focused on materials science and nanotechnology, NM-AIST occupies the downstream segment of the graphite value chain, with potential to advance high-value derivatives such as graphene and battery anodes.

Sokoine University of Agriculture – Provides research support in environmental systems, water management, and sustainable mining practices.

Despite geographic proximity and research capacity, collaboration between these institutions and the Mahenge project remains largely indirect, mediated through national research agendas rather than formalized partnerships. This highlights a structural gap in Tanzania's mining innovation ecosystem.

Associated metallurgical laboratories – Support processing and quality assurance

Ardhi University – Offers expertise in spatial planning and infrastructure management.

Figure 6. Mahenge graphite project, Tanzania

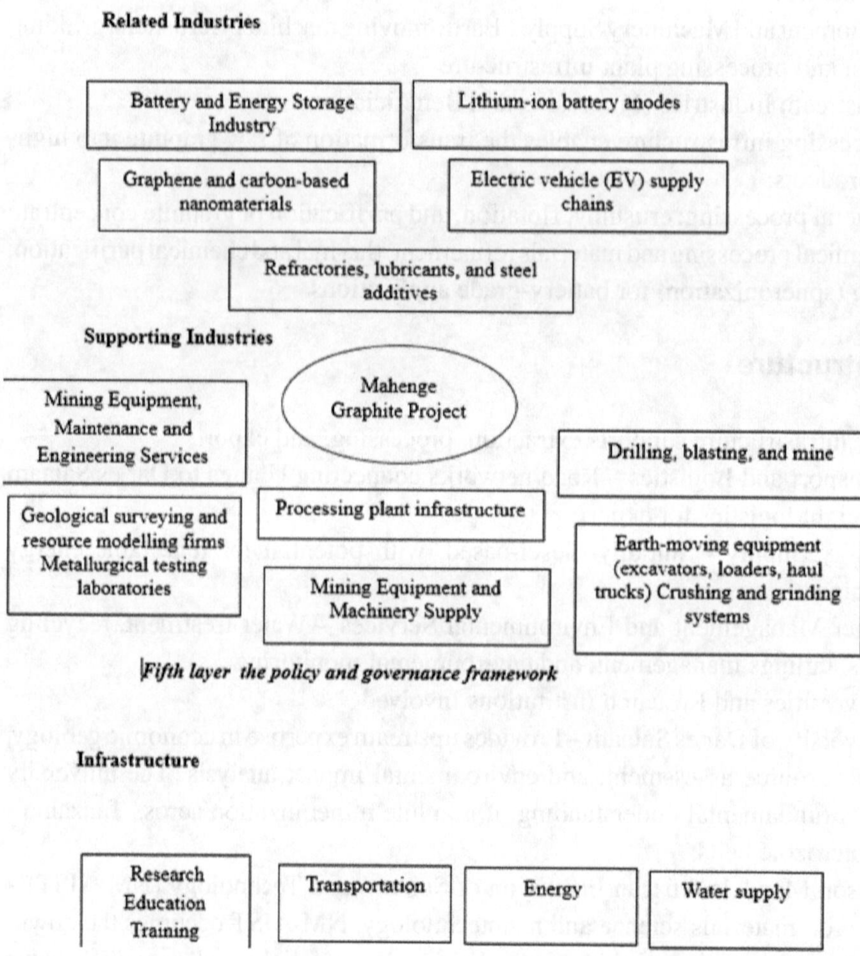

First Layer: The Resource Base

Mines / Deposits within Mahenge Project; Cascade Deposit;

Second Layer: The Industrial Core

Black Rock Mining 84% ownership (indirect) ; Faru Graphite Corporation ; Government of Tanzania 16%

Third Layer: Virtual Innovative Open Incubators

Battery and Energy Storage Industry; Lithium-ion battery anodes; Refractories, lubricants, and steel additives

Figure 7.

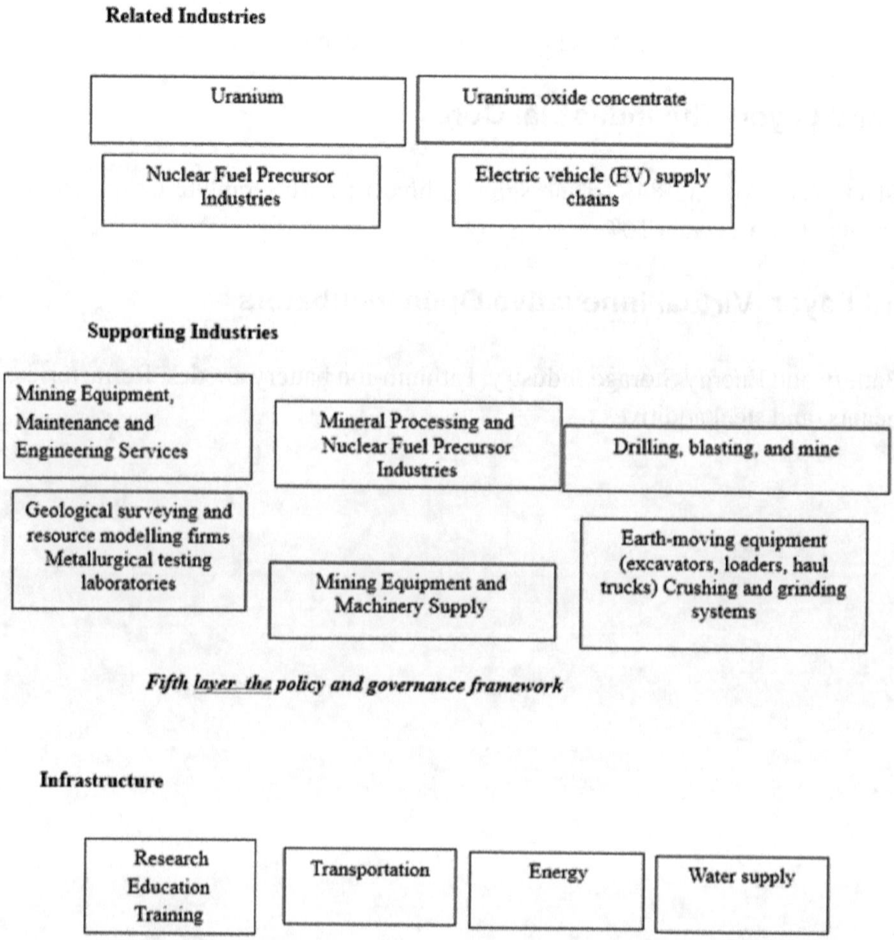

Uranium Extraction in Namibia: Industrial Structure and Supporting Systems

Uranium mining has been a foundational sector in Namibia's economy for nearly five decades, contributing significant export revenue, employment, and industrial activity (Keatom & Tshitereke, 2019). Large-scale production began in the mid-1970s and expanded notably in the early 2000s as global demand for nuclear fuel increased. The industry is geographically concentrated in the Erongo Region, where multiple uranium deposits occur within the Damara Belt, a geologically favorable zone that has enabled clustering of mining and associated industries.

Major Mines and Operators

The following uranium operations form the core of Namibia's uranium production:

Husab Uranium Mine – Operated by a subsidiary of China General Nuclear Power Group (CGN), Husab is one of the largest uranium mines globally, employing mechanized open-pit extraction methods and modern processing infrastructure (CGN Namibia, 2024).

Rössing Uranium Mine – Located near Swakopmund, Rössing has been in continuous operation since 1976. It is historically one of the world's largest open-pit uranium producers. The China National Uranium Corporation (CNUC) holds a majority stake following recent ownership restructuring (Rössing Annual Report, 2023).

Langer Heinrich Mine – Situated in central-western Namibia, this mine is operated by Paladin Energy (Australia). After a period of care and maintenance, operations recommenced in late 2024 with full production expected by 2026 (Paladin Energy, 2025).

These mines produce uranium oxide concentrate (U_3O_8) for export, primarily serving global nuclear fuel markets, and constitute a spatial cluster that supports specialized infrastructure and service industries.

Supporting and Related Industries

The uranium sector's operation depends on a range of supporting industries that enable efficient exploration, extraction, processing, and export:

Geological and Survey Services

Geological surveying and exploration firms provide ore grade control, geostatistical modeling, and resource assessment critical for mine planning (Simpson & Du Plessis, 2018).

Metallurgical laboratories and process engineering specialists assist in optimizing leach and purification methods.

Mineral Processing and Nuclear Fuel Precursor Industries

Uranium processing involves crushing and leaching of ore, followed by solvent extraction and precipitation to produce uranium oxide concentrate (U_3O_8) (Nuclear Energy Agency, 2020).

Radiological safety and waste management systems are essential components of processing operations due to the radioactive nature of uranium ores.

Supporting Equipment and Services

Mining engineering and technical services cover drilling, blasting, mine planning, and heavy machinery maintenance.

Industrial automation and digital mine management systems support real-time operations monitoring.

Environmental impact assessment (EIA) firms and climate/biodiversity monitoring technologies ensure regulatory compliance and environmental stewardship.

Infrastructure and Logistics

Uranium mining and shipment rely on critical national infrastructure:

Transport and Export Logistics: The Port of Walvis Bay serves as Namibia's principal export gateway for uranium concentrate. Road and rail connections link the Erongo mining hubs to coastal ports, enabling efficient freight movement (Namibia Ports Authority, 2024).

Energy Supply: Mining and processing are energy-intensive; operations depend on the national grid managed by NamPower, supplemented by on-site generation where necessary.

Water Systems: In the arid Namib Desert environment, water is a strategic input. Desalination plants and long-distance water pipelines provide the industrial water required for leaching and processing (Water Utility Corporation Report, 2023).

Environmental and Safety Services: Continuous environmental monitoring, tailings management systems, and radiation protection infrastructures are integral to safe operations.

Research, Training, and Innovation Nodes

Institutions in Namibia support technical expertise and research relevant to the uranium cluster:

University of Namibia (UNAM) – Engages in geological sciences, environmental research, and resource management studies.

Namibia University of Science and Technology (NUST) – Offers programs in mining engineering, mineral processing, and radiological science, contributing to workforce development (UNAM & NUST Academic Catalogues, 2024).

Namibian Uranium Association (NUA) – A sector platform that facilitates knowledge sharing, training, regulatory best practices, and environmental stewardship among industry actors.

Namibia's academic and industry institutions also participate in international research collaborations in areas such as radiological safety, advanced processing technologies, and nuclear fuel cycle research, strengthening the country's integration into global uranium science networks.

Figure 8. Uranium extraction in Namibia

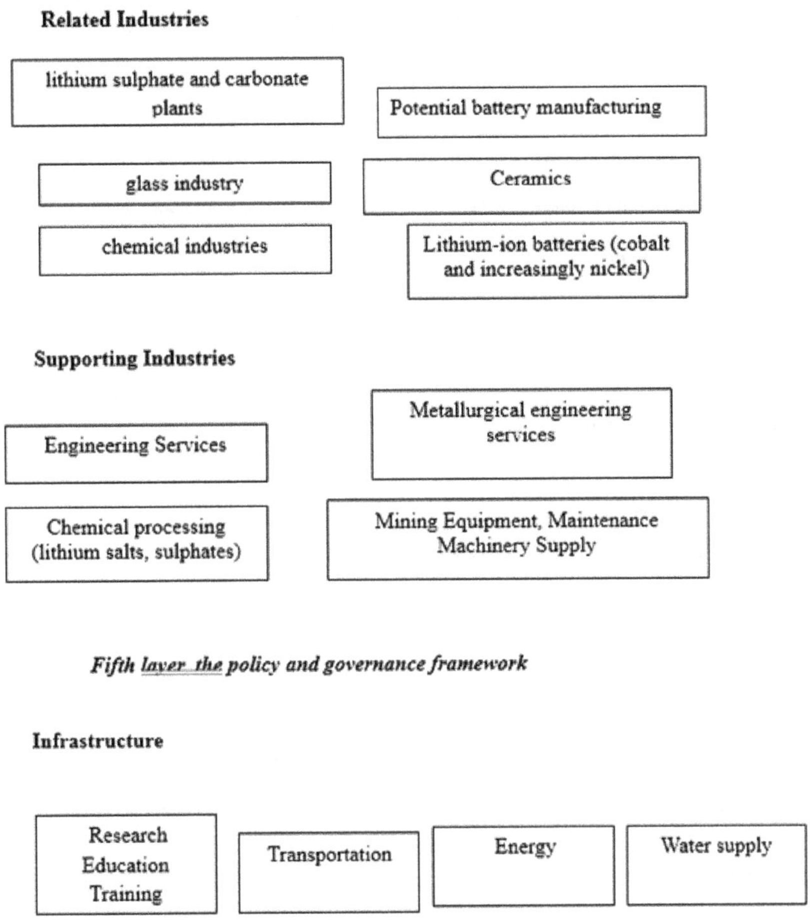

First Layer: The Resource Base

Husab, Uranium Mine; Rössing Uranium; Langer Heinrich Mine.

Second Layer: The Industrial Core

China General Nuclear Power Group (CGN), Mine China National Uranium Corporation (CNUC); Paladin Energy (Australia).

Third Layer: Virtual Innovative Open Incubators

Uranium oxide concentrate (U_3O_8); Nuclear Fuel Precursor Industries

Figure 9.

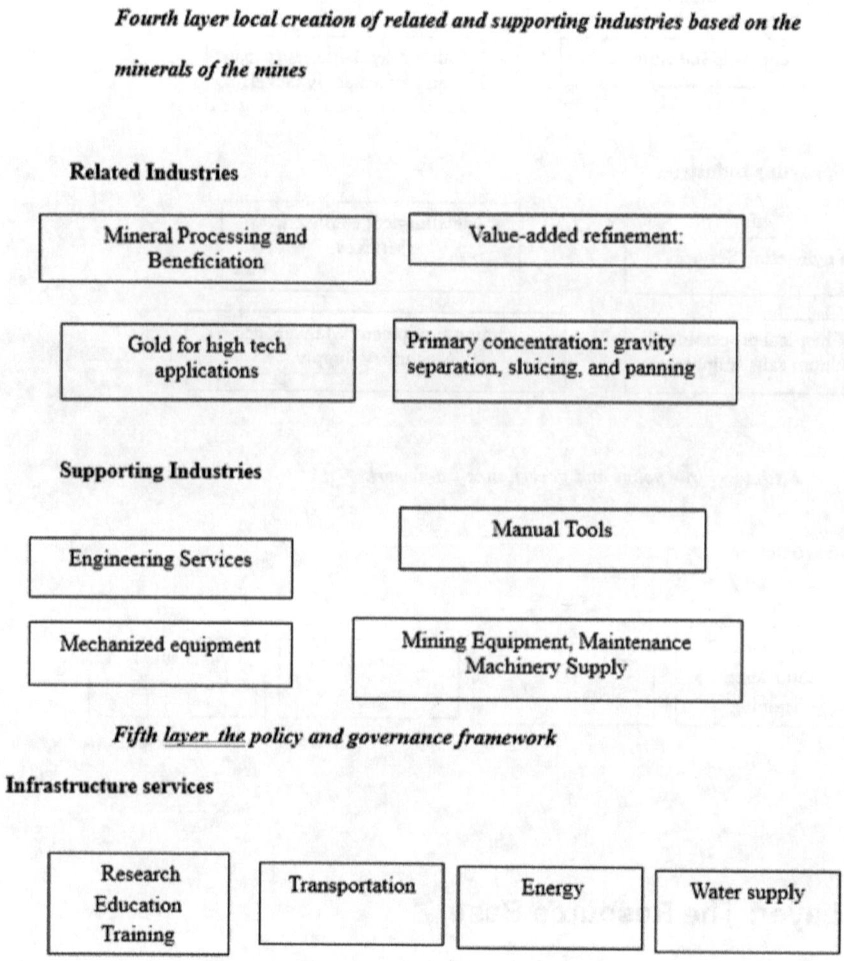

Lithium Resources in Zimbabwe: Mining, Industry, and Innovation Ecosystem

Zimbabwe is endowed with one of Africa's largest lithium resource bases and ranks among the world's top producers (Hatch, 2023; United States Geological Survey, 2024). Lithium deposits are distributed across several key provinces: Manicaland (Bikita and Arcadia), Masvingo (Sandawana belt), and Mashonaland East (Goromonzi lithium corridor). These deposits provide the foundation for both mineral extraction and emerging downstream industrial activities.

Major Lithium Mining Projects

Zimbabwe hosts a range of lithium mining operations, encompassing both primary deposits and tailings reprocessing:

Bikita Minerals – One of the world's oldest lithium mines, producing petalite and spodumene.

Arcadia Lithium Project – A large-scale spodumene resource located near Harare, with significant potential for high-grade lithium concentrate.

Sandawana Mine – Historically an emerald mine, now redeveloped for lithium extraction.

Kamitivi Tailings Project – Focused on reprocessing legacy lithium-bearing tailings to recover additional lithium compounds.

Sabi Star Lithium Mine – Operated primarily by the Chengxin Lithium Group, representing major international investment.

Zulu Lithium and Tantalum Project – Developed by Premier African Minerals, combining lithium and tantalum extraction.

Collectively, these operations have positioned Zimbabwe as Africa's leading lithium producer, accounting for over 10% of global supply by 2024 (United States Geological Survey, 2024; African Mining Review, 2023).

Related Industries and Value Chain Development

Zimbabwe's lithium sector supports the development of downstream industrial activities, with opportunities to create an integrated battery materials ecosystem:

Lithium chemical production – Lithium sulphate and lithium carbonate plants are emerging to supply battery precursor materials.

Battery precursor materials – Lithium hydroxide and carbonate production for electric vehicle (EV) supply chains.

Potential battery manufacturing – National policy aspirations aim to establish local battery assembly, though industrial capacity remains nascent.

Industrial uses – Ceramics, glass production, and specialty chemical industries benefit from lithium-derived products.

Supporting Industries

Efficient mining and mineral processing require specialized technical and industrial support:

Mining services – Drilling, blasting, contract mining, and mine maintenance.

Geological surveying and exploration – Mineral resource modeling and geochemical analysis.

Equipment supply – Crushers, flotation systems, concentrators, and processing plant infrastructure.

Chemical processing – Production of lithium salts, sulphates, and intermediate compounds.

Metallurgical engineering services – Expertise in extractive metallurgy, beneficiation, and process optimization.

Infrastructure and Logistics

Robust infrastructure is critical to sustaining lithium production and industrial development:

Energy systems – High electrical demand for spodumene processing and chemical conversion.

Water supply – Processing-intensive industry requires reliable water infrastructure.

Transport and logistics – Rail and road networks connect mines to ports in Mozambique and South Africa for international export.

Research and Knowledge Ecosystem

Zimbabwe's universities and specialized institutions support innovation and technical capacity in the lithium sector:

University of Zimbabwe – Mineral processing, extractive metallurgy, and environmental sustainability.

Midlands State University – Mining engineering and geoscience research.

Chinhoyi University of Technology – Applied mineral processing and industrial chemistry.

Zimbabwe School of Mines – Practical mining engineering, geosciences, and technical training.

Research focuses on spodumene beneficiation, lithium extraction, environmental impact mitigation, and sustainable mining practices, forming a foundational knowledge base for industrial upgrading and value addition within the lithium supply chain (Chinembiri et al., 2022; Musarurwa et al., 2023).

Figure 10. Lithium resources in Zimbabwe

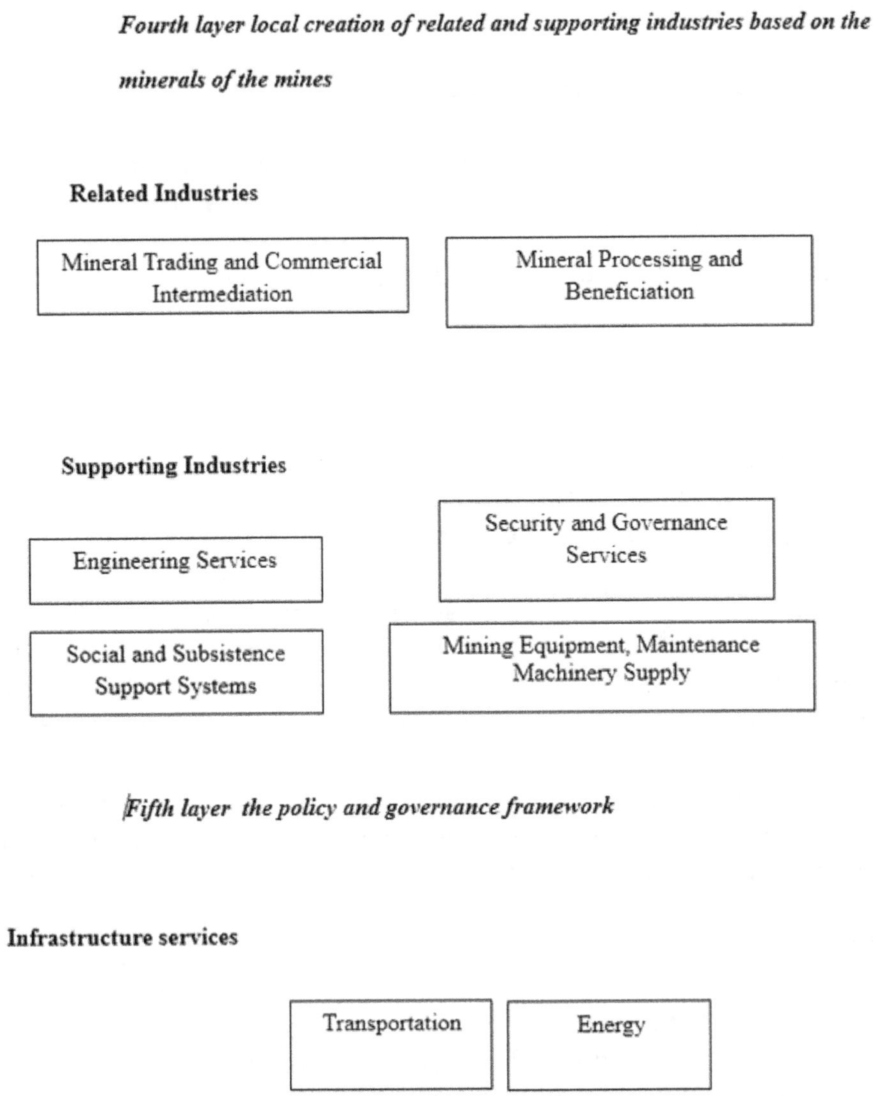

First Layer: The Resource Base

Bikita Minerals, lithium mines (petalite and spodumene); Arcadia Lithium Project – large-scale spodumene resource near Harare; Sandawana Mine, lithium; Kamitivi Tailings Project, lithium tailings. Sabi Star Lithium Mine; Zulu Lithium and Tantalum Project

Second Layer: The Industrial Core

Sinomine Resource Group; : Zhejiang Huayou Cobalt (via Prospect Lithium Zimbabwe); Chengxin Lithium Group (major stake) Premier African Minerals

Third Layer: Virtual Innovative Open Incubators

Lithium sulphate and carbonate; battery precursor materials (lithium hydroxide/carbonate); Ceramics, glass, and industrial chemical industries

Gold Mining in the Democratic Republic of the Congo, Tanzania, Mali, and Burkina Faso: Industry and Supporting Ecosystems

Gold mining is a cornerstone of several African economies, particularly in the Democratic Republic of the Congo (DRC), Tanzania, Mali, and Burkina Faso, where both artisanal and industrial operations coexist. In these countries, gold contributes substantially to export earnings, employment, and local economic development (Hilson & Maconachie, 2020; World Bank, 2023).

Africa remains a preeminent source of global gold production, with mining activities concentrated in countries such as South Africa, Ghana, Mali, Tanzania, and the Democratic Republic of the Congo.

South Africa

Mponeng Gold Mine and South Deep

In South Africa, mines such as the Mponeng (AngloGold Ashanti) and South Deep (Gold Fields) exemplify technologically advanced underground mining, exploiting the rich Witwatersrand Basin. These operations are supported by integrated processing facilities, mechanized transport, and formal labor structures, representing a highly industrialized model of gold extraction

Ghana

Ghana represents one of Africa's most stable gold-producing economies. Multinational mining corporations such as AngloGold Ashanti and Barrick Gold operate large-scale industrial mines, employing advanced extraction technologies and integrating production into global commodity markets.

The University of Mines and Technology (UMaT) plays a strategic role in mining engineering and mineral processing education. Kwame Nkrumah University of Science and Technology (KNUST) has strengths in engineering, applied sciences, and materials research.

Obuasi and Tarkwa Gold Mine

In Ghana, the Witwatersrand-like Birimian greenstone belts host large-scale mines such as Obuasi Gold Mine and Tarkwa Mine, with operations like the Sadiola Gold Mine and the Loulo-Gounkoto complex producing significant quantities of high-grade gold and anchoring Mali's position as a key player in global gold markets.

Mali

Sadiola Gold Mine and Loulo-Gounkoto Gold Mine

Mali host large-scale industrial complexes like the Loulo-Gounkoto (Barrick) and Sadiola mines (AngloGold Ashanti), integrate modern extraction technologies with local labor engagement. These operations rely heavily on supporting industries for equipment supply, mineral processing, and logistical coordination.

Tanzania

Geita and Bulyanhulu Gold Mine

Tanzania's Geita (AngloGold Ashanti) and Bulyanhulu (Acacia Mining) mines exemplify the combination of mechanized open-pit and underground mining, supplemented by processing plants, security provision, and community engagement services to support sustainable production.

DRC

Kibali Gold Mine

In the Democratic Republic of the Congo, the Kibali (Barrick Gold) and Mongbwalu mines (AngloGold Ashanti) illustrate the hybrid nature of African gold mining, where large-scale industrial operations coexist with artisanal and small-scale mining.Société Minière de Kilo-Moto (SOKIMO): Integrates advanced extraction technologies and supports local development programs.

Burkina Faso

Essakane Gold Mine

Essakane Gold Mine (IAMGOLD Corporation) is one of the largest gold operations in Burkina Faso; incorporates modern processing and mechanized operations

Bissa Gold Mine

Bissa Gold Mine (Nordgold) uses conventional crushing, grinding, and carbon-in-leach (CIL) processing; supports local employment and infrastructure development.

Youga Gold Mine

Youga Gold Mine (Endeavour Mining)focuses on semi-industrial operations, integrating local artisanal labor under formalized safety and environmental standards

Houndé Gold Mine

Houndé Gold Mine (Endeavour Mining) combines mechanized extraction with local labor; integrated processing facility with cyanidation and carbon-in-leach (CIL) methods

Bouly Gold Mine

Bouly Gold Mine is a small- to medium-scale mechanized operation with local community engagement programs

Related Industries

African gold-producing regions are increasingly developing local processing capacity to enhance value addition, reduce reliance on raw exports, and integrate into global supply chains:

Primary concentration – Techniques such as gravity separation, sluicing, and panning remain prevalent, particularly in artisanal and small-scale mining (ASM) operations.

Semi-industrial processing – Small- and medium-scale mines often employ milling, cyanidation, and flotation circuits to improve recovery rates.

Value-added refinement – Select industrial hubs, notably in South Africa and Ghana, provide bullion production and further processing for export.

Gold for high-technology applications Increasingly, refined gold from African sources is directed toward electronics, aerospace, and medical industries.

Supporting Industries

Gold mining operations rely on a network of supporting industries that ensure operational efficiency, equipment supply, and technical services:

Equipment Supply, Machinery, and Maintenance

Manual tools (shovels, pans, sluices) for artisanal miners.

Mechanized equipment (crushers, trommels, centrifugal concentrators) for small- and medium-scale mines.

Maintenance workshops, spare-part suppliers, and equipment servicing sustain mining continuity, particularly in remote or logistically challenging areas.

Infrastructure Services

The extraction and processing of gold depend on adequate infrastructure and logistics networks:

Transport and Logistics

Road, river, and rail networks move gold and mining inputs from remote sites to processing or export hubs.

Air transport and secure courier services are frequently used for high-value shipments, especially in conflict-sensitive regions.

Transport systems also facilitate the delivery of fuel, equipment, and provisions to remote mining camps.

Energy and Utilities

Electricity, water supply, and fuel are critical for both mechanized extraction and mineral processing.

Telecommunications and internet connectivity support operational coordination, market intelligence, and financial transactions.

Environmental and Community Support

Environmental monitoring, mine reclamation, and tailings management reduce ecological impact.

Health, sanitation, and education programs support mining communities and workforce development (Armah et al., 2021).

Financial and Governance Services

Gold mining in Africa is underpinned by financial and governance systems that support both artisanal and industrial operations:

Financial services

Trader-financed loans provide working capital for ASM operations.

Local microfinance institutions and mobile money platforms facilitate payments and capital circulation.

Banks and export credit facilities support industrial mining projects and international trade.

Security and Compliance

Oversight mechanisms, including mine audits, certification schemes (e.g., Fairmined, Responsible Gold), and government regulations, ensure compliance with national and international standards.

Security services are critical in conflict-prone regions to protect both personnel and high-value outputs.

First Layer: The Resource Base

Mponeng Gold Mine and South Deep; Obuasi Gold Mine and Tarkwa Mine Sadiola; Gold Mine and Loulo-Gounkoto Gold Mine; Geita and Bulyanhulu Gold Mine; Kibali Gold Min; Essakane Gold Mine; Bissa Gold Mine; Youga Gold Mine; Houndé Gold Mine; Bouly Gold Mine

Second Layer: The Industrial Core

AngloGold Ashanti and Barrick Gold Acacia Mining IAMGOLD Corporation Nordgold Endeavour Mining

Third Layer: Virtual Innovative Open Incubators

Primary concentration;Semi-industrial processing; Value-added refinement; Gold for high-technology applications

The Innovation Layer of the Global Coltan–Tantalum Value Chain: Structure, Power, and Technological Concentration in the DRC–Rwanda Context

Coltan, the principal ore of tantalum, is a critical material renowned for its high melting point, corrosion resistance, and excellent capacitance properties, making it essential for advanced electronic, aerospace, and biomedical applications (Bijaoui, 2025). The global coltan–tantalum sector can be analyzed through the combined frameworks of Global Value Chain (GVC) theory and National/Transnational Innovation Systems. GVC theory emphasizes the fragmentation of production across geographically dispersed yet functionally interconnected stages, where value accrual is uneven and largely dependent on technological capabilities, governance arrangements, and intellectual property (Humphrey & Schmitz, 2002; Gereffi, 2018). Within this framework, technological upgrading is contingent not only on participation in extraction or trade but also on access to high-value segments such as research and development (R&D), advanced materials engineering, and component manufacturing.

The Innovation Layer

The innovation layer of the coltan–tantalum value chain is concentrated among a small set of specialized organizations operating across materials science, refining technologies, and electronic component production. Central to this layer is the Tantalum-Niobium International Study Center (TIC), which coordinates industry actors, establishes technical standards, and facilitates information exchange throughout the global supply chain (Tantalum-Niobium International Study Center, 2024). TIC comprises over 90 members, including mining companies, smelters, component manufacturers, and technology developers, and monitors innovations in tantalum capacitors, thin-film semiconductors (TaN), high-performance alloys, biomedical implants, and sustainability practices (Responsible Minerals Initiative, 2023).

Global regulatory and research networks also intersect with this innovation layer. The OECD provides due diligence frameworks affecting sourcing, while the International Conference on the Great Lakes Region (ICGLR) shapes regional mineral governance. Additionally, the International Atomic Energy Agency (IAEA) addresses transport and safety issues, and initiatives like the Responsible Minerals Initiative (RMI) and CRM Alliance facilitate research and policy coordination in critical raw materials (International Conference on the Great Lakes Region, 2022; International Atomic Energy Agency, 2023).

Mining and Industrial Actors

In Central Africa, governance and extraction are managed by bodies such as the Rwanda Mines Petroleum and Gas Board (RMB) and the Rwanda Mining Association (RMA), alongside mine operators including Société Minière de Bisunzu (SMB) and Samikivu S.A.R.L. (Société Minière de Bisunzu, 2024). Downstream, global smelters and processors—such as H.C. Starck Solutions, Halcyon Inc., Jiujiang Fuxing Tai Trade Co. Ltd., and SAMWOOD NEO Inc.—play pivotal roles in refining and distributing tantalum and niobium products.

At the industrial level, three firms dominate upstream innovation in refining and advanced materials: Ningxia Orient Tantalum Industry Co., Ltd. (China), H.C. Starck Solutions (Germany/USA), and Cabot Corporation (USA). These companies specialize in high-purity tantalum powders, oxides, and engineered metal forms, maintaining proprietary technologies in chemical purification, powder morphology, and nano-scale processing (Global Advanced Metals, 2023). Downstream component manufacturing, led by firms such as KEMET and Kyocera, transforms refined tantalum into capacitors and microelectronic components, with substantial patent holdings and technological influence.

Knowledge Concentration and Value Capture

A defining feature of the innovation layer is the concentration of intellectual property. Approximately 85–90% of patents related to tantalum technologies are held by entities in the United States, Germany, Japan, and China, while African producer countries such as the DRC and Rwanda account for less than 1% (Bijaoui, 2026). This disparity illustrates the structural decoupling between resource extraction and technological innovation, creating a technological dependency where Central African countries remain confined to low-value segments of the value chain.

Value distribution further underscores the centrality of the innovation layer:

Extraction in the DRC: 5–10% of total value

Trade and aggregation (Rwanda): 10–15%

Processing and refining: 20–25% (controlled by firms such as Ningxia, H.C. Starck, and Cabot)

Component manufacturing: 20–30% (KEMET, Kyocera)

Innovation, R&D, and advanced materials engineering: 35–45%

The innovation layer's dominance is reinforced by organizations like TIC, which consolidate technological standards and coordinate global actors, further embedding value and power asymmetries (Tantalum-Niobium International Study Center, 2024; Gereffi, 2018).

Emerging Research Frontiers

Tantalum's strategic significance stems from its high dielectric constant, thermal stability, corrosion resistance, and biocompatibility. Current research focuses on advanced applications including quantum and nanoelectronics, superconducting circuits, next-generation semiconductors, energy storage systems (lithium-ion batteries and supercapacitors), and biomedical engineering (porous tantalum implants and regenerative medicine) (Responsible Minerals Initiative, 2023; International Atomic Energy Agency, 2023).

Main Coltan Mining Regions in Rwanda

North Kivu Province, DRC

North Kivu is a key mineral-producing province in eastern Democratic Republic of the Congo (DRC), containing rich deposits of coltan, gold, tin, and tungsten. The Rubaya mining area in Masisi Territory is the most significant coltan region in the DRC, historically contributing approximately 15% of global supply (Global Witness, 2025). The primary license holder is Société Minière de Bisunzu (SMB) Sarl, associated with Édouard Mwangachuchu, although artisanal and small-scale miners, often organized in local cooperatives such as COOPERAMMA, conduct the majority of extraction (Société Minière de Bisunzu, 2024). Key coltan sites include Luwowo, Gakombe D4, Koyi, Mataba D2, Bundjali, and Bibatama.

The 2025 offensive by the M23 rebel group disrupted control over strategic mining hubs, including Walikale, affecting transport corridors and mineral access. Armed groups continue to dominate many artisanal mining areas, generating revenue through illicit mineral trade and perpetuating regional insecurity.

Impacts on Communities:

Displacement: Civilians near conflict-affected mines have fled to towns such as Goma, overwhelming social services.

Livelihoods: Traditional economic activities, including agriculture, have been disrupted, leaving mining as the primary but high-risk income source.

Government Revenue Loss: Smuggling and illegal extraction reduce state revenues for public services such as healthcare, education, and water infrastructure (Global Witness, 2025).

South Kivu Province, DRC

South Kivu's mining landscape is dominated by artisanal operations producing coltan, cassiterite, and gold, often with limited regulation and safety protocols. Landslides and collapses, such as the 2025 disaster at Lomera, have caused fatalities among miners (Environmental Justice Foundation, 2025).

Key Mining Zones:

Shabunda: Coltan and tin

Mwenga: Gold (primary), coltan, cassiterite; notable industrial mine Twangiza

Kalehe: Cassiterite and coltan; key site Nyabibwe

Fizi: Gold and coltan; sites Misisi and Baraka

Walungu: Cassiterite and coltan; site Nzibira

Urban and Social Impacts:

Migration to cities like Bukavu places pressure on housing, sanitation, and public health services.

Artisanal mining income is irregular, contributing to economic disparity despite local mineral wealth.

Disease outbreaks (e.g., cholera) are common due to poor sanitation and healthcare access.

Ituri and Maniema Provinces

Ituri and parts of Maniema host significant coltan and cassiterite deposits, largely exploited by artisanal and small-scale miners. Towns such as Bunia act as trade hubs. Decades of ethnic and resource-based conflicts, combined with weak governance, have exacerbated insecurity, displacement, and environmental degradation, including deforestation and water pollution (Global Witness, 2025; Environmental Justice Foundation, 2025).

Additional Eastern DRC Deposits

Smaller-scale coltan occurrences exist in Tshopo, Haut-Lomami, and Tanganyika provinces, often explored or mined on an artisanal basis. Armed groups, including M23 and previously active militias, exert influence over mining and export routes, collecting taxes and shaping local economies (Global Witness, 2025).

Goma — Strategic Urban Hub

The city of Goma, capital of North Kivu province, functions as a critical hub for mineral transit, trade, and humanitarian operations. Its location on Lake Kivu and proximity to Rwanda make it strategically and economically significant but highly vulnerable to conflict-driven instability.

2025–2026 Conflict Effects:

M23 Capture of Goma: The January 2025 offensive displaced over 700,000 internally displaced persons (IDPs), adding to pre-existing population pressures.

Infrastructure Disruption: Electricity, water, and transport networks were severely affected, impairing public services and trade.

Health and Humanitarian Crisis: Hospitals were attacked, staff fled, and disease risk increased due to poor sanitation, overcrowding, and disrupted water supplies.

Economic Impacts: Mining-based trade slowed, supply chains were interrupted, and illegal extraction further undermined government revenue.

Environmental Concerns: Mining and artisanal extraction contribute to deforestation, soil erosion, and water contamination, which in turn affect urban agriculture and

Main Coltan Mining Regions in Rwanda

Rwanda's coltan (columbite–tantalite) resources are primarily concentrated in the Western and Northern Provinces, with smaller occurrences in the Southern Province. These regions form part of the Albertine Rift metallogenic belt, hosting pegmatitic systems enriched with tantalum, cassiterite (tin), and wolframite (tungsten) (UN Panel of Experts, 2025).

Western Province

Ngororero District: Site of the Rukaragata mine near Lake Kivu, a formal coltan mining area.

Muhanga and Gakenke Districts: Production is variable, encompassing both artisanal and semi-industrial operations.

Northern Province

Musanze and Burera Districts: Secondary but significant mining zones with dispersed coltan deposits.

Southern Province

Huye District: Contains limited coltan occurrences, generally lower grade and of minor economic significance.

Key Mining Actors and Trade Networks

Boss Mining Solution Ltd.: A Rwandan firm implicated in purchasing coltan that, according to Reuters and UN reports, likely originates from DRC mines under rebel control (UN Panel of Experts, 2025).

Ownership: Eddy Habimana and two businessmen with British/Russian citizenship (Yuriy Tolmatchev and Alexander Konovalchik).

Related Industries

Mineral Trading and Commercial Intermediation

Complex networks of traders, négociants, and export houses operate across South Kivu, North Kivu, and Rwanda, linking artisanal mining sites to regional and global markets.

Urban hubs such as Bukavu and cross-border corridors are pivotal for mineral aggregation, valuation, and export logistics.

Mineral Processing and Beneficiation

Processing at the local level is generally limited to primary concentration: washing, sorting, and grading.

Advanced refining and value addition are largely externalized to international markets, reflecting the classic resource-dependent economy pattern.

Supporting Industries

Equipment supply and machinery maintenance for artisanal and semi-industrial mining operations.

Security and governance services to manage extraction risks in conflict-sensitive zones.

Social and subsistence support systems for mining communities.

Infrastructure and Logistics

Transport networks include road, riverine, and lake transport systems, often relying on motorcycles ("moto-taxis") for last-mile connectivity.

Mineral transit routes along Lake Kivu facilitate movement of ores to regional collection and export centers.

First Layer: The Resource Base

Rubaya Area; Luwowo; Gakombe; Koyi; Mataba;Bundjali; Bibatama; Shabunda; Kamituga and Lulingu;Twangiza and Kamanyola; Misisi and Baraka; Nzibira; Tshopo Tanganyika Regions; Rukaragata mine

Second Layer: The Industrial Core

Ningxia Orient Tantalum Industry Co., Ltd.; H.C. Starck Solutions; Cabot Corporation; Barrick Gold; AngloGold Ashanti; IAMGOLD; Nordgold; Boss Mining; Novacore Mwangachuchu; Hizi International (MHI)

Third Layer: Virtual Innovative Open Incubators

Mineral Processing and Beneficiation

Potential Development

The mining sector in South Kivu Province is underpinned by a complex network of related industries and infrastructural services that extend beyond the extraction of minerals to encompass processing, trade facilitation, financing, and logistical support. These sectors are essential for sustaining both artisanal and industrial mining operations, linking the province's mineral resources—primarily coltan, cassiterite, and gold—to regional and global value chains. Understanding this ecosystem is crucial for assessing the economic, social, and governance dynamics of mining in South Kivu.

Artisanal and small-scale miners depend on traders and négociants who aggregate, grade, and commercialize minerals from remote sites, including Shabunda Territory, Mwenga Territory, and Kalehe Territory. Urban centers such as Bukavu serve as critical nodes where minerals are consolidated, certified, and prepared for export, often via cross-border routes into Rwanda. These trading networks provide essential pre-financing to miners, enabling sustained production despite the absence of formal banking services, but simultaneously reinforce informality and opacity in local supply chains.

Transport and logistics services constitute another critical infrastructural component. The province's mountainous terrain, limited road networks, and seasonal inaccessibility necessitate a combination of transport modalities, including motorcycle and light-vehicle haulage, human porterage in remote zones, and river or lake transport along Lake Kivu. These networks facilitate the movement of raw minerals from remote extraction sites to aggregation and export points but impose high transaction costs and constrain the efficiency of mineral flows.

The provision of equipment and maintenance services forms a complementary industry, supplying miners with both manual and mechanized tools, small-scale crushers, sluices, and spare parts. Most equipment is imported via regional trade channels, particularly from Rwanda, reflecting South Kivu's limited domestic manufacturing capacity. Maintenance services, while rudimentary, are essential for sustaining operational continuity in artisanal and semi-industrial mining contexts.

Mineral processing and beneficiation services are predominantly confined to primary concentration activities such as sorting, washing, and grading. Local processing is limited, and higher-value refinement occurs largely outside the province or country, underscoring a structural gap in local value addition and perpetuating South Kivu's role as a raw-material supplier.

Financial intermediation, primarily through informal credit systems, constitutes an indispensable support mechanism. Traders often provide upfront financing to miners, while mobile money platforms and community-based microfinance initiatives facilitate liquidity and working capital circulation. These mechanisms enable ongoing production but often at high implicit costs, reinforcing the dependency of miners on external actors.

Security and governance-related services are another vital, though complex, component of the supporting infrastructure. Mining regions, particularly in Shabunda Territory and Fizi Territory, require both formal state security provision and informal community-based arrangements to manage site access, labor safety, and the secure transport of minerals. The interplay of these arrangements often shapes revenue flows and local power dynamics.

Essential utilities and infrastructure services—including limited electricity supply, water provision for mineral processing, road and bridge networks, and communications systems—constitute the backbone enabling mining operations. Cross-border trade infrastructure, such as customs posts and logistical corridors, further integrates South Kivu into regional supply chains and facilitates export-oriented mineral flows.

REFERENCES

African Mining Review. (2023). *Zimbabwe lithium mining: Industry trends and prospects*. AMR Publishing.

Armah, F. A., Amponsah, P., & Osei, K. A. (2021). Sustainability and community development in African gold mining regions. *Resources Policy, 70*, 101952.

Bijaoui, I. (2025). Resource-based innovation in African critical minerals: A GVC approach. *African Journal of Industrial Development, 12*(3), 45–68.

Bijaoui, I. (2026). Technological upgrading in Central African mining ecosystems. *Journal of African Mining Studies, 8*(1), 1–34.

China General Nuclear Power Group (CGN) Namibia. (2024). *Husab uranium mine: Operations overview*. CGN Namibia.

Chinembiri, T., Moyo, P., & Chikukwa, R. (2022). Spodumene beneficiation and lithium extraction in Zimbabwe. *Journal of African Mineral Resources, 15*(2), 33–48.

Environmental Justice Foundation. (2025). *Mining and conflict in the eastern DRC: Humanitarian and environmental impacts*. EJF.

Gereffi, G. (2018). *Global Value Chains, Development, and Emerging Economies*. Cambridge University Press. DOI: 10.1017/9781108559423.013

Global Witness. (2025). *Eastern DRC mineral report: Conflict, displacement, and resource governance*. Global Witness.

GlobalDivide.org. (2025). *Urban resilience and resource extraction in Goma*. GlobalDivide Research.

Hatch. (2023). *Global lithium outlook: Zimbabwe's contribution to the supply chain*. Toronto: Hatch Ltd.

Hilson, G., & Maconachie, R. (2020). *Artisanal and small-scale mining in Africa: Economic and environmental perspectives*. Routledge.

Humphrey, J., & Schmitz, H. (2002). How does insertion in global value chains affect upgrading in industrial clusters? *Regional Studies, 36*(9), 1017–1027. DOI: 10.1080/0034340022000022198

International Atomic Energy Agency. (2023). *Materials safety and transport regulations*. IAEA.

International Conference on the Great Lakes Region. (2022). *Mineral governance and due diligence framework*. Bujumbura: ICGLR Secretariat.

Keatom, H., & Tshitereke, C. (2019). Uranium mining as an economic driver in Namibia. *African Mining Journal*, *8*(2), 44–58.

Louvain Cooperation. (2025). *Artisanal mining and urban centers in South Kivu*. Louvain Cooperation.

Musarurwa, C., Nyoni, J., & Tawanda, K. (2023). Sustainable practices in Zimbabwean lithium mining operations. *Southern African Journal of Mining Engineering*, *8*(1), 12–27.

Namibia Ports Authority. (2024). *Walvis Bay export statistics 2023–2024*. Walvis Bay: NPA.

Nuclear Energy Agency. (2020). *Uranium 2020: Resources, production and demand*. OECD/NEA and IAEA.

Paladin Energy. (2025). *Langer Heinrich restart plan and production forecast*. Paladin Energy Ltd.

Responsible Minerals Initiative. (2023). *Tantalum and niobium industry report*. RMI.

Reuters Investigations. (2025). *Rwandan firms and coltan trade links to DRC conflict zones*. Reuters.

Rössing Uranium Ltd. (2023). *Rössing annual report*. Swakopmund: Rössing Uranium Ltd.

Simpson, J., & Du Plessis, A. (2018). *Ore evaluation and mining geology techniques*. Mining Geoscience Publishing.

Société Minière de Bisunzu. (2024). *Corporate sustainability and production report*. SMB.

Tantalum-Niobium International Study Center. (2024). *Global coordination of tantalum and niobium supply chains*. Basel: TIC.

UN Panel of Experts on the DRC. (2025). *Report on mineral flows and armed group financing in the Great Lakes Region*. United Nations Security Council.

UNAM & NUST Academic Catalogues. (2024). *Program offerings in geological and mining sciences*. University of Namibia / Namibia University of Science and Technology.

United States Geological Survey. (2024). *Mineral commodity summaries 2024: Lithium*. USGS.

Water Utility Corporation. (2023). *Industrial water supply systems report*. Windhoek: WUC.

World Bank. (2023). *Gold mining in Africa: Economic contributions and policy challenges*. World Bank Publications.

Appendix

DISCONTINUOUS INNOVATIONS IN THE SAMPLE

Agriculture and Plant Biotechnology

Israel is leveraging genomics, AI, and robotics to enhance crop yield, resilience, and sustainability:

- Genomic Tools & miRNAs: Research at ARO Volcani and Ben-Gurion University (BGU) harnesses miRNAs as genome regulators in crops, improving resistance to diseases like tomato brown rugose fruit virus (TBRFV) and enhancing therapeutic compounds in medicinal plants (e.g., Ocimum, Salvia).
- Kenaf Valorization: Kenaf Green Industries (KGI) develops customized seed varieties for Mediterranean and arid climates, applying full-chain valorization to produce paper pulp, bioplastics, concrete composites, and bioenergy crops.
- Pollinator Monitoring & Robotics: BeeHero's Pollination Insight Platform (PIP) monitors pollinator activity.; Beewise automates hive management with AI-driven robotic "Beehomes" ; BloomX electrostatic pollination devices and Edete's ; Mechanized pollination complement traditional insect-based methods.
- Precision Agriculture Platforms: Agritask aggregates satellite, field, and weather data for farm analytics; Prospera employs AI-powered computer-vision sensors in greenhouses and fields; Netagrow offers a unified IoT-driven farm management suite with soil, pest, weather, and financial analytics; Croptune allows real-time nutrient monitoring (N, P, K) via smartphone and AI analysis; Hydroponics & Controlled. Environment Agriculture: GrowPonics: Modular automated hydroponic greenhouses with 80% water savings; TAP/TAPKIT: Turnkey hydroponic kits with app-guided support and AI cameras for crop monitoring.

- Robotics: MetoMotion's GRoW system: Dual-arm tomato harvesting with AI-based ripeness detection; AI sprayers reducing pesticide use ≥25%; Fleet management for seeding, spraying, cutting, and harvesting.
- Plant-Derived Therapeutics: Sambucol® black elderberry extract demonstrates antiviral activity against H5N1 avian influenza.

Renewable Energy and Energy Efficiency

Israeli innovations optimize energy generation, storage, and efficiency:

- Solar Technologies: SolarEdge Technologies: Distributed "PowerBox" optimizers for panel-level MPPT control, >97% efficiency, remote monitoring; Apollo Power: Lightweight flexible solar panels (~3 kg/m^2) adaptable to rooftops, vehicles, water surfaces, and aircraft; Organic Photovoltaics (OPV): Prof. Nir Tessler and MIGAL Galilee Research Institute increase efficiency (~10–15%) and integrate agrivoltaics into farming systems.
- Energy Storage & Cooling: IceBrick® (Nostromo Energy): Modular ice-based thermal storage capsules for sustainable building cooling;
- SolCold: Nanotech coating enabling passive solar cooling through quantum anti-Stokes emission.
- Advanced Materials: Addionics' 3D porous copper/aluminum current collectors ("Smart 3D Electrodes™") improve battery energy density and power delivery.
- Green Hydrogen Production: Electrochemical–Thermally Activated Chemical (E-TAC) methods enable efficient hematite-based hydrogen generation.

Healthcare and Medical Technologies

Israel is pioneering AI, robotics, regenerative medicine, and wearable diagnostics:

- Imaging & Cancer Detection: Vayyar Imaging: Radar-on-chip 4D imaging for early breast cancer screening; Nucleai, PathAI, and Ibex Medical Analytics: AI-based pathology for early tumor detection and classification.
- Robotic Surgery: Tamar Robotics: Pen-sized robotic endoscope for keyhole brain tumor surgery; Mazor Robotics/Medtronic: Renaissance/SpineAssist for spine and brain surgeries.
- Connected Care Devices: Avoset™ infusion pump: Bluetooth- and cellular-connected ambulatory pump with cloud monitoring; Bariks foldable hyperbaric oxygen therapy (HBOT) chamber: Portable PTSD treatment.

- Regenerative Medicine: Matricelf: 3D-engineered neural implants from autologous stem cells for spinal cord repair; MSC-based platforms for tissue engineering and targeted therapy.
- Precision Oncology: OncoDecipher, Imagene, Sheba Accelerator: AI-enhanced pathology and therapy prediction; OncoHost (PROphet®), Nucleai Spatial Biology Platform, C2i Genomics MRD monitoring, Hadassah+Roche genomic panels.
- Novel Therapeutics: Raziel Therapeutics' RZL 012 for localized fat reduction; Glaucoma drugs: A1 46 targeting $P2Y_6$ receptor; VS 101 latanoprost implant.
- CanBreed and Tikun Olam: CRISPR and cannabis-based medical plant innovations.
- Nano-Drug Delivery: Nano-Ghost, LipoCure, Revium Rx, New Phase (SaNP+EIS), Nanocarry, NurExone: Advanced nanoplatforms for tumor-targeted and blood–brain-barrier delivery.

Food-Tech, Nutrition, and Cosmetics

Israeli companies advance plant-based foods, cellular agriculture, and functional nutrition:

- Reduced-Sugar and Sweet Proteins: Incredo Sugar, Amai Proteins, BlueTree.
- Plant-Based Proteins & Meat Alternatives: Protevin™, Remilk, Alphafarm, SavorEat, InnovoPro, Plantish, Redefine Meat, Aleph Farms.
- Flavor & Natural Ingredients: Gavan Technologies, NutriTech/NextFerm: Fermentation and enzymatic-based flavor production.
- Cosmetics: Lycored, Alguard, Jojoba oil: Cellular agriculture and natural ingredients for skin and hair protection.

Telecommunication, Cloud, and Data Security

Israel's cloud infrastructure and cybersecurity landscape enables enterprise and telco solutions:

- Cloud Providers & Data Centers: Nebius, Vultr, Acronis, Anan Data Centers, ASOCS, Infinida, CTERA Networks, K2view.
- Hybrid/Private Cloud Platforms: On-premises and virtual private cloud solutions, multi-cloud integration, real-time analytics, synthetic data generation.

Digital Imaging and 3D Printing

- Industrial & Construction 3D Printing: Largix, Massivit 3D, 3DM (DM3), Ackerstein/Impact Labs + Thyssenkrupp, Technion Solar AM Center, CMI 3D. Printing: Large-format thermoplastic and metal additive manufacturing for aerospace, defense, and medical applications.
- Bioprinting & Food-Tech: MeaTech/Steakholder Foods: Cultured meat printing; tiny human heart models for regenerative medicine.
- Medical & Surgical Models: Synergy 3DMed: AI-driven patient-specific surgical instruments and anatomical models.
- Consumer & Fashion Printing: Danit Peleg: Customizable 3D-printed clothing and accessories.
- AI-Driven Visual Creation: D-ID, Lightricks, Bazaart: Text-to-video, image-to-video, lip-sync, and multi-language AI visual editing.
- Cortica: Unsupervised visual AI for object and scene recognition.
- Sports and On-Demand Production: Replay Technologies' FreeD system captures live 3D sports; Twine Solutions enables instant thread-dyeing in any color or length.

DISRUPTIVE INNOVATIONS IN THE SAMPLE

Agriculture and Water Treatment

Innovations in agriculture emphasize sustainability, digital monitoring, and genetic advancements:

- Digital Platforms: N-Drip Connect provides intelligent irrigation management, while Croptune offers real-time crop development monitoring.
- Genetic & Biotechnologies: Supree produces semi-dried self-drying cherry tomatoes; Golda Hen develops gene-edited female-only eggs; Soos Technology enables acoustic sex reversal in poultry. Advanced gene-editing tools such as Cas CLOVER (Demeetra Biotech), CRISPR initiatives led by Evogene, CanBreed, ArcBio, and ToolGen facilitate precision livestock and plant breeding.
- Water and Treatment Technologies: Innovations include reverse osmosis (RO) by IDE Technologies, Mekorot, and Aqwise; vacuum freezing vapor compression (VFVC); water-from-air systems by Watergen and H2OLL; and closed-circuit desalination (CCD) solutions by IDE Technologies, ROTec, and Negev Eco Desal.

These interventions reflect disruptive and discontinuous innovations by increasing crop yield efficiency, conserving water, and enabling precision agriculture.

Energy

Energy innovations focus on novel renewable energy systems and automation:

- Osmotic and Solar Energy: Pressure Retarded Osmosis (PRO) produces electricity through reverse electrodialysis heat engines (RED) utilizing osmotic pressure differences between freshwater and seawater or brine (Prof. Sidney Loeb, Ben-Gurion University).
- Automation and Maintenance: Ecoppia's robotic solar panel cleaning system uses microfiber and airflow, powered by solar energy and controlled via a cloud platform.

These innovations exemplify discontinuous innovation, combining mechanical, chemical, and digital technologies to enhance renewable energy efficiency and sustainability.

Healthcare

Healthcare innovations span diagnostics, therapeutics, and regenerative medicine:

- Medical Devices and Diagnostics: PillCam SB capsule enables non-invasive gastrointestinal imaging; HeraBEAT provides smartphone-based fetal heart monitoring; OrSense, GlucoTrack, and HAGAR GWave enable non-invasive glucose monitoring.
- Regenerative Medicine & Bioprinting: Matricelf bioprints 3D hearts; miniaturized human brain replicas allow tumor modeling; Prof. Mahmoud Huleihel's microfluidic systems support sperm production in vitro.
- Therapeutics & Interventions: Corindus robotic PCI systems, Tryton bifurcation stents, and Iron Dome-like protective technologies reflect the integration of robotics and precision medicine.
- Emerging Technologies: "Like a Fish" wearable vest extracts oxygen from water; Virtual Retinal Display (VRD) and EyeJets combine laser displays with eye-tracking; deep brain stimulation (DBS) targets neurological disorders.

Healthcare innovations illustrate disruptive innovation by redefining patient monitoring, diagnostics, and therapeutic interventions using AI, robotics, and biotechnologies.

Telecommunications and Connectivity

Telecommunications innovations focus on end-to-end communication, automotive safety, and cyber operations:

- Enterprise & Consumer Communication: AudioCodes, DriveNets, and Gilat Satellite Networks provide VoIP, VSAT, and cloud-native networking solutions. Viber delivers cross-platform instant messaging and encrypted communications.
- Automotive Safety & V2X: Mobileye, Arbe Robotics, Opsys Tech, and Autotalks develop advanced ADAS, 4D radar, and vehicle-to-everything (V2X) communication systems.
- Cybersecurity & Spyware: NSO Group (Pegasus), Candiru, Cytrox/Intellexa (Predator), Quadream, and Paragon Solutions exemplify zero-click spyware development. Cloud security leaders such as Wiz, Cato Networks, Check Point, CyberArk, Ermetic, Akeyless, Laminar, Cyera, Perimeter 81, and Lightspin secure enterprise infrastructure across multi-cloud environments.

This sector combines discontinuous innovations in secure communications with disruptive innovations in surveillance, autonomous mobility, and global cybersecurity.

Software, Microelectronics, and AI Platforms

Software and AI innovations enhance operational efficiency, testing, and AI lifecycle management:

- Microelectronics: Innovations include Intel EPROM, M-Systems Disc On Key, Mellanox RDMA, SanDisk EEPROM, Saifun Semiconductors (NROM), DSP group DSP-DSPC, EUV lithography by L2X Labs, and novel nano-structures by Dr. Mokari.
- Microservices & Software Platforms: Kong, Solo.io, Tufin, SpectralOps, and StackPulse provide API gateways, service mesh management, and automated remediation for microservices ecosystems.
- Software Testing & Logging: Testim, Applitools, Qyrus, Globitel, Avdor CIS, Lanonyx Telestat, Acmatel/Deepijatel, Glassbox, Cellebrite, and SolidRun CuBox mini-PCs support AI-driven testing, digital forensics, and call/data logging.
- AI Platforms & MLOps: Qodo, Aporia, Run:AI, Pinecone, Navina, Reco, Finout, Exodigo, D-ID, Bria AI, Visionary.ai, aiOla, Beyond Verbal, Chorus.ai, Cortica, Logz.io, MedyMatch, Nexar, Robust Intelligence, FundGuard,

EverC, Optibus, Insilico, and Croptimus™ illustrate AI deployment across healthcare, agriculture, transport, finance, and enterprise operations.

These technologies represent discontinuous innovations improving software development and AI operations and disruptive innovations in enterprise intelligence, generative AI, and domain-specific applications.

Digital Imaging and Nanography

- Printing Technologies: Landa Nanographic Printing & NanoInk, HP Indigo & ElectroInk, PV Nano Cell conductive inks, and Nano Dimension & XTPL enable high-resolution, conductive, and additive manufacturing inks for electronics and industrial applications.
- Applications: Innovations span consumer printing, industrial additive manufacturing, electronics fabrication, and high-performance 3D circuits.

This domain exemplifies disruptive innovation, replacing conventional offset printing and electronics assembly with digital, nano-enabled technologies.

Defense and Homeland Security

Defense innovations integrate UAVs, missile defense, robotics, and sensor technology:

- UAVs & Drones: Albatros UAV, Spear UAV, XTEND, and Reply Technologies deliver autonomous reconnaissance, surveillance, and realverse drone capabilities.
- Missile Defense: Arrow Antimissile System, Iron Dome, and Iron Beam tactical lasers exemplify advanced threat interception.
- Robotics & Sensors: Roboteam robotic systems, Odysight miniature cameras, and R2 Wireless signal processing enhance operational control and situational awareness.

Defense IVOICs showcase discontinuous innovation in sensor integration and robotics, alongside disruptive innovations in autonomous UAV operations and tactical missile defense.

Energy and Renewable Technologies

- Solar & Hydrogen Innovations: Lightweight flexible solar panels, organic photovoltaic cells, IceBrick energy storage systems, and Electrochemical–Thermally Activated Chemical (ETAC) methods for green hydrogen production.
- Automation & Energy Efficiency: Robotic solar panel cleaners and PRO/RED osmotic energy systems increase renewable energy capture and operational efficiency.

Energy sector innovations demonstrate discontinuous innovation in solar, hydrogen, and storage technologies and disruptive innovation in novel energy conversion methods.

NATIONAL COST–BENEFITS ANALYSIS BY MNC

Assessing whether government policies designed to attract multinational corporations (MNCs) generate greater added value for the national economy than their fiscal and opportunity costs requires a multidimensional evaluation framework. Such policies produce both direct economic impacts—including employment, exports, investment, and procurement—and indirect or long-term effects, such as skill formation, technological spillovers, innovation ecosystems, and firm creation.

While opportunity cost analysis is theoretically relevant—public resources allocated to MNC incentives could alternatively be invested in education, infrastructure, agriculture, or biotechnology—empirically determining a superior counterfactual allocation is highly challenging. The diversity of potential investments and their long and uncertain return horizons make precise opportunity-cost comparisons largely indeterminate. Consequently, policy evaluation must rely on observed outcomes across multiple impact dimensions rather than hypothetical alternatives.

Impact Parameters

Key parameters commonly used to evaluate MNC-oriented industrial policy include:

Employment (direct and indirect); Exports; Capital investment; Domestic output; Local procurement; R&D and innovation infrastructure; Academic collaboration; Acquisitions and technology absorption; Startup formation and ecosystem support; Inclusive innovation and workforce diversification.

INTEL

Overview

Intel began operations in Israel in 1974 with a small design center in Haifa. Over five decades, Israel has become Intel's largest R&D and manufacturing base outside the United States. Intel's activities span advanced semiconductor fabrication, processor design, autonomous driving technologies, and AI hardware and software development.

Employment

Intel employs approximately 12,000 workers in Israel, including around 8,000 in R&D and 4,000 in manufacturing, across multiple sites. Estimates attribute an additional ~42,000 indirect jobs to Intel's local operations through suppliers, contractors, and service providers. These positions are characterized by above-average wages, high skill intensity, and long employment duration.

Investment and Procurement

Since 1974, Intel has invested approximately $50 billion in Israel, primarily in fabrication plants, R&D facilities, and infrastructure. In parallel, the company has procured roughly $25 billion from Israeli suppliers, the majority of which are small and medium-sized enterprises. Annual local procurement reached $3.5 billion in 2022, up from $2.2 billion in 2021, reflecting deep integration into domestic supply chains.

Exports

Intel Israel's annual exports reached approximately $8.7 billion in 2022, with cumulative exports since inception estimated at $86 billion.

Intel Israel has been a dominant contributor to Israel's semiconductor exports, including a significant share of exports to China and the United States. Major destination markets include the U.S., Ireland, and East Asia, reflecting Intel Israel's role in global value chains.

Technological Capability and Innovation

Intel Israel has been responsible for the design of several landmark microprocessors, including the Pentium MMX, Core i7, and Ice Lake families. The Kiryat Gat fabrication facilities produce advanced-node semiconductors that are critical to global supply chains. These activities have embedded frontier manufacturing and design capabilities within the national economy.

Academic and Research Collaboration

Intel maintains extensive collaborations with Israeli academic institutions, notably the Technion and the Hebrew University. Initiatives include the Intel Collaborative Research Institute for Computational Intelligence, joint AI research centers, neuromorphic computing programs, and equipment donations supporting advanced materials and nanotechnology research. Programs such as Syllaboost incentivize curriculum innovation and strengthen industry-academia alignment.

Startup Ecosystem and Spillovers

Intel has played a catalytic role in Israel's startup ecosystem through accelerators, mentoring, and technology access. Its activities have contributed to the formation and scaling of startups in AI, cybersecurity, biotechnology, autonomous systems, and deep-tech infrastructure. Alumni of Intel Israel have founded or led numerous high-growth firms, reinforcing cumulative knowledge spillovers.

Strategic Acquisitions

Intel's acquisitions of Israeli firms—including Mobileye ($15.3B), Habana Labs (~$2B), Moovit (~$1B), and Granulate (~$650M)—have anchored global R&D mandates in Israel rather than relocating them abroad. These acquisitions transformed local startups into global technology hubs while preserving high-value employment and decision-making capacity domestically.

Inclusive Innovation

Intel Israel has implemented targeted workforce inclusion programs, increasing participation of Arab- א and Haredi engineers and advancing gender diversity. Arab-Israelis constitute over 14% of Intel Israel's workforce, substantially exceeding national averages in the tech sector. These programs generate broader social returns beyond conventional economic metrics.

Cost–Benefit Considerations

Costs

Intel has received an estimated $2 billion in direct government grants over approximately 50 years, alongside reduced corporate tax rates under Israel's investment incentive laws. While these benefits represent foregone fiscal revenue, they are structured as performance-contingent incentives tied to capital investment and employment.

Benefits

Measured against these costs, the benefits include:

Tens of thousands of high-skill jobs; $86 billion in cumulative exports; $75 billion in combined investment and procurement; Enduring technological capabilities in advanced semiconductors; Deep integration into global innovation and defense supply chains; Long-term ecosystem and human-capital spillovers

GOOGLE

Overview

Google established its Israeli operations in 2006 and has since expanded rapidly through a combination of in-house R&D growth, targeted acquisitions, and the development of innovation and startup-support infrastructure. Today, Israel represents one of Google's most significant global innovation hubs outside the United States, with strategic importance in artificial intelligence, cloud computing, cybersecurity, mapping technologies, and digital infrastructure.

Employment

Google employs approximately 2,000 people in Israel, primarily across its Tel Aviv and Haifa campuses. These sites function as regional centers for advanced R&D, cloud engineering, and AI infrastructure development. Employment is concentrated in high-skilled technical roles, contributing to wage premiums, talent retention, and knowledge accumulation within the domestic labor market.

Research, Innovation, and Technological Capabilities

Google's Israeli teams contribute to a broad spectrum of global products and platforms, including:

- Artificial Intelligence and Machine Learning: Core search technologies, natural language processing, computer vision, generative models (including elements of the Gemini ecosystem), and ethical AI frameworks.
- Cloud Computing (Google Cloud): Infrastructure engineering, security solutions, data platforms (BigQuery), cloud-native services (Anthos), and enterprise AI tooling.
- Cybersecurity: Zero-trust architectures, authentication systems, data privacy technologies, and security automation.
- Mapping and Navigation: Global integration of Waze technologies into Google Maps and mobility platforms.
- Data Infrastructure: Innovations in distributed systems, compression, storage efficiency, and large-scale data management.
- Hardware and AI Chips: Development of Pixel and Nest hardware components, and expansion into custom AI-related silicon.
- Healthcare AI: Medical imaging and predictive analytics.
- Voice and Search Technologies: Hebrew NLP, multilingual ranking, and speech technologies.

Israel also serves as a pilot market for testing AI-enabled services, cloud solutions, and smart mobility applications, with technologies frequently scaled to global deployment.

Semiconductor and Hardware Development

Google has significantly expanded its hardware R&D footprint in Israel, including the development of a new network interface card (NIC) optimized for AI data-center workloads. This effort supports high-bandwidth communication between CPUs and GPUs in large-scale AI systems and reflects Google's broader strategy to reduce dependence on external suppliers such as Nvidia, Intel, and Broadcom.

The NIC initiative builds on earlier in-house chip efforts and aligns with the increasing computational demands of large language models and AI infrastructure.

Academic Collaboration and Talent Development

University Partnerships

Google maintains structured collaborations with Israeli academic institutions:

- Tel Aviv University – Google AI & Data Science Research Program: A three-year initiative launched in 2023, funded with $1 million, supporting interdisciplinary research in AI, sustainability, and education.
- Reichman Tech School: Provides high-tech training and scholarships (up to ~94%) for participants from underrepresented populations, lowering financial barriers to entry into the tech sector.
- Educational and Training Initiatives: Google supports coding bootcamps, internships, mentorship programs, and joint research with global R&D teams.

While some programs target academia directly, others—such as ShoppingIL Academy—focus on upskilling SMEs and entrepreneurs, extending productivity gains beyond the core tech sector.

Startup Ecosystem and Innovation Spillovers

Google for Startups & Campus Tel Aviv

Google operates Campus Tel Aviv, one of the company's flagship global startup hubs. Founded under the leadership of Google Israel's former site lead, the campus hosts accelerators, including Launchpad and AI/ML-focused programs, providing startups with mentorship, cloud infrastructure, and access to global markets.

Sector-Focused Programs

Google for Startups – Growth Academy: Health Israel: A three-month, in-person accelerator supporting health-tech startups with technical guidance, scaling support, and product-market integration.

These initiatives strengthen Israel's role as a launchpad for globally scalable digital technologies.

Ecosystem and Supply Chain Integration

Google's operations have generated a localized ecosystem of cloud, infrastructure, and system-integration partners, including firms specializing in: Data center construction and logistics; Cloud migration and managed services; Cybersecurity, automation, and DevOps; Enterprise AI deployment.

This network amplifies indirect employment and embeds Google Cloud technologies into domestic enterprise and public-sector systems.

Strategic Acquisitions

Google's acquisition strategy has played a major role in anchoring global technological capabilities in Israel. Key acquisitions include:

- Waze: Crowdsourced navigation technology integrated worldwide, also serving as a platform for public safety and environmental initiatives.
- Alooma: Real-time data integration and ETL technologies, enhancing cloud data pipelines.
- SlickLogin: Sound-based authentication technology contributing to passwordless security approaches.
- LabPixies: Personalized web application and user-experience technologies.
- Siemplify: Security orchestration and automation (SOAR), strengthening Google Cloud's cybersecurity portfolio.

These acquisitions transformed Israeli startups into global product lines while preserving high-value R&D functions locally.

Inclusive Innovation and Social Impact

Google has committed $25 million to workforce development initiatives targeting underrepresented communities, including women, ultra-Orthodox, Arab, Druze, and Ethiopian-Israeli populations. Approximately 59% of new hires in certain programs originate from these groups, generating broader social returns alongside economic benefits.

Cost–Benefit Considerations

Project Nimbus

Google, together with Amazon Web Services, won the $1.2 billion Project Nimbus contract to provide cloud and AI services to Israeli government agencies. The contract includes discounted pricing and obligates service provision across civilian ministries, with expanded access to defense-related entities.

The project has generated internal and external controversy, including employee protests and shareholder scrutiny, highlighting the ethical and governance complexities associated with large-scale government cloud contracts.

From a national policy perspective, the benefits associated with Google's presence include: High-skilled employment for ~2,000 workers; Anchoring of frontier AI and cloud capabilities; Acquisition-led technology absorption; Startup ecosystem acceleration; Infrastructure development and supply-chain formation; Talent development and inclusive innovation programs

NVIDIA

Employment

As of early 2025, NVIDIA employs approximately 5,000 people in Israel, which represents around 13–15% of its global workforce. That makes Israel NVIDIA's largest international R&D hub, second only to its U.S. operations.

NVIDIA operates in seven Israeli centers: Yokne'am (headquarters) plus satellite offices in Tel Aviv, Ra'anana, Jerusalem, Kiryat Gat, Be'erSheva, and Tel Hai.

Its workforce has nearly doubled since acquiring Mellanox in 2020, which added roughly 2,000 staff to the Israeli operation. The company has been consistently hiring—adding ~1,000 new employees annually over the past few years, including 640 hires in early 2025 alone.

Exports

India

According to Volza records, India is the top destination for Israeli exports of network equipment, including Mellanox-based hardware—accounting for around 65% of shipments globally (volza site). Recent entries include examples such as:

ConnectX-6/6E HDR HCA/NIC adapters; Various Spectrum-based switch modules

Network cards destined for OEM or integrator YCH Logistics in India; quantities range from tens to hundreds per shipment. The shipments are mostly to OEMs or system integrators like Jabil, Dell EMC, or YCH Logistics.

Vietnam

Vietnam ranks among the top importing countries, receiving around 67 shipments, or roughly 5% of Israeli network-equipment exports (volza site). Specific trades include Mellanox Ethernet switches and network connection cards integrated into Dell EMC servers.

Hong Kong

Hong Kong serves as a transit and trading hub for Mellanox hardware originally manufactured in Israel, although direct ship counts remain limited (volza site). Exported hardware includes specialized enterprise networking switches and adapter cards like the Opal 6 Negev modules.

Academic Institutions

NVIDIA Research Israel (Tel-Aviv Lab, PAR)

The lab works on algorithms, theory, and applications of deep learning, particularly in computer vision, reinforcement learning, perception, action, reasoning.

NVIDIA Deep Learning Institute workshops at Tel Aviv University

Tel Aviv University offers practical certification workshops (free to students, researchers, academic staff with academic email) via NVIDIA's Deep Learning Institute (DLI). These include:

- Fundamentals of Accelerated Computing with CUDA Python
- Generative AI with Diffusion Models

The workshops offer access to cloud-accelerated GPU servers (so hands-on code execution) and on successful completion, participants can get a recognized NVIDIA certification.

R&D Innovation Facilities

The Israeli center drives major global product lines, including NICs, photonic communications chips, Dynamo inference software, and the Blackwell Ultra chip. These innovations are largely led by Yokne'am teams.

Israel-1, built in 2023, was the country's most powerful generative AI supercomputer, layering NVIDIA GPUs and Mellanox networking technology.

In early 2025, NVIDIA invested over $500 million in a new 30-megawatt "Data Center Engineering Facility" near Elyakim (Mevo Carmel Science Park), hosting hundreds of Blackwell, Grace Blackwell, and SuperNIC systems to support local product development.

NVIDIA's Israel-1 supercomputer, among the world's fastest, is located in Israel.

Research in AI & Quantum

The NVIDIA Research Tel-Aviv Lab (PAR), led by Prof. Gal Chechik, publishes cutting-edge work in computer vision, reinforcement learning, diffusion models, and more; notable publications include work accepted at ICML, ICLR, NeurIPS, and SIGGRAPH.

NVIDIA and Israeli startup Quantum Machines jointly developed DGX Quantum, integrating NVIDIA's accelerated computing with OPX quantum control systems for hybrid computing applications.

NVIDIA is investing over $500 million in a new AI research & data center facility near Yokne'am (Mevo Carmel Park), requiring local procurement of infrastructure, utilities, and technical services.

Healthcare AI Partnerships

NVIDIA collaborates with Assuta Medical Centers via its startup program RISE, supporting AI healthcare startups like Aidoc and Rhino Health.

These firms use NVIDIA DGX A100, Clara Holoscan, MONAI, FLARE, and federated learning to accelerate medical imaging diagnostics while protecting patient privacy.

Supply Chain

HIPER Global provided key engineering, server integration, and deployment services for Israel-1 supercomputer, including assembly of Dell PowerEdge XE9680 servers with NVIDIA HGX H100 GPUs and Spectrum-X networking systems. They completed integration in under 30 days.)

OpTeamizer, established in 2015, is NVIDIA's first service delivery partner in Israel and the Middle East. It offers training and consulting for GPU acceleration, deep learning, CUDA, and system migration. It has worked with over 90 Israeli R&D centers.

Acquisitions

Mellanox Technologies ($6.9B)

Mellanox is a leading provider of high-performance networking solutions. The company specializes in Ethernet and InfiniBand connectivity solutions for servers and storage, which are essential for cloud and enterprise data centers. Mellanox's products include network adapters, switches, and cables, designed to enhance data center performance and scalability.

Excelero (~$35M)

Excelero Storage has created a software-defined block storage solution that meets the performance and scalability requirements of large web-scale and enterprise applications. With Excelero's NVMesh, customers can build a distributed, high-performance server SAN for mixed application workloads. The solution has been deployed for hyper-scale industrial IoT services, machine-learning applications, and massive-scale simulation visualization.

Deci (~$300M)

Platform using neural architecture search (NAS) to optimize AI model performance. Deci's deep learning platform helps data scientists eliminate the AI efficiency gap by adopting a more productive development paradigm. With the platform, AI developers can leverage hardware-aware Neural Architecture Search (NAS) to quickly build highly optimized deep learning models that are designed to meet specific production goals.

Startup Inception program

NVIDIA's Inception Program includes 300+ Israeli startups, supporting them with technology stacks, business mentorship, and networking opportunities with global investors and innovators.

Cost benefit analysis

Cost

NVIDIA's current facility in Yokne'am benefits from the Capital Investments Law, which provides substantial tax breaks and grants to companies investing in high-tech infrastructure in designated areas.

Municipalities in northern Israel, such as Haifa and Yokne'am, have actively engaged with NVIDIA to offer tailored incentives for its expansion plans. These incentives include: suitable plots for construction; assisting in the development of necessary infrastructure, such as roads and utilities; Collaborating with educational institutions.

Benefit

- Employment: 5,000 people doubled since acquiring Mellanox in 2020
- Exports from Israel to India, Vietnam and Hong Kong
- Israel-1, built in 2023, was the country's most powerful generative AI supercomputer, layering NVIDIA GPUs and Mellanox networking technology.
- In early 2025, NVIDIA invested over $500 million in a new 30-megawatt "Data Center Engineering Facility.
- Startup Ecosystem & NVIDIA Inceptionincludes around 300 start ups.

Research in AI & Quantum; Healthcare AI Partnerships

PALO ALTO

Employment

Founded in California in 2005 by Israeli-born Nir Zuk, the company has deep roots in Israel's defense and tech ecosystem—including Zuk's tenure in Unit 8200 of the IDF, which is a key origin for many Israeli cybersecurity companies.

1,200–1,400 employees in Israel (as of 2024–2025), making Israel the company's largest R&D hub outside of the U.S.Staff are based primarily in Tel Aviv, with satellite offices near Petah Tikva and Herzliya, especially after major acquisitions.

Academic institutions

BGU (Ben-Gurion University of the Negev) & Palo Alto Networks

BGU's School for Hi-Tech & Cyber has an academic partnership with Palo Alto Networks.

The collaboration includes integration of Palo Alto's technologies in the curricula: Strata, Cortex, SASE, Prisma etc., in courses on cloud & cybersecurity (e.g. cloud/app infrastructure protection, DevSecOps, CISO level) and preparing students for certification.

IDC Herzliya

Direct collaboration between IDC Herzliya and Palo Alto Networks. There are relevant cybersecurity-strategic collaborations at IDC: for example, IDC's International Institute for Counter-Terrorism (ICT) collaborating with Israel Electric Corporation's Cyber Gym to confront cyber terrorism.

Technion

Technion offers a course called *Network Security* which covers threats, defense methods, policy.

R&D Innovation Facilities

Prisma Cloud (cloud security, DevSecOps); Cortex XDR/XSOAR (AI-driven detection, orchestration); Unit 42 threat intelligence feeds; Joint cyber testbeds supported by Israeli government

Acquisitions

Talon Cyber Security

Talon's secure and isolated endpoint environment, enables employees to work from anywhere and from any device, accessing corporate resources from both managed and unmanaged devices.

With Talon, security leaders gain vast visibility and high granularity of control, leveraging the Principle of Least Privilege throughout the organization.

Demisto

Demisto is a security orchestration, automation, and response (SOAR) platform that combines full incident management, security automation and orchestration, and real-time collaboration to improve the efficiency of your security operations and incident response. The orchestration enables to ingest alerts across sources and execute standardized, automatable playbooks across hundreds of security and non-security products.

LightCyber

LightCyber provides a solution designed to identify threats within corporate networks early in the attack lifecycle, facilitating prompt breach remediation and preventing extensive damage caused by malware or hackers.

Secdo

Secdo offers a preemptive incident-response platform designed to help security teams cut incident response time to minutes, remediate attacks surgically without affecting business continuity, and bolster their defenses against future attacks. Secdo uses a powerful set of real-time, granular response tools to enable rapid and surgical response and remediation to any endpoint without affecting business productivity.

Cider Security

Cider Security has developed a platform that provides a unified view of the entire engineering ecosystem, offering security teams an in-depth understanding and comprehensive view of the technologies, systems, and processes unique to every engineering environment. Security teams are provided a highly tailored set of controls and solutions to optimize security and achieve full resilience across the entire CI/CD pipeline from code to deployment.

Dig Security

Dig Security discovers all data assets stored in platform-as-a-service (PaaS), infrastructure-as-a-service (IaaS) and database-as-a-service (DBaaS). It classifies structured and unstructured data and provides the industry's first real-time data detection and response (DDR) solution - a contextualized real-time alerting system that provides insights into the way data is moving and used in the organization. Dig is fully agentless and works out-of-band.

Cost Benefit Analysis

Cost
Grants to Metallox
Benefit
Employment: 1,200–1,400 employees

Prisma Cloud (cloud security, DevSecOps); Cortex XDR/XSOAR (AI-driven detection, orchestration); Unit 42 threat intelligence feeds; Collaborations with Technion, BGU, and IDC Herzliya; Joint cyber testbeds supported by Israeli government.

SIEMENS

Siemens has been active in Israel for decades, with operations in sectors such as energy, mobility, digital industries, and healthcare. Its local footprint is channeled primarily through Siemens Israel Ltd., along with specialized subsidiaries and partnerships. Siemens employs a few hundred people in Israel across its local subsidiaries and project sites. Subsidiaries like Siemens Healthineers Israel (formerly Elscint) contribute to employment in healthcare tech.

R &D Innovation Facilities

- Energy & Smart Grid Technologies: Siemens develops smart grid solutions, energy management systems, and renewable energy integration technologies to modernize Israel's electricity infrastructure.
- Industrial Automation & Industry 4.0: Focus on advanced manufacturing automation, robotics, and IoT solutions for industrial digital transformation.
- Digital Twins & Simulation: Developing digital twin technologies that model real-world systems for predictive maintenance and operational optimization.
- Healthcare Technology: Collaboration on medical imaging, diagnostics, and healthcare IT.
- Transportation & Mobility: Smart transportation systems, including electrification, traffic management, and rail infrastructure.

Table 1. R&D centers

Site	Focus Area	Employees (Est.)	Notes
Caesarea (Mazor Robotics)	Surgical robotics, medtech innovation	~200	Now core to Siemens Healthineers' global R&D in robotic spine surgery
Tel Aviv	Digital industries, smart cities, AI, cybersecurity	~300	Headquarters for Israeli operations; hub for industrial software, Siemens Xcelerator
Haifa (Siemens Mobility & Energy)	Smart grid, predictive maintenance, fiber-optic sensing, rail tech	~150	Partners with Prisma Photonics and Technion on grid intelligence
Yokneam	Chip-level control systems, medtech support	~80	Embedded systems, software engineering
Petah Tikva (Siemens Healthineers)	Medical imaging software, AI diagnostics	~150	Joint research with Zebra Medical Vision and local hospitals
Rehovot (Ecoppia/ clean energy partnerships)	Solar O&M, robotics, energy tech	Strategic collaboration	Siemens Energy R&D piloting robotics via partnership—not owned site

Supply Chain

Siemens sources and supplies components to/from Israel via:

- Energy and rail project inputs, such as turbines, substations, control systems.
- Healthcare imaging systems (e.g., CT/MRI scanners) produced abroad and integrated in Israel.
- Local subcontractors and integrators (in civil works, electronics, system integration) are part of the Siemens ecosystem for project deployment.

Siemens' Israeli supply chain is project-based, involving a mix of imported high-tech systems and localized implementation.

Strategic Partnerships

Siemens partners with Israeli startups, universities, and government bodies through innovation labs and co-development programs.

Participates in MAGNET consortia—public-private partnerships funded by the Israel Innovation Authority to develop next-gen energy and industrial technologies.

Runs accelerator programs to foster startup collaboration in smart infrastructure and energy tech.

Acquisitions

Elscint Medical Imaging (Haifa), acquired via Siemens Healthineers in the early 2000s. Elscint had been one of Israel's premier medical imaging firms.

Siemens has not made recent large-scale acquisitions but continues to form technology alliances and scout startups in areas like: Industrial IoT; Mobility AI; Energy efficiency. The Elscint acquisition remains key to Siemens' medtech integration in Israel.

Mazor Robotics

The Mazor™ system makes it efficient and intuitive to plan and simulate your cages and screws for a more efficient procedure. The automatic recognition feature allows to visualize spinal elements in relation to one another, and an enhanced interface delivers fast and seamless access. Mazor™ planning allows the surgeon to visualize and optimize spinal elements in relation to one another with automatic anatomy recognition.

ECOPPIA

Ecoppia offers robotic cleaning solutions designed to keep PV modules clean and at peak performance year-round. Water-free, fully automated robotic solutions use advanced business intelligence capabilities to prevent soiling losses and potential damage. Managed remotely, Ecoppia's platform allows utility-scale solar sites to achieve optimal performance with minimal human intervention and a lower levelized cost of energy.

Prisma Photonics

Prisma Photonics was founded by a team of experts in lasers, optical fibers, and algorithms (prismaphotonics site). The company helps keep the most critical large-scale infrastructure up & running with a quantum leap in linear infrastructure monitoring.

The PrismaPower suite of solutions enables transmission operators to accurately monitor overhead and underground power lines for thousands of kilometers in real-time with nothing Installed on lines or towers.

PrismaFlow keeps the pipelines up and running, monitoring transportation pipe assets.

PrismaSubsea keeps your underwater cables and pipelines up and running, monitoring submarine infrastructure.

Brenmiller Energy

Brenmiller Energy is a global leader in thermal energy storage, empowering the transition to a cleaner, more resilient energy future.

Thermal Energy Storage (TES) technology enables industrial and energy sector clients to decarbonize heat generation – responsible for over 50% of global energy use – by storing renewable energy and dispatching it as clean heat when needed.

Zebra Medical Vision

Zebra Medical provides specialised healthcare solutions and research-backed technology with a focus on oncology, ultrasound, vascular access and acute pain management – all backed by outstanding service. A single-probe, whole-body ultrasound solution. Butterfly iQ+ is designed to make ultrasound easy to use. Once connected to the iOS or Android app, select from 20+ presets in seconds with the swipe of a finger — and start scanning.

Support to start ups

Tel Aviv (main site): Drives digital twin platforms, industrial IoT, and automation for manufacturing and logistics clients.

Special units for: AI-based predictive maintenance; Cybersecurity for OT (Operational Tech); Industrial control systems design; Implementation of Siemens Xcelerator platform in Israeli industry.

Cost Benefit Analysis

Benefit

Employment: a few hundred people in Israel.

Public sector contracts:

- Support through major government infrastructure projects in transportation (rail), healthcare (imaging systems), and energy.
- Contracted for power grid automation, gas turbine supply, and smart energy solutions, often with the Israel Electric Corporation (IEC).

MICROSOFT

Overview

Microsoft has maintained a continuous and expanding presence in Israel since the late 1980s, evolving into one of the company's most strategically important R&D hubs outside the United States. Israel plays a central role in Microsoft's global activities in cybersecurity, cloud computing, artificial intelligence, developer tools, and applied research. The company's footprint combines large-scale employment, deep academic integration, acquisition-led capability building, and extensive ecosystem engagement.

Employment

As of 2024, Microsoft employs approximately 3,500 people in Israel, with around 2,700 employees working directly in R&D roles as of FY2023. Microsoft's Israeli workforce is distributed across R&D campuses in Herzliya, Haifa, Tel Aviv, and Ness Ziona, with employment concentrated in high-skilled engineering, research, and product leadership positions.

These roles are associated with high wage levels, long job tenure, and significant spillover effects into the broader technology labor market.

Core R&D and Technology Domains

Microsoft Israel's R&D activities span a wide range of globally critical technology areas:

- Cybersecurity: Core security technologies integrated into Microsoft Azure, Microsoft 365, and Windows platforms.
- Artificial Intelligence and NLP: Machine learning systems, conversational AI, language understanding, and privacy-aware AI architectures.
- Developer Platforms: Enhancements to Visual Studio, Azure DevOps, GitHub integrations, and developer productivity tooling.
- Cloud Infrastructure: Distributed systems, analytics, and AI-enabled cloud services.
- Mixed Reality and Computer Vision: Research and product development in AR/VR, natural user interfaces (NUI), and spatial computing.

Three dedicated innovation labs operate as incubation and pilot environments, supporting proof-of-concept development and co-creation with enterprise and public-sector partners.

Azure Israel Central Region

In November 2023, Microsoft launched the Azure Israel Central cloud region, including multiple availability zones. The decision was driven by regulatory requirements for data localization and security, as well as rising demand from Israeli enterprises and public institutions.

The local Azure region supports: National data sovereignty and resilience; Advanced analytics and AI workloads; Public-sector digital transformation; Integration with Israeli cybersecurity vendors, system integrators, and hardware suppliers.

This infrastructure represents a long-term strategic commitment rather than a short-term commercial deployment.

Academic Collaboration and Human Capital Development

University Partnerships

Microsoft maintains extensive collaborations with Israeli academic institutions through structured and sustained programs:

- Academia Outreach Program (Microsoft Israel R&D): Supports joint research, advanced teaching labs, excellence programs for students, and recruitment pipelines.
- Technion – Microsoft Academic Research Center: A multi-year partnership focused on e-commerce technologies, AI, game theory, social networks, and online markets.
- Technion–Microsoft IoT Lab (U.next Program): A startup-style lab environment enabling students to prototype IoT and assistive technologies.
- Ben-Gurion University & Microsoft (2025): Joint research on AI and security, with emphasis on privacy leakage in large language models under Microsoft's Secure Future Initiative.
- Microsoft AI Residency Program (Israel): Trains AI researchers and engineers through industry-led research projects.

Microsoft also supplies higher-education institutions with cloud, productivity, and collaboration platforms, strengthening digital infrastructure across campuses.

Support for Startups

Microsoft operates one of the most extensive startup-support frameworks in Israel through Microsoft for Startups, offering: Azure cloud credits; Technical mentorship; Co-selling and go-to-market support; Integration into Microsoft's global enterprise ecosystem

Hundreds of Israeli startups across fintech, healthtech, cybersecurity, and enterprise software have scaled through this platform. Microsoft also participates directly as an investor via its venture capital activities.

Innovation Community Infrastructure

- Microsoft Reactor Israel: Hosts workshops, hackathons, and developer events.
- The Garage (Herzliya Campus): A hands-on makerspace for rapid prototyping, AI experimentation, and open-source innovation.
- Advanced Technology Lab (ATL) Israel: Focuses on applied computer vision and natural user interfaces, bridging research and commercial deployment.

Inclusive Innovation and Social Impact

Microsoft Israel operates a broad portfolio of inclusion and workforce-diversification programs:

- Hiburim Program (with Appleseeds): Digital-skills training for youth in the Negev and Galilee.
- MakeWhatsNext: Encourages young women to pursue technology careers.
- Cloud School & Coding Bootcamps: Career retraining for women returning to the workforce and ultra-Orthodox professionals.
- Mentorship for Arab Engineers: Academic partnerships supporting Arab students in STEM.
- QueenB and Magshimim Collaborations: Early-stage STEM education for girls and youth in peripheral regions.

Strategic Acquisitions and Capability Anchoring

Microsoft has systematically used Israeli acquisitions to internalize frontier cybersecurity and cloud capabilities. Key acquisitions include: Adallom: Cloud access security broker, now integrated into Microsoft's identity and enterprise security stack; Aorato: Behavioral analytics for Active Directory security; Hexadite:

Automated incident response and SOAR technologies; CyberX: Industrial IoT and critical infrastructure security; RiskIQ: Attack surface management and external threat intelligence; ReFirm Labs: Firmware security and vulnerability analysis; Secure Islands: Data classification and information protection technologies.

These acquisitions anchored advanced security R&D in Israel while scaling technologies into Microsoft's global platforms.

Cost–Benefit Perspective

Costs

Microsoft benefits from Israel's favorable innovation environment, including skilled human capital, research infrastructure, and regulatory support. Direct fiscal incentives are less visible than in manufacturing-heavy MNCs, with public investment primarily concentrated in education, research collaboration, and cloud procurement.

Benefits

Key policy-relevant benefits include: Employment for ~3,500 high-skilled workers; Anchoring of global cybersecurity and AI capabilities; Deployment of sovereign cloud infrastructure; Deep integration with academia and talent pipelines; Startup ecosystem acceleration; Inclusive innovation and regional skill development; Long-term spillovers into public-sector digitalization.

GENERAL ELECTRIC (GE)

Overview

General Electric has maintained a long-standing presence in Israel through its healthcare and energy divisions, positioning the country as a niche global hub for advanced medical imaging, detector technologies, analytics, and energy systems engineering. While GE's Israeli footprint is smaller in employment scale than some digital MNCs, it is highly specialized and capital-intensive, with a strong emphasis on proprietary technologies and global product integration.

Employment

As of 2018, GE employed over 400 professionals in Israel across four primary sites: Haifa, Rehovot, Herzliya, and Tirat Carmel. Employment is concentrated in

R&D, advanced manufacturing support, software analytics, and systems engineering, with a high proportion of engineers, physicists, and applied scientists.

R&D Centers and Specialization

GE Healthcare operates two globally significant R&D hubs in Israel:

Haifa R&D Center

Focuses on medical imaging technologies, including MRI, CT, software analytics, and molecular imaging. The center collaborates closely with hospitals and academic institutions and contributes directly to GE Healthcare's global imaging platforms.

Rehovot – CZT Center of Excellence

Serves as a global hub for Cadmium Zinc Telluride (CZT) detector technology, a core component in GE's nuclear imaging and PET/CT systems. This center develops proprietary detector modules used worldwide, embedding Israel deeply into GE's high-value medical imaging supply chain.

Additional software and analytics activities in Herzliya reinforce GE's capabilities in industrial analytics, IoT-enabled systems, and medical-device algorithms.

Academic Collaboration and Human Capital Development

GE and GE Healthcare maintain active collaborations with Israeli academic institutions:

- Ben-Gurion University of the Negev (BGU): Joint R&D in medical imaging technologies and healthcare solutions.
- Technion – Israel Institute of Technology: Collaboration in biomedical engineering, AI in healthcare, and advanced imaging.
- University of Haifa: Research partnerships exploring AI and machine learning applications for diagnostics and patient outcomes.
- GE Vernova (Energy Division): Training and education partnerships with engineering faculties, focused on power generation, energy systems, and grid efficiency.

These collaborations strengthen translational research pipelines and contribute to workforce upskilling in both healthcare and energy engineering.

Supply Chain

GE's activities extend beyond R&D into local industrial and infrastructure integration, including: Power-generation projects (gas turbines, combined-cycle plants); Water infrastructure and control systems; Substation automation and capacitor banks; Hybrid power units for industrial and defense-related applications.

These activities embed GE technologies within Israel's energy, water, and industrial infrastructure, generating indirect economic and operational spillovers.

Strategic Acquisitions

GE has expanded its Israeli footprint through targeted acquisitions and investments:

- Pulsenmore (2022): Investment of up to $50 million in handheld tele-ultrasound technology, enabling home-based and remote diagnostics.
- DiA Imaging Analysis: Licensing and integration of AI-driven ultrasound image analysis software into GE systems.
- Orbotech Medical Solutions (OMS): Acquisition of CZT detector assets, reinforcing GE's leadership in nuclear imaging.
- Elscint (legacy assets): Integration of nuclear-medicine and MRI expertise, forming the technological foundation of GE's imaging activities in Israel.

These moves anchored proprietary imaging technologies and detector manufacturing know-how domestically.

Cost–Benefit Perspective

Costs

GE Healthcare and related divisions have received conditional R&D grants from the Israel Innovation Authority and the Ministry of Economy. These grants—estimated at tens of millions of dollars over multiple years—were tied to R&D expansion, job creation, and technology development.

Benefits

- Policy-relevant benefits include: Employment for ~400 highly skilled workers
- Global leadership in CZT detector technology; Two specialized R&D centers integrated into global product lines; Academic–industry research spillovers;

- Infrastructure and industrial-system integration; Anchoring of proprietary medical-imaging IP

AMAZON

Overview

Amazon has emerged as one of the most strategically embedded multinational technology companies in Israel, with its presence anchored primarily in cloud infrastructure (AWS), custom silicon design, artificial intelligence, and large-scale distributed systems. Since establishing its first R&D operations in 2014, Amazon has steadily expanded Israel's role from a peripheral engineering site to a core contributor to global AWS and retail platforms.

Employment

As of 2024, Amazon employs over 1,500 people in Israel, distributed across R&D, chip design, cloud engineering, operations, and commercial support functions. Employment is concentrated in high-skilled technical roles, including: Cloud architects and infrastructure engineers (AWS); AI/ML researchers and computer-vision specialists; Custom silicon and systems-on-chip engineers (Annapurna Labs); Data scientists and platform engineers; Product and applied research teams supporting retail, ads, and logistics technologies.

Amazon has also invested in diversified hiring pipelines, partnering with Israeli bootcamps, minority-community initiatives, and reskilling programs supported by government ministries.

R&D Footprint and Functional Specialization

Amazon operates a multi-node R&D network across Israel, with each site contributing to distinct global product lines:

Table 2.

Location	Core Focus Areas	Estimated Employees (2024)
Tel Aviv	AI, cloud security, Alexa, IoT, AWS DevOps tools	~500
Haifa	Machine learning, computer vision, AWS SageMaker	~250
Herzliya	Chip design (Annapurna Labs), Alexa, voice interfaces	~600

continued on following page

Table 2. Continued

Location	Core Focus Areas	Estimated Employees (2024)
Petah Tikva	Retail technology, cashierless checkout (Just Walk Out)	~150
Ramat Gan	Amazon Ads, personalization, experimentation platforms	~200

This distributed model positions Israel as a horizontal capability hub, spanning hardware, cloud infrastructure, and applied AI rather than a single product vertical.

Core Technology Domains

Cloud Computing (AWS)

Israeli AWS teams contribute to: Infrastructure scalability and reliability; Cloud security and compliance tooling; DevOps automation and cloud-native services; Data analytics and machine-learning platforms.

Israel's cloud R&D is closely tied to AWS's global backbone rather than localized adaptations, reinforcing long-term strategic relevance.

AI, Computer Vision, and Conversational Systems

Amazon's Israeli teams play a meaningful role in: Natural language processing and speech recognition for Alexa; Computer vision systems for autonomous retail and logistics; Machine-learning pipelines supporting personalization, fraud detection, and experimentation; Silicon and Systems Engineering

University Partnerships

Amazon has developed a broad educational footprint through AWS-branded programs:

- AWS Academy: University-level cloud curricula delivered at institutions including:
- Ben-Gurion University of the Negev; Technion – Israel Institute of Technology; Tel Aviv University; Hebrew University of Jerusalem; Bar-Ilan University, Reichman University, University of Haifa.
- AWS Educate: Cloud training resources for students and educators, supporting early exposure to cloud careers.

Applied Training

Negev Prime Program (BGU): An Amazon-based e-commerce training initiative enabling students to build private-label businesses on Amazon's platform, developed with Yazamut360 and Negev 19.

Participation in reskilling initiatives with Israeli ministries, supporting workforce mobility into cloud and digital roles.

Startup Ecosystem

Amazon supports Israel's startup ecosystem primarily through platform leverage rather than equity-heavy investment:

- AWS Activate: Cloud credits, mentorship, and go-to-market support for early-stage startups
- Integration pathways into AWS marketplaces and partner networks
- Informal spillovers via alumni mobility from AWS and Annapurna Labs into startups and scale-ups

This model strengthens Israel's cloud-native startup base while reinforcing AWS platform dependency.

Strategic Acquisitions

Amazon's Israeli acquisitions have focused on deep infrastructure technologies rather than consumer-facing products:

- Annapurna Labs (2015, ~$370M)
  Custom chip design; now foundational to AWS's Graviton processors and internal silicon roadmap.
- CloudEndure (2019, ~$200M)

Disaster recovery and cloud migration technologies, integrated into AWS resilience and migration services.

- E8 Storage (2019)

High-performance storage technologies enhancing AWS data services.

These acquisitions embedded long-horizon technical capabilities in Israel and ensured their continued expansion rather than post-acquisition hollowing-out.

AWS Israel Cloud Region

Under Project Nimbus, Amazon committed to operating a local AWS cloud region in Israel through at least 2037. Independent estimates suggest the region could:

- Contribute 51.7 billion to Israel's GDP over its lifecycle
- Support approximately 7,700 jobs annually, directly and indirectly
- The local region enables: Data residency and regulatory compliance; Public-sector and enterprise cloud adoption; Integration with Israel's cybersecurity ecosystem.

Cost–Benefit Analysis

Costs

Public-sector support has largely taken the form of: Cloud procurement commitments (e.g., Nimbus); Workforce training and reskilling programs; Regulatory accommodation for cloud infrastructure; Direct R&D grants appear more limited than in manufacturing-intensive MNC cases.

Benefits

Policy-relevant benefits include: Employment for over 1,500 high-skilled workers; Anchoring of global cloud, AI, and chip-design capabilities; Significant projected GDP and employment multipliers via AWS infrastructure; Human-capital development through academic and reskilling programs; Startup ecosystem acceleration through AWS platform access; Long-term integration into Israel's digital public infrastructure.

SYNGENTA AND HAZERA (LIMAGRAIN)

Overview

Syngenta, via its Israeli subsidiary Zeraim Gedera, together with Hazera Genetics (part of Limagrain), maintains a strong presence in Israel's agri-biotech sector, focusing on plant genetics, crop protection, and digital agriculture.

Employment

Hazera employs around 500–1,000 professionals, with approximately 30% dedicated to research and development.

This workforce strengthens local expertise in genetics, plant breeding, and applied agricultural innovation.

Academic Collaboration

Partnerships with the Hebrew University, Faculty of Agriculture have yielded landmark crop varieties:*Daniela* (1992) – long shelf-life tomato; *Summer Sun* (2007) – yellow tomato with improved shelf-life; *Maggie* (2021) – sweet, disease-resistant tomato.

Collaboration ensures continuous knowledge transfer and development of advanced agricultural technologies.

R&D Facilities

Hazera operates four research centers and eight breeding stations, including a modern hub in Berurim (2025, 80M NIS investment).

Facilities focus on disease resistance, genetic improvement, and global variety testing, supporting exports to approximately 40 markets.

Supply Chain Integration

Close collaboration with local farmers, field trials, and customized seed solutions fosters agricultural know-how and strengthens Israel's agri-tech ecosystem.

Acquisitions

Limagrain acquired Hazera in 2003 and merged with Dutch company Nickerson-Zwaan in 2008, consolidating Israeli R&D capabilities within a global framework.

Cost-Benefit Analysis

Costs: Grants and operational support for R&D.

Benefits: Sustains 500–1,000 skilled jobs; Israel-based research drives global seed innovation and revenue; Anchors agricultural expertise domestically.

APPLE

Employment

Apple employs roughly 2,000 people across R&D centers in Haifa, Herzliya, and Jerusalem.

A hub in Rawabi, Palestinian Authority, employs ~60 engineers via partnership with ASAL Technologies.

Key Acquisitions

Anobit – flash storage solutions; PrimeSense – 3D sensing technology; LinX – miniature multi-aperture cameras; Realface – facial recognition software; Camerai – AR graphics applications; TrueMeeting – digital avatars for video calls.

R&D Centers

Haifa: Processor and semiconductor development; Herzliya: Largest R&D site outside; Cupertino; focuses on sensors, imaging, and hardware innovation; Jerusalem: Mac chip and hardware development

Cost-Benefit Analysis

Benefits: Employs 2,000 engineers in high-value R&D; Local acquisitions fuel innovation in imaging, AR, sensors, and cybersecurity; Contributes to Apple's global product development pipeline

SAMSUNG

R&D and Workforce

Samsung R&D Institute Israel (SRIL), founded 1997, specialized in advanced imaging, AI, and sensor technologies

Samsung Innovation Campus (SIC): ICT education for youth, focusing on underrepresented groups

Samsung SDS Academy: Professional development in digital transformation and customer solutions

Startup Engagement

Samsung Mobile Advance (SMA): Grants ($50K) and technical support for startups in mobile, AI, sensors, XR, health, and ESG

Solve for Tomorrow: STEM and entrepreneurship education for high school students (~250 participants)

Key Acquisitions

TransChip Israel: Camera chips for mobile; Corephotonics (2019): Dual-camera technology; Caaresys: In-cabin automotive monitoring; iOnRoad: AR solutions for vehicles; Red Bend Software: Connected car software; TowerSec & NeuReality: AI and cybersecurity solutions

Cost-Benefit Analysis

Benefits: Strengthened Israel's mobile, AI, and imaging ecosystem; STEM programs enhanced workforce capacity; Technology acquisitions temporarily anchored IP and skills in Israel.

BOSCH

The Bosch Group operates across four main sectors: Mobility, Industrial Technology, Consumer Goods, and Energy & Building Technology (Magen, 2015). As a leading provider in the Internet of Things (IoT), Bosch delivers innovative solutions for smart homes, Industry 4.0, and connected mobility. Leveraging its expertise in sensor technology, software, services, and its proprietary IoT cloud, Bosch offers integrated, cross-domain solutions to its clients.

Employment

Bosch's development center in Israel began with six employees (Automotive World, 2016). The center collaborates with universities and startups in machine learning, robotics, cybersecurity, connectivity, and IoT. Bosch products have been marketed in Israel since 1965 through its long-standing sales partner Ledico.

Acquisitions and Partnerships

- Elmo Motion Control: Bosch acquired the motion control company for $700 million (Hazani, 2022). Elmo develops advanced servo drives and network motion controllers used in industrial and extreme environment automation.
- AnyVision Interactive Technologies: Bosch Building Technologies acquired a 9% stake in this Israeli AI startup, enhancing person- and object-recognition capabilities (blog.midches, 2018).
- Electra Consumer Products Ltd.: Bosch partnered with Electra to establish an HVAC manufacturing and technology park in Ashkelon. The facility exports globally, with projected exports rising from $17.7 million to $177.6 million by 2027 (Yefet, 2020).

Startup Support

Bosch Ventures launched a €250 million ($282 million) fund to support deep-tech startups globally, including quantum computing (Choucair, 2025). The initiative builds on Bosch's track record of over 100 startup investments. Through the "Open Bosch" program, startups can collaborate directly with Bosch business units, receiving funding and co-innovation opportunities. Bosch has previously invested in quantum computing firms such as IonQ and Quantum Motion.

Cost-Benefit Summary

Acquisition of Elmo Motion Control; Stake in AnyVision Interactive Technologies; HVAC manufacturing collaboration with Electra; Investments in quantum computing startups.

IBM

Employment

IBM Israel employs roughly 2,000 staff across multiple sites, with major operations in Petah Tikva for corporate and client engagement. Key R&D locations include Haifa (IBM Research Lab), Be'er Sheva (Cybersecurity Center of Excellence), and additional presence in Tel Aviv and Rehovot.

R&D Focus

IBM Israel develops technologies in: Artificial Intelligence, NLP, and Conversational AI; AI trust, optimization, and business analytics; Quantum computing and fully homomorphic encryption (FHE); Hybrid cloud infrastructure, data governance, and storage

Academia and Student Programs

IBM partners with the Technion and Hebrew University to advance AI research, support doctoral students, and fund research projects. Student opportunities include AI and software engineering internships, research assistant roles, and technical sales positions.

Acquisitions

Databand.ai (2022): Data observability software; Polar Security (2023): Data Security Posture Management (DSPM).

Cost-Benefit Summary

- IBM Haifa Research Lab (cloud computing, chip design, storage, formal verification)
- Strategic acquisitions: Databand.ai, Polar Security
- Research partnerships with leading universities in NLP, drug discovery, and multi-cloud AI

HP

HP Israel contributes to global R&D in cybersecurity, printing technologies, and enterprise IT. Notable focus areas include HP Indigo (digital printing), HP Scitex (large-format printing), and HP Software (cybersecurity, cloud services).

Employment

HP employs over 5,000 people in Israel across multiple sites, including Nes Ziona, Netanya, Ra'anana, Herzliya, Kiryat Gat, Caesarea, and Haifa.

Acquisitions

- Mercury Interactive (2006): Business Technology Optimization software, integrated into HP OpenView, doubling software revenue
- Axis Security (2023): Cloud-based Security Services Edge (SSE)

Cost-Benefit Summary

- Over 5,000 employees
- Key R&D centers: HP Indigo, HP Scitex, HP Software
- Strategic acquisitions: Mercury Interactive, Axis Security

CISCO

Employment and R&D

Cisco has six R&D sites in Israel with more than 800 employees. Centers focus on cybersecurity, networking, cloud & AI, and telecom/mobility solutions. R&D hubs are located in Netanya (ASICs, network software), Tel Aviv & Ra'anana (cloud security, AI), and a dedicated cybersecurity center ($15M investment).

Startup Investments and Acquisitions

Cisco has acquired Israeli companies totaling over $7.2 billion and invested in 35+ startups, collaborating with five local VC funds to drive innovation in AI, cloud, and cybersecurity. Notable companies include: Lightspin: Cloud security for Kubernetes and microservices; Epsagon: Microservice monitoring and optimization; Sedona Systems: Unified network management platform; Portshift: Kubernetes-native security; Intucell: RAN optimization technology; Riverhead Networks: DDoS protection; P-Cube: IP service control platforms; NSD Group / Synamedia: DRM and smart card technologies.

Cost-Benefit Summary

- Six R&D centers employing over 800 people
- Focused on networking, cloud security, AI, and emerging technologies
- $7.2 billion spent on Israeli acquisitions

META

Employment

In early 2025, Meta reduced its Israeli workforce by approximately 5%, affecting around 40 employees out of a total of 900. This was part of a global restructuring effort aimed at streamlining operations and concentrating on core growth areas.

Academic Collaboration

Meta–Hebrew University AI Ph.D. Program

- Hosted at the Hebrew University of Jerusalem, School of Engineering and Computer Science
- Focus areas: Artificial Intelligence, Machine Learning, and Natural Language Processing
- Opportunities for students include: Access to Meta's computational resources; Mentorship from Meta AI researchers; Scholarships for eligible candidates; Integration of academic research with practical applications.

This initiative allows doctoral students to collaborate with Meta while pursuing advanced research.

R&D Innovation Facilities

Meta's primary R&D center in Tel Aviv focuses on: AI & Generative AI: Development of open-source LLMs such as LLaMA 3.1; Augmented Reality (AR): Smart glasses and wearable technologies; Developer Tools: APIs and infrastructure support for creators and startups; Cybersecurity & Privacy: Advanced solutions for data protection and secure messaging

Support to Startups

Meta runs an AI accelerator program in Tel Aviv supporting early-stage Israeli startups. Key highlights include:

- 10 startups selected annually, focusing on AI applications in biotech, ed-tech, publishing, and creative tools
- Access to Meta's FAIR researchers, cloud resources, and mentorship
- Alumni include QRGenetics, Lucid Dreams, and OrCam Hear

Acquisitions

Onavo: VPN apps collecting usage data to inform strategic decisions; discontinued in 2019 due to privacy concerns; Redkix: Team collaboration software; acquisition led to development of Facebook Workplace; Servicefriend: AI-powered customer service chatbots, enhancing automated support capabilities; Snaptu: Mobile apps for feature phones, expanding Facebook's mobile reach; Pebbles Interfaces: Gesture control technology, contributing to Meta's AR and VR initiatives.

Cost-Benefit Summary

- Major R&D center in Tel Aviv focused on AI and Generative AI
- AI accelerator supporting early-stage startups in Israel

MERCK

Academic Collaboration

Merck has established a technology innovation lab at its subsidiary Qlight Nanotech in Jerusalem, hosted on the Hebrew University's Edmund J. Safra Campus. The lab focuses on nanotechnology and advanced materials, particularly cadmium-free quantum materials for display applications. Partnerships with the Hebrew University and support from the Israel Innovation Authority highlight Merck's commitment to advancing local R&D.

R&D Innovation Facilities

Merck's main R&D operations in Israel collaborate closely with universities and startups. Core innovation areas include: Biopharmaceuticals: Immuno-oncology, multiple sclerosis, and cancer therapies; Life Sciences: CRISPR-based tools, cell culture media, and laboratory automation; Electronics & Materials: Quantum dots, nanocrystals, and OLED technologies; AI & Digital Health: Predictive biomarkers, drug toxicity modeling, and digital diagnostics.

Support to Startups

Merck supports early-stage biotech companies in Israel through its BioIncubator program, offering funding, lab space, and mentorship. Other startup initiatives include:

- Merck Serono Israel BioIncubator
- Collaborations with companies such as Neviah Genomics (in partnership with Compugen) for drug toxicity prediction
- Partnerships with the Israel Innovation Authority

Acquisitions

cCAM Biotherapeutics: Immunotherapy for cancer; CM-24, a monoclonal antibody targeting CEACAM1, integrated into Merck's oncology portfolio; Qlight Nanotech: Quantum dot technology for displays, spun out of Hebrew University's tech transfer company Yissum; now Merck's quantum materials research hub in Israel; Serono (2006): Acquisition included Rebif, a multiple sclerosis drug co-developed with the Weizmann Institute.

Cost-Benefit Summary

- R&D center focusing on Biopharmaceuticals, Life Sciences, Electronics & Materials, and AI & Digital Health
- BioIncubator program supporting early-stage biotech startups
- Strategic acquisitions: cCAM Biotherapeutics, Qlight Nanotech, Serono
- Local collaborations, including Neviah Genomics with Compugen

ROCHE

Roche's operations in Israel concentrate on the development and support of several strategic innovation domains. These include in-vitro diagnostics, encompassing advanced laboratory instruments and diagnostic assays for early and accurate disease detection. The company is also active in digital health, where it develops AI-based platforms aimed at personalized treatment, clinical decision support, and remote patient monitoring.

In the field of ophthalmology, Roche advances technologies for retinal disease diagnostics, including home-based monitoring solutions. In addition, Roche is involved in immunotherapy and oncology, with a focus on clinical trials, biomarker discovery, and precision medicine approaches.

Ophthalmology Innovation Initiatives

To strengthen innovation in eye care, Roche launched the *Ophthalmology Innovation Challenge* in collaboration with Beilinson Hospital and Start-Up Nation

Central. This initiative supports Israeli startups developing novel ophthalmic and digital health solutions. Notable participants include Notal Vision, which offers a home-based OCT monitoring platform for age-related macular degeneration, and AEYE Health, which develops AI algorithms for autonomous retinal screening. Other supported companies include GistMD, specializing in personalized patient education and engagement tools, and BioT Medical, which provides cloud-based connectivity solutions for medical devices.

Clinical and Research Collaborations

Roche maintains multiple clinical and research partnerships in Israel. For example, KAHR Medical has collaborated with Roche on human clinical trials in the United States for its immunotherapy drug candidate. More broadly, Roche works with Israeli hospitals and research institutions on genomic testing, personalized medicine, and early-stage drug development programs.

Support for Academia and Talent Development

Roche actively engages with the academic sector by offering apprenticeships, internships, traineeships, and rotational programs for students and recent graduates. These initiatives aim to provide hands-on professional experience while familiarizing participants with the global healthcare and life-sciences industry.

Investments and Strategic Partnerships

Roche has also pursued strategic investments to strengthen its presence in the Israeli biotechnology ecosystem. In 2009, the company partnered with the venture capital firm Pontifax, investing tens of millions of dollars in Israeli biotech startups, with a focus on vaccines, oncology, biomarkers, and infectious diseases. The partnership emphasized early-stage investments with the potential for future acquisitions.

In 2020, Roche collaborated with the venture capital fund aMoon to establish the *StarFinder Lab*, an accelerator program for Israeli health-technology startups. This initiative focuses on AI-driven diagnostics, digital health solutions, and data platforms, providing participating startups with funding, mentorship, and access to international markets.

Cost–Benefit Considerations

Roche's innovation activities in Israel generate strategic benefits through initiatives such as the *Ophthalmology Innovation Challenge*, clinical collaborations with companies like KAHR Medical, and targeted investments via the Pontifax and aMoon partnerships. These efforts enhance Roche's access to cutting-edge technologies, clinical expertise, and early-stage innovations while strengthening its long-term pipeline in diagnostics, digital health, and therapeutics.

ASTRAZENECA

R&D and Innovation Infrastructure

AstraZeneca's activities in Israel are centered on key therapeutic areas, including oncology, cardiovascular, renal, and metabolic diseases (CVRM), as well as respiratory and immunology. The Israeli operation forms part of AstraZeneca's global A.Catalyst Network, which links 17 innovation hubs worldwide.

Within this framework, Israel hosts BeyondBio, a dedicated health-technology innovation hub designed to accelerate collaboration between startups, healthcare providers, and technology companies. BeyondBio functions as a platform for translating digital health and data-driven innovations into scalable healthcare solutions.

ARC and Hospital Partnerships

AstraZeneca collaborates with Sheba Medical Center through the ARC (Accelerate, Redesign, Collaborate) ecosystem. This partnership focuses on the co-development and validation of digital health solutions, integrating clinical expertise with advanced technological capabilities to improve patient care and operational efficiency.

Strategic and Technological Collaborations

Between 2022 and 2024, AstraZeneca partnered with Immunai, an Israeli biotechnology company specializing in AI-enabled drug discovery. The collaboration leveraged Immunai's "digital immune system" model to enhance data-driven approaches to immunology and therapeutic development.

In response to the COVID-19 pandemic, AstraZeneca also entered into a significant agreement with the Israeli government in 2020 to supply up to 10 million doses of its COVID-19 vaccine (AZD1222) on a non-profit basis, reflecting the company's public health commitment during a global crisis.

Academic Engagement and Knowledge Development

AstraZeneca maintains strong ties with the academic sector in Israel. A prominent example is the BEAM-TAU collaboration with Tel Aviv University, which focuses on the use of real-world health data to improve healthcare outcomes. This initiative aims to strengthen Israel's research capabilities through advanced analytics and data-driven medical insights.

In addition, AstraZeneca operates the IMPACT Academy, a global professional education platform for multidisciplinary healthcare professionals. The program delivers evidence-based training in areas such as cardiovascular, renal, and metabolic diseases, supporting continuous medical education through expert-led and interactive learning modules.

Inclusive and Social Innovation Initiatives

AstraZeneca's Young Health Programme (YHP) in Israel promotes healthy lifestyles among young people, with particular attention to individuals with disabilities. The initiative incorporates participatory workshops led by people with disabilities, aiming to raise awareness of healthy behaviors and reduce the long-term risk of non-communicable diseases.

Startup Support and Innovation Ecosystem

Through PlayBeyondBio, AstraZeneca runs a structured startup collaboration program in partnership with organizations such as JVP, Maccabi Healthcare Services, Shaarei Zedek Medical Center, Microsoft, and Cisco. The BeyondBio Health Innovation Hub supports early-stage companies working in AI, data science, and digital health. Participating startups gain access to AstraZeneca's scientific expertise, infrastructure, and global networks, with a strategic focus on diagnostics, personalized medicine, and preventive care.

APPLIED MATERIALS

Employment and Strategic Presence

Applied Materials Israel serves as the company's largest research, development, and manufacturing hub outside the United States, employing more than 2,400 professionals. Despite ongoing geopolitical uncertainty, the company has significantly expanded its footprint since 2021, doubling both workforce size and investment levels. As part of this expansion, Applied Materials is constructing a fourth campus building in Rehovot and actively recruiting talent across physics, software engineering, and algorithm development.

R&D and Innovation Capabilities

Applied Materials Israel plays a central role in advancing technologies critical to next-generation semiconductor manufacturing. A core strength lies in Process Diagnostics and Control (PDC), where the company develops advanced metrology and inspection systems that enhance chip fabrication accuracy and yield.

The R&D portfolio also includes computer vision and deep learning, applied to automated defect detection and yield optimization across complex manufacturing processes. In addition, the site is a global leader in cold field emission electron-beam (eBeam) technology, which supports the production of gate-all-around (GAA) transistors and high-bandwidth memory (HBM). These efforts are complemented by capabilities in optics, scanning electron microscopy (SEM), robotics, and machine learning, enabling semiconductor solutions for applications such as artificial intelligence, the Internet of Things, and autonomous systems.

Reflecting its innovation intensity, Applied Materials Israel holds over 1,000 patents and is recognized as a global leader in semiconductor inspection technologies.

R&D and Operational Centers

Applied Materials operates multiple facilities across Israel. The Rehovot campus functions as the national headquarters and includes advanced cleanroom manufacturing infrastructure. Kiryat Gat specializes in customer support and field engineering, while Migdal HaEmek hosts additional engineering and service operations that support both domestic and international customers.

EPIC Innovation Platform

Applied Materials' EPIC (Equipment and Process Innovation Center) is a global innovation platform designed to facilitate collaboration among R&D leaders, equipment manufacturers, materials suppliers, and research institutions. While EPIC places particular emphasis on advanced semiconductor packaging technologies, it also promotes cross-industry alliances that accelerate innovation throughout the semiconductor manufacturing value chain.

Academic Engagement and Talent Development

Applied Materials Israel maintains strong links with the academic community. The eBeam Horizon Program supports research conducted at Israeli universities and enables researchers and students to visit the Applied Materials campus, fostering hands-on experimentation and knowledge exchange.

In parallel, the company operates internship and university recruitment programs for undergraduate and graduate students, particularly in disciplines such as software engineering, materials science, and supply chain management. These initiatives contribute to workforce development and strengthen long-term industry–academia ties.

Academic and Research Collaborations

Applied Materials collaborates extensively with leading Israeli institutions, including the Technion, Hebrew University of Jerusalem, Tel Aviv University, and Ben-Gurion University of the Negev, often through national frameworks such as MAGNET and Nofar. These partnerships focus on applied research in fields such as nanotechnology, energy systems, and advanced materials. A notable example is the collaboration with the Russell Berrie Nanotechnology Institute at the Technion on multiple joint research projects.

Acquisitions and Capability Integration

Applied Materials Israel has made one notable acquisition relevant to its local innovation trajectory: the purchase of Integrated Circuit Testing GmbH in 1996. Although the acquired company was based in Munich, Germany, its wafer metrology technologies were subsequently integrated into Applied Materials' Israeli operations. These capabilities now form a cornerstone of the company's Israel-based PDC division, which leads global innovation in semiconductor inspection and quality control.

Cost–Benefit Considerations

Applied Materials' substantial employment base of over 2,400 skilled workers represents a major economic and knowledge benefit to Israel. In addition, the integration of advanced wafer metrology technologies through the Integrated Circuit Testing acquisition has significantly strengthened the company's inspection capabilities, reinforcing Israel's position as a global center for semiconductor diagnostics and process control.

BROADCOM

R&D and Innovation Activities

Broadcom's Israeli research and development operations focus on several advanced technology areas, including broadband and fiber optics, telecom processors and network infrastructure, image processing and multimedia integration, 5G wireless communications, and enterprise routing and switching technologies. These capabilities underpin Broadcom's leadership across data center networking, mobile communications, and embedded systems, enabling the company to remain at the forefront of global connectivity solutions.

Strategic Acquisitions

Since 2001, Broadcom has acquired at least ten Israeli technology companies, establishing itself as one of the most active foreign investors in the country's high-tech sector. Several acquisitions highlight the company's strategic focus on communications, semiconductor innovation, and imaging technologies:

- BroadLight – Specializes in Passive Optical Network (PON) solutions, providing integrated semiconductor devices, software, reference designs, and support tools. BroadLight's technology enables equipment vendors to deliver BPON and GPON component solutions for central offices and customer premises with improved speed and reduced risk.
- MagnaCom – Developed a patented WAve Modulation (WAM) technology that increases spectrum efficiency, addressing global bandwidth demand. WAM can be applied across cellular networks, Wi-Fi, satellite communications, cable TV, DSL, fiber networks, and wireless backhaul systems.
- Sightic Vista – Provides image signal processing hardware and software, integrating high-quality imaging capabilities into digital cameras and video systems. Its technologies enhance sensitivity, resolution, dynamic range, digital zoom, video stabilization, and reduce noise and compression artifacts.
- Percello – Fabless semiconductor company offering digital baseband solutions for 3G/HSDPA/HSUPA/HSPA+/LTE femtocells, targeting reductions in cost, power consumption, and development time while increasing integration and flexibility.
- Dune Networks – Fabless semiconductor firm providing traffic management and non-blocking switching fabric solutions, designed for Internet and storage platforms, emphasizing scalability, reliability, and support for next-generation services.

- Provigent – Specialized in high-performance Systems-on-a-Chip (SoC) for broadband wireless transmission, delivering mixed-signal semiconductors for microwave backhaul systems.

Cost–Benefit Considerations

Broadcom's Israeli operations contribute significant technological and economic value. The R&D centers drive innovation in fiber optics, telecom, image processing, 5G, and enterprise networking technologies, while the strategic acquisition of multiple Israeli startups has strengthened the company's global technological portfolio and enhanced its competitive position in semiconductors and network solutions.

PFIZER

R&D and Innovation Facilities

Pfizer Israel, headquartered in Herzliya, concentrates on several strategic therapeutic areas, including immunology and inflammation, oncology, rare diseases, and vaccines and preventive care. The company collaborates with Israeli hospitals, startups, and research institutions to advance digital health solutions, clinical trials, and real-world evidence initiatives. Local partnerships also support AI-driven drug development and remote patient monitoring programs, reflecting Pfizer's commitment to integrating technology with healthcare delivery.

Employment

Pfizer Israel offers a range of professional roles across multiple functions, including medical affairs, sales and field operations, regulatory affairs, clinical research, and digital health strategy, providing a platform for both scientific and business talent development in the life sciences sector.

Academic Collaborations

- Pfizer maintains strong engagement with Israel's academic ecosystem to promote innovation in drug development:
- Technion: In January 2023, Pfizer and the Technion signed a framework agreement to explore intersections of artificial intelligence and drug development, focusing on accelerating discovery and translational research.

- Bar-Ilan University: In 2015, Pfizer entered into an evaluation agreement to investigate DNA nanorobots as carriers for protein-based therapeutics.
- Weizmann Institute of Science: In 2016, Pfizer partnered with the Weizmann Institute to foster early-stage innovation and support advanced research in pharmaceutical development.

Acquisitions

In 2014, Pfizer acquired Prolor Biotech (via OPKO Health) in a deal valued at up to $570 million. Prolor Biotech had developed hGH-CTP, a long-acting human growth hormone therapy. Through this acquisition, Pfizer obtained global commercialization rights, expanding its endocrinology pipeline and offering a treatment that reduces dosing frequency for patients with growth hormone deficiency.

Cost–Benefit Considerations

Pfizer's Israeli operations provide strategic advantages by advancing therapies in immunology, oncology, rare diseases, and vaccines, while the acquisition of Prolor Biotech strengthened its product portfolio in endocrinology. These initiatives enhance Pfizer's local innovation capabilities, clinical expertise, and global market reach.

SANOFI

Employment

Sanofi Israel, headquartered in Yakum, employs over 130 professionals and has been recognized as a Great Place to Work. The company plays a strategic role in global R&D and digital health initiatives, combining local expertise with international capabilities.

R&D and Innovation Focus

Sanofi Israel focuses on key therapeutic and healthcare areas, including immunology and oncology, rare diseases and neurology, diabetes and cardiovascular health, vaccines, and consumer healthcare. The site also emphasizes AI-driven drug discovery, leveraging computational and data-driven approaches to accelerate therapeutic development.

A notable example is the collaboration with CytoReason, a Tel Aviv-based startup that constructs computational models of the human immune system. This partnership targets inflammatory bowel disease (IBD), asthma, and other chronic conditions, allowing Sanofi to predict drug responses, prioritize clinical targets, and optimize treatment strategies using AI-powered modeling.

Academic Collaborations

Sanofi maintains strong ties with Israeli academic institutions to foster research and innovation:

- Bar-Ilan University: In 2015, the company signed an evaluation agreement to explore DNA nanorobots as potential carriers for therapeutic proteins, advancing drug delivery technologies.
- Hebrew University of Jerusalem: Sanofi collaborates on multiple research initiatives, including hepatitis B studies led by Dr. Daniel Shouval, Professor Emeritus of Medicine at the Hebrew University and Hadassah Medical School.
- Talent Development: Alumni like Haya Taitel, a graduate of Hebrew University's School of Pharmacy, have held leadership positions in commercial operations, including at Sanofi, demonstrating the company's role in nurturing local pharmaceutical talent.

Acquisitions and Strategic Investments

Sanofi has made several strategic investments in Israel:

- Biond Biologics (2021): Valued at $125 million upfront plus over $1 billion in milestones, the acquisition focused on BND-22, a novel immunotherapy targeting both adaptive and innate immune cells. This deal is one of the most significant investments in an Israeli preclinical therapy to date.
- Consumer Healthcare (2012): Sanofi-Aventis Israel acquired a local consumer healthcare business specializing in dermocosmetics, nutritional supplements, and lifestyle products.
- KAHR Medical: Sanofi also invested in this Hadasit Bio Holdings portfolio company, supporting early-stage innovations in medical technology.

Cost–Benefit Considerations

Sanofi Israel contributes strategic value through its employment of over 130 skilled professionals, AI-driven drug discovery initiatives, and collaborations with local partners such as CytoReason. Its acquisitions of Biond Biologics and consumer healthcare assets have strengthened the company's pipeline and expanded its presence in both pharmaceutical and health technology markets.

UNILEVER

Employment

Unilever Israel employs approximately 2,000 people across four main production sites—Safed, Acre, Arad, and Haifa—as well as its headquarters in Airport City, Lod. The company produces a wide range of products, from cereals, snacks, sauces, spreads, and ice cream to personal care items. Notable local brands include Telma, Knorr, Klik, and Bagel & Bagel. A significant investment in the Haifa plant of around NIS 12 million (≈US$2.6 million) expanded food processing capacity, demonstrating Unilever's commitment to local production and innovation.

R&D and Innovation Facilities

Unilever Israel operates an Innovation Center, focused on discovering, testing, and deploying locally developed innovations across its portfolio. Since 2015, Unilever has participated in Israel's Multinational Cooperation Program under the Office of the Chief Scientist, fostering partnerships between Israeli innovators and global corporations.

One example is the collaboration with Syneron Medical to develop the Illuminage Beauty line, showcasing Unilever's approach to integrating Israeli technological expertise into its global consumer products.

The company is also involved in broader innovation ecosystem initiatives, including The Kitchen Hub 2, a food technology incubator co-founded with leading firms such as Strauss, Givaudan, and Novozymes and supported by the Israel Innovation Authority. Additionally, Unilever contributes to events like Innovation Nation, sharing insights with local startups and multinational peers. While multiple exploratory projects have been initiated, publicly disclosed active R&D initiatives within Israel remain limited.

Global Open Innovation and AI Pilots

Unilever's global innovation initiatives—including AI-driven product development pilots—present potential opportunities for future collaboration with Israeli tech companies, although these efforts are not currently Israel-focused.

Acquisitions

Vitco Israel (1996): Unilever acquired 60% of Vitco Israel for US$13 million, entering the local personal care and detergents market. The remaining 40% remained with Delek Investments. This acquisition allowed Unilever to leverage its global expertise and brand reputation to establish a foothold in Israel's consumer products sector.

Strauss Ice Cream (1995–2014): Unilever gradually increased its ownership of Strauss Ice Cream, acquiring 50% in 1995, 90% in 2010, and completing full ownership in 2014, fully integrating the brand into its Israeli operations and expanding its presence in the local ice cream market.

Cost–Benefit Considerations

Unilever Israel generates significant local value through employment of 2,000 people, investments in production and processing facilities, and its Innovation Center. Collaborations such as The Kitchen Hub 2 strengthen Israel's foodtech ecosystem, while acquisitions of Vitco Israel and Strauss Ice Cream have expanded Unilever's market share in personal care and consumer food products. These initiatives collectively enhance the company's technological and commercial capabilities in Israel.

Cargill

In May 2019, Cargill participated in a US$12 million Series A funding round for Aleph Farms, an Israeli startup specializing in cell-cultured meat. Aleph Farms, founded in 2017 by Technion researchers and the food-tech incubator The Kitchen Hub, gained international attention for producing a prototype cell-grown steak in 2018, followed by a 3D-bioprinted ribeye in 2021.

Cargill's investment aligns with its global protein strategy, complementing its existing portfolio of animal- and plant-based proteins with innovative cultured meat technologies. This partnership demonstrates Cargill's commitment to supporting alternative protein development and advancing sustainable food solutions.

NESTLÉ

Acquisitions

Nestlé acquired full ownership of Osem Investments in 2016 for approximately €752 million (~US$840 million), becoming the sole owner of Israel's largest publicly traded food manufacturer. Nestlé had previously increased its stake gradually, from 50.1% in 2002 to 58.76% in 2012, while establishing a global snack R&D center in Sderot. Osem produces a wide range of products, including bakery items, snacks, pasta, sauces, and baby foods, and is responsible for iconic Israeli brands such as Bamba and Bisli.

R&D Innovation Facilities

Nestlé's Sderot R&D center functions as a global snack innovation hub, leveraging local talent and technological capabilities to drive product development and experimentation in the food sector.

Food-Tech Partnerships

Nestlé-Osem's subsidiary Tivol has collaborated with the Israeli startup More Foods to develop pumpkin seed–based plant-based meat alternatives. This partnership combines More Foods' plant-based technology with Osem-Nestlé's market knowledge, enabling the expansion of healthy, innovative food offerings on a global scale.

Open Innovation Platform – "Henry"

In 2016, Nestlé-Osem launched the "Henry" Open Innovation platform, named after the company founder, to systematically connect Israeli startups with Nestlé's global R&D and business units. The platform fosters collaboration in areas such as marketing innovation, nutrition science, and process technologies, allowing Nestlé to integrate external technological advances into its internal innovation processes and capitalize on Israel's vibrant food-tech ecosystem.

Cost–Benefit Considerations

Nestlé Israel's strategic initiatives generate value through the full acquisition of Osem, fostering a dominant position in the local consumer food market. Additionally, partnerships like Tivol-More Foods and the Henry platform enhance Nestlé's innovation pipeline, strengthen its engagement with Israel's food-tech ecosystem, and support global product development in healthier and more sustainable food solutions.

DANONE

Acquisitions

Danone re-entered the Israeli market in 1996 through a strategic partnership with Strauss Group, acquiring a 20% stake in Strauss' dairy operations for approximately US$56 million. This collaboration allowed Danone to provide expertise in production, distribution, and R&D, and co-supported the construction of a new dairy plant in Ahihud, strengthening its local presence after previously withdrawing from Israel in the 1980s due to the Arab boycott.

Support for Startups

Today, Danone's innovation activities in Israel focus on strategic venture investments in emerging food-tech companies:

- Wilk Technologies (April 2023): Through Danone Manifesto Ventures, Danone led a $3.5 million funding round, acquiring a minimum 2% ownership (~$2 million). Wilk Technologies develops cell-cultured milk components for human and animal use, holding patents in lab-based milk replication techniques.
- Imagindairy (May 2023): Danone made a strategic investment in this precision fermentation startup, which produces animal-free whey and casein proteins for dairy alternatives. The partnership includes both capital support and potential collaboration with Danone's R&D teams to advance sustainable dairy technologies.

Cost–Benefit Considerations

Danone Israel's initiatives create value by combining historical strategic investments, such as the Strauss partnership, with modern ventures in cell-cultured and precision-fermented dairy. These activities strengthen Danone's local and global innovation capabilities in sustainable food production and support Israel's growing food-tech ecosystem.

TYSON FOODS

Strategic Investment

In May 2018, Tyson Ventures, the venture capital arm of Tyson Foods, co-led a $2.2 million seed investment in Future Meat Technologies, a Jerusalem-based biotechnology company. Future Meat Technologies develops a distributive manufacturing platform for the cost-efficient, non-GMO production of meat directly from animal cells, eliminating the need for conventional livestock raising or harvesting.

The company focuses on producing fat and muscle cells, the fundamental building blocks of meat, using innovative biomanufacturing methods. This technology is based on research conducted by Prof. Yaakov Nahmias at The Hebrew University of Jerusalem and is licensed through Yissum, the university's technology transfer company.

Tyson Foods Overview

Tyson Foods, Inc. (NYSE: TSN) is one of the world's largest food companies and a global leader in protein production. Headquartered in Springdale, Arkansas, Tyson employs approximately 122,000 team members worldwide. The company emphasizes sustainable protein production, global accessibility of food, and innovation in food technology, aligning with initiatives such as its investment in Future Meat Technologies to advance cell-cultured meat solutions.

MIGROS INDUSTRIE

Company Overview

Migros Industrie is the industrial arm of Migros Group, Switzerland's largest retailer. The company focuses on producing private-label products for Migros supermarkets, the discount chain Denner, and the convenience store format Migrolino. Known for high-quality and responsibly produced goods, Migros Industrie offers products with strong brand recognition among Swiss consumers, such as ice tea and Seal ice cream, which are celebrated for both quality and value. It is also one of the largest private-label food producers globally.

Strategic Investment in Food-Tech

In 2019, Migros Industrie acquired a stake in Aleph Farms, an Israeli startup specializing in cultivated meat technology. Aleph Farms develops resource-efficient methods to grow animal cells into steaks within weeks, providing a sustainable alternative to conventional meat production.

By 2023, with support from Migros Industrie, Aleph Farms submitted Switzerland's first regulatory application for cultivated beef to the Federal Food Safety and Veterinary Office (FSVO). This collaboration represents a strategic step toward commercial launch and distribution of sustainable meat products, pending regulatory approval.

ADM (ARCHER DANIELS MIDLAND)

Company Overview

ADM (Archer Daniels Midland) is a global leader in human and animal nutrition, as well as agricultural origination and processing, with headquarters in Chicago, Illinois. Operating across six continents, ADM connects crops to markets worldwide. In 2022, the company reported net sales of $102 billion, reflecting its scale and global reach.

Investments in Alternative Proteins and Food-Tech Innovation

ADM has increasingly invested in alternative protein technologies to diversify its offerings and support sustainable food systems. Key initiatives include:

- New Culture – An animal-free cheese startup.
- Spiber – A biomaterials company specializing in sustainable protein solutions.
- Believer Meats (formerly Future Meat Technologies) – An Israeli cultivated meat company founded by Prof. Yaakov Nahmias, focusing on cell-based chicken and lamb products.

In May 2022, ADM entered a joint development agreement with Believer Meats (a subsidiary of Eat Just) to accelerate cultivated chicken production. The partnership leverages ADM's extensive ingredient expertise and nutrition knowledge to enhance Believer's proprietary cell-cultivation processes. The agreement is non-exclusive, creating opportunities for future commercialization of new cultivated meat products.

Infrastructure and Expansion

ADM announced a $300 million investment in 2022 to expand alternative protein production facilities in Illinois and establish a state-of-the-art Protein Innovation Center. Believer Meats also broke ground on a 200,000 sq. ft. production facility in Wilson, North Carolina, claimed to be the largest of its kind for cultivated meat. The company maintains an additional production plant in Israel and has raised over $320 million in funding, with a reported valuation of approximately $600 million. Believer achieved notable milestones in 2022, including the development of the world's first cultivated lamb.

Cost–Benefit Considerations

ADM's initiatives in alternative proteins strengthen its position as a global leader in sustainable nutrition, leveraging its ingredient and processing expertise to accelerate the commercialization of cultivated meat. Investments in Believer Meats and other startups enhance ADM's technological capabilities, provide entry into the rapidly growing alternative protein market, and support the company's long-term innovation strategy.

SODEXO

Company Overview

Sodexo is a global leader in integrated food and facilities management services, ranked as the 19th largest employer worldwide. The company serves clients across corporate, education, healthcare, senior living, sports and leisure, and government sectors in 64 countries. Sodexo's offerings aim to enhance organizational performance, support local communities, and improve quality of life for millions of customers daily.

Strategic Partnership and Innovation

In 2021, Sodexo partnered with SavorEat, an Israeli food-tech startup founded in 2018 by Racheli Vizman (CEO), Prof. Oded Shoseyov (CSO), and Prof. Ido Braslavsky. SavorEat has developed a Plant-Forward Robot Chef, which produces meat alternatives using a combination of plant-based ingredients and an advanced robotic cooking system capable of preparing multiple products simultaneously.

The technology has completed its development phase and is undergoing pilot testing in Israel at the BBB hamburger chain. The collaboration with Sodexo aims to commercialize the Robot Chef at universities in the United States, using the pilot as a foundation for broader market deployment. This partnership represents Sodexo's commitment to innovative, sustainable food solutions and engagement with Israel's growing food-tech ecosystem.

Cost–Benefit Considerations

Sodexo benefits from the collaboration with SavorEat by gaining early access to advanced plant-based food technologies and robotic food preparation systems. This partnership strengthens Sodexo's innovation capabilities, provides a pathway for commercialization in the U.S., and reinforces the company's commitment to sustainable, scalable food solutions in both institutional and commercial settings.

MEDTRONIC

Employment

Medtronic Israel employs over 1,200 professionals across multiple sites, including Herzliya Pituah (headquarters), Caesarea, Petah Tikva, Jerusalem, Yokneam, and Tel Aviv. Its Israeli operations have expanded largely through strategic acquisitions of local health-tech companies, enabling Medtronic to establish production, R&D, and innovation centers throughout the country.

R&D Innovation Facilities

In 2017, Medtronic established R&D centers in Jerusalem and Yokneam, supported by a NIS 50 million grant from the Israel Innovation Authority (part of a broader NIS 120 million package). These centers focus on imaging technologies for minimally invasive surgery and robotics innovation, positioning Medtronic as one of the first multinationals to expand R&D operations in Israel while hiring local talent through state-supported programs.

Additionally, Medtronic collaborates with the MindUp incubator in Haifa, in partnership with Rambam Hospital, to support early-stage digital medicine startups and foster innovation in healthcare technologies.

Acquisitions

Medtronic has pursued multiple strategic acquisitions in Israel to strengthen its medical device portfolio:

- Mazor Robotics (2018) – Acquired for $1.6 billion, Mazor developed robotic guidance systems for spine surgery, including the Renaissance and Mazor X platforms.
- Given Imaging → Covidien → Medtronic (2014–2015) – Acquired for its PillCam capsule endoscopy technology, later integrated into Medtronic.
- Odin Medical Technologies (2006) – MRI-based brain surgery imaging, later transformed into Medtronic Navigation Israel.
- Ventor Technologies (2009) – Developer of aortic valve prostheses, acquired for $325 million.
- Nutrino Health & Visionsense – Acquired for approximately $100 million and $75 million respectively, focusing on nutrition data analytics and brain surgery imaging.
- Triple Jump (2021–2025) – Developer of an insulin pump patch with mobile connectivity, integrated into Medtronic's artificial pancreas system.

Cost–Benefit Considerations

Medtronic Israel benefits from its 1,200-strong workforce and the strategic integration of multiple Israeli health-tech acquisitions. These investments provide access to advanced robotics, imaging, nutrition analytics, and digital health technologies, enhancing Medtronic's global innovation capabilities and strengthening its position as a leader in minimally invasive surgery, medical devices, and digital medicine solutions.

JOHNSON & JOHNSON (J&J)

Employment

Johnson & Johnson Israel employs approximately 1,000 professionals, combining roles in innovation, research, and manufacturing. Although J&J closed its Israeli headquarters in 2009 and reduced its local workforce by about 20 employees, it continues to maintain a significant operational footprint through partnerships, acquisitions, and innovation initiatives.

R&D Innovation Facilities and Incubation

J&J operates a biotech incubator in Rehovot, established in collaboration with Israel's Office of the Chief Scientist, Takeda, and OrbiMed. This incubator supports early-stage biotech startups, fostering innovation at the intersection of biology and technology. The company focuses on developing smarter, less invasive, and personalized treatments, particularly in the areas of Cardiovascular, Orthopaedics, Surgery, Oncology, Immunology, Neuroscience, and Cardiopulmonary health.

Acquisitions and Strategic Investments

Biosense (1997) – Acquired for $400 million in shares, Biosense was founded in 1993 by Prof. Shlomo Ben-Haim of Technion Medical School. The company specializes in cardiology mapping and diagnostic technologies, using advanced catheters to replace traditional imaging tools like X-rays and scanners. While registered as a U.S. company, the majority of operations are in Israel, employing 60 of 85 total staff locally.

Omrix Biopharmaceuticals (2008) – An Israeli company producing blood plasma products, acquired to expand J&J's biopharmaceutical portfolio.

Cost–Benefit Considerations

Through local acquisitions and incubation initiatives, J&J leverages Israel's strong biotech ecosystem to advance minimally invasive and personalized medical solutions. Investments in companies such as Biosense and Omrix provide access to innovative diagnostic and therapeutic technologies, while the Rehovot incubator fosters collaboration with startups and enhances J&J's R&D capabilities in the region.

BAYER

R&D Innovation Facilities

Bayer Israel operates multiple centers and programs to advance agriculture, climate-tech, and cybersecurity innovation:

- Digital Hub Israel – Focuses on cybersecurity risk management, collaborating with local companies to develop technologies integrated into Bayer's global cybersecurity operations.
- Cybersecurity Center – Planned for 2022, this center is intended to become one of the largest internal cyber units of a multinational in Israel, enhancing Bayer's global cyber capabilities.
- Better Life Farming (BLF) Centers – Support smallholder farmers by providing access to modern farming technologies, training programs, and market linkages.

- Climate-Tech Program – Facilitates partnerships between Israeli startups and Bayer to develop state-of-the-art climate and agritech solutions, including joint R&D and pilot projects.
- Orbia Netafim Collaboration (2024) – Expands digital farming technology initiatives, combining expertise in agronomy, irrigation, digital platforms, and data modeling to support fruit and vegetable growers.

Strategic Investments

TierraSpec (2022) – Bayer's Trendlines Ag Innovation Fund co-invested to establish TierraSpec, an Israeli startup focused on real-time measurement and validation of carbon sequestration in agricultural soils. Leveraging over 30 years of research from Tel Aviv University, TierraSpec uses machine learning and remote sensing technologies to enable cost-effective carbon credit issuance and soil health monitoring.

Cost–Benefit Considerations

Bayer Israel benefits from its strategic investments, R&D centers, and collaborative programs by advancing innovations in agritech, climate technologies, and cybersecurity. These initiatives strengthen Bayer's ability to integrate Israeli technological expertise into global operations, improve farmer access to modern agricultural practices, and support sustainable and data-driven farming solutions.

YARA

Strategic Investments and Innovation

Yara Growth Ventures, the corporate venture capital arm of Yara International, has been actively investing in Israeli startups, with a particular focus on clean hydrogen and sustainable energy technologies.

Key Acquisition / Investment

H2Pro (2022) – Yara Growth Ventures participated in a $75 million Series B funding round for H2Pro, an Israeli startup developing innovative green hydrogen technology. H2Pro's core innovation, the E-TAC (electrochemical-thermally activated chemical) process, enables water splitting without a costly membrane, significantly lowering both capital and operational expenses. Founded in 2019 by Technion researchers and entrepreneur Talmon Marco, H2Pro aims to produce green hydrogen at costs as low as $1 per kilogram by the late 2020s.

Cost–Benefit Considerations

Yara benefits from its Israeli investment by gaining early access to cutting-edge green hydrogen technologies, which could reduce production costs and advance the global transition to sustainable energy. H2Pro's E-TAC process exemplifies scalable, cost-effective innovation with potential global impact on hydrogen production and decarbonization efforts.

VALMONT

Company Overview

Valmont Industries has been a global leader for nearly 80 years in providing infrastructure solutions and agricultural productivity technologies. Traded on the New York Stock Exchange, Valmont currently has a market capitalization exceeding $5 billion.

Strategic Acquisition

Prospera Technologies (2021) – Valmont entered into a $300 million agreement to acquire Prospera Technologies, an Israeli ag-tech company specializing in AI-driven digital and autonomous farming solutions. Founded in 2014 by Daniel Koppel, Shimon Shpiz, and Raviv Itzhaky, Prospera had already partnered with Valmont since 2019 to deploy its technology.

R&D Innovation

Prospera integrates AI technologies with center pivot irrigation systems, enabling real-time crop analysis and anomaly detection. By 2020, the company's solutions monitored five million acres, doubling its adoption compared to the previous year. The company employs approximately 90 people across Israel, the U.S., and Mexico.

Funding and Strategic Partnerships

Prospera raised $22 million in two financing rounds from investors including Cisco, Qualcomm, Bessemer, MoreVC, and private investors such as Mobileye co-founder Amnon Shashua. These partnerships have supported the expansion and enhancement of Prospera's digital farming technologies.

Cost–Benefit Considerations

Valmont benefits from the acquisition by integrating AI-powered irrigation and crop analytics into its global agricultural solutions portfolio. The collaboration with Prospera provides access to cutting-edge ag-tech innovation, enhances operational efficiency for growers, and strengthens Valmont's market position in digital and autonomous farming technologies.

CORTEVA

Company Overview

Corteva Agriscience is a global agricultural leader with approximately 22,000 employees, 400+ production and manufacturing facilities, and operations in over 100 countries. The company manages a comprehensive portfolio of seeds and crop protection solutions, including biologically-derived technologies, designed to improve yields and protect crops. Corteva holds over 16,000 patents and launches 400+ new products annually, including germplasm that produces corn yields exceeding 600 bushels per acre.

Strategic Partnerships and Investments

Evogene Ltd & LaVie Bio (2019) – Corteva signed a strategic cooperation agreement with Israeli agro-tech company Evogene Ltd to invest $10 million in its subsidiary LaVie Bio, which focuses on microbiome solutions to enhance plant growth and crop resilience. As part of the agreement, Corteva acquired 30% of LaVie Bio and will have the right to market some of its products through its global channels.

- LaVie Bio Innovations: Develops bacterial compositions for seed coating, soil integration, or plant sprays to improve crop performance. It leverages Evogene's plant-genetics calculation system, integrating plant and bacterial genetic data to optimize solutions.
- Taxon Biosciences Integration: Corteva transferred its microbiome-focused subsidiary Taxon Biosciences to LaVie Bio, adding a large collection of bacterial samples and development assets.

- Ibi Ag (Corteva Catalyst Platform) – Corteva led a $6.1 million Series A funding round for Ibi Ag, an Israeli crop protection startup. Ibi Ag develops bio-insecticides using single-domain antibody technology, offering solutions that target pests while minimizing ecological impact.

Cost–Benefit Considerations

Corteva's Israeli investments provide access to advanced microbiome and biologically-based crop solutions, expanding its global portfolio with high-margin, scalable agricultural innovations. Partnerships with Evogene, LaVie Bio, and Ibi Ag strengthen Corteva's technological leadership in sustainable crop protection and yield improvement, while also supporting the development of new products for major agricultural markets like corn, wheat, and grapes.

ORACLE

Strategic Acquisitions

Oracle has pursued multiple Israeli acquisitions to strengthen its cloud infrastructure, big data analytics, and telecommunications solutions:

Ravello Systems (2016) – Acquired for approximately $500 million, Ravello Systems specialized in nested virtualization, enhancing Oracle's cloud computing capabilities.

Crosswise (2016) – Purchased for around $50 million, Crosswise was a big data startup focused on cross-device advertising, improving Oracle's data analytics and targeted marketing solutions.

Convergin (2009) – Acquired for an estimated $80–90 million, Convergin provided converged IP services, expanding Oracle's telecommunications service delivery portfolio.

Federos (2021) – Federos, a service and network orchestration company, was acquired to support next-generation network management, including 5G design, monitoring, and configuration.

Cost–Benefit Considerations

Through these acquisitions, Oracle gains advanced technologies and expertise in cloud, big data, and telecommunications, accelerating its global innovation capabilities and enhancing services offered to enterprise customers across multiple sectors.

HITACHI

Cooperations

Table 3.

Type	Israeli company	What the deal was / remarks
Reseller	SparkBeyond (AI startup, Israel)	Hitachi Systems (Japan) signed a reseller contract to offer SparkBeyond's AI problem-solving / data analytics platform in Japan.
Licensing	Accellta (stem-cell technology company, Haifa)	In 2018, Hitachi Chemical licensed patents & know-how from Accellta for stem cell culture media / culture methods.
Investment	Pegasus Technologies / eCogNito etc.	In early 2000s, Hitachi invested via Vertex Management Israel in startups (communications, storage, security etc.).
Smart Cities	Municipal / city authorities in Israel	Hitachi Vantara (part of Hitachi) entered smart city tenders in multiple cities in Israel (Tel Aviv, Raanana, Hadera, Herzliya).

Lockheed Martin

Israel's F-16 and F-35 fighter jets are made by Lockheed Martin, the world's largest defense company (Avcioglu and Ergocun, 2025; lockheemartin site). Lockheed also makes the CH-53K King Stallion heavy-lift helicopter, which ferries Israeli troops and the M270 Multiple Launch Rocket System (MLRS), used for artillery barrages.

In November 2004, Lockheed Martin completed its undertaking for industrial collaboration with Israeli companies and for offset acquisitions in Israel as part of the Peace Marble V program (lockheedmartin site). Originally planned to deliver over the course of 12 years, the resulting work - at a volume of $1.45 billion - was delivered in less than five. Approximately 40 Israeli companies, mainly in defense, technology, venture capital and research and development, were positively impacted by this collaboration.

In the Air

In order to renovate the aging fleet of the original Hercules (Rhinoceros) aircraft, the Air Force decided to acquire the innovative C-130J Super Hercules. In April 2010, Israel ordered the first C-130J and soon exercised the option to acquire an additional six. These were given the Hebrew name "Shimshon". The first Shimshon aircraft landed at the Nevatim Air Force Base in April 2014, and by the end of 2017, the remaining six were supplied to the Israeli Air Force.

Notably, Lockheed Martin has also supplied the Israel Air Force with fifth-generation fighter jets, following the decision of the Israeli government in September 2010 to select the F-35 Lightning II fighter.

Named "Adir" in Israel, the initial acquisition agreement included 19 Adir fighter jets, with the first two planes arriving in December 2016. Between November 2014 and October 2016, the government of Israel ordered an additional 31 aircraft in order to complete a second F-35 squadron. A total of 75 aircraft are projected to be delivered in the coming years.

On Land

Lockheed Martin has also assisted in strengthening the IDF ground forces. The Multiple Launch Rocket System (MLRS) manufactured by Lockheed Martin is used by the IDF ground forces and introduced new capabilities in the 1980s for providing artillery assistance in the battlefield. Lockheed Martin has also supplied radars, rockets, fire control and guidance systems, laser pointers and pods, while also lending support to training, air traffic control and weather forecasting, to name but a few of our diverse activities.

As part of the F-35 program Lockheed Martin signed Industrial Participation agreements with additional Israeli defense companies, worth Billions of dollars. In early November 2014, a new production line for F-35 wing boxes was inaugurated at Israel Aircraft Industries (IAI).

As part of the contract Lockheed Martin, IAI will manufacture over 800 pairs of wing skins over the course of 15 years, at a total financial volume of approximately $2.5 billion. In addition, several agreements of industrial participation are already being conducted with additional Israeli companies, including Elbit Systems, Cyclone, Tadiran and others. The collaboration between Lockheed Martin and Israeli industries is expected to exceed $6 billion.

Boeing

Employment

Boeing has maintained a presence in Israel since 1969, with a corporate office in Tel Aviv serving commercial and military customers. The company collaborates closely with Israeli suppliers and industry partners, supporting both defense and commercial aerospace projects.

Military and Commercial Contributions

Defense Products: Boeing provides Israel with advanced military systems, including the KC-46 Pegasus aerial refueling aircraft, AH-64 Apache attack helicopters, and GBU-39 small-diameter bombs. The Israeli Air Force has operated Boeing Apaches since the early 1990s, with the AH-64D-I Saraph introduced in 2005.

Commercial Aircraft: Boeing has a long-standing relationship with El Al, which transitioned to an all-Boeing fleet starting with the 707 in 1961, and continues to operate 737, 777, and 787 aircraft.

Local Industry Integration

Israeli suppliers provide parts and components for a wide range of Boeing products, including F-15 fighter jets, AH-64D Apache Longbow helicopters, and commercial aircraft models. Boeing has established a reciprocal procurement partnership with Israel, agreeing to invest $3.5 billion in local business if awarded major defense contracts. Over the next decade, Israel is expected to purchase approximately $10 billion in Boeing military products.

Cost–Benefit Considerations

- Boeing's engagement in Israel supports:
- Strengthening the Israeli defense ecosystem with advanced aircraft and weapons systems.
- Enhancing local industrial capabilities through supply chain integration and technology transfer.
- Sustaining a long-term commercial aviation partnership with El Al and other regional operators.

RTX

RTX Corporation supplies Israel with cluster bombs, bunker busters and guided air-to-surface missiles fired from Israeli F-16s. Raytheon, an RTX subsidiary, co-produces Iron Dome interceptors with Israel's Rafael. These interceptors have been included in recent US arms shipments to Israel (rtx site).

Another subsidiary, Pratt & Whitney, makes the engines powering F-15 and F-16 fighter jets.

RTX's commercial manufacturing facilities in Israel remain open and operational and have continued exporting products and importing critical items and raw materials, the company said in an SEC filing.

Raytheon Missiles & Defense, RAFAEL team have signed a joint venture to establish an Iron Dome Weapon System production facility in the United States (August 03, 2020 rtx site). The new partnership, called Raytheon RAFAEL Area Protection Systems, anticipates finalizing a site location before the end of the year.

This is the first Iron Dome all-up-round facility outside of Israel, and it will help the U.S. Department of Defense and allies across the globe obtain the system for defense of their service members and critical infrastructure.

The new facility produces both the Iron Dome Weapon System, which consists of the Tamir interceptor and launcher, and the SkyHunter® missile, a U.S. derivative of Tamir. Both Tamir and SkyHunter intercept incoming cruise missiles, unmanned aerial systems and short-range targets such as rockets, artillery, mortars and other aerial threats.

DAIMLER (MERCEDES-BENZ GROUP)

Overview

Mercedes-Benz Group is a global automotive leader, producing cars, SUVs, and electric vehicles under brands including Mercedes-Benz, Mercedes-Maybach, Mercedes-AMG, Mercedes-EQ, and Smart. The company also engages in technology research via Mercedes-Benz Research & Development and provides financial services such as loans, leasing, insurance, and fleet management. Daimler is headquartered in Stuttgart, Germany.

Strategic Investment in Israel

Daimler has invested in the Israeli battery technology startup StoreDot, a developer of FlashBattery, a fast-charging solution for electric vehicles. This investment was part of StoreDot's third financing round totaling $60 million, which included other investors such as Lucion Venture Capital, Samsung Ventures, and Norma Investments.

Innovation and Technology Impact

FlashBattery Technology: Enables electric vehicles to charge in approximately five minutes, similar to refueling a conventional vehicle. Depending on battery size, vehicles can achieve a range of 300 kilometers or more per charge.

Strategic Value: Daimler's involvement accelerates the commercialization and adoption of FlashBattery technology, particularly for its electric trucks and fleet vehicles, supporting Daimler's electrification strategy.

Cost–Benefit Considerations

- Provides strategic access to cutting-edge battery technology for Daimler's electric vehicles.
- Accelerates market readiness of fast-charging solutions, benefiting fleet operators and EV adoption.
- Strengthens collaboration with Israel's innovation ecosystem, fostering advanced mobility technologies.

VALMONT

Overview

Valmont Industries, a U.S.-based leader in agricultural services and irrigation equipment, has provided infrastructure and productivity solutions globally for nearly 80 years. The company is publicly traded on the New York Stock Exchange with a market capitalization exceeding $5 billion.

Investment & Acquisitions

In 2021, Valmont acquired Prospera Technologies, an Israeli ag-tech AI company, for $300 million. Prospera, founded in 2014 by Daniel Koppel, Shimon Shpiz, and Raviv Itzhaky, specializes in AI-driven digital farming solutions.

Innovation and Technology Impact

- Digital and Autonomous Farming: Prospera integrates AI with center pivot irrigation systems to provide real-time crop analysis and detect anomalies.

- Scale and Adoption: By 2020, Prospera's platform monitored five million acres, up from an initial estimate of one million, with a growing number of growers using its solutions.
- Investment & Support: Prospera has raised $22 million in financing rounds from investors including Cisco, Qualcomm, Bessemer, MoreVC, and private investors like Mobileye's Amnon Shashua.

Employment

Prospera employs approximately 90 people across Israel, the U.S., and Mexico, supporting Valmont's international agricultural technology initiatives.

Cost–Benefit Considerations

- Access to advanced AI technologies for precision agriculture.
- Enhances grower productivity and crop yield optimization.
- Expands Valmont's presence in the global ag-tech sector through Israeli innovation.

CORTEVA

Overview

Corteva Agriscience, a global agricultural company, employs approximately 22,000 people and operates across 100+ crops and 400+ countries. The company holds around 16,400 patents and maintains over 100 production and manufacturing facilities worldwide. Corteva provides comprehensive seed and crop protection solutions, including biologically derived and natural technologies, to help farmers increase yields, improve crop resilience, and protect against pests and diseases.

Collaboration & Investments

In 2019, Corteva signed a strategic cooperation agreement with Evogene Ltd, an Israeli ag-tech company. Under this agreement, Corteva invested $10 million in Evogene's subsidiary LaVie Bio, which focuses on plant microbiome solutions to enhance crop performance.

- LaVie Bio Activities: Develops bacterial formulations for spraying, seed coating, or soil integration to improve plant growth and crop characteristics.

- Ownership & Commercial Rights: Corteva holds 30% of LaVie Bio, with Evogene retaining 70%. Corteva can market select products through its global channels, while LaVie Bio earns royalties.
- Data & Technology: LaVie Bio leverages Evogene's two-decade database on plant genetics, integrated with microbial genetic information, to optimize crop outcomes.
- Subsidiaries & Innovations: Evogene has established four subsidiaries focusing on genetically targeted pesticides, seed improvement, microbiome applications, and medical cannabis products.
- Ibi Ag Collaboration: Corteva, through its Corteva Catalyst program, led a $6.1 million Series A funding round for Ibi Ag, which develops bioinsecticides using single-domain antibody technology. These solutions minimize harm to non-target organisms while maintaining ecological safety.

Cost–Benefit Considerations

- Access to cutting-edge plant microbiome and genetic technologies.
- Supports sustainable crop protection and yield optimization.
- Expands Corteva's global innovation footprint through strategic partnerships with Israeli ag-tech startups.

Compilation of References

Acemoglu, D., Johnson, S., & Robinson, J. A. (2003). An African success story: Botswana. In Rodrik, D. (Ed.), *In search of prosperity: Analytic narratives on economic growth* (pp. 80–119). Princeton University Press.

Acemoglu, D., & Robinson, J. (2012). *Why Nations Fail: The Origins of Power.* Prosperity, and Poverty.

ADNOC. (2022). *ADNOC annual report.* Abu Dhabi National Oil Company.

Ado, A., Osabutey Ellis, L. C., Sinha, P., & Adeola, O. (2025). Africa's international trade paradox, technology transfer, and value chain upgrade. *Technological Forecasting and Social Change*, 213.

African Mining Review. (2023). *Zimbabwe lithium mining: Industry trends and prospects.* AMR Publishing.

African Union. (2025). Driving African Future. the Science, Technology and Innovation Strategy for Africa (STISA 2034). https://au.int/sites/default/files/documents/45087-doc-AU_STISA_2025-2034_Strategy_ENGLISH.pdf

Alberti, F. (2001). The governance of industrial districts: a theoretical footing proposal. *Liuc Papers, 82*(5).

Alden, C., & Alves, A. C. (2009). China and Brazil in Africa: Emerging partners or competitors? *The Journal of Modern African Studies*, *47*(4), 563–586.

Al-Nasser, A. (2025). The Rise of Innovation Hubs in the Middle East. Abu-Ghazaleh Intellectual Property.

Alufer Mining. (2023). *Bel Air and Labé projects overview.* Alufer Mining Limited.

Amnesty International. (2016). *This is what we die for: Human rights abuses in the Democratic Republic of the Congo power the global trade in cobalt.*

Anglo American Platinum. (2022). *Mogalakwena mine overview*. Retrieved from https://www.angloamericanplatinum.com

Angola Ministry of Minerals. (2024). *Tetelo Copper Mine project report*. Government of Angola.

Anser, M. K., Nazir, M., Nassani, A. A., Al-Aiban, K. M., Zaman, K., & Haffar, M. (2025, September). Rethinking Economic Policies: Diversification and Governance Strategies to Address the Resource Curse in Mineral-Rich Economies. *Natural Resource Modeling*, *38*(4), 14. DOI: 10.1111/nrm.70011

Aresti, L., & Panayiotou, G. (2025). Applications and new technologies pertaining to waste heat recovery: A vision article. *Energies*, *18*(8), 2086. DOI: 10.3390/en18082086

Armah, F. A., Amponsah, P., & Osei, K. A. (2021). Sustainability and community development in African gold mining regions. *Resources Policy*, *70*, 101952.

Auty, R. (1993) Sustaining Development in Mineral Economies: The Resource Curse Thesis. Routledge.

Auty, R. M. (2001). *Resource abundance and economic development*. Oxford University Press.

Banda, F. (2020). Zambia's copper sector: Investment challenges and industrial linkages. *Journal of African Economies*, *29*(3), 255–275.

Bargash, M. (2025). Energy, Water and the Cost of Jordan's Dependence on Israel. Merip.

Becattini, G. (1990). The Marshallian industrial districtindustrial district as a socio-economic notion. In *Industrial Districts and Inter-Firm Co-operation in Italy*. International Institute for Labor Studies.

BeeHero. (n.d.). BeeHero. https://www.beehero.io/

bee-io. (2023). *Home*. Bee-Io.com. https://bee-io.com/

Beewise. (n.d.). *Home*. Beewise.ag. https://beewise.ag/home

Bellandi, M. (1996). On entrepreneurship, region and the constitution of scale and scope economies. *European Planning Studies*, *4*(4), 421–438. DOI: 10.1080/09654319608720356

Belussi, F., & Bertini, S. (1998). Evoluzione, apprendimento e modelli di acquisizione delle conoscenze: due sistemi locali a confronto nel settore del mobile imbottito. *Economia e Società Regionale*, (1998/2).

Bijaoui, I. (2025). Resource-based innovation in African critical minerals: A GVC approach. *African Journal of Industrial Development, 12*(3), 45–68.

Bijaoui, I. (2026). Technological upgrading in Central African mining ecosystems. *Journal of African Mining Studies, 8*(1), 1–34.

Bishop, T. (2023). Inside the AI chip race: How a pivotal happy hour changed Amazon's strategy in the cloud. *Geek wire.*

Bloom, I., Pavan, P., & Eitan, B. (2001, November). NROM™ — a new non-volatile memory technology: From device to products. *Microelectronic Engineering, 59*(1–4), 213–223. DOI: 10.1016/S0167-9317(01)00625-6

BlueTree. (2026). *Leaving Nature In, Taking Sugar Out.* Bluetree-Tech.com. https://bluetree-tech.com/

Brautigam, D. (2009). *The dragon's gift: The real story of China in Africa.* Oxford University Press.

Brautigam, D. (2011). Aid 'with Chinese characteristics': Chinese foreign aid and development finance meet the OECD-DAC aid regime. *Journal of International Development, 23*(5), 752–764. DOI: 10.1002/jid.1798

BreifCam. (2024, September 6). *The BriefCam Solution Ecosystem.* BriefCam. https://www.briefcam.com/the-briefcam-solution-ecosystem/

Brenckman, C. M., Parameswarappa Jayalakshmamma, M., Pennock, W. H., Ashraf, F., & Borgaonkar, A. D. (2025). A Review of Harmful Algal Blooms: Causes, Effects, Monitoring, and Prevention Methods. *Water (Basel), 17*(13), 1980. DOI: 10.3390/w17131980

British Geological Survey (BGS). (2018). *Mine water and environmental monitoring in the Zambian Copperbelt.*

Carbonara, N. (2002). New models of inter-firm networks within industrial districts. *Entrepreneurship and Regional Development, 14*(3), 229–246. DOI: 10.1080/08985620210136027

CBG. (2022). *Sangaredi Mine annual report.* Compagnie des Bauxites de Guinée.

Chalco Guinea Co. Ltd. (2025). *Boffa mining and alumina expansion project.* Beijing: Chalco Group.

Chandra S., Lata H., ElSohly M.A., Walker L.A., & Potter D. (2017). Cannabis cultivation: Methodological issues for obtaining medical-grade product. *Epilepsy & Behavior, 70*(B), 302-312.

Chandy, R. K., & Tellis, G. J. (1998). Organizing for radical product innovation: The overlooked role of willingness to cannibalize. *JMR, Journal of Marketing Research*, *35*(4), 474–487. DOI: 10.1177/002224379803500406

China General Nuclear Power Group (CGN) Namibia. (2024). *Husab uranium mine: Operations overview*. CGN Namibia.

Chinembiri, T., Moyo, P., & Chikukwa, R. (2022). Spodumene beneficiation and lithium extraction in Zimbabwe. *Journal of African Mineral Resources*, *15*(2), 33–48.

Cloete, N., Maassen, P., & Bailey, T. (2015). *Knowledge production and contradictory functions in African higher education*. African Minds. DOI: 10.47622/9781920677855

Cloete, N., Maassen, P., & Bailey, T. (2015). *Knowledge production and higher education in Africa*. African Minds.

Codflash Infotec. (2025). Top 10 AI Development Companies in Dubai, UAE | Expert Guide. Codflash Infotec.

Cohen, D. B. (1974). Toward a theory of dream recall. *Psychological Bulletin*, *81*(2), 138–154. DOI: 10.1037/h0037616 PMID: 4359972

Cohen, W. M., & Levinthal, D. A. (1990). Absorptive capacity: A new perspective on learning and innovation. *Administrative Science Quarterly*, *35*(1), 128–152. DOI: 10.2307/2393553

Cohen, Y., & Glater, J. (2010). A tribute to Sidney Loeb—The pioneer of reverse osmosis desalination research. *Desalination and Water Treatment*, *15*(1–3), 222–227. DOI: 10.5004/dwt.2010.1762

Corkin, L. (2013). *Uncovering African agency: Angola's management of China's credit lines*. Ashgate.

Crop, X. (2022, March 23). *CropX Technologies*. CropX Technologies - Data-Driven Farming. https://cropx.com/

Croptune. (2026, March 9). *Your personal nitrogen meter - Croptune*. Croptune. https://www.croptune.io/

CTech (2023). Cleantech startup Tipa acquires Bio4Pack in $8 million deal. *CTech.*

CuBox. (2024). *Cubox: AI Read-It-Later App. Save Once. Know Forever.* Cubox. https://www.cubox.cc/

D'Antonio, M., & Scarlato, M. (2000), Capitale umano e sviluppo economico un modello di equilibrio economico generale per il Centro-Nord e il Mezzogiorno d'Italia. Dipartimento di Economia, Università degli Studi di Roma Tre, Collana di Economia, Working Paper, n.16.

Daily News Egypt. (2025). Egypt, Jordan explore joint projects in water, food, and energy sectors. *Daily News Egypt.*

De la Mothe, J., & Paquet, G. (1998). Local and Regional Systems of Innovation as learning socio-economies. In *Local and Regional Systems of Innovation*. Kluwer Academic Publisher. DOI: 10.1007/978-1-4615-5551-3_1

Debswana. (2023). *Botswana diamond operations: Jwaneng and Orapa*. Gaborone: Debswana Diamond Company.

Dei Ottati, G. (1994). Trust, interlinking transactions and credit in the industrial district. *Cambridge Journal of Economics*, *18*, 529–546.

Devex. (2018). *Devex International Development.* Devex.com. https://www.devex.com/

Di Minin, A., & Corsi, S. (2011). Extending the Uppsala model: Disruptive innovation from a Chinese evolved subsidiary [Paper presentation]. *71st Annual Meeting of the Academy of Management*, San Antonio, TX, United States.

DiGiacinto, V., & Nuzzo, G. (2006). Explaining labour productivity differentials across Italian regions: The role of socio-economic structure and factor endowments. *Papers in Regional Science*, *85*(2), 299–320. DOI: 10.1111/j.1435-5957.2006.00072.x

Dinika, A. A. (2025). Angola and the Isabel Dos Santos web, Good Governance Africa, Jun 6, 2025 https://gga.org/angola-and-the-isabel-dos-santos-web

Dotan, H., Landman, A., Sheehan, S. W., Malviya, K. D., Shter, G. E., Grave, D. A., Arzi, Z., Yehudai, N., Halabi, M., Gal, N., Hadari, N., Cohen, C., Rothschild, A., & Grader, G. S. (2019). Decoupled hydrogen and oxygen evolution by a two-step electrochemical–chemical cycle for efficient overall water splitting. *Nature Energy*, *4*(9), 786–795. DOI: 10.1038/s41560-019-0462-7

Doughman, E. (2022). Automating the broiler sex sorting process in the hatchery could help improve bird growth, welfare and uniformity. *Watt Poultry.*

e&. (2023). *Annual report and corporate overview*. Emirates Telecommunications Group.

eggXYt. (n.d.). *Count Your Chickens Before They Hatch.* Eggxyt. https://www.eggxyt.com/

Enright, M. (1996). Regional clustersclusters and economic development: A research agenda. In U. Staber, N. V. Schaefer, & B. Sharma (Eds.), Business Network Prospects for Regional Development. *de Gruyer.*

Enright, M. J. (2000). Survey of the characterization of regional clusters. Initial results. Institute of Economic Policy & Business Strategy. Competitiveness Program Working Paper, University of Hong Kong.

Environmental Justice Foundation. (2025). *Mining and conflict in the eastern DRC: Humanitarian and environmental impacts*. EJF.

Equinom. (2024). *Consistent Quality, Smarter Milling!* Equi-Nom.com. https://www.equi-nom.com/

Escudero-Cipriani, C., García-del Junco, J., Chafloque-Céspedes, R., & Alvarez-Risco, A. (2024). Frugal innovation in the business environment: A literature review and future perspectives. *Frontiers in Artificial Intelligence*, *7*, 1385522. Advance online publication. DOI: 10.3389/frai.2024.1385522 PMID: 39712468

Farole, T., & Winkler, D. (2014). *Making foreign direct investment work for sub-Saharan Africa*. World Bank.

Farole, T., & Winkler, D. (2014). *Making foreign direct investment work for sub-Saharan Africa: Local spillovers and competitiveness in global value chains*. World Bank.

First Quantum Minerals. (2022). *Kansanshi and Sentinel mines: Overview*. Retrieved from https://www.first-quantum.com

Flocean. (2025). Flocean. https://www.flocean.green

Frantzman, S. J. (2019). The Fight for ISIS's Old Territory Is Just Beginning. Foreign Policy.

Fraser, A., & Lungu, J. (2007). *For Whom the Windfalls? Winners and losers in the privatisation of Zambia's copper mines*. Civil Society Trade Network.

FreshDefrost. (2018). FreshDefrost. https://freshdefrost.wixsite.com/website

Gamsey, E. (1998). The genesis of the high technology milieu: A study of complexity. *International Journal of Urban and Regional Research*, *22*(3), 361–377. DOI: 10.1111/1468-2427.00146

Gereffi, G. (2018). *Global Value Chains, Development, and Emerging Economies*. Cambridge University Press. DOI: 10.1017/9781108559423.013

Gereffi, G., Humphrey, J., & Sturgeon, T. (2005). The governance of global value chains. *Review of International Political Economy, 12*(1), 78–104. DOI: 10.1080/09692290500049805

Gilad, A. (2023). Avigdor Willenz breaks his silence. *Globes.*

Glencore. (2021). *Mopani Copper Mines: Operations overview.* Retrieved from https://www.glencore.com

Global Witness. (2025). *Eastern DRC mineral report: Conflict, displacement, and resource governance.* Global Witness.

GlobalDivide.org. (2025). *Urban resilience and resource extraction in Goma.* GlobalDivide Research.

Goldberg, N. (2024, December 24). Coralogix acquires AI monitoring platform Aporia to strengthen ML observability solutions. *Jewish Business News.* https://jewishbusinessnews.com/2024/12/24/coralogix-acquires-ai-monitoring-platform-aporia-to-strengthen-ml-observability-solutions

Govindarajan, V. (2013, November 18). Reverse innovation starts with education. *Harvard Business Review.* https://hbr.org/2013/11/reverse-innovation-starts-with-education

Grant, R. M. (1996). Toward a knowledge-based theory of the firm. *Strategic Management Journal, 17*(S2), 109–122. DOI: 10.1002/smj.4250171110

Groundwork BioAg. (2024, July 9). *Mycorrhizal Fungi, Carbon Sequestration & Removal Inoculants.* Groundwork BioAg. https://groundworkbioag.com/

GSMA. (2023). *The mobile economy: Middle East and North Africa.* GSMA Intelligence.

H2OLL. (2026). *H2OLL Cyclic Absorption Atmospheric Water Generation.* H2oll.com. https://www.h2oll.com/

Habib-Valdhorn, S. (2025). Wix acquires Israeli vibe coding co Base44. *Globes.*

Haifa Group. (2019). Haifa Group. https://www.haifa-group.com/

Hannan, A., & Mohsin, H. M. (2015). Regional Analysis of Resource Curse Hypothesis: Evidence from Panel Data. *Pakistan Journal of Applied Economics, 25*(1), 45–66.

Han, X., Wan, S., He, L., Zou, J., Mavric, A., Wang, Y., Piotrowski, M., Bandela, A. K., Samorì, P., Wang, Z., Leydecker, T., & Thumu, U. (2024). Tunable Emissive $CsPbBr_3/Cs_4PbBr_6$ Quantum Dots Engineered by Discrete Phase Transformation for Enhanced Photogating in Field-Effect Phototransistors. *Advancement of Science, 11*(32), 2401973. Advance online publication. DOI: 10.1002/advs.202401973 PMID: 39189467

Harrison, B. (1992). Industrial districts: Old wine in new bottles? *Regional Studies, 26*(5), 469–483. DOI: 10.1080/00343409212331347121

Hatch. (2023). *Global lithium outlook: Zimbabwe's contribution to the supply chain.* Toronto: Hatch Ltd.

Hertog, S. (2010). *Princes, brokers, and bureaucrats: Oil and the state in Saudi Arabia.* Cornell University Press.

Hewlett-Packard. (2024). *Laptop Computers, Desktops, Printers, Ink & Toner.* Www.hp.com. https://www.hp.com/us-en/home.html

Hillman, J. E. (2018). *China's Belt and Road Initiative: Five years later.* Center for Strategic and International Studies.

Hilson, G. (2006). Sustainable development in the African mining sector: Experiences and prospects. *Journal of Cleaner Production, 14*(3–4), 305–314.

Hilson, G. (2019). Why is there a large-scale mining "bias" in sub-Saharan Africa? *Land Use Policy, 81*, 352–362. DOI: 10.1016/j.landusepol.2017.02.013

Hilson, G., & Maconachie, R. (2020). *Artisanal and small-scale mining in Africa: Economic and environmental perspectives.* Routledge.

Hodgkinson, G. P., & Sparrow, P. R. (2002). *The competent organization: A psychological analysis of the strategic management process.* Open University Press.

Humphrey, J., & Schmitz, H. (2002). How does insertion in global value chains affect upgrading in industrial clusters? *Regional Studies, 36*(9), 1017–1027. DOI: 10.1080/0034340022000022198

Humphreys, D. (2005). *Natural resources, governance and development: Botswana diamonds in comparative perspective.* Oxford University Press.

Humphreys, D. (2010). Extractive industries and poverty: A review of recent findings and linkages. *The Journal of Development Studies, 46*(4), 517–538.

ICAO. (2022). *Air transport statistics.* International Civil Aviation Organization.

ICMM (International Council on Mining and Metals). (2015). *The role of mining in national economies* (2nd ed.).

ICMM (International Council on Mining and Metals). (2015). *The role of mining in national economies.*

IEA. (2022). *The role of critical minerals in clean energy transitions.* International Energy Agency.

IMF. (2021). *Democratic Republic of the Congo: Staff report.*

Intel. (2023). *Mobileye technology overview.* Intel Corporation.

International Atomic Energy Agency. (2023). *Materials safety and transport regulations.* IAEA.

International Conference on the Great Lakes Region. (2022). *Mineral governance and due diligence framework.* Bujumbura: ICGLR Secretariat.

International Energy Agency. (2023). *World energy outlook 2023.*

International Renewable Energy Agency. (2023). *Renewable energy market analysis: MENA.*

ISRAEL21c (2004). Israel's Emblaze introduces world's first customized multimedia handset. *ISRAEL21c*, https://www.israel21c.org/israels-emblaze-introduces-worlds-first-customized-multimedia-handset

Ivanhoe Mines. (2023). *Platreef project: Mineral resources and development.* Retrieved from https://www.ivanhoemines.com

Japan Oil, Gas and Metals National Corporation. (2020). *Japan's resource strategy and overseas investments.*

Jewish Federation Los Angeles. (2021, June 28). Home. Jewish Federation Los Angeles. https://www.jewishla.org/

Kamoa Copper S.A. (2025). *Operations overview.* Retrieved from company materials. Congo Mining Network. (2025). *Trafigura financing for Kamoa-Kakula copper flow.*

Kaplinsky, R. (2000). Globalisation and unequalisation: What can be learned from value chain analysis? *The Journal of Development Studies, 37*(2), 117–146. DOI: 10.1080/713600071

Kaplinsky, R. (2005). *Globalization, poverty and inequality: between a rock and a hard place.* Polity.

Kaplinsky, R., & Morris, M. (2016). Thinning and thickening: Productive sector policies in the era of global value chains. *European Journal of Development Research, 28*(4), 625–645. DOI: 10.1057/ejdr.2015.29

Keatom, H., & Tshitereke, C. (2019). Uranium mining as an economic driver in Namibia. *African Mining Journal, 8*(2), 44–58.

Kirchgaessner, S. (2023). Washington DC-based group targeted in apparent Pegasus hack. *The Guardian.*

Kiron, M. I. (2021, May 10). *Kenaf Fiber: Properties, Cultivation, Production, Uses and Advantages*. Textile Learner. https://textilelearner.net/kenaf-fiber-properties/

Kitchen Robotics. (2023). Kitchen Robotics Launches an AI-Driven Culinary Revolution for its robotic kitchen Beastro™. *Cision PR Web,* Dec 05, 2023

Klaysom, C., & Vankelecom, I. (2016). Pressure-Retarded Osmosis. In *Encyclopedia of Membranes.* Springer, Berlin, Heidelberg.

Kolstad, I., & Wiig, A. (2009). Is Transparency the Key to Reducing Corruption in Resource-Rich Countries? *World Development, 37*(3), 521–532. DOI: 10.1016/j.worlddev.2008.07.002

Krane, J. (2015). *City of gold: Dubai and the dream of capitalism*. St. Martin's Press.

Leichman, A. K. (2014, June 18). *A two-inch computer for $55 - ISRAEL21c*. ISRAEL21c. https://archive.israel21c.org/a-two-inch-computer-for-55/

Leichman, A. K. (2022, December 28). *Golda, the Israeli hen that lays only female eggs - ISRAEL21c*. ISRAEL21c. https://archive.israel21c.org/golda-the-israeli-hen-that-lays-only-female-eggs/

Levine, U. (2011). Was Selling Waze To Google A Good Decision? Founder Of Waze Reflects On The Deal? *Forbes.*

Levit, M. (2023). ANINA Will Make You Forget Everything You Know About Ready-Made Meals. *Asif.*

Liang, D., Costa, H., Tibúrcio, B. D., Vistas, C. R., & Almeida, J. (2025). High-efficiency solar-pumped lasers. *Advances in Physics: X, 10*(1), 2531056. Advance online publication. DOI: 10.1080/23746149.2025.2531056

Lightspeed. (2025, October). *Eyeview*. Lightspeed Venture Partners. https://lsvp.com/company/eyeview/

Lock Smith Ledger. (2014). Mul-T-Lock's Evolution: Locksmiths Lead the Revolution. *Lock Smith Ledger.*

Lorentzen, J. (2005). The absorptive capacities of South African automotive component suppliers. *World Development, 33*(7), 1153–1182. DOI: 10.1016/j.worlddev.2005.04.006

Louvain Cooperation. (2025). *Artisanal mining and urban centers in South Kivu.* Louvain Cooperation.

Lyngaas, S. (2019). Human rights groups to ask Israeli court to revoke NSO Group's export license. *Cyberscoop.*

Maital, S., & Barzani, E. (2021). The economic impact of the Abraham Accords after one year: Passions vs. interests. Samuel Neaman Institute for National Policy Research.

Majumder, R. (2021). Corruption on exploitation of Bauxite in Guinea, investigation filed against President Alpha Condé and others. *Al Circle.*

Marini, M. (2000). *Le risorse Immateriali. I fattori culturali dello Sviluppo economico.* Carocci Editore.

Markusen, A. (1996). Sticky Places in Slippery Space: A Typology of Industrial Districts. *Economic Geography*, *72*(3), 293–313. DOI: 10.2307/144402

Miller, R., Smith, J., & van der Walt, L. (2018). Geology and mining of South Africa's base-metal deposits. *Journal of African Earth Sciences, 145*, 345–362.

MiningSEE. (2026). *Cobalt in 2026: Global supply chains, DRC dominance, Chinese refining power, and the future of battery metals.*

Morris, M., Kaplinsky, R., & Kaplan, D. (2012). "One thing leads to another" – Commodities, linkages and industrial development. *Resources Policy*, *37*(4), 408–416. DOI: 10.1016/j.resourpol.2012.06.008

Mudd, G. (2015). Sustainable mining in South Africa: Platinum and gold industry insights. *Resources Policy*, *45*, 90–99.

Murphy, E. L., & Bryja, T. (2025). *The Strategic Future of Subsea Cables: Egypt Case Study*. Csis.org. https://www.csis.org/analysis/strategic-future-subsea-cables-egypt-case-study

Musarurwa, C., Nyoni, J., & Tawanda, K. (2023). Sustainable practices in Zimbabwean lithium mining operations. *Southern African Journal of Mining Engineering*, *8*(1), 12–27.

Mutale-J., C., Sbabou, L., & Hicham, E. A. (2023). Microalgae and Cyanobacteria: How Exploiting These Microbial Resources Can Address the Underlying Challenges Related to Food Sources and Sustainable Agriculture: A Review. *Journal of Plant Growth Regulation*, *42*(1), 1–20. DOI: 10.1007/s00344-021-10534-9

MyCrops. (2020). *Farm Management software simplified.* Mycrops.ag. https://www.mycrops.ag/

Namibia Ports Authority. (2024). *Walvis Bay export statistics 2023–2024.* Walvis Bay: NPA.

NetaGenomix. (2026, February 10). *Revolutionizing Plant Genetics.* NetaGenomiX. https://netagenomix.com/

Newman, A. (2023). The Evolution of Voice over Internet Protocol: Uncovering the Innovators.*Phone.com.*

NextHen. (2024, December 9). *Pioneering Poultry's Future.* NextHen. https://www.nexthen.net/

Nobify. (2017). Nobify. https://www.nobify.ai/

Nuclear Energy Agency. (2020). *Uranium 2020: Resources, production and demand.* OECD/NEA and IAEA.

Obi, C. (2010). The changing face of energy governance in Nigeria: Seplat and the Nigerian energy transition. *African Affairs*, *109*(436), 407–426.

OECD. (2018). *Enhancing the contribution of mining to sustainable development.* OECD Publishing.

OECD. (2022). *Economic surveys*. OECD Publishing.

OECD. (2023). *Israel innovation policy review*. OECD Publishing.

Orbach M. (2021). Israeli agtech startup Prospera acquired by Valmont for $300 million. Calcalist, Tech, 05.05.21

ORIX USA. (2026, March 30). *Middle Market Asset Management & Lending*. ORIX Group (USA). https://www.orix.com/

Paladin Energy. (2025). *Langer Heinrich restart plan and production forecast.* Paladin Energy Ltd.

Passiante, G., Elia, V., & Massari, T. (2002). Digital innovation. Imperial College Press.

Pehlivan, M. (2026). Is the resource curse persistent? Dynamic causality evidence from resource-dependent economies. *Resources Policy, 113*(C).

Pepe, C., Mushagalusa Nshombo, J.M., & Risso, M. (2014). Preventing Corruption in Africa: Emerging Challenges in the Mining Sector of the Democratic Republic of Congo. *SYMPHONYA Emerging Issues in Management.*

Picaud, K. (2013). Discontinuous innovation (DI): A review of definitions, theoretical perspectives, and measures – Towards an empirical study of the role of the purchasing department in DI [Conference paper]. https://www.researchgate.net/publication/270744949_Discontinuous_Innovation_DI_A_review_of_definitions_theoretical_perspectives_and_measures

PlantArcBio. (2026, January 19). *Home.* Plantarc. https://plantarcbio.com/

Porter, M. E. (1998). Clusters. *Innovation, and Competitiveness: New Findings and Implications for Policy.*

Prospera Technologies. (2026). *Founder Led Custom Software Development | Prototype Before Contract or Payment.* Prospera Technologies. https://prospera-technologies.com/

Provasi, G. (2002). *Le istituzioni dello sviluppo economico.* Donzelli.

Rabellotti, R. (1995). Is there an industrial district. *World Development, 23*(1), 29–41. DOI: 10.1016/0305-750X(94)00103-6

Rabellotti, R., & Schmitz, H. (1999). The internal heterogeneity of industrial districts in Italy. *Regional Studies, 33*(2), 99–128. DOI: 10.1080/00343409950122909

Ravet, H. (2021). Israel's Zebra Medical acquired by Nanox for just $200 million. *Calcalist Tech,* 10.08.21 https://www.calcalistech.com/ctech/articles/0,7340,L-3914640,00.html

Responsible Minerals Initiative. (2023). *Tantalum and niobium industry report.* RMI.

Reuters Investigations. (2025). *Rwandan firms and coltan trade links to DRC conflict zones.* Reuters.

Roberts, P. (2003, August 25). Sanctum focuses on quality assurance, Web services. *InfoWorld.*

Romano, A., & Passiante, G. (1997). Innovation Territorial System as Learning Organization of Local System Innovation Virtual System. Paper presented at the Regional Science Association 37th European Congress, Rome.

Rosenfeld, S. (1996). Bringing Business Clusters into the Mainstream of Economic Development. *European Planning Studies*, *5*(1), 3–23. DOI: 10.1080/09654319708720381

Rössing Uranium Ltd. (2023). *Rössing annual report*. Swakopmund: Rössing Uranium Ltd.

Ross, M. L. (2012). *The oil curse: How petroleum wealth shapes the development of nations*. Princeton University Press. DOI: 10.1515/9781400841929

Roy, K. (2023). 7 Top Artificial Intelligence Companies in UAE. *Medium.*

RUSAL. (2024). *Fria Alumina Refinery operational report*. United Company RUSAL.

Sachs, J. D., & Warner, A. (1995). Natural resource abundance and economic growth.

Salem, N. M., Jewehan, A., Aranda, M. A., & Fox, A. (2023, September 5). Tomato Brown Rugose Fruit Virus Pandemic. *Annual Review of Phytopathology*, *61*(1), 137–164. DOI: 10.1146/annurev-phyto-021622-120703 PMID: 37268006

Saudi Vision 2030. (2016). *Vision 2030 document*. Government of Saudi Arabia.

Saxenian, A. (1994). *Regional Advantage: Culture and Competition in the Silicon Valley and Route 128*. Harvard University Press.

Scarlato, M. (2001). Capitale sociale e sviluppo economico: Un'analisi empirica per le province italiane. *Economia Pubblica*, *2001*(1).

Schmitz, H. (1995). Collective efficiency: Growth path for the small-scale industry. *The Journal of Development Studies*, *31*(4), 529–566. DOI: 10.1080/00220389508422377

SeeTree. (2019). *SeeTree: Intelligence network for Trees*. Seetree.ai. https://www.seetree.ai/

Senor, D., & Singer, S. (2009). *Start-up nation*. Twelve.

Senor, D., & Singer, S. (2009). *Start-up nation: The story of Israel's economic miracle*. Twelve.

Shah, H., Shah, K., Darji, K., Shah, A., & Shah, M. (2025). Advanced driver assistance system (ADAS) and machine learning (ML): The dynamic duo revolutionizing the automotive industry, *Virtual Reality & Intelligent Hardware,* 7(3) 203-236.

Shapira, A., Noor, N., Oved, H., & Dvir, T. (2020). Transparent support media for high resolution 3D printing of volumetric cell-containing ECM structures. Biomedical Materials (Bristol).

Shelah, S. (2006). EMC buys nLayers for $50m. *Globes*.

Shiny Aura. (2025). 100 Types of Flowers: The Ultimate Guide to Names, Meanings, and Gardening Tips [Review of 100 Types of Flowers: The Ultimate Guide to Names, Meanings, and Gardening Tips]. MorFlora. https://morflora.com/

Shulman, S. (2024). Windward acquired for $270M by FTV Capital, doubling its IPO valuation. *Calcalist.*

Shulman, S. (2025, April 30). *The 50 most promising Israeli startups - 2025.* Ctech. https://www.calcalistech.com/ctechnews/article/923yvb6hw

Sibanye Stillwater. (2023). *Sustainability and corporate responsibility report.* Sibanye Stillwater Ltd.

Sibanye-Stillwater. (2023). *Annual report: South African PGM operations.* Retrieved from https://www.sibanyestillwater.com

Simpson, J., & Du Plessis, A. (2018). *Ore evaluation and mining geology techniques.* Mining Geoscience Publishing.

Situmbeko, T., & Tembo, M. (2019). University-industry linkages in Zambia's mining sector. *African Journal of Science, Technology, Innovation and Development, 11*(6), 737–749.

Slugina, M. A. (2021). Transcription Factor RIPENING INHIBITOR and Its Homologs in Regulation of Fleshy Fruit Ripening of Various Plant Species. *Russian Journal of Plant Physiology: a Comprehensive Russian Journal on Modern Phytophysiology, 68*(5), 783–799. DOI: 10.1134/S1021443721050186

Snesoil. (2024, June 4). Sensoil Protecting Groundwater by Monitoring the Vadose Zone. Sensoil. https://sensoil.com/

Société Minière de Bisunzu. (2024). *Corporate sustainability and production report.* SMB.

Sol-Chip. (2025, June 27). Sol-Chip. https://sol-chip.com/

Solomon, S. (2024, February). Defying war's wreckage, self-drying cherry tomatoes ripen near Gaza. *Times of Israel,* 25.

Soros, G. (2007). *Escaping the Resource Curse* (Humphreys, M., Sachs, J. D., & Stiglitz, J. E., Eds.). Columbia University Press.

South32. (2023). *Hillside Aluminium: Smelter operations and industrial contributions.* Retrieved from https://www.south32.net

Spampinato, E. (2025). Israeli plant-based firm SimpliiGood will commercialize its smoked salmon spirulina analog. *Plant-Based & Cell-Based. Sea food source.*

Standing, A (2007). Corruption and the extractive industries in Africa Can combatting corruption cure the resource curse? Institute of Security Studies, ISS Paper 153.

Sumbul, A., Ansari, R. A., Rizvi, R., & Mahmood, I. (2020, December). Azotobacter: A potential bio-fertilizer for soil and plant health management. *Saudi Journal of Biological Sciences*, *27*(12), 3634–3640. DOI: 10.1016/j.sjbs.2020.08.004 PMID: 33304174

Tamburini, A., Tedesco, M., Cipollina, A., Micale, G., Ciofalo, M., Papapetrou, M., Van Baak, W., & Piacentino, A. (2017, November). Reverse electrodialysis heat engine for sustainable power production. *Applied Energy*, *206*(15), 1334–1353. DOI: 10.1016/j.apenergy.2017.10.008

Tantalum-Niobium International Study Center. (2024). *Global coordination of tantalum and niobium supply chains*. Basel: TIC.

Taranis. (n.d.). Crop & Farm Management Software | Precision Agriculture Technology. Taranis. https://www.taranis.com/

Taylor, I. (2006). *China and Africa: Engagement and compromise*. Routledge.

Tessler, Z. D., Vörösmarty, C. J., Grossberg, M., Gladkova, I., Aizenman, H., Syvitski, J. P. M., & Foufoula-Georgiou, E. (2015). Profiling risk and sustainability in coastal deltas of the world. *Science*, *349*(6248), 638–643. DOI: 10.1126/science.aab3574 PMID: 26250684

The New Arab Staff & Agencies. (2025). *French-led group signs Jordan's 'biggest-ever infrastructure project' for desalination plant*. The New Arab Staff & Agencies.

Trigui, H., Guerfa, F., Harigua-Souiai, E., Qasrawi, R., Atri, Ch., Salem Sokhn, E., El Morr, C., Hammami, K., Souiai, O., Wu, J., Dzevela Kong, J., Rousseau, J.J., & Znaidi, S. (2024). Exploring AI governance in the Middle East and North Africa (MENA) region: gaps, efforts, and initiatives. Data & Policy, 6, e83. DOI: 10.1017/dap.2024.85

Tripsas, M., & Gavetti, G. (2000). Capabilities, cognition, and inertia: Evidence from digital imaging. *Strategic Management Journal*, *21*(10–11), 1147–1161. DOI: 10.1002/1097-0266(200010/11)21:10/11<1147::AID-SMJ128>3.0.CO;2-R

Umicore. (2026). *Responsible sourcing of cobalt*. Retrieved from https://www.umicore.com/en/media/responsible-sourcing-of-cobalt/

UN Panel of Experts on the DRC. (2025). *Report on mineral flows and armed group financing in the Great Lakes Region*. United Nations Security Council.

UNAM & NUST Academic Catalogues. (2024). *Program offerings in geological and mining sciences*. University of Namibia / Namibia University of Science and Technology.

UNCTAD. (2007). *World investment report*. United Nations.

UNCTAD. (2007). *World investment report: Transnational corporations, extractive industries and development*. United Nations.

UNCTAD. (2013). *Economic development in Africa report*. United Nations.

UNCTAD. (2018). *Economic development in Africa report: Migration for structural transformation*. United Nations.

UNCTAD. (2022). *World investment report 2022. United Nations Conference on Trade and Development.*

UNCTAD. (2022). *World investment report 2022*. United Nations.

UNCTAD. (2023). *World investment report 2023*. United Nations.

United States Geological Survey. (2024). *Mineral commodity summaries 2024: Lithium*. USGS.

USGS. (2022). *Mineral commodity summaries: Gold*. U.S. Geological Survey.

van Zyl, P. (2020). Phalaborwa: Carbonatite-hosted copper mining in South Africa. *Mineral Economics*, *33*(2), 167–181.

Vegconomist. (2023). InnovoPro Presents Nutritious Chickpea Solutions for Bakery and Coffee Shop Industries at Fi Europe 2023. *Vegconomist.*

von Eicken, T., Basu, A., Buch, V., & Vogels, W. (1995, December). U-Net: A user-level network interface for parallel and distributed computing (includes URL). *Operating Systems Review*, *29*(5), 40–53. DOI: 10.1145/224057.224061

Water Utility Corporation. (2023). *Industrial water supply systems report*. Windhoek: WUC.

Watts, M. (2004). Resource curse? Governmentality, oil and power in the Niger Delta. *Geopolitics*, *9*(1), 50–80. DOI: 10.1080/14650040412331307832

Whittaker, M. (2026). Dutch disease and the resource curse: Paradoxes of plenty. *Encyclopedia Britannica*. https://www.britannica.com/money/Dutch-disease

Wikipedia contributors. (2024). *Etoile mine*. In Wikipedia, The Free Encyclopedia.

Wikipedia contributors. (2024). *Kamoto mine*. In Wikipedia, The Free Encyclopedia.

Wikipedia contributors. (2024). *Mutanda mine*. In Wikipedia, The Free Encyclopedia.

Wikipedia contributors. (2024). Tenke Fungurume Mine. In Wikipedia, The Free Encyclopedia.

World Bank. (2013). *Barriers to access to payment systems and proposed actions: Special-purpose*. http://hdl.handle.net/10986/21532

World Bank. (2020). *Africa Centres of Excellence project report*.

World Bank. (2020). *Africa mining vision and development frameworks*. World Bank.

World Bank. (2020). Guinea: Country economic memorandum. World Bank.

World Bank. (2020). *Minerals for climate action: The mineral intensity of the clean energy transition*. World Bank.

World Bank. (2020). *Mining sector development in West Africa*. World Bank.

World Bank. (2022). *Digital development in the Middle East and North Africa*.

World Bank. (2022). *Digital development overview: Middle East and North Africa*.

World Bank. (2023). *Gold mining in Africa: Economic contributions and policy challenges*. World Bank Publications.

World Nuclear Association. (2022). *Uranium resources and nuclear fuel cycle*.

Yambayamba, B. (2021). Human capital and technological capacity in Zambia's Copperbelt. *Mining Research Review*, *15*(2), 48–67.

Yang, K., Fu, R., Feng, H., Jiang, G., Finkel, O., Sun, T., Liu, M., Huang, B., Li, S., Wang, X., Yang, T., Wang, Y., Wang, S., Xu, Y., Shen, Q., Friman, V. P., Jousset, A., & Wei, Z. (2023). RIN enhances plant disease resistance via root exudate-mediated assembly of disease-suppressive rhizosphere microbiota. *Molecular Plant*, *16*(9), 1379–1395. DOI: 10.1016/j.molp.2023.08.004 PMID: 37563832

Yasuda, Y., Schillinger, J., Huntjens, P., & Alofs, Ch. (2017). *Transboundary Water Cooperation over the lower part of the Jordan River Basin*. Stockholm International Water Institute (SIWI).

Yu, H., & Wang, G. (2008). A general scheme for velocity tomography. *Signal Processing*, *88*(5), 1165–1175. DOI: 10.1016/j.sigpro.2007.11.007 PMID: 19412317

Yu, Y., Wang, H., You, C., & Chen, X. (2026). Plant microRNA maturation and function. *Nature Reviews. Molecular Cell Biology*, *27*(1), 55–70. DOI: 10.1038/s41580-025-00871-y PMID: 40681920

Zahid, A., Asif, H. M., Zahid, R., Firdous, M., Idrees, H. M., Hasnain, M., & Bashir, U. (2023). Jojoba oil: A best-in-class assessment as cosmetics and forthcoming opportunities. *Journal of Pharma and Biomedics*, *1*(1), 27–34.

Zakari, S., Niels, N. K., Olagunju, G. V., Nnaji, P. C., Ogunniyi, O., Tebamifor, M., Israel, E. N., Atawodi, S. E., & Ogunlana, O. O. (2024). Emerging biomarkers for non-invasive diagnosis and treatment of cancer: A systematic review. *Frontiers in Oncology*, *14*, 1405267. DOI: 10.3389/fonc.2024.1405267 PMID: 39132504

Zoppé, H., Trocmet, L., Rambault, A., Abtroun, Y., Defresne, D., Ansoborlo, M., Hazard, M., & Bonnet-Brilhault, F. (2025). Early detection of neurodevelopmental disorders in children with delayed milestones: Navigating between overlapping trajectories and the limits of a single-diagnosis categorical approach (A Preliminary Study for the CONDOR Cohort). *Asian Journal of Psychiatry*, *109*(July), 104561. DOI: 10.1016/j.ajp.2025.104561 PMID: 40466582

Zvonar, Z. (2000). DSPs' role in cell phones shifting. *EE Times*.

About the Author

Ilan Bijaoui has a PhD. from the Sorbonne Pantheon, Paris II and is a Lecturer in Graduate School of Business Management, Bar Ilan University, Ramat Gan, Israel, teaching courses across marketing, international business and innovation strategy and in the Galilee International Management Institute (GIMI) teaching courses across entrepreneurship, innovation strategy, and project management. He is also a consultant to Ministers and International Organizations. He has written numerous articles in business and economic journals and is the author of the following books: Bijaoui I. (2026). Multinational Companies & Israel National Innovation Strategy, Bijaoui I. (2025). The Open Incubators Cluster Model, Bijaoui I. (2024); Disruptive and Reverse Innovation Challenges for Developing Countries; Bijaoui I. (2023). Innovation Policy for Developing Countries; Bijaoui I. (2022). Reverse Reliance and Inclusive Development in South Saharan Africa (SSA); Bijaoui I. (2021). PPP Models Boosting Economic Development in SSA Nations; Bijaoui I (2021). Education of Youth in Sub-Saharan Nations Challenges and Opportunities; Bijaoui I. (2020). Jobs and Entrepreneurship for Youths in Sub-Saharan Africa Nations ; Bijaoui I.(2019). Innovating for the Bottom of the Pyramid; Bijaoui I. (2017). Multinational Interest & Development in Africa Establishing a People's Economy;Bijaoui I.(2016) SMEs in an Era of Globalization; Bijaoui I. (2015) The Open Incubator Model, generator of viral economic development in the periphery; Bijaoui I. (2014) The economic reconciliation process: Middle Eastern Populations in Conflict.

Index

S

T

U

W

www.ingramcontent.com/pod-product-compliance
Lightning Source LLC
LaVergne TN
LVHW062327300926
849161LV00007B/1600